Take, Lord, and receive:

A Manual
of the
Spiritual Exercises
of
Saint Ignatius of Loyola

"Your reverence knows that there is one outstanding means among those which of their nature are helpful to men. I mean the [Spiritual] Exercises. I remind you, therefore, that you should make use of this weapon."

Saint Ignatius of Loyola

Letter to Father Fulvio Androzzi, July 18, 1556

Take, Lord, and receive:

A Manual
of the
Spiritual Exercises
of
Saint Ignatius of Loyola

Fr. Nathaniel Dreyer, I.V.E.

IVE PRESS

www.ivepress.org

ISBN (paperback): 978-1-947568-41-9
ISBN (ebook): 978-1-947568-42-6

Library of Congress Control Number: 2023943905

Printed in the United States of America

TABLE OF CONTENTS

FIRST WEEK

SECOND WEEK

PREFACE

This book has its origins in the Spiritual Exercises that I preached, particularly throughout 2017-2019, when I was working at the Saint Isaac Jogues and Companions, Martyrs, Novitiate. It would be erroneous to assert that all the materials here are original: so many saints and scholars have taken, preached, and studied the Exercises, with such great insights and fruits, that it would be foolish not to use them. I have tried to make sure that all the citations are present, but it is likely I have missed some.

That being said, a great number of these excellent resources are not available in English translation; the translations of parts or summaries of these texts into English are my own.

My preferred version of the *Spiritual Exercises* text itself, and the one that I follow here, is the edition translated by Louis J. Puhl, SJ. His 1951 work has been reprinted several times, and, while it has some defects, I find the translation far preferable to the one done by George E. Ganss, SJ, as well as superior to others which are meditations on the Exercises and not simply the text itself.

Among the other recourses that I have found useful and that are used extensively here are the following works by Jesuits:

Aloysius Ambruzzi, SJ
- *A Companion to the Spiritual Exercises of Saint Ignatius* (Newman Press: Westminster, MD, 1948)
- *Alla scuola di S. Ignazio: Il completo manuale dei Santi Esercizi* (Luigi Favero: Vicenza, 1961)

José Calveras, SJ
- *Examen de la oración* (Balmes: Barcelona, 1940)
- *The Harvest-Field of the Spiritual Exercises of Saint Ignatius* (Bambardekar: Bombay, 1949)
- *Qué fruto se ha de sacar de los Ejercicios Espirituales de San Ignacio* (Librería Religiosa: Barcelona, 1950)

- *Los tres modos de orar en los Ejercicios Espirituales de San Ignacio* (Librería Religiosa: Barcelona, 1951)
- *Práctica de los ejercicios intensivos* (Balmes: Barcelona, 1955)
- *Ejercicios Espirituales. Directorio y Documentos de San Ignacio de Loyola* (Balmes: Barcelona, 1958)
- *Oración y discernimiento ignaciano: Estudios sobre los Ejercicios de San Ignacio* (BAC: Madrid, 2018)

Ignacio Casanovas, SJ
- *Ejercicios de San Ignacio* (IVEPress: New York, 2012)

Servant of God John Hardon, SJ
- *All my Liberty: Theology of the Spiritual Exercises* (Newman Press: Westminster, MD, 1959)
- *Retreat with the Lord* (Eternal Life: Bardstown, KY, 2012)

Ignacio Iparraguirre, SJ
- *Obras completes de San Ignacio de Loyola* (BAC: Madrid, 1963)

Antonio Oraá, SJ
- *Ejercicios Espirituales de San Ignacio de Loyola: Explanación de las meditaciones y documentos en ellos contenidos* (Razón y Fe: Madrid, 1944)

Likewise, among the non-Jesuits, I found insightful the works by:

Anthony Mary Claret
- *The Golden Key to Heaven* (Immaculate Heart: Location Unknown, 1955)

Alphonsus Liguori
- *Preparation for Death* (Lippincott & Co.: Philadelphia, 1869)

Timothy M. Gallagher, OMV
- *The Discernment of Spirits: An Ignatian Guide for Everyday Living Discernment* (Crossroad: Chestnut Ridge, NY, 2005)
- *Spiritual Consolation: An Ignatian Guide for Greater Discernment* (Crossroad: Chestnut Ridge, NY, 2012)
- *Discerning the Will of God: The Ignatian Guide to Christian Decision Making* (Crossroad: Chestnut Ridge, NT, 2015)

Out of all these authors, two are worth of particular emphasis: while almost unknown in the English-speaking world, José Calveras, SJ, was such an outstanding scholar of the Exercises that sometimes he is referred to as "the man of the Spiritual Exercises."[1] His two works, *Qué fruto se ha de sacar* and *Práctica de los ejercicios intensivos* are, in my opinion, among the best works about the Exercises. Likewise, the explanations given by Timothy M. Gallagher, OMV, in his works regarding discernment and elections, following Ignatius' method, have been the most insightful and clearest that I have read. For the talks in this book concerning the discernment of spirits and the choice of a state of life, I essentially follow his commentary, and add clarifications, explanations, and examples.

While many of these meditations and contemplations were originally preached to religious (priests, seminarians, brothers, and sisters), I hope they will be of use to everyone, religious and lay, married and single.

Lastly, I owe a debt of gratitude to all those who have preached the Exercises to me, taken them with me, and those who have prayed for their fruits. I thank the priests of Miles Christi, who preached the first Exercises I ever took and introduced me to the work of the Servant of God Fr. John Hardon, SJ, and those of my own Institute of the Incarnate Word. Most especially, I thank the one who taught us to "accomplish [the] evangelization of the culture by sanctifying people individually ... preferably by using the Spiritual Exercises" and who encouraged "the priestly attitude proper to the 'third class of man.'"

Fr. Nathaniel Dreyer, IVE
July 31, 2023
Feast of Saint Ignatius of Loyola

1. See, for instance, Josep María Rambla Blanch's article, "José Calveras, S.J., hombre de los Ejercicios espirituales" in *Manresa*, 85, 336 (2013): 291-310.

A (VERY) BRIEF INTRODUCTION
TO THE SPIRITUAL EXERCISES
OF SAINT IGNATIUS OF LOYOLA

The *Spiritual Exercises* is a series of meditations, contemplations, and talks put together by Saint Ignatius of Loyola; the saint told Father Luis Gonzalez (his biographer) that it was done in parts, and not all at once. It was certainly more or less complete (meaning, with all the principal mediations) when Saint Peter Faber took them at the University of Paris in 1533, and a copy from 1541 contains all of the *Exercises*. The text, in its definitive form, was approved by Pope Paul III in 1548.

However, Ignatius began work on it much earlier; some elements can be traced back to his convalescence in Loyola. His contemporaries unanimously assert that it was in Manresa, where the saint arrived in 1522, that the majority of the *Exercises* were written. For this reason Manresa has always been considered the "cradle" of the *Exercises*. Indeed, one tradition says that, while living practically as a hermit there, the Blessed Virgin Mary dictated the *Exercises* to him. In any event, the *Spiritual Exercises* have been approved by the Church for 470 years, and experience has shown that they can produce great fruits in souls that make them generously and openly.

So, what exactly are the *Spiritual Exercises*? They aren't just another retreat. In the introductory observations, at point [001], Ignatius writes: "By the term *Spiritual Exercises* is meant every method of examination of conscience, of meditation, of contemplation, of vocal and mental prayer, and of other spiritual activities that will be mentioned later. For just as taking a walk, journeying on foot, and running are bodily exercises, so we call *Spiritual Exercises* every way of preparing and disposing the soul to rid itself of all inordinate attachments, and, after their removal, of seeking and finding the will of God in the disposition of our life for the salvation of our soul."

There is a lot there. The *Exercises* have a two-fold purpose; it's implied in what we just said, and Ignatius reminds us [021]: "[The Spiritual Exercises] have as their purpose the conquest of self and the regulation of one's life in such a way that no decision is made under the influence of any inordinate attachment." Hence, the Exercises help us, first, to get rid of inordinate attachments (meaning, things that we like too much, are too inclined to, or anything that keeps us away from God, be it a sin, or even something good; in short, when we love something, but not out of pure love for God). Second, once we remove them, then (and only then), can we seek God's will in our lives, meaning, can we see what it is God wants for me, and then follow through with it.

The analogy with physical exercise is useful: for physical exercises, you often have a coach or a trainer. They can help you, answer questions, and explain what you need to do, but, ultimately, the burden falls on you. They can't run laps for you, or do your push-ups for you. *You* have to do them. In the *Spiritual Exercises*, the one preaching the retreat can give you the points (but these aren't the end-all, be-all of the *Exercises*; they're to give you something to help foster your meditation), explain things, and give you elements to think about, but, in the end, you're the one who needs to do the work. It's you and God; hence, the *Exercises* are made ***in silence, both exterior and interior*** (meaning, first, exteriorly, no unnecessary talking, no loud music or firecrackers, but also interior, meaning, you need to be recollected, and not worried about things or thinking about something that's not related to the *Exercises*). It's just you and God. The work is with the intellect, meaning, I think about these things, consider them, engage myself in them, and then with the will, rousing my emotions so that I can more easily move myself to want to reform my life, or imitate Christ, etc.

The *Exercises* are divided into weeks. This is because "the Exercises should be finished in approximately thirty days" [004], and that's about four weeks. That doesn't mean that each week is necessarily seven days (Ignatius says you vary it based on the retreatant), but it does explain why, even in a shorter version of the *Exercises*, we talk about four weeks (so, when we move on to the "second week," or the "third week," even though it's only been a day or two, the one giving the Exercises hasn't lost track of time or gone crazy; he's simply moving on to the meditations of that week).

Each week has a different focus, and a different goal. Ignatius establishes the following scheme:

1st week – Meditation on our own sins and attachments
2nd week – Meditation on the Life of Christ, from the Incarnation until the Passion
3rd week – Meditation on the Passion and Death of Christ
4th week – Meditation on the Resurrection and what follows

A long-standing tradition has assigned the following goals to each week:

1st week: *Deformata Reformare* — to reform what is deformed (by sin)

2nd week: *Reformata Conformare* — to conform
(to Christ's example) what has been reformed

3rd week: *Conformata confirmare* — to confirm, or strengthen
(by Christ's passion) what has been conformed

4th week: *Confirmata Transformare* — to transform
(by divine love) what has been confirmed

You'll notice that Ignatius always gives the same sort of structure for the meditations: he'll give a little introduction, a preparatory prayer (which is always the same), and a number of preludes. The first prelude is the composition of place, meaning, where do I set myself in my mind; it's the mental setting for a particular time of prayer. Ignatius is smart; he gives us a setting as a sort of background, which keeps the imagination engaged and prevents distraction. The second prelude is the petition, the grace we're asking for. This varies based on the week: the first week we want sorrow for sins, the second week to imitate Christ, the third sorrow with Christ in sorrow, and joy in the fourth. Then follows the actual points for consideration. Afterwards, Ignatius ends with a colloquy, a conversation with someone, be it Jesus, Mary or God the Father. This helps us to summarize what we've meditated on, and what we will do to integrate, as it were, that meditation into my life. After this follows an examination of the meditation, as Ignatius explains: "After having finished the Exercise, I will either walk about or sit still, and examine how it has succeeded. If it has not, I will ascertain the cause, sincerely repent, and make firm resolutions for the future. If the success has been satisfactory, I will make acts of thanksgiving, and resolve to follow the same method for the future." I include an examination below (taken, with some modification, and translated from Casanovas).

Two important things: Penance and General Confession

Since the *Spiritual Exercises* is a time to draw closer to God, fasting and penance are encouraged, particularly during the first and third weeks. For those who have spiritual directors, you should consult them about what is appropriate during this time. In general, the rule of *tantum quantum* applies here: you can do as much as you can, provided it doesn't impede the objective of doing the *Exercises* in the first place. In other words, if you are so famished that you can't concentrate at all, or all your meditations revolve around what was eaten (at the Last Supper, at the wedding at Cana, etc.), you've gone too far. However, as Ignatius points out, in that way, you've come to learn "what's suitable for you," meaning, what it is you need, and what is extra. It's a learning process, and also requires that we know ourselves: some people tend to push themselves too hard, while other don't push themselves enough.

Secondly, Ignatius provides for the opportunity to make a general confession, meaning, a confession of all the sins of one's life. In fact, he gives a meditation, the one on *Our Own Sins*, in order to help us prepare for it. This idea of a general confession will be brought up again during the course of the *Exercises*, but there's something worth saying about it, over and over again. We don't make a general confession because we haven't been forgiven when we confessed our sins before; the other confessions, if we made them well, erased those sins. However, Ignatius points out that, since we're on the *Exercises*, our contrition is greater, since we're thinking about just how bad our sins are. Increased contrition produces more grace through the sacrament which reduces the likelihood of falling back into that sin and increases the likelihood of our perseverance in grace. That being said, no one is obligated to make a general confession, but most people do.

An Examination of the Meditation

- Did I give all the time to prayer, or did I cut it short?
- Did I achieve or obtain the fruit proper to each meditation (the fruit found in the petition)?
- Can I pinpoint why or why not? Was I at fault? Or was it something beyond my control? Do I need to move somewhere else? Change my posture?
- Has everything been good, meaning, inclining me to good? (That's a good sign)
- Has it ended in bad, distracting, or less good things, or has it disturbed my peace? (That's a bad sign).
- Do I repeat the petition as many times as I need to?
- How do I speak in the colloquies? With affection, confidence, humility, and reverence?
- To what degree do I have a desire to take advantage of the *Exercises as* much as possible?
- How great is my desire to give everything to God?
- Have I grown in my desire to conquer myself?
- Am I removing those disordered affections so as to order myself to God?
- How is my desire to apply what I've seen to the whole of my daily life?
- Has my sorrow for my sins increased?
- Do I have a desire to do great things for God?
- How deep and intimate is my knowledge of Jesus?

- Am I learning more and more from His life and doctrine in order to grow in holiness?
- Are my love for Him and my desire to imitate Him increasing?
- What effect has this exercise that I've just done exerted in my soul?
- Did I get some concrete fruit or resolution out of this meditation?

Introductory Notes for the Exercises

Fr. Calveras, one of the foremost experts from the last century on the *Spiritual Exercises*, gives the following indication in his book *Practica de los Ejercicios Intensivos*: "The night when the retreatants gather, nothing else need be done but to prepare themselves and dispose themselves with *prayer* in order to make the Exercises perfectly, first by asking Our Lord for three graces: first, to secure the dispositions that are most fitting for the abundant reception of grace, meaning two things: on one hand, the desire to take advantage of the Exercises as much as possible, a liberal surrender of self, meaning, one's person and all that they have, into God's hands, and, on the other, rectitude of intention, attempting only to please God in the Exercises that are to begin. The second grace is that of making the Exercises diligently, overcoming everything that might impede this, and, the third grace, that of obtaining the fruit that gives the most glory to God and is most beneficial to souls.

Second, they should seek to carry themselves as noble soldiers of Jesus Christ in everything that they see. Likewise, they should be very *thoughtful* in cooperating with grace by means of solitude, fidelity to the schedule and method of the *Exercises*, and work in obtaining the proposed fruit. They should be *simple* as doves, always interpreting charitably everything that is done or said to them. Finally they should be as *prudent* as a serpent, not hiding anything in their thoughts that either the devil or the good spirit might give, but rather communicating them with the one who is giving the Exercises, so that they might not be tricked.

Third, since time will be given towards the end of the first week to prepare for the general confession, it should not be thought upon until then. Retreatants can celebrate Mass or receive communion if they usually do so, and go to confession, if they have not done so, before they begins considering the Principle and Foundation."

To help with these preliminary considerations, it may be helpful to think of Jesus' words regarding the vine and the branches during the Last Supper (Jn 15:1-10). "I am the true vine, and my Father is the vine grower. He takes away every branch in me that does not bear fruit, and every one that does he prunes so that it bears more fruit. You are already pruned because of the word that I spoke to you. Remain in me, as I remain in you. Just as a branch cannot bear fruit on its own unless it remains on the vine, so neither can you unless you remain in me. I am the vine, you are the branches. Whoever remains in me and I in him will bear much fruit, because without me you can do nothing. Anyone who does not remain in me will be thrown out like a branch and wither; people will gather them and throw them into a fire and they will be burned. If you remain in me and my words remain in you, ask for whatever you want and it will be done for you. By this is my Father glorified, that you bear much fruit and become my disciples."

The work of the vinedresser is long and hard; it takes time and intimate knowledge of the vines themselves. It would not be an exaggeration to say that the vine owner would know his vines like a shepherd knows his sheep. Vineyard owners would sometimes spend three years teaching their workers how, where, and when to cut the vines. They need constant pruning. While this process is painful, only by this way can the vine produce the best fruit. Even healthy branches would be pruned to give only the very best. The Greek for "every vine that does bear fruit" is emphatic: each and every vine the Lord prunes. No vine is exempt.

This is the work that God wants to do in us; this is what He wants to do in our lives. This is the work of the Spiritual Exercises.

The end of the Exercises [21] Which have as their purpose the conquest of self and the regulation of one's life in such a way that no decision is made under the influence of any inordinate attachment

Presupposition [22] To assure better cooperation between the one who is giving the Exercises and the exercitant, and more beneficial results for both, it is necessary to suppose that every good Christian is more ready to put a good interpretation on another's statement than to condemn it as false. If an orthodox construction cannot be put on a proposition, the one who made it should be asked how he understands it. If he is in error, he should be corrected with all kindness. If this does not suffice, all appropriate means should be used to bring him to a correct interpretation, and so defend the proposition from error.

Dispositions [15, 16]
The director of the Exercises ought not to urge the exercitant more to poverty or any promise than to the contrary, nor to one state of life or way of living more than to another. Outside the Exercises, it is true, we may lawfully and meritoriously urge all who probably have the required fitness to choose continence, virginity, the religious life, and every form of religious perfection.

THE WAY TO MAKE THE MEDITATIONS

The General Method, 45 – 49, with Additional Directions: 73 – 81, 199

"By the term 'Spiritual Exercises' is meant every method of examination of conscience, of meditation, of contemplation, of vocal and mental prayer, and of other spiritual activities that will be mentioned later. For just as taking a walk, journeying on foot, and running are bodily exercises, so we call Spiritual Exercises every way of preparing and disposing the soul to rid itself of all inordinate attachments, and, after their removal, of seeking and finding the will of God in the disposition of our life for the salvation of our soul."

Beginning of Meditation: (75) I will stand for the space of an *Our Father*, a step or two before the place where I am to meditate or contemplate, and with my mind raised on high, consider that God our Lord beholds me, etc. Then I will make an act of reverence or humility.

I will enter upon the meditation, now kneeling, now prostrate upon the ground, now lying face upwards, now seated, now standing, always being intent on seeking what I desire. Hence, two things should be noted:

- If I find what I desire while kneeling, I will not seek to change my position: if prostrate, I will observe the same direction, etc.
- I will remain quietly meditating upon the point in which I have found what I desire, without any eagerness to go on till I have been satisfied.

Prayer: In the preparatory prayer I will beg God our Lord for grace that all my intentions, actions, and operations may be directed purely to the praise and service of His Divine Majesty [this part never changes].

First Prelude: This is a mental representation of the place [also called the *composition of place*].

Attention must be called to the following point:

When the contemplation or meditation is on something visible, for example, when we contemplate Christ our Lord, the representation will consist in seeing in imagination the material place where the object is that we wish to contemplate. I said the material place, for example, the temple, or the mountain where Jesus or His Mother is, according to the subject matter of the contemplation.

In a case where the subject matter is not visible, as here in a meditation on sin, the representation will be to see in imagination my soul as a prisoner in this corruptible body, and to consider my whole composite being as an exile here on earth, cast out to live among brute beasts. I said my whole composite being, body and soul.

The Second Prelude: I will ask God our Lord for what I want and desire. The petition made in this prelude must be according to the subject matter. Thus in a contemplation on the Resurrection, I will ask for joy with Christ in joy. In one on the passion, I will ask for sorrow, tears, and anguish with Christ in anguish.

Note: *The Preparatory Prayer, which is never changed, and the two Preludes mentioned above, which are changed at times according to the subject matter, must always be made before all the contemplations and meditations.*

End of Meditation: The colloquy [Latin *colloquium* "conference, conversation," literally "a speaking together," from *com-* "together" + *-loquium* "speaking," from *loqui* "to speak"] is made by speaking exactly as one friend speaks to another, or as a servant speaks to a master, now asking him for a favor, now blaming himself for some misdeed, now making known his affairs to him, and seeking advice in them. Close with an *Our Father.*
"In the colloquy, one should talk over motives and present petitions according to circumstances. Thus he may be tempted or he may enjoy consolation, may desire to have this virtue or another, may want to dispose himself in this or that way, may seek to grieve or rejoice according to the matter that he is contemplating. Finally, he should ask what he more earnestly desires with regard to some particular interests." [199]

At the end of the hour: After an exercise is finished, either sitting or walking, *I will consider for the space of a quarter of an hour how I succeeded in the meditation or contemplation.* If poorly, I will seek the cause of the failure; and after I have found it, I will be sorry, so that I may do better in the future. If I have succeeded, I will give thanks to God our Lord, and the next time try to follow the same method.

Each meditation should have some sort of concrete fruit as its conclusion: something that needs to be done, or thought about, or discerned, or considered.

General Observations:

After retiring, just before falling asleep, for the space of a *Hail Mary*, I will think of the hour when I have to rise, and why I am rising, and briefly sum up the exercise I have to go through.

When I wake up, I will not permit my thoughts to roam at random, but will turn my mind at once to the subject I am about to contemplate in the first exercise at midnight.... As I dress, I will think over these thoughts or others in keeping with the subject matter of the meditation.

[During this first week] I should not think of things that give pleasure and joy, such as the glory of Heaven, the Resurrection, etc., for if I wish to feel pain, sorrow, and tears for my sins, every consideration promoting joy and happiness will impede it. I should rather keep in mind that I want to be sorry and feel pain. Hence it would be better to call to mind death and judgment.

For the same reason I should deprive myself of all light, closing the shutters and doors when I am in my room, except when I need light to say prayers, to read, or to eat.

I should not laugh or say anything that would cause laughter.

I should restrain my eyes except to look up in receiving or dismissing one with whom I have to speak.

The Principle and Foundation

Man is created to praise, reverence, and serve God our Lord, and by this means to save his soul. The other things on the face of the earth are created for man to help him in attaining the end for which he is created. Hence, man is to make use of them in as far as they help him in the attainment of his end, and he must rid himself of them in as far as they prove a hindrance to him. Therefore, we must make ourselves indifferent to all created things, as far as we are allowed free choice and are not under any prohibition. Consequently, as far as we are concerned, we should not prefer health to sickness, riches to poverty, honor to dishonor, a long life to a short life. The same holds for all other things. Our one desire and choice should be what is more conducive to the end for which we are created.

FIRST WEEK

Meditations and Contemplations

But while one is engaged in the Spiritual Exercises, it is more suitable and much better that the Creator and Lord in person communicate Himself to the devout soul in quest of the divine will, that He inflame it with His love and praise, and dispose it for the way in which it could better serve God in the future. Therefore, the director of the Exercises, as a balance at equilibrium, without leaning to one side or the other, should permit the Creator to deal directly with the creature, and the creature directly with his Creator and Lord.

Hence, that the Creator and Lord may work with greater certainty in His creature, if the soul chance to be inordinately attached or inclined to anything, it is very proper that it rouse itself by the exertion of all its powers to desire the opposite of that to which it is wrongly attached. Thus if one's attachment leads him to seek and to hold an office or a benefice, not for the honor and glory of God our Lord, nor for the spiritual welfare of souls, but for his own personal gain and temporal interests, he should strive to rouse a desire for the contrary. Let him be insistent in prayer and in his other spiritual exercises in begging God for the reverse, that is, that he neither seek such office or benefice, nor anything else, unless the Divine Majesty duly regulate his desires and change his former attachment. As a result, the reason he wants or retains anything will be solely the service, honor, and glory of the Divine Majesty.

Fidelity to the Exercises [12, 13, 14, 17, 20]

While the exercitant is engaged in the First Week of the Exercises, it will be helpful if he knows nothing of what is to be done in the Second Week. Rather, let him labor to attain what he is seeking in the First Week as if he hoped to find no good in the Second.

He who is giving the Exercises must insist with the exercitant that since he is to spend an hour in each of the five exercises or contemplations which are made every day, he must always take care that he is satisfied in the consciousness of having persevered in the exercise for a full hour. Let him rather exceed an hour than not use the full time. For the enemy is accustomed to make every effort that the hour to be devoted to a contemplation, meditation, or prayer should be shortened.

We must remember that during the time of consolation it is easy, and requires only a slight effort, to continue a whole hour in contemplation, but in time of desolation it is very difficult to do so. Hence, in order to fight against the desolation and conquer the temptation, the exercitant must always remain in the exercise a little more than the full hour. Thus he will accustom himself not only to resist the enemy, but even to overthrow him.

While the one who is giving the Exercises should not seek to investigate and know the private thoughts and sins of the exercitant, nevertheless, it will be very helpful if he is kept faithfully informed about the various disturbances and thoughts caused by the action of different spirits. This will enable him to propose some spiritual exercises in accordance with the degree of progress made and suited and adapted to the needs of a soul disturbed in this way.

To one who is more disengaged, and desirous of making as much progress as possible, all the Spiritual Exercises should be given in the same order in which they follow below.

Ordinarily, the progress made in the Exercises will be greater, the more the exercitant withdraws from all friends and acquaintances, and from all worldly cares. For example, he can leave the house in which he dwelt and choose another house or room in order to live there in as great privacy as possible, so that he will be free to go to Mass and Vespers every day without any fear that his acquaintances will cause any difficulty.

There are many advantages resulting from this separation, but the following three are the most important:

First, if in order to serve and praise God our Lord one withdraws from numerous friends and acquaintances and from many occupations not undertaken with a pure intention, he gains no little merit before the Divine Majesty.

Secondly, in this seclusion the mind is not engaged in many things, but can give its whole attention to one single interest, that is, to the service of its Creator and its spiritual progress. Thus it is more free to use its natural powers to seek diligently what it so much desires.

Thirdly, the more the soul is in solitude and seclusion, the more fit it renders itself to approach and be united with its Creator and Lord; and the more closely it is united with Him, the more it disposes itself to receive graces and gifts from the infinite goodness of its God.

Introductory Notes for the Exercises (2)

As we did last night, this talk will not really be a *meditation,* in the strict sense of the word, but rather a continuation of some of the considerations we thought about last night, in order to help us enter more fully into the Exercises. Here are some preliminary thoughts that we should bear in mind throughout this month.

I would like to consider, briefly, two points: first, the nature of holiness in general, meaning, what does it mean to be holy, and, second, what does holiness mean in particular during the Exercises.

What is holiness? What does it mean to be holy? Fr. Casanovas, writing a commentary on the Exercises, but with a meaning that can be applied to the Christian life in general, says, "Holiness, in the broad sense of the word, means moral perfection, and this is what everyone, even the most degenerate and debased civilizations, has understood. . . ." Christian holiness, though, follows a very particular sort of perfection: "Christian holiness is that holiness that takes our Lord Jesus Christ as teacher and model. . . . [and thus] one word defines [Christian holiness] completely: it is the *divinization* of man here in this present life by supernatural participation in the divine life."[1] In other words, as the *Catechism* has it:

> The Word became flesh to make us *partakers of the divine nature.* [As Saint Irenaeus puts it]: "For this is why the Word became man, and the Son of God became the Son of man: so that man, by entering into communion with the Word and thus receiving divine sonship, might become a son of God." [Or, in the words of Saint Athanasius]: "For the Son of God became man so that we might become God." [And, lastly, as the great Saint Thomas Aquinas states]: "The only-begotten Son of God, wanting to make us sharers in his divinity, assumed our nature, so that he, made man, might make men gods."[2]

On one hand, Christ became man because we needed to have forgiveness of our sins; that's the section that precedes this one in the *Catechism.*

1. Ignacio Casanovas, *Ejercicios Espirituales de San Ignacio.* Vol. 1, 30.
2. CCC, 460.

Nonetheless, Christ also came to give us a model, since, absolutely speaking, Christ did not need to become incarnate. God could have arranged for our salvation in another manner but, if He arranged it through the incarnation, there is a reason why that was the best option, the most fitting choice.

Part of this reason is because, as the Word Incarnate, Jesus reveals to us what holiness is. This understanding of Christian holiness needed to be revealed, continues Casanovas, since it is a holiness that relies on grace, which is supernatural. We receive this holiness not only through sanctifying grace, but also in the actual graces that we receive, day in and day out, that lead to my perfection, to my divinization, to my becoming more like God.

In his book, *The Father Revealed by Jesus Christ*, Fr. Miguel Angel Fuentes gives an insightful explanation of what this means; it's the same thought, but expressed differently. In the chapter entitled, "A Father to Imitate," he writes (this is a lengthy section):

"So be perfect, just as your heavenly Father is perfect" (Mt 5:48).

It's a law of life that children are like their parents: not only in their physical characteristics but rather—and perhaps even more—in their movements, gestures, language, mannerisms, reactions, thought processes, psychology, etc.

This similarity is owed to imitation (generally unconscious) and this, in turn, to frequent contact (the daily living together).

Here Jesus is speaking of a need: "*Be.*"

It's an imperative.

It's as if He were to have said: "You are God's children; therefore, be like your Father."

May others "recognize" Whose children you are from your traits.

As Jesus told the Pharisees and the scribes who persecuted Him: "You are doing the works of your father [*the devil*]!" (Jn 8:41); "You belong to your father the devil and you willingly carry out your father's desires. He was a murderer from the beginning and does not stand in truth. . . . But because I speak the truth, you do not believe me" (Jn 8:44-45). Because of their disbelief and their rejection of the truth, those adversaries of the Lord showed that they were children of "The Rejecter of the Truth," of him "who did not remain in the truth," that is, the devil.

Jesus ordered us to imitate our Father's perfection. The Lord thus judges that we are able to know God, and even to know Him "perfectly," in a certain sense, and, even more, to *imitate* Him.

From here we can conclude that if we do not know our Father, the fault is ours. Likewise, if we don't imitate Him, the fault is also ours.

Perhaps we think that we don't know Him, even though He is in front of us. A tree can be in front of our eyes, but if we look for it somewhere else, we will think that we have never encountered it before. Philip tells Jesus at the Last Supper: "Master, show us the Father, and that will be enough for us" (Jn 14:8). And Jesus replies with a reproach: "Have I been with you for so long a time and you still do not know me, Philip? Whoever has seen me has seen the Father" (Jn 14:9).

Imitate God! This seems to be an impossible task. Nevertheless, there are some general features of God to which we may aspire.

The perfection of God is, first of all, to be Spirit; therefore, to imitate His perfection is to become spiritual as much as possible by detachment from all created things, achieving that freedom of which Saint Louis Marie Grignion de Montfort spoke: "free: souls raised above this earth like heavenly dew who, without impediment, fly to and fro in accordance with the breath of the Holy Spirit. It was they, in part, Your Prophets spoke of when they asked: *Who are these that fly as clouds?* [Is. 60:8]. *Wherever the spirit would go, they went* [Ez 1:12]" (*The Fiery Prayer for the Apostles of the Latter Times*).

The Father's perfection consists in being God; thus, to imitate His perfection is to let oneself be divinized by Him as much as is possible; it is to live His very life, which we receive through participation in the sanctifying grace which He infuses into our hearts.

The Father's perfection is to give Himself whole and entire; therefore, to imitate His perfection is to set off on the path to the total gift of oneself.

Jesus says: "But the hour is coming, and is now here, when true worshipers will worship the Father in Spirit and truth; and indeed the Father seeks such people to worship him" (Jn 4:23). *These are the ones that He seeks to have worship Him.* The perfection that Jesus Christ demands of us in order to be like the heavenly Father is to live "in spirit and truth," that is, explains Saint Thomas, in "the fervor of love [and in] the truth of faith" (*Commentary on Saint John*). The Father wants His Adorers, His children, to be transformed by the truth (which comes to us through faith in the Truth revealed by God the Father) and pierced by love.

By means of these two virtues, we resemble the Father who is Love and Truth."[3] Thus far Fr. Fuentes.

Going back to holiness, and what it means for the Exercises, Casanovas continues by giving a couple of basic points regarding holiness. We can break them into four[4]:

---

3. Miguel Angel Fuentes, *The Father Revealed by Jesus Christ* (Chillum: IVEPress, 2018), 39-42.

4. Casanovas, 32-34.

First, the laws of holiness don't change and shouldn't be changed because they come directly from God or indirectly from God through our human nature. Attempting to change the laws of holiness is where heresies start, like Pelagianism which diminishes the role of grace, and Lutheranism, which denies free will. In this sense, we could say that what Casanovas means is that grace builds on nature; it doesn't destroy it. We need to cooperate with God; He takes the first step and then, together, we advance on the path to holiness. Grace builds on nature: in the introduction to *Saints are not Sad*, Frank Sheed notes that the saints are more perfectly themselves, because they come to resemble the idea that God has of them. Sinners tend to all be the same, since sin bleeds the color out of people.

Second, the example and path to holiness should be taken from the life and example of Jesus Christ. I am not the measure of holiness; my judgments are not infallible; I am not the Second Coming. I need to conform myself to Christ, and not vice versa: either making Christ conform to my likings and my whims, or conforming myself to what I think Christ is, or what I think He should be.

Third, God has graces prepared for each and everyone one of us, which He wants to give so that we can become saints. It is this connection, God working with us and us working with God, that produces holiness. This means, too, that we don't need to look for or await great supernatural graces (as if grace could somehow not be great!) like levitation, or visions, or speaking in unknown languages. Sometimes God does grant those gifts, but *holiness does not consist in such things*. Holiness is the conformity of ourselves with Christ: nothing more, but also nothing less.

Fourth, there is a great difference between knowing what holiness is, and being holy in practice. In fact, you can have the knowledge, and know all the lives of so many saints, and yet be a horrible sinner.

In the Exercises then, and throughout your lives, I would call attention to two impediments that can creep up and really wreak havoc on the search for holiness. One impediment is found in the intellect, and the other in the will.

In the intellect, we sometimes find the vice of *spiritual pride*. In Spanish, they use the word *juicio propio*, which is very apt, because it implies being attached to your own judgment, the way you see things. This is deadly because it prevents us from being able to see anything clearly.

In his book, *The Three Ages of the Interior* Life, Fr. Garrigou-Lagrange explains that spiritual pride "gives us such confidence in our reason and judgment that we are not very willing to consult others, especially our superiors, or to enlighten ourselves by the attentive and benevolent examination of reasons or facts which may be urged against us. This state of mind leads to manifest imprudent acts that will have to be painfully expiated. It leads also to asperity in discussions, to stubbornness in judgment, to disparagement which excludes in a cutting tone all that does not fit in with our manner of seeing things. This pride may lead a person to refuse to others the liberty he claims for his own opinions, and also to submit only very imperfectly to the directions of the supreme Shepherd, and even to attenuate and minimize dogmas under the pretext of explaining them better than has been done hitherto."

In his book, *He Blinded Their Eyes,*[5] Fr. Fuentes notes some typical examples of "spiritual pride":

- The one who never asks the advice of the person who knows more than they do
- The one who asks for advice, but has already decided what to do
- The one who scorns spiritual direction or is negligent in doing it
- The one who scorns the advice that comes from others
- The one who doesn't willingly accept corrections
- The one who disputes (at least interiorly) the directions of their superiors
- The one who obstinately defends their opinion in things that are debatable
- The one who does not change their opinions, even when their errors are pointed out
- The one who makes everything subjective, judging from a partial and particular point of view
- The one who forms their judgments starting from the passions that dominate them

Be aware of this: if you have spiritual pride, your Exercises will be very difficult, and perhaps, I dare say, even useless.

A second impediment, again, considering this as a preparation for the Exercises, is *a weak will* that refuses to make the effort needed to work towards becoming a saint. There is a great deal that could be said here, but I will simply note that *laziness, acedia, emotional instability, an unhealthy reliance on the feelings and support of others*, and many other things, can result in a weakening of our will.

Again, in very summarized form, what we need to do is be convinced that holiness is *something good*, that it is *something good for me*, and that I can achieve it. This is what we need to have in mind.

I need to see holiness as a good *in the abstract or universal sense*. I need to see it as something good in general, for everyone. It is a good *in general*, and,

---

5. Miguel Angel Fuentes, *He Blinded Their Eyes* (Chillum: IVEPress, 2019). This is the translation of the Spanish Virtus book *Cego sus ojos*.

in general, then, it should be desired and sought after. However, I cannot remain on that general level. I need to bring myself to consider that *it is something good for me*; if I don't individualize it, it doesn't help. It remains on the abstract level. Lastly, once I am convinced that it is a good for me, I must be convinced that, with God's grace I can achieve it, and thus I will put the means into place to obtain that holiness.

We should ask our Blessed Mother, Mother of All Religious and Help of Christians, to help us obtain these graces from her Son, so that we might truly take advantage of these Exercises to grow into holiness.

Introductory Notes for the Exercises (3)

Once again, this talk will not really be a *meditation*, in the strict sense of the word, but rather a continuation of some considerations about the Exercises, and now we will focus on some practical applications. What are the fruits that we should get out of the Exercises? For this, we will follow a book by Fr. Calveras, entitled precisely that *What Fruits Should be Obtained from the Spiritual Exercises of Saint Ignatius.*[1]

Following what Ignatius says in the Exercises, Calveras proposes three fruits, which we can list, and then consider the first more in depth (since it is linked to the first week). We do this because this will really help us to direct our efforts and to see what sort of things we should be aiming to fix and improve.

1st: *To conquer oneself*: by means of subjecting our reason, our will, and our understanding to God, and by dominating, in the sense of controlling, our sensuality (imagination, interior senses, and sensitive appetites) and the lower parts of man (exterior senses and parts of the body), to the point of achieving a transformation of heart and a stable and certain peace of soul.

2nd: *To order one's life*: by disposing for a right choice of a state of life (if that is needed) and the principal occupations of a person in it, and reforming and reordering the exercise of all internal and external activity, without forgetting the other things to be done in life, and

3rd: *Spiritual formation*: and this in the different practices of the interior life, like the experience and discernment of the different spirits and interior motions that come upon the soul.

If all of these are achieved, then the result is that a person will be able to *love and serve the Divine majesty in everything.*

The first fruit of the Exercises, and the one that we will focus on during this meditation, is victory over oneself, which we can see in the very title of the Exercises themselves, as we read in [21]: "The Spiritual Exercises, which have as their purpose the conquest of self."

To conquer oneself means to obtain control and dominion over one's interior kingdom, a kingdom comprised of body and soul, with their members, with the interior and exterior senses in the sensitive and spiritual order; in

1. Jose Calveras, *Que fruto se ha de sacar de los Ejercicios Espirituales de San Ignacio.* 45-71.

other words, it means to take our fallen human nature and, by the work of grace in our souls, restore to it, as much as possible, the internal peace and harmony of that original state of innocence, the fruit of our original integrity.

The perfect victory, as we read in the *Imitation of Christ* "is to triumph over self. For he who holds himself in such subjection that sensuality obeys reason and reason obeys [God] in all matters, is truly his own conqueror and master of the world." Ignatius specifies that another object of this victory is "to make our sensual nature obey reason, and to bring all of our lower faculties into greater subjection to the higher" [87]. Thus, when we speak of victory over ourselves, we mean, as included in this, a descending order of subjection: our reason is subjected to God, our sensuality is subjected to reason, and the lower parts are entirely subjected to what is above.

How does one subject their reason to God? This work entails two parts: subjecting not only reason to God, but also the will, since the will, as the queen of the other potencies, orders and commands them.

Let's begin then, with the will. The work to be done here isn't simply with the will *as such*, meaning, just the will and its ability to make decisions, to act or not act, to want or not want, but rather even the "*sensible side of the will*" as Calveras calls it. He means how the will can be affected by the lower appetites, in the sense that they can draw it, by means of the intellect, to want this or that in a disordered way. We could say, in perhaps more Thomistic terms, that he is referring to how the passions can cause problems for the higher faculties, and we need to subject the will so it doesn't fall into those errors.

So, how is the will subjected to God? "By ordering our love perfectly," which means pulling up any evil or dangerous "loves" to the point where we despise those things, and taking things that are honest and good loves and transforming them into spiritual loves so that, in this way, we might love, with one same love, ordered and purified, God in Himself, in us, and in other creatures, and love ourselves and other creatures in Him.

From this one purified love, will come true, stable, and efficacious desires to please Him in everything. This stable love won't permit us to be shaken by those emotions which are produced in us by the actions of others or by circumstances.

So, practically speaking, how can we reach this one, undivided love for God during the Exercises? First, we should hate our sins, mortal and venial, and even things that, without being sins, are disordered; we should also hate the world in the sense of the worldly spirit of show and appearance. This hatred or scorn will destroy whatever particular love or attachment we have in the will.

Second, we should, as much as possible, try to extinguish in our wills any feeling of repugnance or rejection of a real or imagined sacrifice or cross.

Third, we should order all of our loves and particular attachments to things that are good or indifferent of themselves when we see that God is not the reason we love them.

Fourth, we should strive and ask for a deep love of the person of Jesus Christ, so that we can intensely feel His pains and sufferings and rejoice in His triumph as if all these things were our own.

Fifth, we should order our natural love of ourselves, so that even while we are seeking excellence and perfection, we should do so only in God.

Lastly, we should place all of our love of self and complacency in God Himself, since He is the source of all good.

How is this possible? Only by grace, because in order to seek the things of God, I need to experience a sort of delight in them, and this only comes from prayer.

As we mentioned earlier, this work on the will must go hand in hand with a work on the intellect, in reforming our judgments. So, we can re-consider all of the steps of the will and examine what role the intellect must play in them.

On one hand, this means changing the judgments that I have formed. For example, this means changing "the formal concepts" I have. For instance, I can only really hate my sins and the disorder in my life when I have a real understanding of the ugliness and malice of each sin committed, of the lack of conformity between my actions and right reason, and the irrationality of the worldly spirit.

To overcome a repugnance for the cross and sacrifice, I should correct my "natural" judgments that see those things as bad or harmful, and instead examine them under the light of the benefits that come to me from them, of the good that they do me, and how they make me perfect.

To love Jesus Christ profoundly, I must develop a profound and intimate knowledge of what Christ has done for me, becoming man and dying for me.

To perfectly order my self-love in God, to seek Him and only Him in everything, I should correct my natural judgment that thinks, erroneously, that happiness and love is found in worldly greatness and in loving and delighting in creatures.

Lastly, a love of God must come from an internal knowledge of His infinite perfections. The limited goods of earth which the Divine goodness has given, all fade away in the face of infinite divine perfection.

This reform of intellect also entails a reform of my *practical judgments*, adjusting my judgments to match those of God, who is the true judge of all things. The Bible tells us that we must "Love the Lord our God with all our heart, all our soul, all our mind, and all our strength." Hence, I should reform my judgments so that:

- I judge as disordered and to be avoided, everything that is not based on the reason of pure service of God;
- I set, as a first practical principle of my actions, valid everywhere and always, without any possible exception or dispensation, to do in every setting what is more conducive to my last end, what is most pleasing to His divine goodness, and His most holy and ever pleasing will.

This is useful for the two higher faculties of the soul, the will and the intellect. However, we must also conquer and submit our sensuality, meaning, the lower parts of our soul. This means:

- Regulating the sensible appetite's influence, in such a way that the emotions and the passions serve the will in accord with the dictates of reason. On the one hand, this means to try to intervene when the emotions get worked up, but also to use them to help us achieve our goals, thinking of things that rouse the emotions and inspire us.
- Subjecting the imagination and avoiding all disorder in the use of our senses, rejecting the desire to see, to hear, to experience, to imagine whatever is pleasant, and even more what exposes to danger and temptations.
- Dominating the fickleness of our will, acting against our desires or lack of desire to not act or to act; those desires that come and go at whim, and that move us to engage ourselves in useless, superficial, or disordered things.
- To restrain our tongue and to moderate our gestures, so that we do everything with modesty and dignity, without the least sign of impatience or pride, in this way correcting bad habits that we might have
- To control ourselves in our eating and drinking, never giving way to temptation or to desire, and in the same way controlling our desire for sleep and any other natural need.
- To obtain perfect chastity and defend it by means of mortification and penance.

These are difficult things to do, first because our flesh rebels against them, but also because we have a natural tendency in our fallen nature to seek what is easy and our reason naturally judges things backwards from God's way of seeing them.

Fortunately, a month of Exercises will help, especially if we really try to live out this time generously, offering sacrifices and penances, and taking advantage of every moment to die to ourselves so as to live for God.

Introductory Notes for the Exercises (4)

For our last set of introductory points before we embark onto the meditations on the Principle and Foundation, we will consider the 1st and the 3rd method of prayer. These can be found in the book of the Exercises, points 238 to 248, and then 258 to 260.

These methods of prayer aren't assigned a particular time or place. However, Ignatius himself and commentators on the Exercises emphasize the need to explain them to retreatants, especially those who are making the month-long Exercises for the first time, but also and even to those who are only taking the "Exercises of the First Week." The reason for this is that these forms of prayer are usually meant not only for during the Exercises, but also beyond, aiding the perseverance of the retreatants. So, we will present these two methods of prayer here.

One might ask, why are these methods here? As Calveras notes,[1] following the historical study of the Exercises, these methods have three main goals:

First, they provide *ample material* for meditation in an *easy and relaxed* way, in order to assure continued prayer after the Exercises end and thus to assure the spiritual refreshment of the exercitant.

Second, to give a form and a way *to carry forward the ordering of one's life,* progressively continuing the work of self-knowledge and perfection in everyday works,

Third, to begin the *practice of perfect vocal prayer* by uniting it to mental prayer, to give life to liturgical prayer which then refreshes the soul.

We will see more as we consider the methods themselves; also, bearing this history in mind, we should know that it isn't mandatory to practice these methods of prayer during the Exercises, but it can be useful and you should feel free to use them if you would like.

"The first mode of prayer, with its four topics," says Calveras, "gives an easy but complete, full, and efficient exercise, inasmuch as it advances the whole of self-knowledge and strengthens the will in order to improve itself, and hence is very appropriate for monthly retreat days. In the commandments, complimented by the particular obligations of one's state, we make an examination

---

1. Calveras, *Practica de los Ejercicios Intensivos,* 411-500.

of the whole of God's will that has been revealed to us, both directly and indirectly. In the seven capital sins with their contrary virtues, we examine the affective (emotional) dispositions of the heart, and in the three potencies and five senses we make a complete run through of all our potencies and faculties. At the same time that the will acts by repenting, asking for forgiveness and grace in order to change, vocal prayers are multipled, begging to obtain graces in order to effectively amend our lives."

Let's consider, first, the text itself:

[238] Three Methods of Prayer

The First Method of Prayer
The First Method of Prayer is on the Ten Commandments, the Seven Capital Sins, the three powers of the soul, and the five senses. This manner of praying is not meant so much to provide a form and method of prayer, but rather to supply a way of proceeding and some practices by which the soul may prepare itself and profit so that its prayer may be acceptable to God.

On the Ten Commandments
[239] Additional Direction
First an equivalent of the second Additional Direction as given in the Second Week is to be observed, that is, before entering on the prayer I recollect myself for a while, and either seated or walking up and down, as may seem better, I will consider where I am going, and for what purpose. The same direction should be observed at the beginning of all the methods of prayer.

[240] **Prayer:** A preparatory prayer should be made, for example, I ask God our Lord for grace to know how I have failed in the observance of the Ten Commandments, and also for grace and help to amend for the future. I will beg for a perfect understanding of them in order to observe them better and glorify and praise the Divine Majesty more.

[241] **Method:** In this first method of prayer I should consider and think over the First Commandment, asking myself, how I have observed it, and in what I have failed. I will use as a measure of this consideration the space of time it takes to recite three times the *Our Father* and the *Hail Mary* [and how, might we ask, do we know how long it takes? Because we actually recite them during that time]. If during this time I find faults I have committed, I will ask forgiveness and say an *Our Father*. This same method will be followed with each of the Ten Commandments.

Notes

I. **[242]** If one comes to the consideration of a Commandment against which he is not in the habit of committing any sins, it is not necessary to delay so long on it. According as he finds that he sins more or less against a Commandment, he should devote more or less time to the examination and consideration of it. The same rule should be observed with regard to the Capital Sins.

II. **[243]** After one has finished the consideration of all the Commandments as indicated above, and has accused himself of his faults, and asked for grace and help to amend for the future, he should close with a colloquy to God our Lord, adapted to the subject matter.

[244] On the Capital Sins
Method

With regard to the Seven Capital Sins, after the Additional Direction, the preparatory prayer should be made in the way prescribed, but with the modification that the object is the sins to be avoided, whereas before, it was the Commandments to be observed. In like manner the method prescribed, the regulation of the time, and the colloquy are to be observed.

- It is worth recalling that the seven deadly sins are gluttony, lust, avarice, pride, despair, wrath, vainglory, and sloth, and their opposing virtues are chastity, temperance, charity, diligence, patience, kindness, and humility.

[245] Note

In order to understand better the faults committed that come under the Seven Capital Sins, let the contrary virtues be considered. So also, the better to avoid these sins, one should resolve to endeavor by devout exercises to acquire and retain the seven virtues contrary to them.

[246] On the Three Powers of the Soul
Method

With regard to the three powers of the soul, observe the same method, measure of time, and additional direction as for the Commandments. As there, use a preparatory prayer and colloquy.

- By this Ignatius means the understanding, the memory, and the will.

[247] On the Five Senses of the Body
Method

With regard to the five senses of the body, the same method should always be observed, only the subject matter is changed.

[248] Note

If anyone wishes to imitate Christ our Lord in the use of the senses, he should recommend himself to His Divine Majesty in the preparatory prayer, and after the consideration of each sense say a *Hail Mary* or an *Our Father*.

If he wishes to imitate our Lady in the use of his senses, he should recommend himself to her in the preparatory prayer that she obtain for him this grace from her Son and Lord, and after the consideration of each sense say a *Hail Mary*.

- Great! So, there we have the first method of prayer. Here, "the whole of our conduct is reviewed, in order to know our own sins, both mortal and venial, our failings, imperfections, and even the natural defects of our character and temperament, with the goal of bringing about the work of correcting them and ordering our lives, a task begun in the first week.

    Essentially this method of prayer is an examination of conscience, with repeated acts of the will with interjected vocal prayers. It is different from the general examination of conscience, though, because the general examination is made in order to 'be cleansed' from one's daily faults, 'throwing them out,' that is, 'erasing them' from our consciences by asking sincere forgiveness for them and making amends for the future. This method of prayer, on the other hand, scrutinizes the habitual faults that are present in our souls, not necessarily ones committed today, in order to correct them, as well as to develop a perfect knowledge and understanding of the commandments, the capital sins and their contrary virtues, powers and senses of the soul, in order to observe the commandments more perfectly each day, and to acquire virtues. Hence, this method of prayer also includes a progress in the knowledge of the perfect keeping of God's law and of the ordered use of our faculties, a fruit of considering each commandment that is ordered and sin that is prohibited, and in the right use and abuse of each sense and potency. Thus, there is a two-fold intellectual growth: I consider, first, the commandment in itself, what it commands and what it forbids, and, second, I can examine how I have kept or have broken it. The same could be said of every sin, potency, and sense."
- This leads, then, to the third method of prayer, "a measured rhythmical recitation." One might ask, "Why?", but again Calveras states that

the point is to "say the words of each prayer rhythmically, one word per breath, in order to give oneself time to be impressed or struck by their meaning, in such a way that the idea of the word be accompanied by the imagination, and this, in turn, should awaken a corresponding reflection in the sensibility . . . in order to pray with greater fervor."

[258] Third Method of Prayer - A Measured Rhythmical Recitation

Additional Direction: The same Additional Direction will be observed here as in the First and Second Methods.

Prayer: The preparatory prayer will be as in the Second Method of Prayer.

Method: This is as follows: With each breath or respiration, one should pray mentally while saying a single word of the *Our Father,* or other prayer that is being recited, in such a way that from one breath to another a single word is said. For this same space of time, the attention is chiefly directed to the meaning of the word, to the person who is addressed, to our own lowliness, or the difference between the greatness of the person and our own littleness. In this way, observing the same measure of time, he should go through the other words of the *Our Father.* Let the other prayers, the *Hail Mary,* the *Soul of Christ,* the Creed, and the *Hail Holy Queen,* be recited in the ordinary way.

[259] Rule I

On another day, or at some other time, when he wishes to pray, he may recite the *Hail Mary* in this measured rhythm, and the other prayers in the ordinary way.

[260] Rule II

He who wishes to spend more time in this measured prayer, may say all the prayers mentioned above, or a part of them in this way. But let him keep the same method of a breath for the measure as has been explained above.

- Again, the point that Ignatius is trying to make "is to help us to pray these vocal prayers with devotion, that is, more slowly and with more attention and delight, and thus we can find spiritual refreshment in them."

Principle and Foundation Talk #1
In the Book of the Exercises:

[23]. "Man was created to praise, reverence, and serve God our Lord, and by this means to save his soul; and the other things on the face of the earth were created for man's sake, in order to aid him in the prosecution of the End for which he was created. From this it follows that man is to use them as much as they help him on to his end, and ought to rid himself of them so far as they hinder him as to it."

Usual Preparation Prayer.

First Prelude: The Composition of Place: Heaven opened above me and Hell yawning under my feet; also myself placed on this earth, halfway between Heaven and Hell, and saying to myself: "For all eternity I'll either be in Heaven with God, Mary, and all the saints, or else in Hell suffering the torments of Satan; and it depends on me alone, which of these two conditions will be my lot within a few years, perhaps within a few months, weeks, or days; it depends on me alone whether I am to gain so great a good or to incur so great an evil."

Second Prelude: The Petition I need to ask for light to know clearly, to realize intimately the supreme importance of this matter of my salvation and sanctification, as well as strength to adopt resolutely all the means that will most surely bring it to a successful issue. This, then, I must implore with all the energy of my being, with the utmost earnestness and fervor.

That truth we just heard is called "The Principal and Foundation," and early Jesuit books on the Exercises call it "the groundwork of the entire spiritual and moral edifice."[1] This point, then, is the foundation of the entire Spiritual Exercises, and must be the foundation of my entire life.

Let's hear those words again: "Man was created to praise, reverence, and serve God our Lord, and by this means to save his soul; and the other things on the face of the earth were created for man's sake, in order to aid him in the prosecution of the End for which he was created. From this it follows that

---

1. Directory of 1599.

man is to use them as much as they help him on to his end, and ought to rid himself of them so far as they hinder him as to it."

There are three things we can consider: first, the end for which we were created, second, the means to attain this end, and thirdly, the difficulties that we encounter in choosing the right means. So the end itself, the means to it, and the difficulties in choosing it.

The end of man: Why are we even here on this planet in the first place? Why are we here at all? Why aren't we nothing? We know that God created us, and that He did so out of love. He didn't and doesn't *need* us, He didn't do Himself a favor by creating us, but rather He called us into being to show forth His greatness and love. God, who is the Eternal Being, Infinite Perfection, Love Itself, wanted me to come into this world, to share in His love and His perfection. I belong entirely to Him, and therefore my life must be entirely concerned with doing whatever it is He asks of me.

If you're familiar with the Baltimore Catechism, you probably recognize these points as the first four questions: 1. Who made us? God made us. 2. Who is God? God is the Supreme Being, infinitely perfect, who made all things and keeps them in existence. 3. Why did God make us? God made us to show forth His goodness and to share with us His everlasting happiness in Heaven. 4. What must we do to gain the happiness of Heaven? To gain the happiness of Heaven we must know, love, and serve God in this world.

These are simple truths! There's nothing tricky about them. *But we forget them!* One of God's most common commands in the Old Testament is "Do not forget!" All I have to do in this world to get to Heaven is to love and serve God: that's my whole purpose. As Christ Himself says: "What profit is there for one to gain the whole world and forfeit his life?" his eternal life? This is a matter of supreme importance; in fact, it's really the only important thing in this life: I must serve God and save my soul. That's it: I must save my soul. But how? For this, God has given me a number of things, a great number of things, so I can serve Him.

What are the means to attain this end? The means are "all other things on the face of the earth; all of created reality." Absolutely everything created on this planet is made to help me get to Heaven. This is their sole purpose: to help me get to my eternal home with God. My vocation, my job, my savings account, my family, my skills, my talents, my friends, my education, absolutely everything is supposed to help me get to Heaven. These are the means that I use to serve God, to do His will as He desires. God, who is the author of creation, wants me to get to Heaven; He wants me to be there with Him for all eternity, and so He provides everything that I need in order to get there. How wonderful! How loving!

This all sounds so simple! Yet ... it's hard, the hardest thing we have to do in this life: "Whoever wishes to come after me must deny himself, take up his cross, and follow me." I so desire to serve God with all my heart and all my soul, but ... things stop me. What are these difficulties?

The difficulties are these very same things that God gave me: all of these means are good if I use them for that end, in order to get myself to Heaven, but if I don't, if I make them my end, instead of God, then they become harmful for my soul and my salvation. If I serve created things, be that in some vice that I have, in some job that keeps me from doing God's will, the pride I take in my work or my talents, I can't serve God. "No one can serve two masters ... you cannot serve both God and the riches of this world." It's a hard, cold fact. When this happens, I have an inordinate (meaning, unordered or disordered) attachment to that thing.

If I make my end something other than God, I become a slave to that thing. I become inordinately attached to it; it becomes *my precious, my idol*, the focus of my life and energies to the exclusion of God's will. Having an attachment is like wearing sunglasses: it distorts everything, the way I think, the way I see things. My will is caught up with it, my mind is fixated on it, and I can't do God's will. This doesn't mean that I can't have things, or can't use things, but the problem is when I become more attached to them than I am to God's will.

Ignatius defines the Spiritual Exercises this way: "We call Spiritual Exercises every way of preparing and disposing the soul to rid itself of all inordinate attachments, and, after their removal, of seeking and finding the will of God in the disposition of our life for the salvation of our soul" [1]. This ridding of attachments is one of the key purposes of the Exercises.

For now, we must see what it is we are inordinately attached to, so we can break those attachments, and seek the will of God. Again, many times these things are good in themselves: money, for instance, can be a good thing if we use it well. However, as Saint Henry wrote to his son, "the riches of this world are fleeting and meaningless, while [they are] possessed, unless we can glimpse something of Heaven's eternity" in them. Everything has to help me to my end, and if a created thing doesn't do that, I need to leave it behind.

How do we know when something has become an inordinate attachment? We can consider three criteria given by Fr. Thomas Dubay in *Fire Within* which just take from what Ignatius says, and makes it more concrete. First, *is that the activity or thing is diverted from the purpose God intends for it*. Many things in this world are good, to a point, but when sleep, food, study, or whatever gets away from its purpose, there is a disorder. *The second sign is excess in use. As soon as we go too far in eating, drinking, recreating, speaking, or working, we show that there is something disordered in our activity. We cannot honestly direct to the glory of God what is in excess of what He wills.* Excess is a clear sign of disordered attachment. *The third sign of attachment is making means into ends. . . . As soon as honesty requires us to admit that this* [or that thing] *is not directly or indirectly aimed at Father, Son, and Spirit, we have made ourselves into an idol. We are clearly clinging to something created for our own self-centered sake.*

Again, we can be attached to pretty much anything: physical things like objects or places or work, spiritual things like a gift or talent, and even just my way of seeing things and doing things. Certainly things like vices, or attachments to sin, need to be given up: these are the easiest to see, and the first things to be broken with.

However, if we're free from attachment to grave sin, this work of looking for attachments must be thoughtful and attentive. In a letter to her spiritual director, Saint Gemma Galgani recounts how she was attached to something sort of odd. She writes that she was completely detached from everything, that she had nothing, and yet Jesus found something: "But Jesus – Padre, do you know what He said? – 'That tooth of Ven. Gabriel, tell Me, My daughter, are you not too much attached to that?' (This tooth was a relic of Saint Gabriel Possenti and had been given to her by her director). I was silent for a moment, and then began to complain: 'But Jesus,' I said, almost in tears, 'that's a precious relic!' And Jesus answered rather seriously, 'Daughter, it is your Jesus who tells you so, and that should be sufficient for you.' Alas, it is true Padre. Jesus is right. Sr. Maria asked me for it in order to show it to the nuns, and when I had given it to her I cried because I wanted to have it always near me. But Jesus, Jesus, it is to Him that I must be attached!" I won't ask who has a saint's tooth hidden away, and having a saint's tooth isn't necessarily a bad thing, but it reminds us that even the smallest things can be a hindrance to our holiness.

Some other things worth considering:
- The esteem of others: "I am only that which I am before God," said Saint Francis of Assisi. Of what use is it to be esteemed by men, says Alphonsus, if we are contemptible in the sight of God? And what does it matter if we are despised by the world, provided we are acceptable before God? "What does it matter," exclaims St. Teresa, "if we are loved or hated by creatures, provided we are without blame before you, O God!" How often do we worry about what others think about us, about what our friends would say or do if we gave ourselves fully to God! How often we are concerned about what others think, and we let the fear of what they would do or say get in the way of what we need to do in our lives.
- Our studies, or our works: how often do we consider things to be *my* work, *my* accomplishments, and lose sight of what really matters: that

I need to save my soul . . . Could I leave this behind? Sometimes when we're asked to take on another task, we say what we're doing is too important. Remember that cemeteries are full of indispensable people. Saint Joseph Cottolengo, despite his great accomplishments, never lost sight of the fact that he was a mere instrument; he never became attached to his success. Once he commented: "There is nothing of mine in the Little House, not an inch of ground has been purchased, not a wall has been raised, not a garden fenced, but by the command of Providence: I am ready to tear down with my own hands every brick and fling every tile, were such the Divine bidding." Again, it's not that work or studies are bad things, but if I'm more attached to them than I am to God's will, I won't be free to do what God wants.

– My own opinion, my way of doing things, my way of seeing things: Saint John Climacus says: "He who follows his own ideas in opposition to the direction of his superiors needs no devil to tempt him, for he is a devil to himself." Or, as Saint Bernard put it, "He who is his own master is a scholar under a fool."

– The list goes on: these are all created things as well. What is our saint's tooth? Again, these aren't necessarily bad things; they're great things, if they help us get to Heaven. But, as St. Gemma said, "But Jesus, Jesus, it is to Him [alone] that I must be attached!"

The things of this world, the created goods that are at my disposal, are like scaffolding. When a building is under construction, there's scaffolding all over it so the workers can climb to where they need to go and finish the building. We'd worry about a person if they said, "My, what beautiful scaffolding! I hope it stays like that!"

The things of this world are simply scaffolding: they are the means I use to get myself to Heaven. If they aren't getting me to Heaven, if they aren't letting me do God's will, then they're not fulfilling their purpose.

What is it that we're attached to? What is our saint's tooth? What keeps us from doing God's will?

Colloquy: We can end by conversing with our Lord upon the Cross. Saint Thomas Aquinas wrote that "Whoever wishes to live perfectly should do nothing but disdain what Christ disdained on the cross and desire what he desired." Ask Him for the grace to love what He loves, to desire what He desires, and to disdain what He disdained.

Principle and Foundation Talk #1 – Repetition
In the Book of the Exercises:

[23]. "Man was created to praise, reverence, and serve God our Lord, and by this means to save his soul; and the other things on the face of the earth were created for man's sake, in order to aid him in the prosecution of the End for which he was created. From this it follows that man is to use them as much as they help him on to his end, and ought to rid himself of them so far as they hinder him as to it."

Usual Preparation Prayer.

First Prelude: The Composition of Place: Heaven opened above me and hell yawning under my feet; also myself placed on this earth, halfway between Heaven and hell, and saying to myself: "For all eternity I'll either be in Heaven with God, Mary, and all the saints, or else in hell suffering the torments of Satan; and it depends on me alone, which of these two conditions will be my lot within a few years, perhaps within a few months, weeks, or days; it depends on me alone whether I am to gain so great a good or to incur so great an evil."

Second Prelude: The Petition I need to ask for light to know clearly, to realize intimately the supreme importance of this matter of my salvation and sanctification, as well as strength to adopt resolutely all the means that will most surely bring it to a successful issue. This, then, I must implore with all the energy of my being, with the utmost earnestness and fervor.

Throughout the Exercises, Ignatius instructs that the same meditation be repeated, which he calls, aptly, "a repetition." Usually I will give points for these repeated Exercises, and so here, we will once again consider the principle and foundation and, in particular, the end of man: what is it that man is to do upon this earth?

I will follow, very loosely, some thoughts of Fr. Calveras, as we consider that "man was created to praise, reverence, and serve God our Lord, and by this means to save his soul."

Calveras offers the following note: "God has created us, not in order to escape punishments (meaning, those of purgatory and hell), but rather to be great and happy saints in this life and in the next, so that we might be employed in His service for His glorification and our holiness, without neglecting our neighbors. For these ends, He has given us all other creatures; all of us, without exception, are called to the perfection of the Christian life, regardless the state of life we find ourselves in."[1]

We can look at this both from a negative perspective as well as a positive one, and these will be the two points for this meditation: negative, in the sense that a part of the end of man is to avoid sin, but, positively, it's far more: to seek and strive after holiness.

First, let's consider the negative aspect of man's end, what he has been called to avoid: "It is disordered to separate or get away from the intention that God had in creating us, and this is punished by the voluntary privation of a greater perfection in our actions and the corresponding merit and joy in this life and in the next. Moreover, it is sinful to go against what God has ordered and what He has prohibited, which is positively punished by a temporal or eternal punishment that divine justice imposes on those who act in this way."

There are people in this world who act simply to *avoid mortal sin*. That's their only goal. However, as we see in the Principle and Foundation, that is a very poor goal. In fact, it's not even in keeping with the reason God created us. People will say, "Well, if it's not a sin, then I can do it." This mistake is attractive because it has an element of truth in it: it's true that we should avoid mortal and venial sins. However, there are many things that, even though they aren't sinful, take us away from the goal that God has in creating us. These are, as we said last night, disordered attachments, the disordered use of creatures.

Some people are a little better, and try to avoid all *venial sins*. Again, that's a higher, more generous, disposition, but, still, there are many things that are disordered that are not sinful. Consider an example on the natural level: you could try to clean your hands with motor oil or bacon grease. You could try: it's not sinful, but it just doesn't make any sense, since the point of "cleaning your hands" is to, well, make them clean, and motor oil and bacon grease aren't meant for that. It seems dumb, *but this is precisely what we do when we use creatures in the wrong way.*

In short, we would be wrong to say that the end of man is "simply to avoid sin." That is a very negative outlook on human nature and, really, on the whole universe. The avoidance of sin, the "following of the rules," is a part, just like basketball and soccer have rules that should not be broken. However, the greatness of a basketball star or soccer champion doesn't consist in their unrivalled ability to follow the rules. The rules give a framework, but, within that

1. Jose Calveras, *Practica intensiva*, 38-39.

framework, they excel, and do far more than the minimum suggested by the rules. This is exactly what Ignatius is pointing out in the Principle and Foundation: he doesn't say "man was created to avoid sin, and thus he will save his soul." No, the wording is positive, things man should do: "man was created to praise, reverence, and serve God our Lord, and by *this means* to save his soul."

I would note, as a conclusion, that this wording is far more important than it seems, and it touches on a truth that has far deeper ramifications than we might see at first. The founder of the Schoenstatt movement, Blessed Joseph Kentenich, said that "the one who only wants to avoid sin, will fall into it." The person who has, as their only goal, to avoid sin, will fail and fall into it. This truth follows from what we've said, and we could say, if you will permit me the expression, that to live a life based simply and solely upon avoiding sin *is impossible*; I dare say it is even *anti-natural*, since it goes against our nature, because our nature comes from God, and God didn't make us that way. That is a point worth meditating on, especially because sometimes this point gets us into trouble: if we are seeking to form children in catechism, adults in marriage, or young people discerning, and all we do is hammer home the fact that they shouldn't be sinning, it's not enough. It is a part, but we always need to have the idea of holiness before us. Examine yourselves on this, because this is often at the base of scrupulosity and misinformed consciences.

This leads us, then, to the positive consideration of the Principle and Foundation as regards man's end. Again, Ignatius tells us that "man was created to praise, reverence, and serve God our Lord, and by this means to save his soul."

In this we see that man's vocation is not a vocation to mediocrity: praising, reverencing, and serving God might have a bare minimum, but they have no maximum. My very nature is a call to perfection and to holiness, since God has made me for this end, and He calls me constantly to achieve that end, to seek Him by means of these activities. Again, we could say that *mediocrity is anti-natural*. In spite of the fact that so many people live mediocre lives, *mediocrity is not what we were created for*, and hence it goes against our nature.

What is, then, the proper attitude of man, based solely on the purpose God created him for? Man's natural, proper attitude must be one of *generosity*, of *magnanimity*, of *striving for greatness*.

We can consider, what this greatness of soul consists in, following a writing of Fr. Fuentes (*Duc in altum*):

As its name indicates, magnanimity refers to greatness of soul, *anima magna*. Therefore, Aristotle said that magnanimity is the characteristic of the souls that aspire to what is best, to the highest things. Its object is "what is great," and, more properly, "what is greatest," the "best": the things that, although great, are not "the greatest," are only the secondary matter of this virtue.

Saint Thomas defined it as *extensio animi ad magna,* stretching forth of the soul to great things. Pieper translates this expression as "the striving of the mind towards great things." It is, therefore, a true desire for greatness. Nonetheless, it is essentially different from that desire for greatness which is pride, since pride is a desire for an apparent greatness: greatness based on the recognition of others, in applause, in fame, or in power. On the other hand, magnanimity is a desire for true greatness, that is, for the greatness of a virtue; it is an aspiration to the greatness proper to virtuous works. For this reason, it is called "the flower of virtue," and for this reason too only the virtuous man can be magnanimous, as Saint Thomas says. Beauty is something proper to every virtue, because every virtue has its own specific beauty; but to this, magnanimity adds a beauty that comes from the greatness of the work performed: "further adornment results from the very greatness of a virtuous deed through magnanimity, which makes all virtues greater." Even further, Saint Thomas affirms that to act with magnanimity isn't a characteristic of all the virtuous, but rather proper only to those who are very virtuous, the ones who practice virtue to an eminent degree. This is why he says that Jesus Christ, since He was the most virtuous of all, was also the most magnanimous.

It is said that the magnanimous person seeks greatness. To understand this in the right way, it must be understood that he principally seeks interior greatness, that is, the glory that is intrinsic to virtue. What Saint Bernard said, that love is its own reward, can also be applied to every virtue: the greatness and the reward of every virtue is the exercise of the virtue itself. Magnanimous people believe that they have been sufficiently repaid by the simple fact that they have done something magnanimous. Only as a secondary end, and then according to the circumstances, does the magnanimous person aspire to the exterior glory of the virtue, that is, to the honor that the virtue deserves. Regarding that exterior glory, the magnanimous person should, and indeed does if he is virtuous, desire human glory; however, he also knows that the exterior tribute redounds to the honor of the virtue itself; thus, in a secondary and subordinated way, the person can sometimes aspire to a certain exterior recognition. This is what Saint Paul says: *Your kindness should be known to all* (Phil. 4:5). Christ Himself says: *Your light must shine before others* (Mt 5:16).

Saint Thomas says that the magnanimous person seeks honor for three possible ends. First, it is for his own good, in the sense that the honor that is given him because of his virtue affirms him in his desire for greatness, and it encourages him on to reach perfection. Second, it is for his neighbor's good, because he knows that that in which he excels is a gift from God who has given it to him for the benefit of his neighbor, exciting the neighbor to virtue with his outstanding example of virtue. Finally, it is for God, because he who is virtuous directs all honor to the true cause of virtue, which is God Himself: *What do you possess that you have not received? But if you have received it, why are you boasting as if you did not receive it?* (1 Cor 4:7)."

As we continue our meditation on the Principle and Foundation, and particularly on the end of man, we can consider how we live: are we really living in accord with our nature, with the end God has created us for? Is our attitude one of mediocrity, or of generosity?

Colloquy: We can end with the same colloquy as last night, conversing with our Lord upon the Cross. We can recall what Saint Thomas Aquinas wrote: "Whoever wishes to live perfectly should do nothing but disdain what Christ disdained on the cross and desire what he desired." Ask Him for the grace to love what He loves, to desire what He desires, and to disdain what He disdained.

Principle and Foundation Talk #2 – The End of Creatures

In the Book of the Exercises:

[23]. "Man was created to praise, reverence, and serve God our Lord, and by this means to save his soul; and the other things on the face of the earth were created for man's sake, in order to aid him in the prosecution of the End for which he was created. From this it follows that man is to use them as much as they help him on to his end, and ought to rid himself of them so far as they hinder him as to it."

Usual Preparation Prayer.

First Prelude: The Composition of Place: Heaven opened above me and hell yawning under my feet; also myself placed on this earth, halfway between Heaven and hell, and saying to myself: "For all eternity I'll either be in Heaven with God, Mary, and all the saints, or else in hell suffering the torments of Satan; and it depends on me alone, which of these two conditions will be my lot within a few years, perhaps within a few months, weeks, or days; it depends on me alone whether I am to gain so great a good or to incur so great an evil."

Second Prelude: The Petition I need to ask for light to know clearly, to realize intimately the supreme importance of this matter of my salvation and sanctification, as well as strength to adopt resolutely all the means that will most surely bring it to a successful issue. This, then, I must implore with all the energy of my being, with the utmost earnestness and fervor.

Again, the commentators on the Exercises often give three days dedicated to the Principle and Foundation: one day dedicated to the end of man, another to creatures and their end, as well as their right use, and a third dedicated to indifference. Although we mixed the two last night, tonight we will consider solely creatures and their end.

So, for this meditation, let us consider, simply, some basic truths about creatures, and some practical considerations regarding them.[1]

Regarding some basic truths about creatures, let us begin by considering three points: first, that God has absolute dominion over creatures, second, that creatures have an essential and necessary relation to Him, and, thirdly, that misusing creatures is an injustice and something anti-natural.

Considering the first, that God has absolute dominion over creatures, we must remember that all creatures belong to God as to their owner. God creates them from nothing, He holds them in being, and He directs them to their end, usually through their very nature. This is part of God's providence, that ordering of the universe for an end. In His infinite wisdom, God has established that creatures can be causes with Him, and that they participate in His goodness by means of that ordering.

To man, God gives the use of creatures, but not possession, as it were. They are still "His creatures," we could say. Creatures belong to God; they are His. On one hand, if creatures belong to God, and not to us, we don't really own them like property; we are simply beneficiaries of them, taking advantage of them, like a tenant might lease a vineyard, or like a person might lease a car. If I misuse a creature, no matter what it is, I'm like the slug that messes up the train. True story: it happened in June that a little slug got onto the wires of the high speed trains in Japan, and because it was fried, that little one inch slug shut down huge portions of the railway system.[2] When we misuse creatures, we're slugs that get in the way of the well-ordered providence of God, and distort them for our purposes. Electrical boxes aren't homes for slugs; they just aren't. Nor are creatures meant for my own ends, but rather for God's.

On the other hand, having these creatures speaks to us also of God's goodness and providence. He provides us with what we need, and so we could say that God's wisdom, omnipotence, and goodness are really the root of our obligation to use creatures for God. He is their owner, and, since He adopts us as His children, He transforms us and elevates us. In each creature, then, again, no matter what it is, we should be able to see an image or reflection of God's love for us.

Secondly, we should note that creatures have an essential and a necessary relation to God (necessary, in the sense of a mixed relation: God does not depend on creatures, but creatures do depend on Him). For this reason, just like us men, creatures are meant to tend to God's glory. We know that God does

1. These notes are taken, more or less, from Luis Gonzalez and Ignacio Iparraguierre, *Ejercicios Espirituales – Comentario Pastoral*, 160-162,
2. https://nypost.com/2019/06/24/slug-shorts-out-huge-section-of-japans-high-speed-railway/

nothing without seeking some good, and, when He acts outside of Himself, extrinsically, what He seeks is His glory. This is because, as He is infinitely perfect in Himself, He doesn't need creatures to make Him happy or to perfect Him. Rather, He creates creatures in order to make His own perfections known, adored, and loved.

Hence, all created beings tend to that end, that is, to God's glory, in virtue of a natural ordering, almost a natural virtue, we could say, because perfection consists precisely in seeking that end.

Thirdly, we should consider, then, if creatures are naturally meant to tend towards God's glorification, then to abuse creatures is an injustice, an inversion of the right order, a sort of idolatry.

It follows that creatures that separate us from God are vain and useless. This is because whatever we use to accomplish an end, that is, whatever we use as a mean, has no goodness in itself outside of the end. Since all things have been created so that, as means, they help us to reach our end, it follows necessarily that there is no goodness in them if they are separated from their end; all goodness would be merely vain, false, or deceptive.

Again, we can consider the example we used earlier: you can try to clean your hands with motor oil or bacon grease, but it doesn't work. Those things have a purpose; they have an end, but cleaning hands isn't it.

It's worth noting what the *Catechism* says about idolatry; at 2113 and 2114 we read: "Idolatry not only refers to false pagan worship. It remains a constant temptation to faith. Idolatry consists in divinizing what is not God. Man commits idolatry whenever he honors and reveres a creature in place of God, whether this be gods or demons (for example, satanism), power, pleasure, race, ancestors, the state, money, etc. . . . Idolatry rejects the unique Lordship of God; it is therefore incompatible with communion with God. Human life finds its unity in the adoration of the one God. The commandment to worship the Lord alone integrates man and saves him from an endless disintegration. Idolatry is a perversion of man's innate religious sense. An idolater is someone who transfers his indestructible notion of God to anything other than God."

When we worship God alone, and keep Him in His place, our life is integrated. To abuse creatures is to lose that union and order, and to replace it a cheap imitation.

So, practically speaking, then, what does this mean? This is our second topic.[3] It means that all creatures have one sole purpose in my life, that is, to help me get to Heaven. I am to use them like the tools that they are.

---

3. For this section, I follow, loosely, Coppens, *The Spiritual Exercises of Saint Ignatius*, 13.

Now then, just like the tools we have here in the garage are used differently, so, too, creatures are not all to be used the same way. We could think of four ways creatures are used: some are to be considered, some are to be used, some are to be endured, and some are to be abstained from. Considered, used, endured, and abstained.

First, some things are to be considered and meditated upon so as to bring our hearts to consider God and reverence and serve Him. "The heavens declare the glory of God; the firmament proclaims the works of his hands. Day unto day pours forth speech; night unto night whispers knowledge" (Ps 19).

In a Wednesday audience regarding the gift of knowledge, Pope Saint John Paul the II explained it this way: "We . . . discover the theological meaning of creation, seeing things as true and real, although limited, manifestations of the Truth, Beauty, and infinite Love which is God, and consequently we feel impelled to translate this discovery into praise, song, prayer, and thanksgiving. This is what the Book of Psalms suggests so often and in so many ways. Who does not recall some instances of this raising of the soul to God? 'The heavens are telling the glory of God; and the firmament proclaims his handiwork' (Ps 18 [19]:2; cf. Ps 8:2). 'Praise the Lord from the heavens, praise him in the heights.... Praise him, sun and moon, praise him, all you shining stars!' (Ps 148:1, 3)." This is an excellent point: the natural world, in simply doing what it does, praises God, but we, through the gift of knowledge, can join in this "Canticle of Praise," or, rejecting that gift, we can decide not to.

Other creatures are for the use of man, as food, drink, clothing, etc. Usually when we think of creatures and their "use," this is usually what we have in mind, and, again, we spoke yesterday about signs of disorder in use.

Others creatures are to be endured, so that we can practice submission to God's most holy will. In his book, *Uniformity with God's Will*, Saint Alphonsus Liguori makes this point very well. He writes: "We should wish with the divine will for heat and cold, storm and calm, and all the vagaries and inclemencies of the elements. We should in short accept whatever kind of weather God sends us, instead of supporting it with impatience or anger as we usually do when it is contrary to what we desire. We should avoid saying, for instance, 'What awful heat!' 'What terrible cold!' 'What shocking weather!' 'Just my bad luck!' and other expressions of the same kind which only serve to show our lack of faith and of submission to God's will. Not only should we wish the weather to be as it is because God has made it so but, whatever inconvenience it may cause us, we should repeat with the three youths in the fiery furnace: *Cold, heat, snow and ice, lightnings and clouds, winds and tempests, bless the Lord; praise and exalt him above all forever.* The elements themselves are blessing and glorifying God by doing His holy will, and we also should bless and glorify Him in the same way. Besides, even if the weather is inconvenient for us, it may be convenient for someone else. If it prevents us from doing what we want to do, it may be helping another. And even if it were not so, it should be enough for us that it is giving glory to God and that it is God who wishes it to be as it is."

"An incident in point would be this one: Late one night St. Francis Borgia arrived unexpectedly at a Jesuit house, in a snowstorm. He knocked and knocked on the door, but all to no purpose because the community being asleep, no one heard him. When morning came all were embarrassed for the discomfort he had experienced by having had to spend the night in the open. The saint, however, said he had enjoyed the greatest consolation during those long hours of the night by imagining that he saw our Lord up in the sky dropping the snowflakes down upon him." This gives us a good example of how things that must be endured can bring us closer to God. Creatures of this sort would be the failings and defects of others, sickness, death . . . really anything that we cannot change and simply must accept as it is, even though perhaps we might like it to be different. We can even, and eventually, transition from seeing these things as things to be endured to seeing them as things that make me praise God.

Lastly, some creatures are simply to be abstained from, meaning, their use implies sin. This would be like the forbidden fruit in Eden, but also any number of things in this world that would be sinful.

We can ask ourselves then: what are the goods that we are using? Do we act like we own them, or that they're mine, when in reality they are God's? Do I have any idols? Are the things I use helping me to praise God? To serve Him? To revere Him? If not, why?

Colloquy: We can end with the same colloquy as last night, conversing with our Lord upon the Cross. We can recall what Saint Thomas Aquinas wrote: "Whoever wishes to live perfectly should do nothing but disdain what Christ disdained on the cross and desire what he desired." Ask Him for the grace to love what He loves, to desire what He desires, and to disdain what He disdained.

Principle and Foundation Talk #2 –
The End of Creatures – Repetition
In the Book of the Exercises:

[23]. "The other things on the face of the earth were created for man's sake, in order to aid him in the prosecution of the End for which he was created. From this it follows that man is to use them as much as they help him on to his end, and ought to rid himself of them so far as they hinder him as to it."

Usual Preparation Prayer.

First Prelude: The Composition of Place: Heaven opened above me and hell yawning under my feet; also myself placed on this earth, halfway between Heaven and hell, and saying to myself: "For all eternity I'll either be in Heaven with God, Mary, and all the saints, or else in hell suffering the torments of Satan; and it depends on me alone, which of these two conditions will be my lot within a few years, perhaps within a few months, weeks, or days; it depends on me alone whether I am to gain so great a good or to incur so great an evil."

Second Prelude: The Petition I need to ask for light to know clearly, to realize intimately the supreme importance of this matter of my salvation and sanctification, as well as strength to adopt resolutely all the means that will most surely bring it to a successful issue. This, then, I must implore with all the energy of my being, with the utmost earnestness and fervor.

Last night and this morning we were able to meditate on the end of creatures, and what they mean for us and our salvation. Today, we will focus on the famous principle of Ignatius, contained in the second half of the text we just read: "From this it follows that man is to use them as much as they help him on to his end, and ought to rid himself of them so far as they hinder him as to it." : "As much as" is commonly known in Latin as *tantum quantum*. We are to use creatures as much as they help us get closer to God, and we are to abstain from using them as much as they impede us to that end.

"In order to really conform ourselves with God's divine plan, and to avoid all disorder in our lives, we should not use anything whatsoever without making sure that its use fulfills the double end for which we and that thing are created: to glorify God and to save and perfect my soul. This must be the *only end and intention* in my use or privation (meaning, not using) of creatures."[1] "The use of any creature whatsoever is not arbitrary; they need to be used for their end, which simply follows" from the considerations we had last night.[2]

Many commentators say that here, the point isn't so much that we discern, here and now, what would be a balanced use of creatures for us; that will come in the future meditations. What we really need to have in mind is this *principle*, since, as part of the principle and foundation, it should really form my way of thinking at every moment; it should just be part of the machinery of my mind and my will. With that in mind, we can consider some general rules of this doctrine of *tantum quantum,* and then offer some examples of how they might be applied to our own lives.

These three points to be considered are *the simple intention we should have,* we should choose *what is most conducive to our end,* and, third, we must always remember *that what is most conducive to our end, is God's will.*[3]

First, *our intention must be simple.* Given that God has established an end for us, and an end for creatures, our intention must be simple. In his book *Childlikeness before God,* Blessed Joseph Kentenich writes about the simplicity of the child, and notes that "in Latin, the word *simplex,* means 'one-fold.' The child's person is truly 'one-fold,' that is, relatively uncomplicated."

I mention this because, yes, on one hand, from the principle and foundation it follows logically that "all love, desire, thought, word, action, omission, anything, any personal act and positive or negative use of creatures that isn't done for spiritual reasons is disordered." However, on the same token, and this is Kentenich's point in his book, Christ tells us "Amen, I say to you, unless you turn and become like children, you will not enter the kingdom of Heaven" (Mt 18:3). To live according to the *tantum quantum* requires a childlike love and trust in God which makes and keeps things simple. Again, we can consider what Ignatius says from a negative standpoint, namely the things that I cannot do, but, on the other hand, we need that positive attitude, to become like children, because really only in this way will I be always and everywhere able to live out what Ignatius proposes. We can probably see in our lives how we complicate things: a child doesn't do that. If you've worked with children, you know that they *are very simple;* there is very little concealment or complication. Think, for instance, of how children wear their emotions on

1. Cf. Calveras, *Practica intensiva,* 92-97.
2. Cf. Oraa, *Ejercicios Espirituales de San Igancio,* 53-57.
3. In what follows, I follow, loosely, Calveras.

their sleeves; if you look at a kid, you pretty much know how they are feeling. I'm not saying we need to be *childish*, like lacking maturity, but we need to be *childlike* in our simplicity: look at things the way they are, trust in God who, as a good Father, wants me to get to Heaven and gives me what I need, and then use things in accord with that love. It's simple.

Returning to our topic at hand, that of having a simple intention, there are a couple of corollaries that follow:

- First, the *choice to use any good or indifferent thing is* disordered if I don't look at the end, meaning, if I don't consider the service of God and salvation of my soul;
- It is disordered if I *don't look at that end rightly,* meaning, wanting it, and only it, so, allowing my heart to be contaminated as it were by human motives, and
- It is disordered if that end isn't *the only thing that I'm looking at,* meaning, I might have God's service in mind, but with a mixture of ulterior motives and desires.

Likewise, *all love and affection towards persons and things,* when such a love and affection isn't for the sole purpose of loving and serving God, is also disordered. Sometimes, such love and affection can't be directed to God at all, for instance, when it is a love for mortal or venial sin, or an occasion of sin. In these cases, that love is not only *disordered,* but also *bad.*

In other cases, when the object of our affection isn't bad, then the affection is *simply disordered,* and we need to rectify our love, putting it in order, to love people and things in God and for God.

From here follows our second point: once I make sure that my intention is simple, that the only thing I have in mind is the service of God and the salvation of my soul, then I can use them *as much as is fitting for my end.* Again, my use of creatures cannot be something arbitrary; I should use them *as much as,* and not more; *as much as,* and not less. This implies a choice, a discernment.

I would call your attention, as Calveras does, to what Ignatius *doesn't* say here. Here, he doesn't say "what is best or more perfect"; he says, "that which is most conducive to his end." Calveras says that Ignatius' point isn't so much to be concerned about what is most perfect in itself, in the sense of being scrupulous about whether this is the most perfect thing in itself, but rather what, here and now, leads me to my end.

Let me explain this: we usually know, because we study our faith and want to live it, what is more perfect *objectively.* Yet, it could be *subjectively* that something in the moment is better for our path. For instance, some people might like to sleep on the floor every night as penance, but, if they do that, they will be destroyed the following morning, and useless for all their meditations. Yes, we could say that *objectively* doing penance is better but, *subjectively*, for me, here and now, that is not what is most conducive to my path to God.

Consider a passage from *Story of a Soul*. Saint Therese, as sacristan, had to return the keys for the communion grate, but since the mother, her blood-sister, was sick with bronchitis and asleep, she wanted to go to her room, leave the keys (and see her sister), and do so quietly. However, another sister, motivated by the same desire, said she would take the keys. Therese admits that she should've just let her go, but she was not happy, and instead followed her up to Mother's room, where the noise did in fact wake her up. As the other sister began a long discourse blaming Therese, the Little Flower simply walked away. But, it's interesting to note what she writes about the incident: "I thought that if I began to justify myself I should certainly lose my peace of mind, and *as I had too little virtue to let myself be unjustly accused without answering*, my last chance of safety lay in flight. No sooner thought than done. I hurried away, but my heart beat so violently, I could not go far, and I was obliged to sit down on the stairs to enjoy in quiet the fruit of my victory. This is an odd kind of courage, undoubtedly, but I think it is best not to expose oneself in the face of certain defeat."

In other words, the point isn't that Therese did what was *objectively more perfect*, meaning, she didn't stay and take the unjust accusations. She knew herself and her lack of virtue too well; it wouldn't have happened. So, she just left. That was what was objectively best for her. She didn't fall into a lack of charity or gossip.

Tantum quantum: I use things in as much as they help me to my end, and I avoid them insofar as they don't. To really be able to use this principle and apply it, I need to be aware, painfully aware, of my strengths and my weaknesses, my virtues and lacks of them.

This leads into our third point: what will really lead me to the end for which I was created *is what is most conducive to God's glory, praise, and service* and the *health, salvation, and perfection* of my soul. This is what is most pleasing to the Divine goodness, and it is always united with God's will.

Hence, when I live out the rule of *tantum quantum*, I am able to live out God's will at each and every moment. It is my ticket to union with God in everything.

As a sort of concluding note, I would simply point out that we must really be careful of our judgments, as I said earlier. These can keep creeping in and affecting what I do and the way I measure things. For instance, what is my idea of God? What is my understanding of myself, of my neighbors, my family, my brothers in religious life? Are my judgments set according to the norm of Jesus Christ, or to a norm of my own choosing? This is where *juicio propio*, spiritual pride, will destroy us and keep us from advancing. I dare to say that either our pride will be destroyed, or our vocations. There isn't a middle ground.

We can ask ourselves: how pure are our intentions? What people, places, and things do I love or am I attached to? Are my attachments ordered? Do I make use of them as much as is necessary, not more nor less? What are my weaknesses and defects?

Colloquy: We can end with the same colloquy as last night, conversing with our Lord upon the Cross. We can recall what Saint Thomas Aquinas wrote: "Whoever wishes to live perfectly should do nothing but disdain what Christ disdained on the cross and desire what he desired." Ask Him for the grace to love what He loves, to desire what He desires, and to disdain what He disdains.

Principle and Foundation Talk #2
In the Book of the Exercises:

[23 con't.]. "Therefore, we must make ourselves indifferent to all created things, as far as we are allowed free choice and are not under any prohibition. Consequently, as far as we are concerned, we should not prefer health to sickness, riches to poverty, honor to dishonor, a long life to a short life. The same holds for all other things. Our one desire and choice should be what is more conducive to the end for which we are created."

Usual Preparation Prayer.

First Prelude: The Composition of Place: Heaven opened above me and hell yawning under my feet; also myself placed on this earth, halfway between Heaven and hell, and saying to myself: "For all eternity I'll either be in Heaven with God, Mary, and all the saints, or else in hell suffering the torments of Satan; and it depends on me alone, which of these two conditions will be my lot within a few years, perhaps within a few months, weeks, or days; it depends on me alone whether I am to gain so great a good or to incur so great an evil."

Second Prelude: The Petition I need to ask for light to know clearly, to realize intimately the supreme importance of this matter of my salvation and sanctification, as well as strength to adopt resolutely all the means that will most surely bring it to a successful issue. This, then, I must implore with all the energy of my being, with the utmost earnestness and fervor.

By indifference, Saint Ignatius means a quality of the will whereby it is able to choose, not based on some preference it has for this or that thing, or out of fear of losing something, but rather solely for love of God. Indifference therefore means freedom of spirit; indeed, some commentators on the Exercises even go so far as to say that indifference is simply another word for freedom.[1] When we become indifferent to created things, we see that we embrace a radical and all-encompassing freedom, a freedom that touches on the very heart

1. Cf. *God Finds Us* by Jim Manney

of our vocations as Christians. As Saint Paul writes to the Galatians (5:13): *in libertatem vocati estis* "You were called for freedom."

In a sense, we could say that freedom is the "other side of the coin" of indifference, since the two go hand in hand: if I'm not indifferent to created things, then it means that I have my preferences and likes; I'm bound to things, and if I'm bound, I'm a slave: I'm not free. This is, we could say, the negative aspect: freedom means not being bound to things.

By the same token, though, we can look at this indifference from the positive light: being indifferent doesn't mean saying "Ok, whatever" to anything that happens; nor does it mean being indifferent for indifference's sake, as if indifference were an end unto itself (as if we were Buddhists). Freedom isn't apathy. Case in point: when God asks Abraham to sacrifice Isaac, his father takes him up the mountain, and it pains him, because he loves Isaac, but he loves God more. We'd wonder about his love for his son if he just said: "Ok, whatever." He'd be a psychopath, and not a father. Rather, when I am indifferent to all created things, it's for a reason. That reason is that I'm completely and profoundly in love with God and with His will. It means being totally and completely at God's disposal, to be free for what He wants, when He wants it, and how He wants it. Indifference isn't apathy; it's not a universal "whatever" to anything and everything. Rather, it's a stripping away of everything, a detachment from everything that's not God because of a profound and all-encompassing love which can only be profound and all-encompassing because, through indifference I am free to love that way. When that love of God calls me to use a creature to serve Him, I do, and when it calls me to leave it behind, I leave it. In the future meditations, we'll see concretely how to live out that love, but, for now, we must work on gaining that indifference so as to get that freedom to love completely.

When considering how indifference leads to freedom, we can consider two points: first, the nature of freedom, and second, the perfect freedom that is meant to be ours as religious. So, the nature of freedom, and perfect freedom.

1. Nature of freedom

Indifference is directed to making us free, to making us be the ones in control of our actions: to be the one who chooses.

To be free means:

- To be without chains, without any impediments that hold us back. Listen to what Saint John of the Cross writes: "The soul that is attached to anything, however much good there may be in it, will not arrive at the *freedom* of divine union. For whether it be a strong wire rope or a slender and delicate thread that holds the bird, it matters not, if it really holds it fast; for until the cord be broken the bird cannot fly." – True freedom is found in our union with God. Union, or, as Alphonsus Ligouri likes to say, uniformity.

But just as in order to be pure, water needs to be more than simply free from dirt, so too to be free also means

- to be able to see what the end is and to be able to choose it and the means to it. To be free means to be able to choose Jesus, no matter what He asks: when Blessed Chiara Luce Badano lay dying and was in great pain, she continually refused medicine for the pain and instead offered everything to Jesus. A few days before her death, she said, "I'm not asking Jesus to come and take me to Heaven with Him. I don't want Him to get the impression that I don't want to suffer for Him anymore."[2] She was 19, and died in 1990.
- We could say the same of Venerable Montserrat Grases, who died at the age of 17. When her parents told her that she had been diagnosed with an aggressive form of cancer, she took the news calmly, went to her room, made her usual examination of conscience, kissed her crucifix and said, "*Serviam* – I will serve," looked at an image of Our Lady and said, "[I accept] whatever you want," and went to sleep, with a calm that her parents could only describe later as supernatural.[3]

Indifference, then, frees us so that we can be concerned about the things of God.

On the other hand, the slave is one who is chained, perhaps blinded by their own judgments or likes, one who doesn't have the strength to love and choose, the one who is bound by their tastes, fears, disordered desires, and so on.

Even the littlest things can enslave us: they are like the little foxes in the Song of Songs (2:15): "Catch us the foxes, the little foxes that damage the vineyards." The foxes are small, but their damage is great, since they destroy the greatest of treasures. It doesn't matter what the attachment is; someone in prison could care less if their chains are gold or silver or platinum studded with diamonds. The end result is always the same: to be bound.

2. The Law of Perfect Freedom

This leads to our second point. In his letter, Saint James says that we are called, not to just any sort of freedom, but perfect freedom: "For if anyone is a hearer of the word and not a doer, he is like a man who looks at his own

---

2. Ann Ball, *Young Faces of Holiness*, 27.

3. Cf. Mercedes Eguíbar Galarza, *Montserrat Grases: Una vida sencilla* (Madrid: Ediciones Palabra, 2016).

face in a mirror. He sees himself, then goes off and promptly forgets what he looked like. But the one who peers into the *perfect law* of freedom and perseveres, and is not a hearer who forgets but a doer who acts, such a one shall be blessed in what he does." Our English word *perfect* comes from the Latin *perfectus*, meaning, *completely.* Our freedom is *perfect* when it completely embraces absolutely every aspect of my life.

That perfect freedom is to be found in indifference, and is freedom, of course, from slavery to sin, death, and hell, but also from any secondary end that we might place in front of or in the way of God.

Indifference gives us that freedom because it gives us a four-fold control or dominion (*señorío* – lordship):

a) First, control over ourselves: as we submit our souls to God and strip away our attachments, our intellect sees clearly what is most important, and our will becomes free to attach itself entirely to God. Everything else, then, falls into place. We can think of Saint Dominic Savio, whose motto was "Death, but not sin!" Not just mortal sin, mind you, but all sin. Imagine the detachment that let him see things in their proper light, and the control he must have had over himself to not only say that, but live it. For the record, Savio died when he was 14.

b) Second, dominion over others. This doesn't mean that we get to boss them around, but rather that, by giving ourselves entirely to the service of Jesus Christ, we have a certain spiritual authority over them. Case in point: there is a well-known incident with Saint Theresa of Calcutta. While out asking for donations, she asked a man for something for her orphans and held out her open hand. The man spat in it, and she, very gently, drew her hand back and stuck out her other one. "Thank you," she said, "that was for me; now please give me something for my orphans." From that moment on, the man became one of her biggest benefactors. How do you argue against that? This woman wasn't attached to her pride, her feelings, or anything: she had a mission from God and she was going to fulfill it, and there's something about that that will always inspire awe.

c) Third, dominion over the world: and this in two senses: one, by collaborating with it through our apostolates, but, at the same time, rejecting it when it tries to become an end unto itself. Again, being indifferent means being free, and being free means being able to serve God whenever, wherever, and however He calls us. When Blessed Titus Brandsma, a Dutch Carmelite, was warned that the Nazis would imprison him, he would reply, "Well, now I am going to get what I've always wanted—a cell of my own. At last I shall be a real Carmelite."

d) Lastly, dominion over the devil: when we're free from attachments, the devil has no tools he can use against us.

In short, Saint Alponsus Ligori writes that "this is the beautiful freedom of the sons of God, and it is worth vastly more than all the rank and distinction of blood and birth, more than all the kingdoms in the world." It is worth so much because it is the key to Heaven, but it is a key that is gained only by walking through the doors of indifference and detachment. In the Song of Songs we read "Set me as a seal upon your heart." Indifference is that seal that keeps our hearts safely shut, to be opened only by God, when He asks, how He asks, and for what He asks.

Lastly, we can consider those four examples Ignatius gives as particularly paradigmatic examples of indifference: "Consequently, as far as we are concerned, we should not prefer health to sickness, riches to poverty, honor to dishonor, a long life to a short life. The same holds for all other things. Our one desire and choice should be what is more conducive to the end for which we are created."

Again, the goal of this life is to get me to Heaven, to be a saint, so, whatever it is that God wants to use to get me there, has to be fine by me. We're talking, not just about avoiding sin, (as Blessed Joseph Kentenich said, "He who only tries to avoid sin, will fall into it"), but about becoming saints. God knows exactly what I need to become a saint, and I have to trust that, and accept it. Therefore, I shouldn't prefer:

Health to sickness: Some saints have been healthy. Others have been quite sick, but, submissive to God's will, they became saints through their sufferings. Saint Gabriel Lalemant was inspired to offer himself for the missions because of his uncle, Father Jerome Lalemant, who was the Jesuit superior of the Canadian missions. Yet, Lalement's health was always poor; reporting his death, the Jesuit superior wrote that Lalemant's had been a "very delicate constitution, and [it was a] fact that his body had no strength except what the spirit of God and the desire of suffering for his name could give him." Nevertheless, Lalemant offered himself wholeheartedly to the mission, but his uncle still had to be careful in assigning him. Lalemant quickly picked up the language, but, after a mere six months, he was martyred along with John de Brébeuf. Interestingly enough, as weak as his body might have been, Lalemant endured torture for 15 hours, while de Brébeuf, who was so strong and tough that the native called him "Echon," "The Strong One" in Huron, died after three. Lalemant accepted his mission, as well as his physical limitations, as coming from God. Ultimately, his poor health had no impact on his ability to serve in the missions, since he wasn't there long.

Likewise, Saint Elizabeth of the Trinity died at a young age after great suffering, so much so that "upon her death, the prioress described her body as being 'like a skeleton.'" Yet, shortly before her death, "Elizabeth pressed her profession crucifix to her heart and said, 'We have loved each other so much.'" Perhaps the greatest example of this is Saint Therese of Lisieux, the Little Flower. While she was literally suffocating from tuberculosis, was asked whether she wanted to die or to live. Her reply is the crystallization of indifference. She said: "I desire neither death nor life. Were our Lord to offer me my choice, I would not choose. I only will what He wills; it is what He does that I love. I do not fear the last struggle, nor any pains – however great – my illness may bring. God has always been my help. He has led me by the hand from my earliest childhood, and on Him I rely. My agony may reach the furthest limits, but I am convinced that He will never forsake me." *"I desire neither death nor life. Were our Lord to offer me my choice, I would not choose. I only will what He wills; it is what He does that I love."*

I will just mention in passing, that sometimes we are attached to our fears, our "what if's." Indifference means loving God above all things and so requires that we abandon ourselves to Him and trust in Him and in His will.

Riches to poverty: Some saints have been rich, but made good use of that wealth. Some, like Saint Francis, simply gave it all up. Poverty is not an impediment to God accomplishing His work. After all, He says, "Mine is the silver; mine is the gold."

Archbishop Fulton. J. Sheen (1895-1979), in his renowned book, *Way to Happiness* narrates an incident in the life of a pious nun residing in a cloistered Carmelite convent (chapter 31). The nuns were leading a simple, silent and austere life and were practicing penance, prayer and meditation without access to the outside world. Once, during the feast of St. Therese, the cloister of the convent was opened to visitors who wanted to witness their lifestyle. Among the visitors was an industrialist who could not appreciate the silent lifestyle of the sisters. He met a young, beautiful and highly educated nun and showed her a large, palatial house on the opposite hill. It was large and luxurious with all modern amenities, a gorgeous garden, beautiful buildings, expensive cars and fine furniture. He asked her, "If you had the fortune to be born in and own such a house with all facilities for a luxurious modern life, would you have left it and joined this convent with only poverty, penance and prayer?" The nun gave a short but firm reply, "Sir, that was my home!"

Honor to dishonor: The young Saint Aloysius Gonzaga, and many other early Jesuits, gave up royal titles to become religious. How many saints have suffered dishonor and humiliations!

An example of this trust can be found in the life of Saint Louis de Montfort: the fiasco of the Calvary at Pontchâteau. After having preached eight popular missions in the vicinity of Pontchâteau, "Montfort dreamed of building a gigantic Way of the Cross, which would dominate the entire countryside." He obtained the land, and in May of 1709 work began. The labor was all volunteer; inspired by de Montfort, over 20,000 people from as far away as Italy and Spain came to help. Everything was donated as a gift to God. The work was finished, and the date for the blessing was set for September 14th, 1710.

However, there were some who were angry at Montfort, for whatever reason. They and those in power managed to convince the king that the Calvary was to be a fortress, a threat to national security. Thus, on September 13th, while he was preaching a mission, Montfort was told that the blessing had been called off. He hurried on foot through the night in order to see the bishop, arriving exhausted the next morning. He was given the sad news: there was nothing that could be done. The king ordered the Calvary, so painstakingly and lovingly built by volunteers, to be taken down, block by block, by the peasants under the army's watchful eye. "Montfort's personal humiliation must have been nothing compared to the anguish he felt for all those who had invested so much of their energy and time in the Calvary of Pontchâteau." On the bishop's advice, Montfort went on retreat, but, in that time of silent suffering, the Jesuits who ran the retreat house were amazed at his attitude. As one wrote later:

I thought I would find him downcast and disappointed; I had prepared myself to do as much as I could to console him; but I was astonished to find him happier and more peaceful than I myself was. I said to him jokingly, "My, you are acting like a strong and courageous fellow!" . . . "I am neither strong nor courageous," he replied, "but, thanks be to God, I am neither grievously pained nor desolate; I am at peace." [I asked him] "You are content, then, that they have destroyed your Calvary?" "I am neither content nor discontent. The Lord allowed me to have it built; but now He has allowed it to be destroyed. Blessed be His Holy Name! If it had depended on me, the Calvary would have stood till the end of time, but since it depends upon God, may His will be done and not mine. I would prefer, o My God, to die thousand times . . . than to oppose your Holy Will."

Or, closer to our days, we can think of Servant of God Jérôme Lejeune, the French geneticist who discovered the cause of Down Syndrome. Pope Saint John Paul the Second reportedly called him "the most intelligent man [he] had ever met." In 1969, when he was awarded the top prize of the American Society of Human Genetics, rather than give a lecture on his research, which was the norm, he instead gave an impassioned speech about the dignity of human life, and begged that genetics not be used as a reason for abortion. The powers that be informed him that if he wanted to win the Nobel Prize for medicine, for which he was certainly a candidate, he should keep his mouth shut about prolife issues. After the speech, Lejeune is said to have called his wife and remarked, "Today, I lost my Nobel Prize in medicine." His tireless defense of life would cost him funding for his research, friendships, his reputation in the scientific community, and earn him the hatred of many. When France was debating liberalizing their abortion laws, graffiti appeared on the walls of the Sorbonne, proclaiming: "Death to Lejeune!" Yet, none of this mattered to him; his sole concern was God's will and to defend the truth.

A long life to a short life: How many saints reach holiness after a short life! We already mentioned a number, but think of the Fatima visionaries. A clear example of this is Venerable Antonietta Meo, who died from cancer at the age of six and a half. She had just learned how to write, wrote 105 letters to Jesus. As her illness progressed she would dictate to her mother. Her last letter is dated June 2nd, 1937. This is what her mother had to say: "I sat by her bed and wrote down what Antonietta struggled to dictate: 'Dear Crucified Jesus, I love you and am so fond of you! I want to be with you on Calvary. Dear Jesus, tell God the Father that I love him, too. Dear Jesus, give me your strength for I need it to bear this pain that I offer for sinners.'" Her mother said: "At this point Antonietta was consumed by a violent fit of coughing and vomiting but as soon as it was over she went on dictating: 'Dear Jesus, tell the Holy Spirit to enlighten me with love and to fill me with his seven gifts. Dear Jesus, tell Our Lady that I love her and want to be near her. Dear Jesus, I want to tell you again how much I love you. My good Jesus, look after my spiritual father and grant him the necessary graces. Dear Jesus, look after my parents and Margherita. Your little girl sends you lots of kisses. . . .'"

Colloquy: We can end with the same colloquy as in the last meditation, by conversing with our Lord upon the Cross. Saint Thomas Aquinas wrote that "Whoever wishes to live perfectly should do nothing but disdain what Christ disdained on the cross and desire what he desired." Ask Him for the grace to love what He loves, to desire what He desires, and to disdain what He disdained.

Principle and Foundation Talk #3 – Indifference – Repetition In the Book of the Exercises:

[23 con't.]. "Therefore, we must make ourselves indifferent to all created things, as far as we are allowed free choice and are not under any prohibition. Consequently, as far as we are concerned, we should not prefer health to sickness, riches to poverty, honor to dishonor, a long life to a short life. The same holds for all other things. Our one desire and choice should be what is more conducive to the end for which we are created."

Usual Preparation Prayer.

First Prelude: The Composition of Place: Heaven opened above me and hell yawning under my feet; also myself placed on this earth, halfway between Heaven and hell, and saying to myself: "For all eternity I'll either be in Heaven with God, Mary, and all the saints, or else in hell suffering the torments of Satan; and it depends on me alone, which of these two conditions will be my lot within a few years, perhaps within a few months, weeks, or days; it depends on me alone whether I am to gain so great a good or to incur so great an evil."

Second Prelude: The Petition I need to ask for light to know clearly, to realize intimately the supreme importance of this matter of my salvation and sanctification, as well as strength to adopt resolutely all the means that will most surely bring it to a successful issue. This, then, I must implore with all the energy of my being, with the utmost earnestness and fervor.

Once again, we return to the same point that we made last night, that of the need for indifference as our spiritual attitude in the face of created things. When Ignatius speaks of "conquering ourselves, the majority of the work is to be done here, in reaching for perfect indifference with respect to creatures, which means not having any preference [for using or not using them] that comes from human motives, but rather only the desire to take what helps us to best serve God and to become saints ourselves. This comes about as we convert all of the love that we naturally feel for creatures into a spiritual love in God and for God.

Again, this is something necessary if we really want to live out the Principle and Foundation. During this first week, our goal is really to form our minds to think according to this principle, to really want to be indifferent. The meditations of the first and second weeks will help up to attain this indifference in practice, and those of the third and fourth will reinforce it." [1]

In this meditation, I want to consider in a particular way God's providence, and what our attitude should be towards it. Some Jesuit authors and commentators on the Exercises present indifference as a more *passive attitude*; it was their way of expressing a docility to God's will. We can think, for instance, of Saint Thomas More's last letter from the Tower of London, to his daughter Margaret, where he writes, "And, therefore, my own good daughter, do not let your mind be troubled over anything that shall happen to me in this world. Nothing can come but what God wills. And I am very sure that whatever that be, however bad it may seem, it shall indeed be the best." In other words, we should eagerly await and accept from God whatever He give us from His hands. [2]

Nonetheless, there is more to indifference than just being passive. If all I do is just suck up everything like a sponge, or, worse yet, with a "Whatever," my indifference isn't as perfect as it could be. What we should do is make our indifference *active*, meaning, not only seeking to rid our soul of its disordered attachments, but also, and everywhere, embracing God's will for us. This attitude that we must cultivate is one of "seeing the hand of Providence in the government of the world and in all the events of our lives, whether prosperous or adverse." [3]

We can start by simply considering what divine providence is. As we mentioned before, the word *providence* itself come from the Latin *pro* – ahead, and *videre* – to see. God sees ahead of us, or, rather, in His eternity He sees all things as present. Aquinas says beautifully that God is "stationed as it were at the *arce aeternitatis*, the summit or mountaintop of eternity" (*Peri. Herm.*, 14, 20). When we climb mountains during *convivencia* and reach the summit, and we see everything going on at the base, and here and there and everywhere, we catch a glimpse, a faint glimmer, of the way God sees everything. For instance, if we see hikers on the north face of the mountain, and another group on the south face, we know they'll meet on the summit. They have no idea, but we see it coming. Or, to use another example of Aquinas, "if two servants are sent by their master to the same place, the meeting of the two servants in regard to themselves is by chance; but as compared to the master, who had

---

1. Cf. Calveras, *Que fruto se ha de sacar*, 166-167.
2. Cf. Iparraguirre, *Ejerecicios Espirituales – Comentario pastoral*, 178-180.
3. I think this is from Royo-Marin, *The Great Unknown*.

ordered it, it is directly intended" (ST I, q. 116, 1). God's Providence, we must say time and time again, is concrete, perhaps the most concrete and constant expression of His love for us, since it touches on absolutely every element of our lives. When we talk about how creatures help us to reach Heaven and sanctity, this is a large part of it.

Saint Edith Stein explains this wonderfully in her masterpiece *Finite and Eternal Being*. Speaking of essence and accidents, of all things, she writes, "The coherence of our own life is perhaps best suited to illustrate what we mean. In ordinary speech we distinguish between what is 'planned' or 'well-designed' — and this appears simultaneously as 'meaningful' and 'intelligible' — from what is merely 'accidental' and which seems by itself meaningless and unintelligible. For example, I intend to pursue certain studies and to this end select a university which promised to provide some special incentive in my chosen field. Here we have a meaningful and intelligible coherence of motives and circumstances. But the fact that in that particular university town I make the acquaintance of a person who is 'accidentally' matriculated at the same institution and that one day I 'accidentally' become engaged in talking on questions regarding an outlook on life — this seems at first glance hardly a thoroughly intelligible coherence of events. And yet when, many years later, I reflect upon my life, it becomes clear to me that this particular conversation turned out to be of decisive significance for my life, that it was perhaps more 'essential' than all my studies so that now I am inclined to think that this encounter may have been 'precisely the reason' why I 'had to go' to that town. In other words, what did not lie in my plan lay in God's plans. And the more often such things happen to me the more lively becomes in me the conviction of my faith that — from God's point of view — nothing is accidental, that my entire life, even in the most minute details, was pre-designed in the plans of divine providence and is thus for the all-seeing eye of God a perfect coherence of meaning. From God's point of view — nothing is accidental, my entire life, even in the most minute details, was pre-designed in the plans of divine providence and is thus for the all-seeing eye of God a perfect coherence of meaning. Once I begin to realize this, my heart rejoices in anticipation of the light of glory in whose sheen this coherence of meaning will be fully unveiled to me."[4]

Nothing is accidental; God knows everything, and whatever happens, happens because He makes it happen or because He allows it to happen. That is Caussade's *Abandonment to Divine Providence* summarized in one sentence. God knows everything: He knows the struggles we faced yesterday, the joy

---

4. Edith Stein, *Finite and Eternal Being: An Attempt at an Ascent to the Meaning of Being* (Washington, D.C.: ICS Publications, 2002), 113.

we experienced years ago, our weaknesses and defects, the things to which we're attached, the way to call our attention, the problems that will come up in three months, the sorrow that awaits us around the corner or in the mission. He knows, and because He loves us and wants us to go to Heaven, He already has it worked out so that everything, absolutely everything, will help us get to Heaven.

In his book entitled *Interior Freedom*, Fr. Jacques Philippe makes very clear what this active indifference looks like. He writes: "The exercise of freedom as a choice among options, plainly is important. However, to avoid making painful mistakes, we also need to understand that there is another way of exercising freedom: less immediately exciting, poorer, humbler, but much more common, and one immensely fruitful, both humanly and spiritually. It is *consenting to what we did not originally choose*. It is worth stressing how important this way of exercising our freedom is. The highest and most fruitful form of human freedom is found in accepting, even more than in dominating. We show the greatness of our freedom when we transform reality, but still more when we accept it trustingly as it is given to us day after day. . . . To achieve true interior freedom we must train ourselves to accept, peacefully and willingly, plenty of things that seem to contradict our freedom."

He goes on to clarify that this *consent* is not the same as *resignation* (or, in our words, indifference is active, not merely passive): "Resignation," he writes, "is a declaration of powerlessness that goes no further," whereas "the attitude to aim for is *consent*. Compared with registration, consent leads to a completely different interior attitude. We say yes to a reality we initially saw as negative, because we realize that something positive may come from it. This hints at hope. We can say yes to the poorest and most disappointing human raw materials, because we believe that 'love is so powerful in deeds that it is able to draw good out of everything, both the good and the bad that it finds in me,' as St. Therese of Lisieux said. The ultimate difference between resignation and consent is that with consent, even though the objective reality remains the same, the attitude of our hearts is very different. They already contain the virtues of faith, hope, and love in embryo."[5]

I might dare to say, even more than consent, we should aim at *uniformity* with God's will, as the title of Alphonsus Ligouri's book suggests. We should embrace God's will, even in things that seem to contradict our freedom and His love for us.

A story from the life of Saint Ignatius gives us a good insight into the saint's indifference, how *he himself lived it out*.

5. Jacques Philippe, *Interior Freedom* (New York: Scepter, 2007), 28-29, 30-31.

The early Jesuits recall that once, when Ignatius was sick, the doctor told him to avoid anything that could cause sadness or painful thoughts. After thoroughly examining himself, Ignatius found that there was only one thing that really could upset him: it was the thought that the Society of Jesus might be dissolved. He examined it more and more, and then, upon considering it, he said that even if the Company were to be dissolved, if it were not through his fault, fifteen minutes in prayer would be enough to reestablish his peace.

Indeed, on May 23rd, 1555, a new pope was elected: Gian Pietro Carafa, who took the name Paul IV. Carafa was no friend of the Jesuits (he had a leading role in the Inquisition), and his companions noticed that Ignatius's face changed and was upset. Indeed, all the bones of his body seemed to shake. Without a word, Ignatius stood up and went to pray in the chapel. A little while later, Ignatius returned, as happy and as content as if the election had been to his liking. When the people began complaining about Paul IV as being too strict, Ignatius began looking to discover his good qualities and good works, and would recount them to anyone who spoke about the Pontiff.[6]

As we wind down our meditations on the Principle and Foundation, we can ask ourselves[7]:

- How is my desire to take *advantage of everything* as much as possible in my spiritual life?
- How resolute is my *desire* and my *generosity* to give myself entirely to the will of my Creator and Lord? Especially as a religious, have I kept that flame of charity alive, that spirit with which I first entered?
- How clear in my mind is the golden rule of *tantum quantum*, meaning, of not seeking to use or to abstain from the use of creatures except as God's service and my sanctification demand it?
- How is my desire to make this norm the sole *rule of my life?*
- How great is my desire for *indifference*, meaning, to prepare myself and dispose myself to remove from my life all my bad and disordered affections?

Colloquy: We can end with a colloquy speaking with Jesus Christ as He hangs upon the Cross. From the worst crime man ever committed, to kill the Son of God, God worked the greatest good: our salvation. Ask Jesus for the grace to love the cross, to trust in His infinite knowledge and infinite love, so that you can embrace with indifference anything and everything that He sends to you.

---

6. Cf. Tejada, *Los Ejercicos Espirituales de San Ignacio de Loyola – Comentario y textos afines*, 180-181

7. Calveras, *Practica intensiva*, 104.

The Three Sins [045-053]

Usual Preparation Prayer.

First Prelude: The composition of Place: The representation will be to see in imagination my soul as a prisoner in this corruptible body, and to consider my whole composite being as an exile here on earth, cast out to live among brute beasts. I said my whole composite being, body and soul.

Second Prelude: The petition: Here the petition will be to ask for shame and confusion, because I see how many have been lost on account of a single mortal sin, and how many times I have deserved eternal damnation, because of the many grievous sins that I have committed.

Here Saint Ignatius asks us to call to mind three sins: that of the angels, that of Adam and Eve, and that of a soul condemned to hell for a single mortal sin. In each case, we'll consider that sin, the effects, and then compare it to ourselves. We want to consider the destruction caused, and the devastation wrought, by one sin.

[050] **The First Point:** "This will consist in using the memory to recall the first sin, which was that of the angels, and then in applying the understanding by reasoning upon this sin, then the will by seeking to remember and understand all to be the more filled with shame and confusion when I compare the one sin of the angels with the many sins I have committed. I will consider that they went to hell for one sin, and the number of times I have deserved to be condemned forever because of my numerous sins.

I said we should apply the memory to the sin of the angels, that is, recalling that they were created in the state of grace, that they did not want to make use of the freedom God gave them to reverence and obey their Creator and Lord, and so falling into pride, were changed from grace to hatred of God, and cast out of Heaven into hell.

So, too, the understanding is to be used to think over the matter more in detail, and then the will to rouse more deeply the emotions."

Saint Peter tells us in his second letter that "God did not spare the angels when they sinned, but condemned them to the chains of Tartarus and handed them over to be kept for judgment" (2 Pt 2:4).

Let us consider the angels, created in paradise. As pure spirits, they don't need matter for anything, so no food, no drink, no need to sleep, no need to rely on material things for knowledge. Their knowledge was wonderfully sublime, keen, and comprehensive; the energy of their will was proportioned to the loftiness of their intelligence. "The angelic intelligence is quite different from the human intelligence. . . . The angel does not receive its knowledge from things. Rather, ideas are poured into the angel by God. Man knows from the bottom up; an angel knows from the top down. We . . . have to unwrap the ideas that God put into things. An angel never has to wait until a package in unwrapped; it already knows what is in things. An angel is far more brilliant than man. An angel knows more science than Einstein. When an angel has an idea, for example, the idea of man, the angel knows every individual man in the world in virtue of that idea. Human beings do not. We just know humanity in general."[1]

In addition to that powerful intellect was a will that was equally as powerful and its power outstripped that of the whole physical world. We can think of the angel who came to visit Gideon: "The angel of God said to Gideon, 'Put the meat and the unleavened bread on that rock over there. Then pour the broth on them.' And Gideon did as he was told. The angel of the Lord touched the meat and the bread with the end of the stick that was in his hand. Then fire jumped up from the rock and completely burned up the meat and the bread!" (Jdgs 6:20-21).

We can think of the power of the angel that killed Sennacherib's army. In 2 Kgs 19:35, we read: "That night the angel of the LORD went forth and struck down one hundred and eighty-five thousand men in the Assyrian camp. Early the next morning, there they were, dead, all those corpses!" One night, 185,000 soldiers, without so much as a whimper or complaint, no resistance or fight.

Or at the Passover, in Ex 12:29, "And so at midnight the LORD['s angel] struck down every firstborn in the land of Egypt, from the firstborn of Pharaoh sitting on his throne to the firstborn of the prisoner in the dungeon, as well as all the firstborn of the animals." In an instant, he kills the firstborn male everywhere in the entire nation.

Besides, from the first moment of their creation they had been endowed with sanctifying grace and adorned with various virtues, preeminently with charity. And what was their purpose, their destiny? The same as ours, to show reverence and obedience to their Lord and Creator. Hence they were

---

1. Fulton J. Sheen, *Thinking Life Through* (New York: McGraw-Hill, 1955), 29-30.

unceasingly singing the praises of the Most High, rapt in loving adoration before the throne of His Majesty.

How did so many come to fall? What a tragic story! Saint Thomas Aquinas (ST, I, q. 63, aa. 1-3) tells us that the angels desired to be like God, but in a very specific way: they knew they couldn't ever be equal to God, since their keen intelligence told them that only God is God. They wanted to be like Him, *but through their own power.* They didn't want to receive what God had prepared for them as a gift.[2]

That's all it took. From that moment, the moment when Lucifer said, "*Non serviam* – I will not serve," he was cast into hell and was transformed. Lucifer, who, as Milton describes him, was "brighter once amidst the host. / Of angels, than that star the stars among, Fell with his flaming legions through the deep / Into his place" (*Paradise Lost,* VI, 131-135).

In this rebellion he was at once joined by numerous other Spirits. They refused to glorify their Creator, because they had become in love with themselves and inflated with pride. This sin was committed in the very presence of the Infinite Majesty. But that same instant, meaning, no delay, they also heard the awful sentence: "Depart from Me, you cursed, into everlasting fire." No longer adopted Sons but degraded Rebels, they are stripped of sanctifying grace and supernatural virtue. Their beauty is changed into ugliness; just think of how this is portrayed in art, the image of an angel compared with an image of a demon. Their wisdom has become madness, their love is turned into hatred, and from Angels they are transformed into Demons. Driven from before the throne of God they are hurled into the abyss of Hell.

As often as I deliberately transgressed any Commandment of God in a grievous manner, I committed an act of rebellion similar to that of the Angels as to deserve no less a punishment than Hell. If the Angels were cast into Hell for one single sin, what have I not deserved for so many; especially after obtaining pardon, not only once, but over and over again, through the Blood of Jesus Christ, in the Sacrament of Penance? Where should I be most justly, at this very moment, except for the Inexhaustible Mercy of God? Instead of being allowed to live on this earth, a member of Holy Church, I have deserved, perhaps many times over, to be at the bottom of Hell, an object of scorn to the very Demons and the other Reprobates.

[051] The Second Point: "In the same way the three powers of the soul are to be applied to the sin of Adam and Eve. Recall to memory how on account

2. Summary given at http://readingthesumma.blogspot.com/2012/03/question-63-sin-of-angels.html

of this sin they did penance for so long a time, and the great corruption which came upon the human race that caused so many to be lost in hell.

I said recall to mind the second sin, that of our First Parents. After Adam had been created on the Plain of Damascus and placed in the Garden of Paradise, and Eve had been formed from his side, they sinned by violating the command not to eat of the tree of knowledge. Thereafter, they were clothed in garments of skin and cast out of Paradise. By their sin they lost original justice, and for the rest of their lives, lived without it in many labors and great penance.

So too, the understanding is to be used to think over the matter in greater detail, and the will is to be used as explained above."

All the benefits that Adam had received were intended for one sole object, namely, that both Adam and Eve together with their entire offspring, by praising, revering, and serving God, might bring human nature to its highest perfection and complete in themselves the Divine likeness. Thus also this earthly Eden was but an entrance to the heavenly Jerusalem. How great God's goodness in giving them such a wonderful place! How great the graces they possessed! How their every need was met! And to think, as Genesis says, the "LORD God walk[ed] about in the garden at the breezy time of the day" (Gn 3:8).

To test the obedience of our First Parents, God had forbidden them to eat of the fruit of the tree of knowledge. We see at once how just this prohibition was easy, but substantial. By respecting this kind command, Adam would have obtained, both for himself and for his posterity, the gift of sanctifying grace together with many other extraordinary favors. He was offered a choice between the fullness of life, natural as well as supernatural, and a miserable death of both body and soul; a choice between perfect happiness and utter affliction.

However, they did eat of the forbidden fruit and sinned. Lucifer, the leader of the fallen angels, appeared to them under the form of a serpent. He began by tempting Eve, in order through her also to seduce Adam. First he suggested to her imagination that the restriction put upon them by the Almighty was against their happiness; next he instilled into her heart a desire of becoming completely independent of the Most High; and then he drove her from this inward disloyalty into open disobedience. Eve in turn, by her bad example and insinuating manner, prevailed upon Adam to set aside the Divine Prohibition.

Their eating of the forbidden fruit, though in itself a very small thing, was nevertheless a deliberate and willful rejection of God's Supreme Authority. Nor was the threatened penalty long in being inflicted: "Then the eyes of both of them were opened, and they knew that they were naked; so they sewed fig leaves together and made loincloths for themselves" (Gn 3:7). That same moment our First Parents were deprived of all their heavenly graces and special gifts; they were driven out of paradise into the wide world which thenceforth was to yield only thistles and thorns; and, filled with shame at the lustfulness of their bodies, they were obliged to cover them with the skins of animals. They too had decided to have their own way and to be their own masters, but they found that their flesh had revolted against their spirit and that the whole earth had shaken off their former supremacy. Before, everything in them was subjected to God: their intellects and wills had perfect control over their passions and lower faculties, and these, in turn, had control over everything in the created world. Man was the ruler of all reality. Now, all that was turned upside down.

The remainder of their lives was spent in constant and manifold misery, which finally culminated in the terrible ordeal of death. Yet all these sufferings would have availed them nothing to escape eternal perdition, had it not been for the infinite merits of their promised Redeemer. But even so, what terrible consequences this one sin entailed for all their descendants: loss of sanctifying grace and other precious gifts; darkness of the mind and weakness of the will; subjection of the soul to a threefold concupiscence; numberless hardships and ailments of the body rapidly preparing the way for death.

What dire consequences, and all this for one small sin, one little act of disobedience! It was a small thing, and yet how much suffering and destruction it has brought the world! How many souls have suffered the consequences of this one little decision! What do I deserve, then, for my many grave sins, for my many acts of disobedience? What should the consequences of my many mortal sins be?

Adam and Eve were given all the goods of the earth, all the created reality, to serve God. However, they used a creature to do their own will and to act against God. See the destruction and the disorder that results! And me, and my life . . . how many times I have abused, not one, but many creatures! How much disorder and destruction has resulted from my sins!

[052] Third Point: In like manner, we are to do the same with regard to the third sin, namely, that of one who went to hell because of one mortal sin. Consider also countless others who have been lost for fewer sins than I have committed.

I said to do the same for the third particular sin. Recall to memory the gravity and malice of sin against our Creator and Lord. Use the understanding to consider that because of sin, and of acting against the Infinite Goodness, one is justly condemned forever. Close with the acts of the will as we have said above.

The third sin to be considered is a still more striking instance of Divine Justice; namely, the loss of "a soul who for one mortal sin has gone to Hell, and of many others without number that have been condemned for fewer sins than I committed." And yet I am still alive.

St. Alphonsus Ligouri gives the example of a little boy, just barely the age of reason, who, when passing in front of a church where Alphonsus stood, uttered a blasphemy. At that very moment, he fell down, dead. But, who will say that God was unjust in such a case? Who would say that the boy didn't deserve such a punishment, or that God was harsh?

As God says through the prophet Ezekiel: "You say, 'The LORD's way is not fair!' Hear now, house of Israel: Is it my way that is unfair? Are not your ways unfair? When the just turn away from justice to do evil and die, on account of the evil they did they must die. . . . But the house of Israel says, 'The Lord's way is not fair!' Is it my way that is not fair, house of Israel? Is it not your ways that are not fair?" (Ez 18:25-29).

In the light of this fact that so many are lost for one single sin, how silly appears the presumption that it is easy to avoid Hell after committing a grievous offense, and what utter folly it was for me to remain so long on the brink of perdition or even within the reach of temptation. Where should I be now, if God had wished to deal with me as He most justly dealt with countless other sinners perhaps far less guilty than myself? If God had treated me as was only right and just, I should long since have been a prisoner in Hell, abandoned to perpetual torment and infamy.

[053] *Colloquy:* Imagine Christ our Lord present before you upon the cross, and begin to speak with him, asking how it is that though He is the Creator, He has stooped to become man, and to pass from eternal life to death here in time, that thus He might die for our sins.

I shall also reflect upon myself and ask:

"What have I done for Christ?"

"What am I doing for Christ?"

"What ought I to do for Christ?"

As I behold Christ in this plight, nailed to the cross, I shall ponder upon what presents itself to my mind.

The Three Sins [045-053] – Repetition

Usual Preparation Prayer.

First Prelude: The composition of Place: The representation will be to see in imagination my soul as a prisoner in this corruptible body, and to consider my whole composite being as an exile here on earth, cast out to live among brute beasts. I said my whole composite being, body and soul.

- Why this composition of place? What is Ignatius trying to accomplish with this? "What Ignatius is insinuating is that life in this world ends with the corruption of the body (death) and that this valley of tears in which we live is not our final destiny, but rather an exile, a fate shared with the beasts. Furthermore, the corruptible body, with its needs, weaknesses, and sicknesses, aggravates the soul, which feels imprisoned and impeded from freely raising itself to heavenly things. It is in the consideration of truths such as these that we can come to understand our situation, so as to free ourselves from the tricks and misunderstandings of the world, and detach ourselves from excessive concern about our bodily well-being."[1]

Second Prelude: The petition: Here the petition will be to ask for shame and confusion, because I see how many have been lost on account of a single mortal sin, and how many times I have deserved eternal damnation, because of the many grievous sins that I have committed.

As we mentioned last night, in this meditation Saint Ignatius asks us to call to mind three sins: that of the angels, that of Adam and Eve, and that of a soul condemned to hell for a single mortal sin.

Again, because these are meditations, the work is done primarily with the *intellect* and the *will*. First, I use the memory to recall what it was that happened. Second, I use the understanding to think it over, and, third, I use the will to rouse the emotions.

We can consider, then, using the memory first, what the point is that Ignatius is trying to make:

1. Calveras, *Practica intensiva*, 153.

"First, in every mortal sin, there are two major aspects. First, there is a *serious disorder* in the sinful act itself, meaning, that sets the one sinning outside of the order and end indicated in the very nature of the thing and the sinner, a nature established by God Himself (and hence something serious against the Creator); secondly, a mortal sin implies *a conscious, malicious disobedience* to the Lord of the Universe, who also gravely prohibits that disorder (meaning, it is also a malice against the Lord, who expresses forbids it)."[2] It is a turning from God, from the end He established for us, from the good that He has intended towards us, and a turning towards creatures, making some creature our end, and not His most adorable and loving will.

Then, we are to use the understanding to think the matter over in more detail: "God has reinforced His prohibition by the loss of His friendship and the enjoyment thereof which is a sharing in His happiness. By sinning, the sinner prefers to delight of sin rather than happiness with God. Thus the sinner has freely renounced his friendship with God. It is in the sinner's power, it lies in his hands, to break his friendship with God, but not to restore it once it has been lost. It is restored only through the Divine condescension, that fact that God Himself comes to the sinner to return to him his status as adopted son. That privation of friendship with God, which becomes definitive with death in sin, is what the suffering of hell primarily consists of. Here, we can stop and think, for a moment, of what an eternity of pain and suffering in hell would be like, thousands, millions, billions, of years ... forever."[3].

Thirdly, then we are to use the will to rouse the emotions: "we should use our wills so as to be filled with shame and confusion when we see how many times we have deserved to be condemned, and justly so, for our many sins. This is because I, too, in each sin have acted seriously and maliciously against my Creator and Lord, and I have done so against God's infinite goodness, preferring the delight of sin so much so as to freely renounce my friendship with God, and in this, somehow I have been favored over the many souls that are in hell, souls who have perhaps committed only one single mortal sin, or at least fewer sins than I have committed."[4]

"St. Ignatius works out this line of thought in the three points which follow, placing sin before us in striking and terrible examples, drawn from creatures of different orders, that we may fully realize the dreadful injustice, folly, and misery contained in a single sin. Before the tribunal of God, of history, of our reason, we condemn sin as something utterly shameful and debasing; we view,

2. Ibid, 157.
3. Ibid, 157-158.
4. Ibid, 158.

as in a mirror, the deformed mass of our folly and sinfulness and, trembling at the depth of wickedness in one mortal sin, we consider what we must have been in God's sight, at the time when we had the misfortune to commit not merely one, but many, indeed, countless mortal sins. The injustice, malice, and baseness of sin find short and concise expression in the words of the three points: *the angels . . . were created in the state of grace, that they did not want to make use of the freedom God gave them to reverence and obey their Creator and Lord, and so falling into pride, were changed from grace to hatred of God . . . Our first parents sinned by violating the command not to eat of the tree of knowledge. . . . [When thinking of the one who was condemned because of one mortal sin] recall to memory the gravity and malice of sin against our Creator and Lord . . . sinning and acting against the Infinite Goodness.*

The folly and misery of the sinner are seen in the expressions: *The angels were cast out of Heaven into hell. . . . Our first parents were clothed in garments of skin and cast out of Paradise. By their sin they lost original justice, and for the rest of their lives, lived without it in many labors and great penance. . . . The one with only one mortal sin is justly condemned forever.*"[5]

"Consider the first sin we know of, that by which the angels fell.

Apply to it: 1st the memory, recalling the facts. They were created by the same Lord that made me, and for the same end, to praise, reverence and serve Him, and by this means to attain eternal bliss. They, like me, were put to a trial of their obedience; they were free to serve or no, as they chose. A multitude of the angels refused to obey: they sinned. These were cast out of Heaven into Hell, and punished with the worst suffering forever.

2nd: The understanding takes in the striking points of analogy between their history and that of man: If they were so severely punished, what must man expect when he imitates their rebellion? What a dreadful evil sin must be, since a good and just God hates it so. Their great number did not save the angels, nor will the number of bad men be a protection; all men are like a little dust before the infinite God. Man's excellence is below that of the angels, in power, in knowledge and in all natural gifts. They sinned but once; perhaps I have sinned repeatedly. What must I think of myself? of my past? of my future?

3rd: My will is gradually moved by these and similar considerations to detest sin, to dread sin, to detest my self if I have sinned, to beg God to spare me. I must stir up my will to hate sin more and more, to protest to God my hatred of it, my self-reproach.

Consider now the sin of our first parents:

5. Maurice Meschler, *The Spiritual Exercises of Saint Ignatius*, 44-45.

1st: My memory recalls the facts. They were created by the same God and for the same end as I; they were loved by Him and placed in a garden of delights, in Paradise, destined to enjoy the vision of God forever. They were free. God allowed Satan to tempt them, as He allows him to tempt me. But after falling, as a consequence, they were cast out of Paradise, condemned to years of toil and suffering, and to death, and all the evils that have befallen them and their posterity have been the punishment of sin.

2nd: My understanding must weigh these facts and reason on them, so as to realize the boundless evil of rebelling against our sovereign Lord and Master. It is not only the words of God but even more His deeds that show us what He is and how He acts. His severity in punishing sin in creatures for which He had shown such generous love exhibits the utter abomination He has for moral evil.

3rd: I must stir up my will to detest that same evil, to dread my own weakness which exposes me to sin again, to regret my past offenses, and to form strong resolutions for the future, praying earnestly for God's help.

Then, St. Ignatius bids us consider a third sin, namely that of some person who has gone to Hell for one mortal sin.

1st: The memory must recall the facts: it matters not whether the stories that we heard last night from Alphonsus Ligouri (and apparently he has many) are well authenticated or not, since the doctrine is certain that one mortal sin unpardoned is enough to damn the soul.

2nd: The understanding reasons on the case, so as to realize vividly the sad results of dying in sin.

3rd: The will is thus stirred up to hate sin as the greatest of all evils, and to avoid it at any sacrifice, according to the warning of Christ: "If your eye causes you to sin, cut it out and throw it away."[6]

"One who by his own folly and wickedness has brought upon himself such well-deserved unhappiness, has certainly no ground for self-complacency. The mere thought that here below we are continually exposed to so deplorable a fall, ought to be enough to cover us with shame. Our confusion is brought to a climax in the colloquy, wherein is shown hat our Lord had to suffer for us and for our sins; and wherein we see ourselves, in spite of our wickedness, the object of God's wondrous love and mercy. Here every word is to be weighed. Whoever makes this meditation earnestly, and in the right way, comes to look upon himself as a condemned criminal escaped from prison. And so it should be; otherwise the soul will not make an unconditional surrender to God. This feeling of confusion will be tempered by the humble confidence awakened

6. Charles Coppens, *The Spiritual Exercises of Saint Ignatius*, 26-30.

in the colloquy. We should, in fact, conclude every meditation in a spirit of confidence."[7]

[053] *Colloquy:* Imagine Christ our Lord present before you upon the cross, and begin to speak with him, asking how it is that though He is the Creator, He has stooped to become man, and to pass from eternal life to death here in time, that thus He might die for our sins. "How is this? We already know the answer: Christ came because He loved me, and wants me to be in Heaven with Him; this love, then, is a special love for me, a preference over many other sinners who are less sinful than I").[8]

I shall also reflect upon myself and ask:

"What have I done for Christ?"

"What am I doing for Christ?"

"What ought I to do for Christ?"

As I behold Christ in this plight, nailed to the cross, I shall ponder upon what presents itself to my mind.

7. Maurice Meschler, *The Spiritual Exercises of Saint Ignatius*, 45.

8. Calveras, *Practica intensiva*, 159.

Our Own Sins [055-061]

Usual Preparation Prayer.

First Prelude: The composition of Place: The representation will be to see in imagination my soul as a prisoner in this corruptible body, and to consider my whole composite being as an exile here on earth, cast out to live among brute beasts. I said my whole composite being, body and soul. Likewise, if it's easier, you can present yourself before God in the state of a criminal who appears before the judge at court, and is going to hear his sentence.

Second Prelude: The petition: Here the petition will be to ask for a growing and intense sorrow and tears for my sins.

Here Saint Ignatius asks us to call to mind our own sins. This meditation is the best preparation for our general confession and, again, we don't make a general confession because we don't think that we've been forgiven. We make a general confession because it forces us to realize how our lives are deformed and how often we have abused God's gifts; it makes us see what needs reforming in our lives, and renews our appreciation and thankfulness for God's mercy.

In fact, Ignatius discusses this at point 44, saying:

"Among many advantages of a general confession, which one makes of his own accord during the time of the Spiritual Exercises, there are especially these three:

- It is true that one who confesses every year has no obligation to make a general confession. But if one is made, there will be much greater merit and profit, because of the greater sorrow experienced for all the sins and perversities of his whole life.
- While one is going through the Spiritual Exercises, a far deeper insight into his sins and their malice is acquired than at a time when he is not so engaged with what concerns his inner life. Since at this time he attains to a deeper knowledge and sorrow for his sins, there will be greater profit and merit than he would otherwise have had.
- As a consequence of having made a better confession, and of being better disposed, he will find that he is more worthy and better prepared to receive the Most Blessed Sacrament. This reception will strengthen him

not only against falling into sin, but will also help him to retain the in-crease of grace which he has gained.

It will be better to make this general confession immediately after the Ex-ercises of the First Week."

Likewise, sometimes a general confession helps with scrupulosity. This was the experience of Saint Peter Faber, who suffered from such terrible scruples that he said that if by going out into the desert and living in solitude on bread and water would have taken them away, he would've done it. Ignatius wisely told him to make the Exercises and make a good general confession, and the rest is, as they say, history.

You can also combine your general confession with a regular one, but you should start off by saying, "Ok, it's been how many ever weeks since my last confession, and these are my sins . . . " and then start by saying, "And I'd like to make my general confession."

[056] The First Point: "This is the record of my sins. I will call to mind all the sins of my life, reviewing year by year, and period by period. Three things will help me in this: First, to consider the place where I lived; secondly, my dealings with others; thirdly, the office I have held."

So, at this point, we're to review our entire lives, examining them year by year, to see how and when we've fallen short of what God has asked of us. If we think of the place we lived (or maybe the place we went to school, if that's easier), the people we dealt with, and the job or tasks we were engaged in, we'll see lots of sins. We can also break it down into sins of thought, word, and deed, if that's easier.

We could say that this review isn't done in the first-person singular, mean-ing, I'm not trying to go back and re-live those sinful experiences, or bring back memories from the past that could be a source of temptations. I don't need to examine my sins that way. Instead, we want to review our sins like "a court record of a trial" (in fact, the specific word that Ignatius uses, *proceso de los pecados*, means just this, like, the trial proceedings), or like an eagle sees things from above; it sees them, but not in agonizing detail. The point isn't to have a detailed record of every little sin that we've ever committed, with all the little elements; the point is to focus on the big sins, the mortal sins, which have made us lose sanctifying grace and have turned us and our gifts against God.[1]

---

1. The early Jesuit directories emphasize that a focused list of mortal sins is more ef-fective in generating contrition and sorrow than a long list of all the sins one has ever committed.

"Sins of childhood, sins of early youth, sins of later. Examine all your years; what day was there that you didn't sin? Ask all the laws of God; is there a single one that you didn't break? Ask all your past temptations; are there many times you didn't fall? Ask all your faculties; is there any that's not guilty of sin? Ask all your senses: your eyes, your ears, your mouth, your sense of touch, your sense of smell: which is there that hasn't served as an instrument of iniquity?"[2]

[057] The Second Point: "I will weigh the gravity of my sins, and see the loathesomeness and malice which every mortal sin I have committed has in itself, even though it were not forbidden."

The loathsomeness and malice of each mortal sin: "Mortal sin is a supreme contempt for the infinite majesty of God. The creature despises the laws the Creator has made for him, for his good, and instead laughs God to scorn. The one who sins mortally would kill God if he could, since God and sin cannot exist close together. Those who live in mortal sin act as if God didn't exist. Infinite Love, Power, Goodness, Wisdom, and Mercy could be dead, as far as the grave sinner is concerned. He or she simply isn't interested."[3]

"How loathsome sin is! It is supreme ugliness, since it is infinitely opposed to supreme beauty, which is God. How ungrateful sin is! You withhold everything from God, and dare to tell Him, 'Go away from me! Leave me alone; get out of my heart, which is created to love You. Get out of my being, which I was given only to serve You!"

Blessed Joseph Kentenich says it well when he writes that in mortal sin, "I lose the beauty of my soul. There are mystics who have marvelously profound things to say about the singular beauty of the soul in the state of grace. They stress that, next to God, hardly anything is as beautiful as the soul in the state of grace. If this is true, we can likewise infer how ugly a soul must be that lacks this divine life! Perhaps I can begin by asking you to compare God with Satan. We can understand how souls in the state of grace shudder when they see the Devil, an image, a horrendous image of the Devil. If I can take my parallel further: must not a soul held captive by Satan, who has delivered himself up to him, be singularly ugly? Be that as it may, the soul in the state of grace certainly loses its marvelous beauty when it falls from grace."[4]

2. *Manresa, or, the Spiritual Exercises of St. Ignatius for General Use*, 305.
3. Cf. Rev. Fr. Francis J. Ripley *This Is the Faith: A Complete Explanation of the Catholic Faith*
4. *Childlikeness before God*, 110-111.

"How bold sin is! You dare to tell God, 'I will not serve; I will not obey.' And you dare to say it to God's face, right as you stand on the edge of the grave, on the brink of hell, where you are held suspended by a thin thread called life."[5]

This malice would be there "even though [these sins] were not forbidden." In other words, the point isn't just that we've broken the law. Sin isn't bad simply because God forbids it. Sin, and mortal sin in particular, is horrible because of the disorder it implies, the hatred it entails, and the perversion it means. There is an ontological problem with sin; it is a lack of being, a parasite, an intrinsic lack of perfection. In themselves, sins are horrible, and in forbidding them God is doing us a favor by telling us to avoid them. And yet, we go ahead and do them anyways.

[058] Third Point: "I will consider who I am, and by means of examples humble myself: What am I compared with all men? What are all men compared with the angels and saints of paradise? Consider what all creation is in comparison with God. Then I alone, what can I be? I will consider all the corruption and loathsomeness of my body. I will consider myself as a source of corruption and contagion from which has issued countless sins and evils and the most offensive poison."

What I am compared with all the men and women who have ever lived? There's around 7 billion people alive right now, and 108 billion have been born on this planet. What percentage of the population am I? "What is a leaf in comparison with the forest? A grain of sand compared with the beach? Considered this way, little me is nothing."

Consider all these people, though, compared with one angel, in all its glory, all its power, all its strength. All those people are nothing compared to a single angel.

And yet, what are all men and women, all angels, and all creation, when compared with God? Absolutely nothing. They are nothing. And yet little me, in my littleness and insignificance, have dared to rebel against God, like a spoiled child who throws a tantrum. It is like "when a parent feels the strangeness of the power of the obstinate will of his children to resist and spurn persuasion, love, hope, or fear of punishment. A power so strong resides in a body so small and a mind so childish; yet it is a faint picture of men when they have willfully sinned."[6]

5. *Manresa, or, the Spiritual Exercises of St. Ignatius for General Use*, 306-7.
6. Fulton Sheen, *Life of Christ*.

[059] Fourth Point: "I will consider who God is against whom I have sinned, going through His attributes and comparing them with their contraries in me: His wisdom with my ignorance, His power with my weakness, His justice with my iniquity, His goodness with my wickedness."

Consider God's attributes: "For the foolishness of God is wiser than human wisdom, and the weakness of God is stronger than human strength" (1 Cor 1:25).

Or, as God tells Job (Chapters 38-40): "Who is this who darkens counsel with words of ignorance? Where were you when I founded the earth? Tell me, if you have understanding. Who determined its size? Surely you know? Who stretched out the measuring line for it? Into what were its pedestals sunk, and who laid its cornerstone? Have you ever in your lifetime commanded the morning and shown the dawn its place for taking hold of the ends of the earth, till the wicked are shaken from it? Have you entered into the sources of the sea, or walked about on the bottom of the deep? Have the gates of death been shown to you, or have you seen the gates of darkness? Have you comprehended the breadth of the earth? Tell me, if you know it all. Have you entered the storehouses of the snow, and seen the storehouses of the hail which I have reserved for times of distress, for a day of war and battle? What is the way to the parting of the winds, where the east wind spreads over the earth?

Then Job answered the LORD and said: "Look, I am of little account; what can I answer you? I put my hand over my mouth. I have spoken once, I will not reply; twice, but I will do so no more. Then the LORD answered Job out of the storm and said: I will question you, and you tell me the answers! Would you refuse to acknowledge my right? Would you condemn me that you may be justified? Have you an arm like that of God, or can you thunder with a voice like his? Adorn yourself with grandeur and majesty, and clothe yourself with glory and splendor. Let loose the fury of your wrath; look at everyone who is proud and bring them down. Look at everyone who is proud, and humble them. Tear down the wicked in their place, bury them in the dust together; in the hidden world imprison them."

[060] Fifth Point: "This is a cry of wonder accompanied by surging emotion as I pass in review all creatures. How is it that they have permitted me to live, and have sustained me in life! Why have the angels, though they are the sword of God's justice, tolerated me, guarded me, and prayed for me! Why have the saints interceded for me and asked favors for me! And the heavens, sun, moon, stars, and the elements; the fruits, birds, fishes, and other animals—why have they all been at my service! How is it that the earth did not open to swallow me up, and create new hells in which I should be tormented forever!"

See what mercy God has had! See all the creatures placed on this earth that, rather than destroy you, have instead kept you in being! How all creation, the natural world, which, by its very nature, serves God, has been placed at your disposal! The sun, the moon, and the stars, instead of falling upon you, have given you light and joy! The earth, rather than swallow you up like Dathan, Abiram, and Korah (cf. Numbers 16:31), has supported you and kept you alive! How the waters, rather than rush over you and end your life, as happened to so many in Noah's day, have sustained you in being! How the animals, rather than throw themselves at you to destroy you, have served you with their lives! How the angels, who cannot stand iniquity, have tolerated your sins, as though they turned a blind eye to them! How the saints, seeing your terrible deeds, rather than condemn you, interceded for you! Such is the mercy and greatness of God!

For our many sins, what punishment haven't we deserved! And yet, God sustained us, and ordered all creation to our good!

[061] *Colloquy*: I will conclude with a colloquy, extolling the mercy of God our Lord, pouring out my thoughts to Him, and giving thanks to Him that up to this very moment He has granted me life. I will resolve with His grace to amend for the future. Close with an Our Father.

Our Own Sins [055-061] Repetition

Really, here we are doing the *Third Exercise* [62-63], which is a "repetition of the first and second exercises with three colloquies.

After the preparatory prayer and the two preludes, this exercise will consist in repeating the First and Second Exercise. In doing this, we should pay attention to and dwell upon those points in which we have experienced greater consolation or desolation or greater spiritual appreciation. After the repetition, three colloquies are to be used in the following manner:

First Colloquy

The first colloquy will be with our Blessed Lady, that she may obtain grace for me from her Son and Lord for three favors:

I. A deep knowledge of my sins and a feeling of abhorrence for them;

II. An understanding of the disorder of my actions, so that filled with horror of them, I may amend my life and put it in order;

III. A knowledge of the world, so that filled with horror, I may put away from me all that is worldly and vain.

Then I will say a *Hail Mary*.

Second Colloquy

I will make the same petitions to her Son that He may obtain these graces from the Father for me.

After that I will say *Soul of Christ*.

Third Colloquy

I will make the same requests of the Father that He Himself, the eternal Lord, may grant them to me.

Then I will close with the *Our Father*.

Usual Preparation Prayer.

First Prelude: The composition of Place: The representation will be to see in imagination my soul as a prisoner in this corruptible body, and to consider my whole composite being as an exile here on earth, cast out to live among brute beasts. I said my whole composite being, body and soul.

Likewise, if it's easier, you can present yourself before God in the state of a criminal who appears before the judge at court, and is going to hear his sentence.

Second Prelude: The petition: Here the petition will be to ask for a growing and intense sorrow and tears for my sins.

- We can consider, for a moment, those three words, "growing," "intense," and "tears." "'Growing' means that it is a sorrow that becomes very vehement, from the strength of my will, and that it becomes so strong that it bursts forth in a firm resolution to change my life from here on, with, of course, the help of grace.
- 'Intense,' meaning that by the understanding I live with an appreciation of the reasons for this sorrow; done by the understanding; the understanding shouldn't be content with a superficial examination of these reasons, but should, rather, penetrate and delve into their depths, and
- 'Tears' are the external manifestation of the first two. Tears aren't necessarily an unmistakable sign of real and interior contrition; some people can cry at the drop of a hat! These sort of tears aren't usually the sort of ones that make us firm and constant in our proposals, but, nonetheless, even these tears, inspired by an intense imagination or whatever, can help that sorrow to penetrate deep into the soul. For some people, tears are hard to come by, but it should be remembered that tears are a gift from God, and they should be asked for. Oftentimes those who do not cry are proud of their strong temperament, that appears tough as iron and unyielding as diamond. These should humble themselves to ask, humbly, for the gift of tears."[1]

Last night and this morning, you had the opportunity to meditate on your own sins and now, as is usually the case, we will have a repetition of that same meditation.

To have it clear in mind, the fruits we want to obtain are the following:

- "first, *internal contrition, sorrow, and pain* for our own sins, accompanied by perfect internal penance with the firm resolve not to commit them or any other sins in the future;
- second, *hatred* and scorn of those sins, because of our deep interior knowledge of how ugly and malicious sin is, a knowledge which strengthens our resolution to avoid them and destroys the disordered affection we have for them, and;

1. Cf. Oraa, *Los Ejercicios Espritiaules*, 97-98.

- third, *tears*, to cry much over them, in order to feel the bitterness that is sin, and to correct the erroneous natural judgments we have regarding sin, judging it to be something pleasant and attractive, and that, as these tears will be accompanied by a love for our Creator and Lord, we might be filled with appreciation and gratitude towards Him, and thus the void that is left when we leave sin might be filled with a love for Him."[2]

So with that in mind, let us return to the points again.

[056] The First Point: "This is the record of my sins. I will call to mind all the sins of my life, reviewing year by year, and period by period. Three things will help me in this: First, to consider the place where I lived; secondly, my dealings with others; thirdly, the office I have held."

Again, the point is not to have a detailed list with all of the little mores and lesses of our sins; the preparation for a general confession is, as it were, more general than for a weekly confession.[3]

Likewise, we recall the seriousness of that word "record," or "*proceso*" in Spanish. We should think of the seriousness and severity with which we should do this examination, not hiding anything; we should go about it with the rigor of a well-formed judge, or a very astute, very precise District Attorney.

Let us consider, then:

- "The years of our childhood: how did we behave towards our parents, teachers, brothers and sisters, classmates and friends? How did we take advantage of the time we were given, and the means of salvation that were so generously poured out upon us? How did we protect our innocence? As Saint Augustine puts it so well in the *Confessions* (I, 7, 12): 'Where, I pray you, O my God, where, Lord, or when was I, Your servant, innocent?'
- The years of our youth and adolescence, when our passions were violently awakened. Let us remember the people with whom we had interactions, the places we would go, the jobs or the studies that we undertook. What path did we follow? The wide one to perdition, or the narrow one to Heaven? *Remember no more the sins of my youth*, says Psalm 25 (7), *remember me according to your mercy, because of your goodness, LORD.*
- Finally, in adulthood, and in the religious life (for those of us who are in it). Did I always keep my eyes fixed on my last end? In everything, was I seeking my salvation and God's glory? When I received graces from God,

---

2. Cf. Calveras, *Practica intensiva*, 161-162.
3. Ibid., 163, but also Oraa, *Ejercicos Espirituales*, 98.

how did I take advantage of them? As Job tells God, *What are my faults and my sins? My misdeed, my sin make known to me!* (13:23)."[4]

We can consider the rebuke that Christ makes of the soul in the fourth book of the *Imitation of Christ:*

Lament grievously and be sorry, because you are still so carnal and worldly, so unmortified from your passions, so full of the motion of concupiscence, so unguarded in your outward senses, so often entangled in many vain fancies, so much inclined to outward things, so negligent of internal things; so ready to laughter and dissoluteness, so unready to weeping and contrition; so prone to ease and indulgence of the flesh, so dull to zeal and fervor; so curious to hear novelties and behold beauties, so loth to embrace things humble and despised; so desirous to have many things, so grudging in giving, so close in keeping; so inconsiderate in speaking, so reluctant to keep silence; so disorderly in manners, so inconsiderate in actions; so eager after food, so deaf towards the Word of God; so eager after rest, so slow to labor; so watchful after tales, so sleepy towards holy watchings; so eager for the end of them, so wandering in attention to them; so negligent in observing the hours of prayer, so lukewarm in celebrating, so unfruitful in communicating; so quickly distracted, so seldom quite collected with thyself; so quickly moved to anger, so ready for displeasure at others; so prone to judging, so severe at reproving; so joyful in prosperity, so weak in adversity.

[057] The Second Point: "I will weigh the gravity of my sins, and see the loathesomeness and malice which every mortal sin I have committed has in itself, even though it were not forbidden."

- Let us first consider the loathsomeness of sin, the ugliness of it. We could say that this speaks more to the intellect, the way I abuse my understanding when I sin because it implies a lack of conformity with right reason: "All sin is something ugly for the rational being and for the Christian; by committing it, man surrenders the use of his reason, he acts against the right judgments of his understanding, he thinks according to his desires, and he acts according to his appetites. In this, man lowers himself to the level of the beasts, of the animals. Man, who was created in honor, thus, as Psalm 49 (13) tells us, this *man does not abide in splendor. He is like the beasts—they perish.* In sin, man, created in splendor, is reduced

4. Cf. Oraa, *Ejercicos Espirituales,* 99-100.

to the level of the beasts over which he was to have authority. He becomes a beast."[5]

- The malice of sin: here, we can mention more the disorder we find in the will when we sin: "First, sin is a *monstrous ingratitude*: Jesus seems to tell the soul, as He told the children of Israel in John's Gospel, *I have shown you many good works from my Father. For which of these are you trying to stone me?* (10:32). I have received so many blessings and benefits from God the Father, who created me out of nothing, and to whom I owe absolutely everything. I owe Him my undivided obedience and, yet, when I sin, I throw myself against Him and usurp His dominion.

- But there's more: God is a father, and a most loving father, who loves me as no one else can or does, and what cruelty it is to sin against one so loving! The son of a good mother thinks on her constantly, and tries to avoid sin in order to not cause her pain. If he does fall through passion or wicked companions, how sorrowful he feels afterwards when he thinks upon her, and how he throws himself at her feet, full of remorse and sorrow!

- But there's more: not only is God a loving father, He is also our Redeemer! Only by looking at the cross can we really come to understand the profound malice, the price of sin and disobedience. It is my sins that have put Christ there!

- Sin is therefore *a despising of God, a despising that is unfit to render towards God.* And why do we sin? Because we don't love God! We sin for stupid reasons, little nothings!

- Sin is insolence! Sin is madness!"[6]

[058] Third Point: "I will consider who I am, and by means of examples humble myself: What am I compared with all men? What are all men compared with the angels and saints of paradise? Consider what all creation is in comparison with God. Then I alone, what can I be? I will consider all the corruption and loathsomeness of my body. I will consider myself as a source of corruption and contagion from which has issued countless sins and evils and the most offensive poison."

- "What am I compared to all men? What is my knowledge, my abilities, my strength, my power, compared to all men together? What would happen if I declared war on all the other people in the world? If I were to

5. Ibid., 101-102. However, the attribution of *ugliness* to reason, and *malice* to the will comes from Calveras, *Practica intensiva*, 163-164.

6. Ibid., 101-106.

disappear, who would notice in Maryland or California? Who would notice in the United States? Who would notice in Africa, or Asia . . .

- But, now, what is all the knowledge, all the abilities, all the strength, all the power, of all men combined when compared with that of all the angels and all the saints? Nothing. Imagine if all men were to declare war against the angels and saints: a single blast of light would blind all men, as it did when the angels visited Sodom, or a single angel could slay them all, as happened to the 185,000 Assyrians in one night. So, then, me alone, what could I possibly be?

- But now, compare all men, all angels and saints, all creation, to God! Of course, they would never declare war on Him, but we can see the difference. As the Book of Wisdom says so clearly (11:28): *Indeed, before you the whole universe is like a grain from a balance, or a drop of morning dew come down upon the earth.*

- What then, am I? Nothing. Well, actually, worse than that. Anything that seems to be mine, my body, my soul, all of that is really a gift from God. What I am, what I have done on my own, are my sins. When I want to see what I have done, what I am capable of doing by myself, that's where I can look. I am just dust and ashes . . . and sin. Sins come from me like a poison, like toxic waste."[7]

[059] Fourth Point: "I will consider who God is and against whom I have sinned, going through His attributes and comparing them with their contraries in me: His wisdom with my ignorance, His power with my weakness, His justice with my iniquity, His goodness with my wickedness."

- "My ignorance has despised the precious divine order established by God, rejecting His laws and wanting to correct them, to change them to suit my likings.

- My weakness has thrown itself into rebellion against His power, against His goodness.

- My iniquity has thrown itself in the face of His justice, to whom *not even the heavens are pure in His sight.*

- My wickedness has offended His goodness, shown like a father to me, time and again, without ceasing. Even if the offense was small, the offense is measured against the one who was offended, and hence, with God, there is no small sin. When I really consider all this, the fifth point should simply follow naturally."[8]

7. Ibid., 101-106.
8. Ibid., 108.

[060] Fifth Point: "This is a cry of wonder accompanied by surging emotion as I pass in review all creatures. How is it that they have permitted me to live, and have sustained me in life! Why have the angels, though they are the sword of God's justice, tolerated me, guarded me, and prayed for me! Why have the saints interceded for me and asked favors for me! And the heavens, sun, moon, stars, and the elements; the fruits, birds, fishes, and other animals—why have they all been at my service! How is it that the earth did not open to swallow me up, and create new hells in which I should be tormented forever!"

- "Why? Why this mercy? In short, so that I might return to Him, throw myself into His arms, and reform my life. That is why. Mercy, and only mercy, unmerited, undeserved, can explain this. Will I continue to resist His love and goodness?"[9]

[061] *Colloquy*: I will conclude with a colloquy, extolling the mercy of God our Lord, pouring out my thoughts to Him, and giving thanks to Him that up to this very moment He has granted me life. I will resolve with His grace to amend for the future. Close with an Our Father.

9. Ibid., 108-109.

Hell [65-71]

Usual Preparation Prayer.

First Prelude: The composition of Place: Here it will be to see in imagination the length, breadth, and depth of hell.

Second Prelude: The petition: I should ask for what I desire. Here it will be to beg for a deep sense of the pain which the lost suffer, that if because of my faults I forget the love of the eternal Lord, at least the fear of these punishments will keep me from falling into sin. – Of course, we should add that it's far, far better to love God, and to not want to sin because we love Him, but if the fear of hell keeps us from sinning, it has accomplished its purpose.

Then, in the points, Ignatius will have us use our five senses to really envision ourselves in the depths of hell, suffering for our sins.

[66] First Point: This will be to see in imagination the vast fires, and the souls enclosed, as it were, in bodies of fire.

[67] Second Point: To hear the wailing, the howling, cries, and blasphemies against Christ our Lord and against His saints.

[68] Third Point: With the sense of smell to perceive the smoke, the sulfur, the filth, and corruption.

[69] Fourth Point: To taste the bitterness of tears, sadness, and remorse of conscience.

[70] Fifth Point: With the sense of touch to feel the flames which envelop and burn the souls.

Holy Mother Church has always taught that hell is real, and that it is a real possibility for each of us to end up there for all eternity. This isn't something the Church made up; rather, Jesus Himself talks about hell on a number of occasions. In Matthew's Gospel, ch. 10 (v. 28), Jesus tells His listeners "Do not be afraid of those who kill the body but cannot kill the soul; rather, be afraid of the one who can destroy both soul and body in Gehenna." Later, in chapter 25, He warns that those who refuse to practice charity will hear the terrifying sentence: "Depart from me, you accursed, into the eternal fire prepared for the devil and his angels." The *Catechism of the Catholic Church* tells us [1033-1035]: "We cannot be united with God unless we freely choose to love him. But we cannot love God if we sin gravely against him, against our neighbor or against ourselves. . . . To die in mortal sin without repenting and accepting God's merciful love means remaining separated from him for ever by our own free choice. This state of definitive self-exclusion from communion with God and the blessed is called 'hell.' Immediately after death the souls of those who die in a state of mortal sin descend into hell, where they suffer the punishments of hell, 'eternal fire.' The chief punishment of hell is eternal separation from God, in whom alone man can possess the life and happiness for which he was created and for which he longs."

The Catechism tells us that going to hell is a choice; it's a choice we make. We can say, and correctly, that God doesn't throw people into hell; we throw ourselves there by refusing to do what He asks and then, by refusing to repent. We were made for God, and so we were also made for Heaven, but if we refuse to leave behind our sins and refuse to love God, God won't force us to be with Him for all eternity. We can choose to separate ourselves from Him forever, and that's what hell is.

This is all true, but sometimes to hear the experiences of the saints who have had visions of hell can help us to visualize this better and understand the seriousness of this eternal condemnation.

Servant of God Sister María Josefa Menéndez, who died at the age of 33, had a number of visions of hell. In fact, her fellow sisters used to know when she had had a vision of hell because the entire chapel would reek of sulfur. She describes it this way:

My soul fell into abysmal depths, the bottom of which cannot be seen, for it is immense. . . ; Then I was pushed into one of those fiery cavities and pressed, as it were, between burning planks, and sharp nails and red-hot irons seemed to be piercing my flesh. I felt as if they were endeavoring to pull out my tongue, but could not. This torture reduced me to such agony that my very eyes seemed to be starting out of their sockets. I think this was because of the fire which burns, burns . . . not a finger nail escapes terrifying torments, and all the time one cannot move even a finger to gain some relief, not change posture, for the body seems flattened out and [yet] doubled in two. Sounds of confusion and blasphemy cease not for an instant.

A sickening stench asphyxiates and corrupts everything, it is like the burning of putrefied flesh, mingled with tar and sulfur . . . a mixture to which nothing on earth can be compared ... although these tortures were terrific, they would be bearable if the soul were at peace. But it suffers indescribably..."

She concludes this way: "All I have written is but a shadow of what the soul suffers, for no words can express such dire torment" (September 4, 1922).[1]

Likewise, **Saint Faustina**, the saint of Divine Mercy, had visions of hell. As she writes: "I, Sister Faustina Kowalska, by the order of God, have visited the Abysses of Hell so that I might tell souls about it and testify to its existence.... What I have written is but a pale shadow of the things I saw. But I noticed one thing: That most of the souls there are those who disbelieved that there is a hell" (Diary 741).

"I was led by an angel to the Chasms of Hell. It is a place of great torture; how awesomely large and extensive it is! The kinds of tortures I saw:

The First Torture that constitutes hell is: the loss of God.

The Second is: perpetual remorse of conscience.

The Third is: that one's condition will never change.

The Fourth is: the fire that will penetrate the soul without destroying it. A terrible suffering since it is a purely spiritual fire, lit by God's anger.

The Fifth Torture is: continual darkness and a terrible suffocating smell, and despite the darkness, the devils and the souls of the damned see each other and all the evil, both of others and their own.

The Sixth Torture is: the constant company of Satan.

The Seventh Torture is: horrible despair, hatred of God, vile words, curses and blasphemies. These are the Tortures suffered by all the damned together, but that is not the end of the sufferings.

There are special Tortures destined for particular souls. These are the torments of the senses. Each soul undergoes terrible and indescribable sufferings related to the manner in which it has sinned.

There are caverns and pits of torture where one form of agony differs from another. I would have died at the very sight of these tortures if the omnipotence of God had not supported me.

Let the sinner know that he will be tortured throughout all eternity, in those senses which he made use of to sin. I am writing this at the command of God, so that no soul may find an excuse by saying there is no hell, or that nobody has ever been there, and so no one can say what it is like... how terribly souls suffer there! Consequently, I pray even more fervently for the conversion of sinners. I incessantly plead God's mercy upon them. O My Jesus, I would rather be in agony until the end of the world, amidst the greatest sufferings, than offend you by the least sin" (*Diary* 741).

1. See her book, *The Way of Divine Love.*

Lastly, we have the vision of **Saint Teresa of Jesus**: she saw the very place that had been reserved for her in hell. As she writes:

I was one day in prayer when I found myself in a moment, without knowing how, plunged apparently into hell. I understood that it was our Lord's will I should see the place which the devils kept in readiness for me, and which I had deserved by my sins. It was but a moment, but it seems to me impossible I should ever forget it, even if I were to live many years.

The entrance seemed to be by a long narrow pass, like a furnace, very low, dark, and close. The ground seemed to be saturated with water, mere mud, exceedingly foul, sending forth pestilential odors, and covered with loathsome vermin. At the end was a hollow place in the wall, like a closet, and in that I saw myself confined. All this was even pleasant to behold in comparison with what I felt there. There is no exaggeration in what I am saying.

But as to what I then felt, I do not know where to begin, if I were to describe it; it is utterly inexplicable. I felt a fire in my soul. I cannot see how it is possible to describe it. My bodily sufferings were unendurable. I have undergone most painful sufferings in this life, and, as the physicians say, the greatest that can be borne, such as the contraction of my sinews when I was paralyzed, without speaking of others of different kinds, yea, even those of which I have also spoken, inflicted on me by Satan; yet all these were as nothing in comparison with what I felt then, especially when I saw that there would be no intermission, nor any end to them.

These sufferings were nothing in comparison with the anguish of my soul, a sense of oppression, of stifling, and of pain so keen, accompanied by so hopeless and cruel an affliction, that I know not how to speak of it. If I said that the soul is continually being torn from the body it would be nothing,--for that implies the destruction of life by the hands of another; but here it is the soul itself that is tearing itself in pieces. I cannot describe that inward fire or that despair, surpassing all torments and all pain. I did not see who it was that tormented me, but I felt myself on fire, and torn to pieces, as it seemed to me; and, I repeat it, this inward fire and despair are the greatest torments of all.

Left in that pestilential place, and utterly without the power to hope for comfort, I could neither sit nor lie down: there was no room. I was placed as it were in a hole in the wall; and those walls, terrible to look on of themselves, hemmed me in on every side. I could not breathe. There was no light, but all was thick darkness. I do not understand how it is; though there was no light, yet everything that can give pain by being seen was visible."[2]

2. Saint Teresa of Jesus, *Life*, Ch. 32.

In the supplement to the Tertia Pars of the *Summa*, Thomas Aquinas confirms everything that these saints say: I would point out several of his conclusions:

In question 98, a. 4, Aquinas asks, "Do the damned in hell wish that others, who are not damned, would be damned as well?" In other words, are the damned so filled with hate, that they wish the saints would be damned with them, in hell? He answers, "Even as in the blessed in Heaven there will be most perfect charity, so in the damned there will be the most perfect hate. Wherefore as the saints will rejoice in all goods, so will the damned grieve for all goods. Consequently the sight of the happiness of the saints will give them very great pain; hence it is written (Isaiah 26:11): 'Let the envious people see and be confounded, and let fire devour Thy enemies.' Therefore they will wish all the good were damned."

That makes sense, but, in an objection Aquinas points out how wicked this is. He notes, that, if in Heaven, the saints increase in joy as the number of the blessed increases, so in hell the punishment suffered increases as the more people end up in hell. It would seem like the damned shouldn't want more people to end up there, because it just means they'll be suffering more. Aquinas replies: "Although an increase in the number of the damned results in an increase of each one's punishment, so much the more will their hatred and envy increase that they will prefer to be more tormented with many rather than less tormented alone." They are so hate-filled, that they prefer to suffer worse torments with many people than be tormented less alone.

In q. 97, a. 4, we can also consider what he says about the darkness there, which all the saints have touched upon: the place is dark, and yet there's a certain amount of light. He says: "The disposition of hell will be such as to be adapted to the utmost unhappiness of the damned. Wherefore accordingly both light and darkness are there, in so far as they are most conducive to the unhappiness of the damned. Now seeing is in itself pleasant for, as stated in *Metaph.* i, the sense of sight is most esteemed, because thereby many things are known."

Yet it happens accidentally that seeing is painful, when we see things that are hurtful to us, or displeasing to our will. Consequently in hell the place must be so disposed for seeing as regards light and darkness, that nothing be seen clearly, and that only such things be dimly seen as are able to bring anguish to the heart. Wherefore, simply speaking, the place is dark. Yet by Divine disposition, there is a certain amount of light, as much as suffices for seeing those things which are capable of tormenting the soul. The natural situation of the place is enough for this, since in the center of the earth, where hell is said to be, fire cannot be otherwise than thick and cloudy, and reeky as it were."

Let us consider that there is a place in hell for us as well, a place with our name on it, reserved for us and our particular sins. Whether that spot will be occupied or empty for all eternity depends on the way I live my life from now on.

Again, as we said earlier, it is far better to serve God out of love than out of fear of hell but, if love of God doesn't keep us from sinning, then at least fear of the torments of hell should.

To this, I will add one short story that involves my mom and one of her friends. My mom was raised Protestant, so I do most of her theological vetting when there is a question. Anyways, she once asked me to tell her what I thought about a particular event that took place at the hospital. Her friend is a nurse in the cardiac intensive care unit at a major hospital, and, being a devout Catholic and a mother, she would try, subtly, to convince the other nurses, many of them young, to stop living wild lives, and really focus on God. Of course, this approach met rather dismal results, until one day, a fellow nurse stopped her and said, "Sue,[3] could you tell me about Jesus and God and what I need to do to be a good person?" My mom's friend looked at her, surprised, and said, "Of course! But . . . what happened? Why the change?" The other nurse began to recount that she had been caring for a patient in the ward when suddenly he went into cardiac arrest, meaning, his heart stopped. Of course, they are prepared for that in the ward, and they were able to revive him, but, when he came around, he was extremely agitated, and so the nurse tried to calm him down, saying, with all her professional ability, "Sir, your heart stopped and we revived you. You're ok now, but you need to calm down." But the man was not to be calmed, and was shouting, "No! You don't understand! You have no idea how awful it was! It was terrible! It hurt so much! Please, you can't let me die! Don't let me die! I don't want to go back there!" At this, the nurse was shaken, but told the patient to remain calm, that he was going to be fine, but the patient insisted and insisted . . . until his heart stopped again. And again, the nurses and doctors came and revived him, and, again, the nurse told him to remain calm, but the patient, even more frantic, replied, "No! You don't understand! It was awful! He was there! It hurt so bad! Help me! Don't let me die! I can't go back there!" And this continued . . . until his heart stopped a third time. Only this time, they couldn't revive him, and he died, with a horrific expression on his face, one of sheer horror and agony. The nurse then added: "The look on his face convinced me that, whatever he had seen, was real."

---

3. Not her real name, I think!

[71] Colloquy: Enter into conversation with Christ our Lord. Recall to memory that of those who are in hell, some went there because they did not believe in the coming of Christ; others, though they believed, because they did not keep the Commandments. Divide them all into three classes:

Those who were lost before the coming of Christ;

Those who were lost during His lifetime;

Those who were lost after His life here on earth.

Thereupon, I will give thanks to God our Lord that He has not put an end to my life and permitted me to fall into any of these three classes.

I shall also thank Him for this, that up to this very moment He has shown Himself so loving and merciful to me.

Close with an Our Father.

Hell [65-71] – Repetition

Usual Preparation Prayer.

First Prelude: The composition of Place: Here it will be to see in imagination the length, breadth, and depth of hell.

Second Prelude: The petition: I should ask for what I desire. Here it will be to beg for a deep sense of the pain which the lost suffer, that if because of my faults I forget the love of the eternal Lord, at least the fear of these punishments will keep me from falling into sin.

[66] First Point: This will be to see in imagination the vast fires, and the souls enclosed, as it were, in bodies of fire.

[67] Second Point: To hear the wailing, the howling, cries, and blasphemies against Christ our Lord and against His saints.

[68] Third Point: With the sense of smell to perceive the smoke, the sulfur, the filth, and corruption.

[69] Fourth Point: To taste the bitterness of tears, sadness, and remorse of conscience.

[70] Fifth Point: With the sense of touch to feel the flames which envelop and burn the souls.

"The Lord's special love for me should be sufficient for me to change my ways for the future, with the help of His grace. However, precisely because of my sins, little by little, I might come to forget Him, since our wills weaken. Hence, if I think of hell, this will support me in my endeavor to not fall into sin.

If my fear of hell should also waiver, then my ruin is certain. This is why it is important to have a holy fear of God and to think on hell occasionally.

Saint Ignatius wants us to think of the sensible torments of hell because usually temptations are presented as something sensibly good, as something delightful or enjoyable, and so, by focusing on the sensible pains of hell, we are more easily able to overcome temptation."[1]

We can consider what the Fatima visionaries say in their vision of hell. Sr. Lucia described it this way:

[Mary] opened Her hands once more, as She had done the two previous months. The rays [of light] appeared to penetrate the earth, and we saw, as it were, a vast sea of fire. Plunged in this fire, we saw the demons and the souls [of the damned].

The latter were like transparent burning embers, all blackened or burnished bronze, having human forms. They were floating about in that conflagration, now raised into the air by the flames which issued from within themselves, together with great clouds of smoke. Now they fell back on every side like sparks in huge fires, without weight or equilibrium, amid shrieks and groans of pain and despair, which horrified us and made us tremble with fright (it must have been this sight which caused me to cry out, as people say they heard me).

The demons were distinguished [from the souls of the damned] by their terrifying and repellent likeness to frightful and unknown animals, black and transparent like burning coals. That vision only lasted for a moment, thanks to our good Heavenly Mother, Who at the first apparition had promised to take us to Heaven. Without that, I think that we would have died of terror and fear.

This vision of hell marked a turning point in the spiritual life of the three Fatima visionaries. "The sight of Hell had horrified Jacinta so much that all the penances and mortifications seemed as nothing so long as she could save a few souls from going there."

Likewise, too, the great Saint John Bosco had a very lengthy vision of hell. He had had several nightmares, but on the night of April 18th, 1868, as Bosco slept, a "distinguished person" came to him, and showed him, not only the path that leads to hell, but also hell itself. The entire dream is worth reading, but I would like only to present two parts: first, his vision of hell, and, second, the curious ending.

Describing hell, as he sees children from his oratory running towards hell, and then falling in, the saint recalled that his distinguished guest led him, and "he stepped through that gate into a corridor at whose far end stood an observation platform, closed by a huge, single crystal pane reaching from the pavement to the ceiling. As soon as I crossed its threshold, I felt an indescribable terror and dared not take another step. Ahead of me I could see something like an immense cave which gradually disappeared into recesses sunk far into the bowels of the mountains. They were all ablaze, but theirs was not an earthly fire with leaping tongues of flames. The entire cave --walls, ceiling, floor, iron,

1. Cf. Calveras, *Practica intensiva*, 172-178.

stones, wood, and coal -- everything was a glowing white at temperatures of thousands of degrees. Yet the fire did not incinerate, did not consume. I simply can't find words to describe the cavern's horror. 'His firepit made both deep and wide, with fire and firewood in abundance, And the breath of the LORD, like a stream of sulfur, setting it afire' (Isaiah 30:33).

I was staring in bewilderment about me when a lad dashed out of a gate. Seemingly unaware of anything else, he emitted a most shrilling scream, like one who is about to fall into a cauldron of liquid bronze, and plummeted into the center of the cave. Instantly he too became incandescent and perfectly motionless, while the echo of his dying wail lingered for an instant more.

Terribly frightened, I stared briefly at him for a while. He seemed to be one of my Oratory boys. 'Isn't he so and so?' I asked my guide.

'Yes,' was the answer.

As I looked again, another boy came hurtling down into the cave at break-neck speed. He too was from the Oratory. As he fell, so he remained. He too emitted one single heart-rending shriek that blended with the last echo of the scream that came from the youth who had preceded him. Other boys kept hurtling in the same way in increasing numbers, all screaming the same way and then all becoming equally motionless and incandescent. I noticed that the first seemed frozen to the spot, one hand and one foot raised into the air; the second boy seemed bent almost double to the floor. Others stood or hung in various other positions, balancing themselves on one foot or hand, sitting or lying on their backs or on their sides, standing or kneeling, hands clutching their hair. Briefly, the scene resembled a large statuary group of youngsters cast into ever more painful postures. Other lads hurtled into that same furnace. Some I knew; others were strangers to me. I then recalled what is written in the Bible to the effect that as one falls into Hell, so he shall forever remain 'wherever it falls, there shall it lie' (Ecclesiastes 11:3).

More frightened than ever, I asked my guide, 'When these boys come dashing into this cave, don't they know where they are going?'

'They surely do. They have been warned a thousand times, but they still choose to rush into the fire because they do not detest sin and are loath to forsake it. Furthermore, they despise and reject God's incessant, merciful invitations to do penance. Thus provoked, Divine Justice harries them, hounds them, and goads them on so that they cannot halt until they reach this place.'

'Oh, how miserable these unfortunate boys must feel in knowing they no longer have any hope,' I exclaimed. 'If you really want to know their innermost frenzy and fury, go a little closer,' my guide remarked.

I took a few steps forward and saw that many of those poor wretches were savagely striking at each other like mad dogs. Others were clawing their own faces and hands, tearing their own flesh and spitefully throwing it about. Just then the entire ceiling of the cave became as transparent as crystal and revealed a patch of Heaven and their radiant companions safe for all eternity.

The poor wretches, fuming and panting with envy, burned with rage because they had once ridiculed the just. 'The wicked sees and is angry; gnashes his teeth and wastes away' (Psalms 112:10). 'Why do I hear no sound?' I asked my guide,

'Go closer!' he advised.

Pressing my ear to the crystal window, I heard screams and sobs, blasphemies and imprecations against the Saints. It was a tumult of voices and cries, shrill and confused.

'When they recall the happy lot of their good companions,' he replied, 'they are obliged to admit: 'We fools esteemed their life madness, and their end without honor. Behold, how they are numbered among the children of God, and their lot is among the saints. Therefore we have erred from the way of truth, and the light of justice has not shined unto us, and the sun of understanding has not risen upon us' (Wisdom 5:4-6) 'We wearied ourselves in the way of iniquity and destruction, and have walked through hard ways, but the way of the Lord we have not known. What has pride profited us? Or what advantage has the boasting of riches brought us? All those things are passed away like a shadow' (Wisdom 5: 7-9).

Here time is no more. Here is only eternity."

At the very end, as Bosco is leaving hell, his guide makes a request: "But as soon as we stepped across the last bronze portal, he turned to me and said, 'Now that you have seen what others suffer, you too must experience a touch of Hell.'

'No, no!' I cried in terror.

He insisted, but I kept refusing.

'Do not be afraid,' he told me; 'just try it. Touch this wall.'

I could not muster enough courage and tried to get away, but he held me back. 'Try it,' he insisted. Gripping my arm firmly, he pulled me to the wall. 'Only one touch,' he commanded, 'so that you may say you have both seen and touched the walls of eternal suffering and that you may understand what the last wall must be like if the first is so unendurable. Look at this wall!' I did intently. It seemed incredibly thick. 'There are a thousand walls between this and the real fire of Hell,' my guide continued. 'A thousand walls encompass it, each a thousand measures thick and equally distant from the next one. Each measure is a thousand miles. This wall therefore is millions and millions of miles from Hell's real fire. It is just a remote rim of Hell itself.'

When he said this, I instinctively pulled back, but he seized my hand, forced it open, and pressed it against the first of the thousand walls. The sensation was so utterly excruciating that I leaped back with a scream and found myself sitting up in bed. My hand was stinging and I kept rubbing it to ease the pain. When I got up this morning I noticed that it was swollen. Having my hand pressed against the wall, though only in a dream, felt so real that, later, the skin of my palm peeled off.

Bear in mind that I have tried not to frighten you very much, and so I have not described these things in all their horror as I saw them and as they impressed me. We know that Our Lord always portrayed Hell in symbols because, had He described it as it really is, we would not have understood Him. No mortal can comprehend these things. The Lord knows them and He reveals them to whomever He wills."

Lastly, I would warn, as Fr. Calveras does, that if our fear of hell waivers, if we think nothing of the torments there, our ruin is assured.

This was the case of the atheist A. J. Ayer, who suffered heart failure. He had what was presumably an experience of hell: "I was confronted by a red light," he later wrote of his experience in an article entitled "What I Saw When I Was Dead," "exceedingly bright, and also very painful even when I turned away from it."

And what was this light? "I was aware that this light was responsible for the government of the universe. . . . [and as time went on] I became more and more desperate, until the experience suddenly came to an end."

One of his doctors later claimed Ayer had confided to him, "I saw a Divine Being. I'm afraid I'm going to have to revise all my books and opinions." His experience rattled him some. That article concludes by saying: "My recent experiences have slightly weakened my conviction that my genuine death, which is due fairly soon, will be the end of me, though I continue to hope that it will be." Unfortunately, he said it did not affect his atheism: "[These experiences] have not weakened my conviction that there is no god."

Ayer died the following year. That experience, presumably of hell, did him no good. Let the same not be said of us.

We can ask ourselves: do I really live out that *holy fear of God* which helps me to flee from sin?

[71] Colloquy: Enter into conversation with Christ our Lord. Recall to memory that of those who are in hell, some came there because they did not believe in the coming of Christ; others, though they believed, because they did not keep the Commandments. Divide them all into three classes:

Those who were lost before the coming of Christ;

Those who were lost during His lifetime;

Those who were lost after His life here on earth.

Thereupon, I will give thanks to God our Lord that He has not put an end to my life and permitted me to fall into any of these three classes.

I shall also thank Him for this, that up to this very moment He has shown Himself so loving and merciful to me.

Close with an Our Father.

Death [71]

Saint Ignatius doesn't give a meditation on death, *per se*, but in point 71 he says that "If the one giving the Exercises judges that it would be profitable for the exercitant, other exercises may be added here, for example, on death and other punishments of sin, on judgment, etc. Let him not think this is forbidden, though they are not given here."

Thinking about death has a way of sobering us up, and making us realize that our time on earth is limited, and we need to make the best use of it that we can.

Let us, first, consider the meaning of death, and two separations that it entails: separation of the soul from the body, and the soul from possessions. Then we can consider its characteristics and, lastly, how to prepare for it.

Death means the separation of the Soul from the Body, which entails many sufferings. It is not only physical pain and mental anguish, but perhaps also violent temptations stirred up by our enemy, the Devil.

As soon as the Soul has departed, sometimes even much earlier, the Body becomes an object of disgust and horror; then it turns into a shocking mass of corruption that serves as food to the worms; and after a few years there is nothing left of it but a heap of dust, which in the course of ages will be scattered to the four winds.

"Imagine to yourself a person, whose soul has just departed," writes Alphonsus Ligouri. "Behold that pale corpse, which is still upon the bed, the head fallen upon the breast; the hair disheveled and bathed in the sweat of death; the eyes sunken; the cheeks hollow; the face of ashy paleness; the tongue and the lips of a leaden hue; the body cold and heavy. Those who see it grow pale and tremble. How many there are who, upon seeing a relation or friend in this condition, have changed their life, and have left the world!

But still more dreadful is it when the body begins to decay. A few hours or days will hardly have passed and it will become offensive. Behold to what that proud, that voluptuous man is reduced? In life he was the favorite, the one who was sought after in society; now he makes all those who look upon him shudder. His relations hasten to have him removed from the house, and men are hired to bear him, shut up in a coffin, to his grave. He was once famous for his great talent, for his great politeness, for his courteous behavior, and for his facetiousness; but now that he is dead, his memory will soon pass away.

"One day, as a young girl, Saint Raphaela Mary of the Sacred Heart was vainly admiring herself in the mirror, rearranging her curls and smiling at how attractive she was. Suddenly, her tutor, a priest, came up behind her and said, 'Raphaelita, how do think you will look a quarter hour after your death?'"... Years later, as she told the story, Raphaela said, 'That was my conversion.'"[1]

Death means also the separation from the goods of this world, earthly possessions, earthly amusements, earthly distinctions, popularity, standing, influence. For the man of the world this will be a frightful ordeal! None of these things can be taken along; others will enjoy what he has gathered with so much anxiety; and soon his very name will be forgotten.

We can see this beautifully reflected in the ceremony for the burial of Hapsburg emperors and princes. The Hapsburgs were one of the longest and most influential royal families in all of Europe.

When one of their family died, the coffin would be carried to the Capuchin Cloister in Vienna, where the Imperial Crypt is. However, there is a special ceremony that takes place as they bring the casket with the body. Most recently it took place in 2011, with the death of Otto von Hapsburg.

The grand chamberlain, with a silver cane, knocks three times on the door, and the prior, from within the cloister, behind the shut door, asks: "Who desires entry?"

The chamberlain replies: "Otto of Austria; once Crown Prince of Austria-Hungary; Royal Prince of Hungary and Bohemia, of Dalmatia, Croatia, Slavonia, Galicia, Lodomeria and Illyria; Grand Duke of Tuscany and Cracow; Duke of Lorraine, Salzburg, Styria, Carinthia, Carniola and the Bukowina; Grand Prince of Transylvania, Margrave of Moravia; Duke of Upper and Lower Silesia, of Modena, Parma, Piacenza, Guastalla, of Oświęcim and Zator, Teschen, Friaul, Dubrovnik and Zadar; Princely Count of Habsburg

---

1. Ann Ball, *Modern Saints, Vol. 1* (Charlotte, NC: TAN, 2011), 272-3.

and Tyrol, of Kyburg, Gorizia and Gradisca; Prince of Trent and Brixen; Margrave of Upper and Lower Lusatia and Istria; Count of Hohenems, Feldkirch, Bregenz, Sonnenburg etc.; Lord of Trieste, Kotor and Windic March, Grand Voivod of the Voivodeship of Serbia etc. etc."

And the prior simply replies: "We do not know him."

The grand chamberlain, with his silver cane, again knocks three times, and, again, the prior from within asks: "Who desires entry?"

The chamberlain replies: "Dr. Otto von Habsburg, President and Honorary President of the Paneuropean Union, Member and quondam President of the European Parliament, honorary doctor of many universities, honorary citizen of many cities in Central Europe, member of numerous venerable academies and institutes, recipient of high civil and ecclesiastical honours, awards, and medals, which were given him in recognition of his decades-long struggle for the freedom of peoples for justice and right."

And again, the prior replies, simply: "We do not know him."

So again, the grand chamberlain, with his silver cane, knocks three times, and from within the prior asks: "Who desires entry?"

The chamberlain replies, simply: "Otto, a mortal and sinful man."

To which the prior answers: "Then let him come in." The doors open, and the casket enters the cloister.

In death, everyone is equal. You leave everything behind when you die.

St. Aloysius Gonzaga, with practical wisdom, would often say, "What is this compared with eternity?" and St. Stanislaus, used to exclaim, "I was born for something better and nobler."

All things end with death. This experience of death is what rattled Saint Francis Borgia and Saint Margaret of Cortona. "This saint Francis Borgia was obliged to accompany the body of the Empress Isabella to Granada. When the coffin was opened, all those present fled, because of the dreadful sight and smell; but St. Francis, led by Divine light, remained to contemplate, in that body, the vanity of the world, and while looking upon it, said "Are you that great one to whom so many great ones bowed the knee? O my mistress, Isabella, where is your majesty and your beauty now?"

After these separations, from the body, from earthly goods, and from friends and relatives, the Soul has entered upon a new and unchangeable phase of its never-ending existence; it has stood in the presence of the All-Holy, Almighty, inevitable Judge; it has seen in one intellectual flash all the good omitted and all the evil committed; it has been called to a strict account for every word and action, for its most brief thoughts as well as for its most hidden desires, for the use of every natural gift and every super-natural favour bestowed on it during this earthly period of probation; and it has already heard the Divine, final Sentence that determines its lot for all Eternity, either in Heaven or in Hell. There will be no room for defence, no call for explanation, just as there will be no plea for mercy, no appeal for pardon. Every sin not atoned for here below shall receive its full measure of punishment, and the whole debt will have to be paid to the last penny. Such is the Particular Judgment that will be passed upon us at the very moment of our Death.

Second Point. Characteristics of Death.

Death is most certain as to fact. All men without exception are to die; either in the ordinary way through sickness, or in some unusual way through accident. Many people nowadays boast that they will not accept anything as true unless borne out by actual experience; yet, though nobody now living ever had the actual experience of death, every one holds it for certain that he is going to die.

It's true that people try to escape it, delay it, put it off, but they often end up hurting themselves; they are their own worst enemies, because rather than prepare well for death, they simply try to avoid it, and all the while it comes closer. In *Man's Search for Meaning*, Viktor Frankel recounts the following story: *A rich and mighty Persian once walked in his garden with one of his servants. The servant cried that he had just encountered Death, who had threatened him. He begged his master to give him his fastest horse so that he could make haste and flee to Teheran, which he could reach that same evening. The master consented and the servant galloped off on the horse. On returning to his house the master himself met Death, and questioned him, "Why did you terrify and threaten my servant?" "I did not threaten him; I only showed surprise in still finding him here when I planned to meet him tonight in Teheran," said Death.* All the avoidance of death . . . to what end? Just to meet it anyways.

But Death is most uncertain as to Circumstances. Death comes most of the times as a surprise; even very sick people usually fail to realize that their end is so near. Hence our Lord tells us that Death will come upon us as a thief in the night. The when, the where, and the how of our death, are completely hidden from our view. We do not know anything about the time, place, and manner of our departure from this world.

To this truth there is but one exception. There is one important circumstance which we can foresee with a fair amount of probability, almost with certainty. It is whether a person is going to die in the State of Grace or in the State of Sin. For both reason and faith tell us plainly, "*talis vita, finis ita*" "your death will be as your life has been." "As a man lives so shall he die." The story is told of my first spiritual director, back home, who was called to assist a woman who was dying. The woman harboured a great deal of resentment towards her husband, and she refused to forgive him. The priest kept insisting, "You need to forgive him," and she kept refusing, "No, he's hurt me too badly!" Finally, the priest said, "If you don't forgive him, you will go to hell!" And she replied, "Well, then I'll see him there!" And she died. And did she, at that moment, go to hell? No. She was already there. On earth, she lived in hell, a hell of her own making, of her own choices. She just moved into her permanent residence. "As a man lives so shall he die."

Consequently, if we wish to die in the friendship of God, we must never deal with a temptation to grievous sin. If we want to die with a prayer on our lips, we should pray often and fervently during our daily occupations. If we wish to die with the Sacraments, the surest way is to receive Holy Communion as far as we can every morning, with the best possible preparation and thanksgiving.

Finally, the moment of death is most decisive. We die but once. Death is the great crisis of our whole existence. On that one moment will depend everything forever after: the salvation or perdition of our Immortal Soul. Our last agony, instead of being "the beginning of the end," is rather the end of the beginning, the close of the initial period of our existence, the conclusion of our preparation for eternity. You can never make up for a bad death. Hence, to ensure a good death, it is absolutely necessary to be always ready. Are we ready to die right now? Is there any task we should prefer to have accomplished, any resolution we should wish to have taken, any sacrifice we should like to have made? Yet we may die much sooner; even before the end of this month or this week; in fact, at any moment within the next twenty-four hours.

Third Point. Preparations for Death.

The most obvious preparation we can make for a holy death is to live each moment for God, giving Him our all at every instant. Life is too short. Therefore we should be watchful not to lose one single instant. From the moment we awake, we should strive to give ourselves entirely to God, in sentiments of adoration, contrition, confidence, and love.

Confession also is an excellent Preparation for Death, provided we labor to make it every time as well as we can, not so much by searching the inmost recesses of our soul — which ought rather to be done in our daily Examinations of Conscience — but especially by conceiving real and deep confusion blended with fervent and practical contrition.

However, the best preparation for a happy death undoubtedly consists in the worthy reception of Holy Communion, since this Sacrament is a Divine Pledge of Everlasting Life. An intense desire springing from a vivid realization of our manifold shortcomings, and a boundless trust arising from a lively faith in this Mystery — these form the chief dispositions with which we should strive to welcome our Heavenly Guest. It is in particular this Sacrament that will enable us to die to ourselves and thus render our physical Death more peaceful and more meritorious. "Blessed are they who die in the Lord." These words of Holy Scripture will apply literally to us if, every time we prepare for Communion, we take care to do so as though it were to be our Viaticum.

In a number of sacristies, you see a message for priests: "Priest of God, celebrate this Mass as though it were your first Mass, your last Mass, and your only Mass." Imagine how well we would receive communion if we received it as our first communion, our last communion, and our only communion. What devotion and love we would have!

The saints lived constantly in the face of death. Often they are pictured with a skull near them, reminding them of that moment when they, too, will be just a skull. *Momento mori*, remember that you must die. If the thought of death bothers us, the problem isn't with death; it's with the way we're living. The saints saw death for what it was: the passage to eternal life.

When the doctor who was treating Saint Alberto Hurtado realized the priest had cancer and would die soon, he was concerned about how to break the news to him, knowing that Hurtado had many important apostolates. Finally, he told him in no uncertain terms that he would die soon. Hurtado looked serious, and asked to make a phone call. He called his provincial, and, with a smile that spread from ear to ear, he told him: "Father, today is the happiest day of my life: they've just told me that I am going to die."

Likewise, when Saint Therese of Lisieux realized that she was sick with tuberculosis because she woke up at night coughing up blood, she described that moment, the first sign of her approaching death that she knew would be prolonged and agonizing: "It was like a sweet and distant murmur announcing the arrival of the Bridegroom."

Or, we can consider Saint Elizabeth of the Trinity. As she lay on her deathbed, "Elizabeth did not try to hide from the doctor the overflowing delight that she felt because of her faith. The doctor was so astonished at her happiness that she tried to explain it to him by speaking in a moving way about how we are all God's children. After she finished speaking, tears flowed among many of her listeners. Exhausted by her efforts, she entered for the last time into her cherished silence. We only heard her murmur in a sort of chant: 'I am going to the light, to love, to life!; They were her last intelligible words."

In short, let us consider the words of Saint Camillus de Lellis: "When Camillus de Lellis beheld the graves of the dead, he said within himself, 'If all these dead bodies could come back again to life, they would do anything to gain eternal life. And I, who have now the opportunity what am I doing for my soul?'"

Colloquy: first, with St. Joseph, patron of a happy death in the sweet embrace of Jesus and Mary; then, with the Blessed Virgin, our Mother, whose death was the effect of her most ardent love; and lastly, with our Savior on the Cross exclaiming, "Father, into Your hands I commend My spirit." End with an Our Father.

Mercy [71]

Usual Preparation Prayer.

First Prelude: The composition of Place: Here it will be to see the story of the Prodigal Son, as his father lovingly welcomes him back into his arms (Lk 15:11-32).

Second Prelude: The petition: I should ask for what I desire, and that is grace to correct and repair whatever was worldly, inordinate, or sinful in my past life; and to regulate my remaining years in such a manner as will ensure a happy death, full of confidence in God's mercy.

Saint Ignatius doesn't give a meditation on mercy, *per se*, but it's a good follow-up to the considerations of sins, hell, and death.

A good priest friend of mine once insisted that "Mercy means womb, and what do you do in the womb? You grow." That phrase might strike us as rather odd, because most of the time we hear about mercy either in its Latin or Greek etymology, or in another, different, Hebrew word (*hesed*). However, in the Old Testament one of the words used for mercy has this meaning, and, in fact, Pope Saint John Paul the Second points this out in a massive footnote in *Dives in Misericordia*. In footnote 52, the saint notes that "in describing mercy, the books of the Old Testament use two expressions in particular, each having a different semantic nuance. . . . The second word which in the terminology of the Old Testament serves to define mercy is *rahamim*. This has a different nuance from that of *hesed*. While *hesed* highlights the marks of fidelity to self and of 'responsibility for one's own love' (which are in a certain sense masculine characteristics), *rahamim*, in its very root, denotes the love of a mother (from *rehem*, meaning mother's womb—[hence Father's comment]). From the deep and original bond—indeed the unity—that links a mother to her child there springs a particular relationship to the child, a particular love. Of this love one can say that it is completely gratuitous, not merited, and that in this aspect it constitutes an interior necessity: an exigency of the heart [we'll come back to this]. It is, as it were, a 'feminine' variation of the masculine fidelity to self, expressed by *hesed*. Against this psychological background, *rahamim* generates a whole range of feelings, including goodness and tenderness, patience and understanding, that is, [as if to summarize] readiness to forgive.

The Old Testament attributes to the Lord precisely these characteristics when it uses the term *rahamim* in speaking of Him. We read in Isaiah: 'Can a mother forget her infant, be without tenderness for the child of her womb? Even should she forget, I will never forget you. [See, upon the palms of my hands I have written your name]' (Is 49:15). This love, faithful and invincible thanks to the mysterious power of motherhood, is expressed in the Old Testament texts in various ways: as salvation from dangers, especially from enemies; also as forgiveness of sins—of individuals and also of the whole of Israel; and finally in readiness to fulfill the (eschatological) promise and hope, in spite of human infidelity, as we read in Hosea: 'I will heal their apostasy, I will love them freely; for my anger is turned away from them' (Ho 14:5)."[1] Thus far JPII.

We can examine more in depth three characteristics that the Pope has pointed out. First, God's mercy is a particular love, meaning it's something for me personally: "God the Father loves *me*, knowing who I am, how I am, where I'm coming from, what I can do, and what limitations I have. He knows me by name. He has loved me with those characteristics; He hasn't loved me 'in bulk,' '*en masse*,' or generically."[2] A mother doesn't love just any child; she loves *her* child. If you don't believe it, try swapping a child on a mom and trying to convince her that it's all just the same. "Look, one kid for another, no big deal. This one's quieter and better behaved. He doesn't eat as much!" Any mother will want and far, far prefer her own child, no matter how loud and obnoxious her child is, no matter how much he eats, and no matter how quiet and well-behaved the other one is.

Secondly, God's mercy is gratuitous: in other words, quoting the Pope, it's "not merited, and that in this aspect it constitutes an interior necessity: an exigency of the heart." A mother loves her child, and if we tried to come up with a reason why, probably the best we could say is that she just *has* to: it just follows from the nature of being a mother. If we think about this from just a purely logical or empirical standpoint, there's really no reason for this: the child doesn't *do anything* to deserve the mother's love. Especially in the beginning, as a newborn, the child does things that, objectively, are annoying, like crying in the middle of the night. It's just who the child is, and the place that he or she occupies in the heart of his or her mother.

---

1. *Dives in Misericordia*, n. 52.
2. Miguel A. Fuentes, *Meditations on God the Father* (Chillum, MD: IVEPress, 2017), 34.

This unconditional love of God is the foundation of our joy and, indeed of our entire lives. The brilliant German theologian, Pope-Emeritus Benedict XVI, said the following in an audience (remember, he's German; we're not known for our overwhelmingly loving, sentimental, and affectionate natures. What he says is just the cold, hard, truth): he said, "[Where does joy come from? There are many factors.] But in my view, the crucial one is this certainty, based on faith: I am wanted; I have a task in history; I am accepted, I am loved. . . . Those who are unloved cannot even love themselves. This sense of being accepted comes in the first instance from other human beings. But all human acceptance is fragile. Ultimately we need a sense of being accepted unconditionally. Only if God accepts me, and I become convinced of this, do I know definitively: it is good that I exist. It is good to be a human being. If ever man's sense of being accepted and loved by God is lost, then there is no longer any answer to the question whether to be a human being is good at all. Doubt concerning human existence becomes more and more insurmountable. Where doubt over God becomes prevalent, then doubt over humanity follows inevitably. We see today how widely this doubt is spreading. We see it in the joylessness, in the inner sadness, that can be read on so many human faces today. Only faith gives me the conviction: it is good that I exist. It is good to be a human being, even in hard times. Faith makes one happy from deep within."[3] So much hinges on this: God loves and accepts us unconditionally, not just when we're good people doing good things, but at all times and all moments, even at the worst parts of our lives.

We know this from Scripture and from first-hand experience: God's merciful love is "a prior love: *He loved us [first]* (1 Jn 4:10). I wasn't anything but rather nothing, and He loved me before I existed. He gave His Son to save me, even before I was called into existence. [Think about this for a moment; God paid a debt for me before I had even racked it up. To think, too, that He called us into existence *fully knowing* how sinful we would be *before* we were that sinful. He didn't have to, but He did, fully knowing the ugly thing that I would become through my sins. That says something about our dignity as children of God, and what great hopes He has for us]. He gave me His life in baptism, before my mind had been opened to knowledge. He has always taken the initiative in my life."[4]

This shows itself in a very particular way in those of us who have been chosen as members of the Church. We can count on one hand the number

---

3. Address of His Holiness Pope Benedict XVI on the occasion of Christmas greetings to the Roman Curia, Clementine Hall, Thursday, 22 December 2011.

4. Ibid., 34.

of people in this room who are worthy of the call that they've received. . . . It would look like this: none. Zero. None of us can say that we earned this vocation or that we deserved it. None of us. And yet, here we are, with the graces that we need to get through life, and advance on the way to holiness.

Thirdly, this sort of merciful love is shown in a particular way through the forgiveness of sins: it emphasizes God's readiness to forgive. The Pope mentions this characteristic twice, and almost places it as a sort of summary of what *rahamim* means. Sometimes, though, this is perhaps the most difficult thing for us to grasp. I mean, we talk about God's love and mercy and forgiveness, but oftentimes there's this lingering sort of doubt that maybe God will spring something on me at the end of time, a sort of bad surprise, like "Oh, you forgot about this one thing you did wrong once. Sorry: off to the fiery abyss."

"The one who thinks that God holds grudges or keeps a book with sins and good deeds, [a ledger with good deeds and bad ones hoping they balance out], doesn't understand God's fatherhood, God's mercy, or God's love." To doubt God's mercy is the "greatest falsification that can be made of God," because it says that there is a sin that's greater than He is, that there's something He can't forgive. God *wants* to save us; He *wants* us to get to Heaven. Even if I didn't want to go to Heaven, He still *wants* me to get there. So . . . how much more will He help me since I really *do* want to get to Heaven?

This affects the way we live our lives: we could say that this is the point of transition between servile fear and filial fear. Do I obey the commandments so I don't get punished, or do I love God, and so obey the commandments because I love Him? It makes the difference between living in what I like to call survival mode, where I'm just getting by day by day, and living it fully, ready for anything and everything, because "I know him in whom I have believed and am confident that he is able to guard what has been entrusted to me until that day" (2 Tm 1:12) when I see Him again, face to face. We can think of some words of Jesus to Saint Faustina: "The graces of My mercy are drawn by means of one vessel only, and that is — trust. The more a soul trusts, the more it will receive" (1578). "I never reject a contrite heart" (1485) – note the categorical nature: "never." No exceptions, no little lines at the end of the contract. Never. "Sooner would Heaven and earth turn into nothingness than would My mercy not embrace a trusting soul" (1777). To be in the womb of God's mercy, as it were, is to be entirely dependent on God, but also entirely protected.

This, of course, leads us to consider some Scriptural passages that can help us shed some light on this. There are many parables and sayings of Jesus that reveal God the Father's mercy, but often we can just let them pass unnoticed.

For instance, we can consider the parable in Matthew's Gospel of the unforgiving servant (Mt 18:23-35): "That is why the kingdom of Heaven may be likened to a king who decided to settle accounts with his servants. When he began the accounting, a debtor was brought before him who owed him a huge amount. Since he had no way of paying it back, his master ordered him to be sold, along with his wife, his children, and all his property, in payment of the debt. At that, the servant fell down, did him homage, and said, 'Be patient with me, and I will pay you back in full.' Moved with compassion the master of that servant let him go and forgave him the loan.'"

The first thing to consider here is the unforgiving servant who owes his master "a huge amount." That translation doesn't do justice to the original, which reads μυρίων ταλάντων, or literally, 10,000 talents; records tell us that all of the annual taxes paid to the Romans by all the citizens of the regions of Judea, Idumea, Samaria, Galilee, and Perea, all together, came to 800 talents per year, and, more pertinent to the steward, a talent would've been the wages of 16 years of work. In order to pay the debt, then, he would have needed to work 160 thousand years, provided he doesn't spend anything on food and clothing for himself or his wife and kids.

There's a lot of things we could ask: how on earth did he rack up such a debt? Any reason we can find doesn't look good for the steward: maybe he was an addict to something, or built an amazing house . . . but, ultimately, there's really no reason except his stupidity and probably his sinfulness.

The steward throws the best plea he has at the master: "Be patient with me, and I will pay you back in full." Yeah . . . patient, like . . . two hundred thousand years. Yet, what is the master's response? "Moved with compassion the master of that servant let him go and forgave him the loan." The word for "moved with compassion" is σπλαγχνίζομαι splagchnizomai, which derives from the Greek *splanxna*, meaning, the deep interior organs; it's related to this idea of mercy as a womb. Notice that the master simply forgives the debt; he doesn't take the steward up on his offer, or even negotiate. Instead he goes far beyond what the steward had dared to ask or even hope for. This calls to mind some quotes of Saint Therese of Lisieux: "O God, you have surpassed all my expectations." Or, "We can never have too much confidence in the Good God, He is so mighty, so merciful. As we hope in Him so shall we receive."

We also have the parable of God's mercy in Luke 15, which contains the images of the lost sheep, the lost coin, and the prodigal son. Cardinal Van Thuan, in the Spiritual Exercises he preached to Pope Saint John Paul the Second, mentioned this incident when he spoke of Christ's "five defects," which aren't really defects, *per se*, but comments on Jesus' way of doing things. We'll consider three. Van Thuan wrote: "[One defect is that] Jesus didn't know math.

If Jesus would have had to take a mathematics exam, he might have failed. He indicates this in the parable of the lost sheep. . . . For Jesus, one is equal to ninety-nine – and perhaps more! Who could ever accept this? But his mercy reaches from generation to generation.'" Some church fathers have also noticed that the shepherd "sets the sheep on his shoulders," a very affectionate gesture. In the same way, Christ will carry the cross on His shoulders out of love for all of His wayward sheep.

Likewise, "Jesus doesn't know logic [citing the story of the woman who has a celebration over finding her missing coin]. This is truly illogical—to disturb your friends over one silver piece and then to plan a feast to celebrate the find! Even more, by inviting her friends, she is bound to spend more than the one silver piece. . . . Here we can truly say, with the words of the French philosopher, Blaise Pascal, 'The heart has its reasons that the reason doesn't know.'"

Finally, Jesus has a terrible memory. Citing as evidence Jesus' promise to the thief crucified with Him that he will be in paradise, he writes: "If I had been Jesus, I would have told Him, 'I certainly will not forget you, but your crimes have to be expiated with at least twenty years in purgatory.' Instead Jesus tells him, 'Today you will be with me in paradise.' He forgets all the man's sins. . . . Jesus does not have a memory like mine. He not only pardons, and pardons every person; he even forgets that he has pardoned."[5] I would add that this "Divine forgetfulness" is also verified in stories that are told of lives of Saint Teresa of Jesus and Saint Bernard of Clairvaux, among many others. For instance, the story is told that once Teresa was upset about something she had done. She confessed it, but, still upset, she was berating herself for it. Christ appeared to her, and she apologized for her failing. Christ looked at her and said, "My Child, I don't know what you're talking about." She replied, "Well, you know, the thing I did." "I don't know what you're talking." It went back and forth, again and again, with Teresa apologizing, and Jesus denying. Finally Christ said, "Oh, that! You mean that thing . . . My Child, that's been forgiven. It's so far from my mind that it's forgotten." Likewise, the story is told that once Saint Bernard had an apparition of Jesus, and Christ asked him, "Bernard, I want you to give me a gift." Bernard replied, "Ask, but I've given you everything." Christ replied, "No, you haven't. There's still one thing you hold on to. Your sins. Give them to me Bernard; you don't need to hold on to them."

Such is the greatness of the mercy of our God.

5. Francis Xavier Nguyen Van Thuan, *Testimony of Hope* (Boston: Pauline, 2000), 14-16.

Colloquy: We can end this meditation with a three-fold colloquy: first, by speaking with our Lord Jesus Christ, who suffered and died, not to condemn us, but to save us. Second, we can talk with the Blessed Virgin Mary, the Mother of Mercy, who has interceded for us time and time again. Lastly, we can talk with God the Father, who loves us so much that He sent His Son to pay the price for our redemption. We can ask ourselves:

What have we done for Christ? What are we doing for Christ? What will we do for Christ?

FIRST WEEK

Conferences

The Particular Examination of Conscience

For this conference, we will consider the particular examination, the general examination, and the material regarding which this should be done. The points in the book of the Exercises are [24-31], [43], and [32-44], respectively. We will also follow the book by Fr. Fuentes entitled, *The Particular Examination of Conscience and the Dominant Defect*. This was required reading this year for the novices, but the book is of great help for everyone: lay people, religious, priests, and spiritual directors.

"The classics of Christian spirituality, beginning from the desert monks in the first centuries of our era, but especially starting from Ignatius of Loyola in the 16th century, have considered daily work on one well-established point in our spiritual or emotional life to be the most outstanding way to educate the will, that is, to acquire virtues, to uproot vices, and to correct defects.

I think that this is the *most useful* way a person can combat not only common defects, but also deeply rooted vices and even problems of addiction (provided that, in this case, it is done *in conjunction* with the necessary or appropriate therapies).

It seems to me that this method, which is at once simple but demanding, is most fitting for the one who wants to progress in the spiritual life. Moreover, it is absolutely indispensable for anyone who wants to resolve emotional conflicts. Each spiritual director—just like each therapist—is free to choose his own methods, and perhaps many of them do not like this one ("to each his own," as the saying goes). Respecting the freedom of each one to choose for himself, I propose this instrument which has already given abundant spiritual and psychological results throughout the centuries. In fact, as Pope Pius XII wrote to priests: "Let him also not omit his daily examination of conscience which is undoubtedly the most efficacious means we have for taking account of the conduct of our spiritual life during the day, for removing the obstacles which hinder or retard one's progress in virtue, and finally, for determining the most suitable means to assure to our sacred ministry greater fruitfulness and to implore from the Heavenly Father indulgence upon so many of our deeds wretchedly done" (Pius XII, *Menti Nostrae*, 52).

Saint Ignatius himself, its great organizer and promoter, carefully practiced it. As Fr. Laínez reported to Fr. Polanco: Ignatius took "so much care of his conscience that each day he compared week with week, month with month, day with day, seeking daily to advance." Fr. Narciso Irala cites "Dr. Schleich, a Protestant, professor of the Faculty of Medicine at Berlin, [who] asserts even more. 'I say with all assurance and conviction that with these norms and exercises in our hands we could even today transform our asylums, prisons, and mental institutions, and prevent the commitment of two thirds of the people who are today within their walls.'"

This method is at once the measure of one's will and productive of the will: "this is truly a control and stimulus to the will." By this he means that it focuses a person's attention and energies on one precise point, which increases the will's capacity to per- form acts that will culminate in the achievement of the desired goals.

It is a shame that so few people resort to this method, which is truly a walking stick for the journey in the formation of the will, for the effective uprooting of defects, and for growth in virtue. It's a still greater shame that this is the sad reality that we observe in so many lay Catholics, men and women in religious life, and priests who, all the while knowing and being fully aware of its importance and necessity, nonetheless disregard it, perform it with amazing indifference, and even abandon it entirely – then they are surprised when they continue dragging their vices and defects with them or, even more simply, that their spiritual life is at a standstill! Royo Marín writes: "There is no doubt that the faithful practice of examination of conscience will have profound effects on one's spiritual life. But in this, as in so many things, its efficacy depends to a great extent on perseverance. To omit the examination frequently or to make it in a purely mechanical fashion is to render it absolutely sterile. The soul that earnestly desires to become holy must be convinced that many of the other means of sanctification are frustrated if one does not make the daily examination of conscience" (Royo Marín, Antonio, *The Theology of Christian Perfection* (Eugene, Oregon: Wipf & Stock, 1962), 570).

This is to be attributed to several factors: in part it is a result of the general abandonment of the spiritual life, both on the part of the faithful as well as the pastors. Likewise, it is owed in part to the prejudice against any serious spiritual project, and this examination is undoubtedly an essential element of a serious spiritual project. It's also in part a consequence of ignorance regarding the examination's nature and end. Indeed, as Casanovas points out, the examination "becomes a complicated and fastidious device, like a sort of spiritual penance," when the reason for it is unknown.

What is the particular examination? What does it consist of? "The examination is at once both a "state" and an "operation of the spirit." It is a *state of the spirit* in the sense that it is "a general disposition of man that makes him always and intensely interested in knowing, discerning, and perfecting the reactions produced in his soul when they arise." Here we have the first benefit for a person with deeply rooted defects or emotional disorders: the person's *attitude* becomes an *interest in changing, improving, and consciously living their life and its interior movements* (which doesn't happen when a person is drowning in the well of unhinged emotions). The examination is also an *operation* that "requires set times and precise rules for carrying it out. The operation without the spirit ends up becoming an annoying and sterile routine; the spirit without the operation has no practical efficacy."

Casanovas continues by pointing out that "there are two classes of people who err in the understanding of Saint Ignatius's examination: those who only seek to multiply the practical details, demanding their fulfillment in an almost superstitious way, and those who scorn it, taking it for a system of accountability, improper for spiritual affairs and one that weakens hearts. Both positions are equally superficial and unjust."

In short: the examination "seeks to keep the spirit awake and active at all hours of the day, so that man might achieve the end he has proposed for himself, in the way that is most serious and effective. This is what is primary and principal, since it is, we could say, the spiritual life of the soul. Whatever comes after this is secondary, no matter how important it might be, and it should be seen and treated as secondary by whoever wants to give things their proper value, without sinning either by excess or defect."

How does one make a particular examination? "The best *way* to practice this examination is the way that Saint Ignatius of Loyola explains it in his *Spiritual Exercises*. The saint distributes the work into three fundamental moments [these are points 24, 25, and 26]:

1st: In the morning, after getting up, among the very first things that must be done, the goal of the work must be precisely determined, meaning, the *resolution or personal spiritual project* that is at hand, that is, that which must be corrected, uprooted, or acquired, be it this or that defect, this or that virtue, this or that habit or custom. It is an awareness of the work at hand. Moreover, every Christian knows that the success of the work depends on God's help, and must therefore also ask for that help in this first moment so that he can perform his work well. For those for whom this step is very difficult, it can be very beneficial for them to write a small prayer that makes mention of what they want to achieve and why. For example, for a person who wants to work on *humility*, the prayer could be something like this:

"My Lord Jesus Christ, I ask for Your light and grace in order that this day I might direct my efforts to obtain and grow in the virtue of humility. Today I want to be humble especially by practicing humility in words, both in those that I say of myself, as well in those that I use to speak of my neighbor. I want to live in humility in imitation of Your Most Gentle and Humble Heart. I ask for this grace through the intercession of your holy and humble Mother."

Note that in this possible prayer, I have not only pointed out the virtue that is to be sought, but also the concrete act in which we want to incarnate or realize it today. Further on we will see the importance and the way to determine the possible concrete acts that we practice *one by one*.

2nd: At the middle of the day (before or after lunch, more or less, or whatever is easier in each case) two things should be done:

a)   Recall how many times I have failed in the particular resolution (or if positive acts that were proposed were carried out). For this, it might be convenient to *review* what was done during the morning, hour by hour, or place by place, and to *record it* in a little book or notebook. Some complain about the "materiality" of this work, and prefer not to lower themselves to such a detail, limiting themselves to keeping their work in their memory. However, they forget that the end of this task is to overcome *laxity* and *laziness*. For this reason, I advise that the examination be made as it is indicated here, at least by those who suffer from emotional illnesses or have very deeply rooted defects. On the other hand, it is appropriate not only to *observe and write down* how many times one has fallen, but also the *reasons* why these falls occurred, in order to correct them and to build up prudence for the future.

b)   In addition to this step, one should renew the resolution for the rest of the day. Saint Ignatius proposes the following method of writing down the falls (which each person can adjust as best suits them). You can find this, and the little drawing, at [31], where 'G' stands for *giorno*, or day.

There are two lines for each day: on the first line, the falls (or, on the contrary, the fulfillment of acts that were proposed) of the morning should be noted, whereas those of the afternoon on the second.

3rd: Lastly, as the day reaches its end, one should make the examination again, considering the falls that have occurred since mid-day until that moment. Record this on the corresponding line.

Saint Ignatius himself teaches that it is appropriate, when one realizes that he or she has failed in the resolution, to make some external sign, the meaning of which only the one with the resolution knows (for example, to gently beat the chest), in such a way as to manifest one's sorrow at having fallen. The same could be said when one performs an action that had been proposed. Casanovas indicates that this *being aware* of the act itself by means of which one falls into their defect (that we had proposed to avoid) or practices a virtue (that we had proposed to practice) has great importance: "after said foresight [that is, of foreseeing the acts that we will do or avoid], there is nothing more important than being aware of one's own actions; likewise, there is nothing more fatal than being unaware of one's falls or falling into routine in one's actions. . . . This being attentive to the falls must be *entirely conscious*, and that careful awareness must be manifested even with an external action, leading one to, for example, place one's hand on their chest. This external gesture indicates repentance, if one has fallen into their defect, and it is, furthermore, a renewal of the resolution not to fall. It is simply not possible for someone to get used to falling if they are aware of every time that they do, they repent after each slip-up, and they take strength from each fall in order to renew their spirit. If this renewal is made as is appropriate, perhaps the very slip itself will serve as a stimulus and incentive to take a step forward, as tends to happen in physical slips." This is not far from the so-called *healthy rituals* of those who fight against serious and deeply rooted problems.

I am aware that some spiritual directors (often clumsy ones) consider this type of work as a *mechanization* of the spiritual life; nevertheless, even good psychologists consider it at least an effective method. It is beyond doubt that this examination, when poorly carried out, can convert spiritual or psychological work into a useless automation; this is why we warned about the need to create a *spirit*, since the letter without the spirit kills (cf. 2 Co 3:6).

Furthermore, in the nightly examination, the person must examine if his or her conduct has improved when compared to that of the morning. Each day (or at least once a week) a comparison should be made between that day and other days, seeing if the behavior has improved or worsened. Then the person should look for the reasons why: if it has improved, the person should continue working in that direction; if it has worsened, the person will know how to correct those things that have made him or her slide back in the work. Lastly, every so often compare one week with the previous ones, in order to see if the goals are nearer to or further from being accomplished.

– This is a key part of the examine. If people do not write things down, then they will never know if they are improving or not. Often people will tell their spiritual director, "I feel like I am improving," but feelings are not a good way to order your spiritual life. Likewise, sometimes an analysis of when people fall helps us to see the *why* behind it. Do you fall every Wednesday into anger? Perhaps that is because it's sports day, and you are particularly aggressive then.

With a solid work by means of this method, in a few months even defects that have been deeply rooted for a long time can be corrected. However, this requires perseverance and tenacity, as well as sufficient humility in order to start anew when the person becomes aware that they have fallen again.

The effects of this examination are so important for behavior that I firmly believe that this type of work must be incorporated even into the treatment of those people with addictions and emotional disorders."

So, what should we examine ourselves on? "In regards to the *matter* of the examination, it should always be something very precise and specific, as well as sufficiently known by the one who is doing the examination.

First and foremost, it must be some *specific good*. The main mistakes in work regarding the will (and also in other areas) comes from proposing very general plans (for example, "to want to be humble," or "to want to be generous"). Even if humility and generosity are concrete virtues, they are still just general resolutions. Dealing with things in a generic way can never lead to advancement in the spiritual life. For this reason, the particular resolution must always be something concrete, and the more particular, the better. If, for example, a person desires to grow in humility, the resolutions must be focused: which concrete acts of humility (in looks, words, or deeds?), or with respect to whom (superiors, subordinates, spouse, friends, parents), or in which moments of the day, etc. After a time of work, once a certain habit with respect to this act has been formed, the person can move on to new acts of humility. What is true in other fields is true here as well: the fundamentals (meaning, the little things) must be mastered in order to later master the big things.

Secondly, how does one *choose* the matter on which they should work? I reproduce a text from the above-cited Casanovas:

Generally ascetical authors emphasize the need to choose with certainty the particular defect or virtue regarding which the particular examination should be carried out. In order to be certain about this point, they established the theory of the dominant passion, affirmed that first the principal vice should be attacked,[1] then secondary ones, and then, lastly, the virtues should be sought.

All of this is very well established when seen as a theory based on the value of the vices and virtues; *however, if attention is paid to the end* towards which the

---

1. Although we will deal with this topic in the second part of this work, let's look ahead, in order to understand well what we have been saying: by dominant passion or defect, Casanovas means the propensity or proclivity to a specific sinful act produced by the frequent repetition of the act itself. All of us are born with a natural disposition to certain acts that are good and others that are bad, a disposition which is part of our temperament. If the will does not oppose these con-natural predispositions to evil from the very beginning, these quickly acquire a great vigor and become true defects. The "dominant defect" in a person is that proclivity whose impulse is most frequent and strongest, even though it might not always be externally observed. It is usually the source of the other defects and sins that each person falls into most often.

spirit of Saint Ignatius's particular examination is ordered, *perhaps it is fitting to follow a different criteria*. Given that the end of the particular examination is to keep the desire for holiness alive and active, what pertains to the person's class and circumstances that surround them is to be given preference since it is more effective in stirring up that desire, even though this might break the molds of the objective order with which we give value to the vices and virtues. The variety of circumstances in which souls find themselves, even with respect to the same degree of perfection and imperfection, is so great that it is very difficult to decree *a priori* which is the most beneficial method. Let us never lose sight of the fact that holiness is a life and not a theory, no matter how well-thought out that theory might be, and that the particular examination is not an end to which a soul's life must be conformed, but rather a means to maintain and perfect that life.

Thus, what a person should examine themselves about must be determined according to the needs of that concrete person "here and now." For this reason, for example, a person dominated by a vice like lust or alcohol, despite the fact that their dominant passion or vice is lust or alcohol, should perhaps examine themselves, at least at some point in their lives, regarding their confidence in and abandonment to God (since without these attitudes recovery is impossible), or regarding humility (when there is some inferiority complex at the root), or regarding other, different acts when the examination is being used primarily to strengthen or intensify the will."

How do I work on this, in particular? "Again, I maintain that a virtue cannot be acquired, nor a vice fought, if the territory upon which one will work is not well known. A good military officer studies his own army, his enemy, and the land upon which the battle will take place in great detail: if he doesn't, his defeat is all but assured. In our case, something similar happens; if a person wants to acquire a virtue, he or she must become, in a certain sense, an "expert" in it. When someone tells me, for example, "I think that I need to work on meekness, because my biggest problem is anger," I usually reply, "That seems like a good idea; now give me fifteen different acts that you could put into practice in order to achieve this goal." The majority of people are simply left confused; at most, one or two actions come to mind. This means that they know little or nothing about that virtue. If that's the case, however, then serious work isn't possible, because the people won't realize when opportunities to practice that virtue arise if they don't know, and know well, what that virtue is and the different situations in which it acts. The same can be said of vices. Anyone who wants to work hard must (according to their possibilities and abilities) study the topic.

Thus, for a serious work, I recommend, before anything else, reading what the classics of spirituality of moral theology have to say about the virtue that is sought or the vice that needs to be uprooted (for example, some of the works of Antonio Royo Marín, Tanquerey, Garrigou-Lagrange, Merkelbach, Prümmer, etc.).

Once this is done, the person will be able to make a list, as exhaustive as possible, of all the acts that they see as connected both *directly* and *indirectly* with the virtue or vice that is their subject matter, and this as it is found in the daily life *of the person who is doing the work.* A list of fifteen to twenty acts is the ideal.

As can be seen, in order to come up with a list for the other virtues or vices, it's enough to make a list of the main elements of that virtue: its nature, cause, ways to acquire it, main acts, secondary acts, effects, occasions to practice it, the vices that are opposed to it, and so on. Later the various concrete acts can be determined in order to feed that particular aspect or to uproot it. The afore-mentioned examples are eloquent enough in themselves.

With these ideas in mind, the person who is to work on this attitude must examine themselves *on only one of those points* during whatever amount of time is needed until that element is uprooted. After that, he or she can move on to another. A person must not work on several points at a time, because this would be contrary to the goal of the particular examination (since the objec-tive is to concentrate the will's energy and the intellect's attention on only one focus). It's understood as well that when the person begins to examine a new act to perform, *the exercise of those acts that have already been acquired must be kept alive.* The person should gain new ground with each examination. In this way, in a short time, a person can completely change, from apathetic to ener-getic, and from vicious to virtuous."

What are the effects of these examinations of conscience? "The work car-ried out in this way not only conquers or overcomes a defect or vice, or makes that virtue upon which attention had been centered grow, but rather, at the same time, it has another important effect: it strengthens the will itself, which, with each firm and energetic act, becomes more invigorated and consolidated.

Moreover, above and beyond this benefit in the will, it also produces anoth-er, more important effect which, according to some authors, is its main fruit: it keeps the interest in one's personal sanctification and perfection awake and alive.

Above all, we must remember a great truth: with great frequency (to avoid saying, "almost always"), without a serious particular examination, all good desires and efforts, are condemned, sooner or later, to utter failure, and the Christian ends up incarcerated in lukewarmness and mediocrity. For this rea-son, not giving the examination the importance that it deserves could be taken as a sign of foolishness."

Methods of Prayer

For this conference, we will consider the different methods of prayer that Ignatius gives throughout the Exercises and that you will be using throughout the month. We will consider five different sorts: meditation, contemplation, repetition, summary, and application of the senses:[1]

Meditation: "With the word meditation, we should understand a form of prayer using the three potencies of the soul. Whenever we act like men, we naturally use our three potencies of our soul, that is, memory, understanding, and will, and when we do this in prayer, applying the aforementioned faculties in an orderly and reflective way on a particular point or fitting matter, with a spiritual end, we can call what we are doing *meditation.*"

Hence, if you pay attention, you will notice that Ignatius has some things labeled as "meditations" while others are "contemplations." These meditations make use of memory (to recall the scene to mind), the understanding (to think the matter over more profoundly), and the will (to excite the emotions).

Contemplation: "The majority of the Exercises that Ignatius proposes are contemplations, and among these we should count all of the exercises regarding the life, passion, and resurrection of Christ. . . .

[For those of you who are familiar with John of the Cross, Teresa of Jesus, and other great contemplatives] we should understand that here Ignatius is referring to what they would call *acquired contemplation* [and not *infused contemplation*]. The material for contemplation is/are visible things, and the form we can understand as the particular way we use our faculties on that matter.

In contemplations, Ignatius will say things like, 'see the people,' 'hear the people,' and 'see what they are doing.' On one hand, this means that we shouldn't be looking at, hearing, and seeing these people as if we were separated by great distances either of time or of space. For instance, consider the way Ignatius presents the contemplation on the Nativity: 'This will consist in seeing the persons, namely, our Lady, St. Joseph, the maid, and the Child Jesus after His birth. I will make myself a poor little unworthy slave, and as though

1. Commentary taken from Ignacio Casanovas, *Ejercicios de San Ignacio*, 178-202.

present, look upon them, contemplate them, and serve them in their needs with all possible homage and reverence.'"

In other words, the point is that we are interacting with the scene. I am seeing it, hearing it, and participating in it. I am *involved in it*.

"Ignatius's mind couldn't be clearer: the saint doesn't want our contemplation to be purely speculative, esthetic, sentimental, or a gloss, rather practical and of great spiritual strength."

Repetition and Summary: "Both the repetition and the summary are based on a single fundamental concept, which is that of taking another hour of prayer on the same matter that was already contemplated or meditated upon.

A repetition, as Ignatius says in [62], consists in going over the points that were previously considered, and 'we should pay attention to and dwell upon those points in which we have experienced greater consolation or desolation or greater spiritual appreciation.'

The point of the repetition is directed to reinforcing the feel of the meditation or contemplation, either by allowing oneself to be fully satisfied by drinking at the fountains that were already opened, or by knocking again on the rock that, during the first time through, obstinately resisted our efforts.

In a summary, as Ignatius notes in [64], 'the intellect, without any digression, diligently thinks over and recalls the matter contemplated in the previous exercises.'

The point of the summary, then, is to leave ideas firmly established in the understanding, drilling them in, as it were. The summary is more suited to meditations, and, in fact, we will notice that Ignatius only has us do summaries during the first week; repetitions are more fitting for contemplations, and that's what we have in the second, third, and fourth weeks."

Application of Senses: Lastly, we have the application of the senses. Ignatius tells us, in [121], that "it will be profitable with the aid of the imagination to apply the five senses" to the matter at hand.

Casanovas says that "the application of the senses doesn't involve any discourse" (meditation tends to be more intellectual), but rather "contents itself to see, hear, touch, etc., the sensible things, in which it delights with great spiritual joy and fruit."

The early Jesuits debated about what Ignatius meant by this sort of application of senses. However, the 1599 *Directory* of the Exercises (recall that Ignatius died in 1556) says that this application has two fruits: first, "when the soul cannot contemplate more profound things, by contenting itself with the sensible, it prepares itself, little by little, to be raised to higher things," or, secondly, and in the contrary case, "when the soul is filled with devotion because of the knowledge it has of the highest mysteries, lowering itself to these sensible things, it will find in everything abundant material, consolation, and fruit, and because of this great love, the soul comes to appreciate in even the smallest things (like a simple movement of the head, for example) matter for love and consolation."

In points 121 – 125, Ignatius explains how this is done:

[121] This [application of senses] will consist in applying the five senses to the matter of the contemplations:

After the preparatory prayer and three preludes, it will be profitable with the aid of the imagination to apply the five senses to the subject matter of the First and Second Contemplation in the following manner:

[122] This consists in seeing in imagination the persons, and in contemplating and meditating in detail the circumstances in which they are, and then in drawing some fruit from what has been seen.

[123] This is to hear what they are saying, or what they might say, and then by reflecting on oneself to draw some profit from what has been heard.

[124] This is to smell the infinite fragrance, and taste the infinite sweetness of the divinity. Likewise to apply these senses to the soul and its virtues, and to all according to the person we are contemplating, and to draw fruit from this.

[125] This is to apply the sense of touch, for example, by embracing and kissing the place where the persons stand or are seated, always taking care to draw some fruit from this.

So . . . taste gets shorted, but, no matter. Four out of five senses isn't bad.

Addition Directions 1 – 9
[73-81]

We've already seen most of these points, because they are included on the sheets regarding *How to Make the Meditations*. However, I reminded you of them because they are useful in order to provide remote preparation for the Exercises, as well as to give us something to make our particular examination on.

[73] The purpose of these directions is to help one to go through the exercises better and find more readily what he desires
- This is the point of the additional directions. These first nine additions can be divided in four groups: preparation for prayer [73-75]; position during prayer [76]; exam [77]; and the general environment or setting [78-81]. The point is to have the best possible setting for making the Exercises.

After retiring, just before falling asleep, for the space of a *Hail Mary*, I will think of the hour when I have to rise, and why I am rising, and briefly sum up the exercise I have to go through.

[74] When I wake up, I will not permit my thoughts to roam at random, but will turn my mind at once to the subject I am about to contemplate in the first exercise at midnight. I will seek to rouse myself to shame for my many sins by using examples, let us say, of a knight brought before his king and the whole court, filled with shame and confusion for having grievously offended his lord from whom he had formerly received many gifts and favors. Similarly, in the Second Exercise, I will consider myself a great sinner, loaded with chains, that is, I will look upon myself as bound with fetters, going to appear before the supreme and eternal Judge, and I will recall the way prisoners, bound and deserving of death, appear before an earthly judge. As I dress, I will think over these thoughts or others in keeping with the subject matter of the meditation.

[75] I will stand for the space of an *Our Father*, a step or two before the place where I am to meditate or contemplate, and with my mind raised on high, consider that God our Lord beholds me, etc. Then I will make an act of reverence or humility.

- There is an interesting text that Aquinas gives in ST II-II, q. 83, a. 13, wherein he asks if attention is a necessary condition for prayer. After making a clarification, he makes a point of explaining how important making the intention of our prayer is. He writes: "A thing is said to be necessary when without it something cannot obtain its effect. Now the effect of prayer is threefold. The first is an effect which is common to all acts quickened by charity, and this is merit. In order to realize this effect, it is not necessary that prayer should be attentive throughout; *because the force of the original intention with which one sets about praying renders the whole prayer meritorious, as is the case with other meritorious acts.* The second effect of prayer is proper thereto, and consists in impetration: and again the original intention, to which God looks chiefly, suffices to obtain this effect. But if the original intention is lacking, prayer lacks both merit and impetration: because, as Gregory [Hugh St. Victor, *Expos. in Reg. S. Aug.* iii] says, "God hears not the prayer of those who pay no attention to their prayer." The third effect of prayer is that which it produces at once; this is the spiritual refreshment of the mind, and for this effect attention is a necessary condition: wherefore it is written (1 Corinthians 14:14): "If I pray in a tongue . . . my understanding is without fruit."

[76] I will enter upon the meditation, now kneeling, now prostrate upon the ground, now lying face upwards, now seated, now standing, always being intent on seeking what I desire. Hence, two things should be noted:
a) If I find what I desire while kneeling, I will not seek to change my position: if prostrate, I will observe the same direction, etc.
b) I will remain quietly meditating upon the point in which I have found what I desire, without any eagerness to go on till I have been satisfied.

[77] After an exercise is finished, either sitting or walking, I will consider for the space of a quarter of an hour how I succeeded in the meditation or contemplation. If poorly, I will seek the cause of the failure; and after I have found it, I will be sorry, so that I may do better in the future. If I have succeeded, I will give thanks to God our Lord, and the next time try to follow the same method.

[78] I should not think of things that give pleasure and joy, as the glory of Heaven, the Resurrection, etc., for if I wish to feel pain, sorrow, and tears for my sins, every consideration promoting joy and happiness will impede it. I should rather keep in mind that I want to be sorry and feel pain. Hence it would be better to call to mind death and judgment.

[79] For the same reason I should deprive myself of all light, closing the shutters and doors when I am in my room, except when I need light to say prayers, to read, or to eat.

[80] I should not laugh or say anything that would cause laughter.

[81] I should restrain my eyes except to look up in receiving or dismissing one with whom I have to speak.

We spoke about how to make the particular examination, meaning, how to examine ourselves regarding our faults or failings. Although many of us have a dominant defect that we are working on throughout the year or normally, during the Exercises, we should be examining ourselves regarding our meditations and how, in particular, we are fulfilling the directions that we've just read. Calveras, very nicely, makes a sort of particular examination with questions that we can use in order to do this particular examination.

Let's consider what Calveras has to say, and especially the questions he gives:[1]

"The particular examine of the four weeks of the Exercises is to be done in order to *remove failings and defects* in the practice of each one of the *Exercises* in particular, and regarding *negligence* in keeping the additional directions. The point of this is to keep up our general interest, as a sort of prevention, in order to do everything with the greatest possible perfection and to take great care to keep the additions, the object of which is to make the Exercises themselves better and to better find what we desire. This general interest unifies many particular things that are proposed for the matter of making this particular examination, in such a way that, in spite of the number of things to examine, the examination can still be called *particular*." In other words, usually a *particular examination* concerns one point only; here, we are dealing with a number of little questions, but all are related to the Exercises, and united in one examine.

"Questions to make the examination easier:

Failings and defects with respect to the Exercises: Have I meditated *the whole hour*, adding something more if I left the temptation to cut it short? Did I make my meditation *at the indicated hour*? In my *interior reverence and my exterior bodily position*, have I taken care that these elements are in accord with the working of my understanding and my will, and with my interior disposition? Did I make the *preparatory prayer* with great interest and desire? Did I faithfully follow *preambles, points, and considerations* that are proposed by the text,

---

1. Calveras, *Practica intensiva*, 105-112.

directed at *obtaining the fruit* of each particular Exercise? Was I *lukewarm* or *lazy* in what concerns my work? Did I cooperate with the action *of the good spirit, and resist the evil one*? Did I make the *colloquy* or colloquies with fervor?

Negligence in following the additional directions:

1st additional direction: After retiring, just before falling asleep, for the space of a *Hail Mary*, did I think of the hour when I have to rise, and why I was rising, and briefly sum up the exercise I had to go through?

2nd additional direction: When I woke up, did I not permit my thoughts to roam at random, but rather turned my mind at once to the subject I was about to contemplate by using examples to rouse myself to shame for my many sins (like that of an ungrateful knight, before his king, and prisoners, before an earthly judge)?

3rd additional direction: A step or two before the place where I was to meditate or contemplate, did I stand for the space of an *Our Father*, and with my mind raised on high, consider that God our Lord beholds me, etc. Did I make an act of reverence or humility?

4th additional direction: Did I enter upon the meditation, kneeling, prostrate upon the ground, lying face upwards, seated, standing, always being intent on seeking what I desire? Did I take note of two things, namely, that if I found what I desired while kneeling, I didn't seek to change my position, and did I remain quietly meditating upon the point in which I had found what I desired, without any eagerness to go on till I had been satisfied?

5th additional direction: After an exercise is finished, either sitting or walking, did I consider for the space of a quarter of an hour how I succeeded in the meditation or contemplation, and, if poorly, did I seek the cause of the failure in order to find it and be sorry so as to do better in the future, and, if the meditation went well, did I give thanks to God our Lord, and propose to try to follow the same method the next time?

6th additional direction: Did I seek not to think of things that give pleasure and joy, as the glory of Heaven, the Resurrection, etc., but rather try to keep in mind that I want to be sorry and feel pain, calling to mind more death and judgment (because, in order to feel pain, sorrow, and tears for our sins, any consideration of joy and happiness is an impediment)?

7th additional direction: Did I deprive myself of all light, in order to feel sadness and sorrow for my sins, closing the shutters and doors when I was in my room, except when I needed light to say prayers, to read, or to eat?

8th additional direction: Did I laugh or say anything that would cause laughter?

9th additional direction: Did I restrain my eyes except to look up in receiving or dismissing one with whom I had to speak?

Additional Direction 10 and Notes:
Penance and the Spiritual Exercises
[82-86] and [87-90]

For today's conference, we return to consider the last additional direction, 10, and some further notes that regard the practice of penance during the Exercises.

The practice of penance has a long history in, not only the Catholic Church, but also even before it.

For example, in the Old Testament we read: "Then the Israelites, all the people, went up to Bethel, and there they sat weeping before Yahweh. They fasted that day until evening and presented burnt offerings and fellowship offerings to Yahweh" (Jdg 20:26).

Likewise, we read that "when Ahab heard these words, he tore his clothes, put on sackcloth and fasted. He lay in sackcloth and went around meekly. Then the word of Yahweh came to Elijah the Tishbite: 'Have you noticed how Ahab has humbled himself before me? Because he has humbled himself, I will not bring this disaster in his day, but I will bring it on his house in the days of his son'" (1 Kgs 21:27-29).

In the New Testament as well, we see Christ performing acts of penance, although He has no need to atone for personal sins. We can consider His fasting in the desert for 40 days and 40 nights, for instance. Saint Padre Pio says it well: "Anyone who wants to be a true Christian . . . must mortify his flesh for no other reason than devotion to Jesus, who, for love of us, mortified His entire body on the cross."

Likewise, penance was the norm in the early Church. In the Acts of the Apostles we read: "While they were worshipping the Lord and fasting, the Holy Spirit said, 'Set apart for me Barnabas and Saul for the work to which I have called them.' So after they had fasted and prayed, they placed their hands on them and sent them off" (Acts 13:2-3). And, a little later we read "Paul and Barnabas appointed elders for them in each church and, with prayer and fasting, committed them to the Lord, in whom they had put their trust" (Acts 14:23).

Saint Paul tells the Corinthians in his first letter (9:25-27): "Every athlete exercises discipline in every way. They do it to win a perishable crown, but we an imperishable one. Thus I do not run aimlessly; I do not fight as if I were shadowboxing. No, I drive my body and train it, for fear that, after having preached to others, I myself should be disqualified." The word the NABRE translates as "drive" is the Greek ὑπωπιάζω (hypōpiazō), which literally means "to strike under the eye," and to make black and blue; it implies a lot more severity than just "driving."

Paul makes it clear that this discipline is necessary for salvation, and Saint John of the Cross notes, *"The world is the enemy least difficult to conquer; the devil is the hardest to understand; but the flesh is the most tenacious, and its attacks continue as long as the old self lasts."* Hence, we must conquer the flesh just like we conquer any other temptation or challenge.

It shouldn't surprise us, then, that Ignatius tells us about doing penance, and especially about doing penance during the Exercises so as to continue it throughout our lives.

[82]: The tenth Additional Direction deals with penance. This is divided into interior and exterior penance. Interior penance consists in sorrow for one's sins and a firm purpose not to commit them or any others. Exterior penance is the fruit of the first kind. It consists in inflicting punishment on ourselves for the sins we have committed. The principal ways of doing this are three.

Thus far Ignatius. Before we begin to discuss them, however, it is important to keep what we've just read in mind. The point is not that I do great penances because I want to be acknowledged or become tough. It is a fruit of my internal sorrow, my internal penance, which is much more pleasing to God.

This is an extremely important point. Teresa of Jesus said that interior mortifications are "the means by which every other kind of mortification may become much more meritorious and perfect." As Our Lord told Saint Faustina: "The greatest works are worthless in My eyes if they are done out of self-will, and often they are not in accord with My will and merit punishment rather than reward. And on the other hand, even the smallest of your acts, done with the confessor's permission is pleasing in My eyes and very dear to Me."

In fact, the saints have strong words for those who perform corporal penances without the intention of eradicating their self-will and attachments:

Saint John of the Cross writes, "The ignorance of some is extremely lamentable; they burden themselves with extraordinary penances and many other exercises, thinking these are sufficient to attain union with divine Wisdom. But such practices are insufficient if these souls do not diligently strive to deny their appetites. If they would attempt to devote only half of that energy to the renunciation of their desires, they would profit more in a month, than in years with all these other exercises. . . . I venture to say that without this mortification, all that is done for the sake of advancement in perfection and in knowledge of God and of oneself is no more profitable than seed sown on uncultivated ground (that is, only producing weeds). Accordingly, darkness and coarseness will always be with a soul until its appetites are extinguished."

Saint Alphonsus De Ligouri adds, "There are some religious who perform a great many exercises of devotion, who practice frequent Communion, long meditations, fasting, and other corporal austerities, but make no effort to overcome certain little passions for example, certain resentments, aversions, curiosity, and certain dangerous affections. They will not submit to any contradiction; they will not give up attachment to certain persons, nor subject their will to the commands of their Superiors, or to the holy will of God. What progress can they make in perfection? Unhappy souls! They will be forever imperfect."

Again, penance isn't a bad thing; it's a good thing, but we need to make sure of our motives for it, and that it is a reflection and a result of our interior penances. We can continue with Ignatius:

[83] The first kind of exterior penance concerns eating. In this matter, if we do away with what is superfluous, it is not penance, but temperance. We do penance when we deny ourselves something of what is suitable for us. The more we do this, the better the penance, provided only we do no harm to ourselves and do not cause any serious illness.

[84] The second kind of exterior penance concerns sleep. Here, too, it is not penance when we do away with the superfluous in what is pampering and soft. But it is penance when in our manner of sleeping we take something away from what is suitable. The more we do in this line, the better it is, provided we do not cause any harm to ourselves, and do not bring on any notable illness. But we should not deny ourselves a suitable amount of sleep, except to come to a happy mean in case we had the habit of sleeping too much.

[85] The third kind of penance is to chastise the body, that is, to inflict sensible pain on it. This is done by wearing hairshirts, cords, or iron chains on the body, or by scourging or wounding oneself, and by other kinds of austerities.

[86] *The more suitable and safe form of penance seems to be* that which would cause sensible pain to the body and not penetrate to the bones, so that it inflicts pain, but does not cause sickness. For this reason it would seem more suitable to chastise oneself with light cords that cause superficial pain, rather than in any other way that might bring about a serious internal infirmity.

- We can consider what Saint Catherine of Siena writes in a letter: "Penance to be sure must be used as a tool, in due times and places, as need may be. If the flesh, being too strong, kicks against the spirit, penance takes the rod of discipline, and fast, and the cilice of many buds, and mighty vigils; and places burdens enough on the flesh, that it may be more subdued. But if the body is weak, fallen into illness, the rule of discretion does not approve of such a method."

Notes [87]

The principal reason for performing exterior penance is to secure three effects:

I. To make satisfaction for past sins;

II. To overcome oneself, that is, to make our sensual nature obey reason, and to bring all of our lower faculties into greater subjection to the higher;

III. To obtain some grace or gift that one earnestly desires. Thus it may be that one wants a deep sorrow for sin, or tears, either because of his sins or because of the pains and sufferings of Christ our Lord; or he may want the solution of some doubt that is in his mind.

- We shouldn't ignore this important aspect of our vocations, as Catholics in general and as religious in particular. Christ told Saint Faustina: "You will save more souls through prayer and suffering than will a missionary through his teachings and sermons alone."

[88] Note that the first and second Additional Directions are to be observed for the exercises at midnight and at daybreak, and not for the exercises made at other times. The fourth Direction is never to be followed in the church before others, but only in private, for example, at home.

- Recall that the first directive deals with, "After retiring, just before falling asleep, for the space of a *Hail Mary,* I will think of the hour when I have to rise, and why I am rising, and briefly sum up the exercise I have to go through," and the second, "When I wake up, I will not permit my thoughts to roam at random." It should be fairly obvious, then, that these directions only apply for the first two meditations.

- The fourth direction is "I will enter upon the meditation, now kneeling, now prostrate upon the ground, now lying face upwards, now seated, now standing, always being intent on seeking what I desire," which, again is sort of awkward if done in public.

[89] When the exercitant has not found what he has been seeking, for example, tears, consolation, etc., it is often useful to make some change in the kind of penance, such as in food, in sleep, or in other ways of doing penance, so that we alternate, for two or three days doing penance, and for two or three not doing any. The reason for this is that more penance is better for some and less for others. Another reason is that we often quit doing penance, because we are too much concerned about our bodies and erroneously judge that human nature cannot bear it without notable illness. On the other hand, at times we may do too much penance, thinking that the body can stand it. Now since God our Lord knows our nature infinitely better, when we make changes of this kind, He often grants each one the grace to understand what is suitable for him.

[90] The Particular Examination of Conscience will be made to remove faults and negligences with regard to the Exercises and the Additional Directions. This will also be observed in the Second, Third, and Fourth Week.

With these points in mind, following Fr. Calveras,[1] we can make an examination of sorts regarding our practice of penance during these Exercises:

- Have I done penance, not only internally, with sorrow for my sins and with firm resolution not to commit those nor other sins, but also external penance, as a fruit of the first, as a punishment for the sins committed, and as a means to subject my sensuality to reason and better control my lower faculties, or in order to seek and obtain grace or the gift of interior contrition for my sins and to mourn greatly over them?
- Have I performed penance in its different manners, in eating, in my way of sleeping, but without losing the appropriate amount of sleep, unless I have the vice of sleeping too much and thus overcoming that vice and punishing my body in this way?
- Regarding my way of eating and of sleeping: have I removed only what is superfluous, or also what is necessary as much as I can, without harming my person and without causing illness?
- Regarding punishing my flesh, have I sought to cause sensible pain to the body and not penetrate to the bones, so that it inflicts pain, but does not cause sickness, chastising myself with light cords that cause superficial pain, rather than in any other way that might bring about a serious internal infirmity?

---

1. Jose Calveras, *Practica intensiva*, 111-112.

- Have I ceased doing penance for sensual love or for erroneous reasons, like that the human body cannot tolerate it, or, on the contrary, do I do too much, thinking my body can take it?
- If I still have not found what I have been seeking, for example, tears, consolation, etc., have I made some change in the kind of penance, such as in food, in sleep, or in other ways of doing penance, doing penance for two or three days, and not doing any for two or three days, so that God can show me what is fitting for me?

Especially in the month-long Exercises, we have an excellent opportunity to see what is fitting for us: what we can tolerate, and what is too much. We should take advantage of this time and of these rules to do, as Ignatius says, *tantum quantum*, as much as possible within the limits that he has set down.

Annotations (Introductory Observations)
[2-10], [14, 15, 18, and 19]

For today's conference, we will consider some of the introductory observations that Ignatius gives in the beginning of the Exercises. Puhl translates this section as "introductory observations." However, since the Spanish is literally *"annotaciones,"* sometimes you will see it translated as "annotations." Be that as it may, the point of these observations is, as Ignatius says [1]: "The purpose of these observations is to provide some understanding of the spiritual exercises which follow and to serve as a help both for the one who is to give them and for the exercitant."

[02] "The one who explains to another the method and order of meditating or contemplating should narrate accurately the facts of the contemplation or meditation. Let him adhere to the points, and add only a short or summary explanation. The reason for this is that when one in meditating takes the solid foundation of facts, and goes over it and reflects on it for himself, he may find something that makes them a little clearer or better understood. This may arise either from his own reasoning, or from the grace of God enlightening his mind. Now this produces greater spiritual relish and fruit than if one in giving the Exercises had explained and developed the meaning at great length. For it is not much knowledge that fills and satisfies the soul, but the intimate understanding and relish of the truth."

- What does this mean? As we've mentioned before, the work of the Exercises is really the work of the one making them, not of the one preaching them. I can give you points, and give you some things to think about, but as Casanovas writes, "the Director doesn't need to invent or even look for any material for the meditation whatsoever; the material is already very well established in the Exercises."[1] We do write things to help, a brief clarification here or there, but really if all we did was read the book, that would, in the mind of Ignatius, be enough. Contained implicitly here,

---

1. Casanovas, *Ejercicios de San Ignacio,* 300 and following. All the commentary and notes are summarized from this text.

though, is a great rule of the spiritual life: it isn't knowing a lot of things that fills and satisfies the soul, but rather to feel and savor few things internally. Fr. Diego Lainez, one of Ignatius' first followers and the second superior general of the Jesuits, said that this direction is like "a portrait of the interior of Saint Ignatius: he was a man of few truths, but he profoundly penetrated them and let them sink their roots into his soul." The Exercises are like this: there are few truths, none are complicated, but they are all certain, and can become the motor of our spiritual lives, the light, love, and strength of our souls. The word that Puhl translates as "intimate understanding" is *sentir* in Spanish, which Ignatius uses a lot. It doesn't mean just feel or to know, but rather, by knowing, and knowing profoundly, to come to love and esteem that truth, so much so that it penetrates and inspires all the spiritual and sensible strengths, in every place where we work.

[03] In all the Spiritual Exercises which follow, we make use of the acts of the intellect in reasoning, and of the acts of the will in manifesting our love. However, we must observe that when in acts of the will we address God our Lord or His saints either vocally or mentally, greater reverence is required on our part than when we use the intellect in reasoning.

- Here Ignatius is reminding us of the great reverence we should have when speaking with God; this is an act that is particularly Christian and something proper to the saints. Reverence is an act of adoration, mixed with filial love and servile humility. To really be reverence, it must come from the intellect, pass through the will, and affect even the feelings. Any sort of piety that forgets this reverence is a piety of dubious character.

[04] Four Weeks are assigned to the Exercises given below. This corresponds to the four parts into which they are divided, namely: the first part, which is devoted to the consideration and contemplation of sin; the second part, which is taken up with the life of Christ our Lord up to Palm Sunday inclusive; the third part, which treats of the passion of Christ our Lord; the fourth part, which deals with the Resurrection and Ascension; to this are appended Three Methods of Prayer.

However, it is not meant that each week should necessarily consist of seven or eight days. For it may happen that in the First Week some are slower in attaining what is sought, namely, contrition, sorrow, and tears for sin. Some, too, may be more diligent than others, and some more disturbed and tried by different spirits. It may be necessary, therefore, at times to shorten the Week, and at others to lengthen it. So in our search for the fruit that is proper to the matter assigned, we may have to do the same in all the subsequent Weeks. However, the Exercises should be finished in approximately thirty days.

- At first, this seems just to be a sort of calendar or material outline of the Exercises. We've already mentioned the setup in the brief history, and so it seems like we could just pass over this note. However, I want to call your attention to a couple of things:

  · First, Ignatius intended that the Exercises be preached one on one, meaning, one director, one exercitant. If it's hard to organize a month-long Exercises, imagine how hard it would be to do 16 of them, so that each of you could do it one on one! But, if you can do it one on one, then the director can see precisely where you are at spiritually, and adjust the Exercises as need. As Casanovas says nicely, this avoids "superstition," as it were: it's not that the Exercises are a magical formula; we preach as written and, magically, like a rabbit's foot (which, incidentally, wasn't that lucky for the rabbit), you become a saint. The individual conditions of each person must be taken into account.

  · Second, a good director of the Exercises knows the end of each week and of each meditation or contemplation. Only in this way would they be able to adjust accordingly.

[05] It will be very profitable for the one who is to go through the Exercises to enter upon them with magnanimity and generosity toward his Creator and Lord, and to offer Him his entire will and liberty, that His Divine Majesty may dispose of him and all he possesses according to His most holy will.

- Casanovas says that, of all the introductory observations, this is the main one, since it tells us the dispositions of the person who wants to make the Exercises perfectly. Such a one will open wide the doors of their soul. The problem is that often people want spiritual things, but only to a certain point and with only a limited intensity. They want to be holy, but only "if it doesn't cost too much." Ignatius gives the example of a man who has spent his entire life working towards obtaining some position of honor and prestige, or working honestly to have a good economic status. Naturally, if he were to lose those things, he would feel ashamed and see it as his biggest failure and disgrace. It wouldn't even cross his mind that God might be asking it as a voluntary sacrifice, and that God will reward him greatly for making that sacrifice for Him. This is the position of the person who wants to serve God: what should they care about anything else? The only thing that matters is giving everything to Him, and letting Him sort out the rest.

[06] When the one who is giving the Exercises perceives that the exercitant is not affected by any spiritual experiences, such as consolations or desolations, and that he is not troubled by different spirits, he ought to ply him with questions about the exercises. He should ask him whether he makes them at the appointed times, and how he makes them. He should question him about the Additional Directions, whether he is diligent in the observance of them. He will demand an account in detail of each one of these points. Consolation and desolation are treated in # 316–324; the Additional Directions are given in # 73–90.

- This instruction is written for the director, but it is also of use to the one making the Exercises. Ignatius here is assuming that, if someone is making the Exercises as they ought, they should also experience spiritual consolation and desolation (we will discuss the meaning of these words tomorrow). If one is faithful, God will make the exercitant feel His presence, and this by means of these spiritual movements. Casanovas asks, "Isn't a little presumptuous for Ignatius to assume that God will do this? No, and the reason why is clear. If someone really enters into the Exercises seeking to do God's will, and they faithfully fulfill everything that God is asking of them, seeking God in everything, is it possible that God wouldn't make Himself be found? From here, too, follows the insistence of Ignatius on making the meditations well and at the right times; it's as though God needs to know where to find you, and He will be looking for you according to what the schedule has posted.

[07] If the director of the Exercises observes that the exercitant is in desolation and tempted, let him not deal severely and harshly with him, but gently and kindly. He should encourage and strengthen him for the future by exposing to him the wiles of the enemy of our human nature, and by getting him to prepare and dispose himself for the coming consolation.

- This note, along with the three that follow, are special moments of temptation and fights that must be endured. If the director gets sad or angry, it will just make it worse. What needs to be done, rather, by both *parties,* is to recognize that they are dealing with a temptation and fight with the devil, and not with a failing of the one on the Exercises. They should be reminded of the rules for discernment and that desolation will soon pass, and consolation will return.

[08] If the one who is giving the Exercises should perceive from desolations, from the wiles of the enemy, and from consolations that the exercitant has need of them, he should explain to him the rules of the First Week and of the Second Week for the understanding of different spirits, # 313–327, and 328–336.

[09] It should be observed that when the exercitant is engaged in the Exercises of the First Week, if he is a person unskilled in spiritual things, and if he is tempted grossly and openly, for example, by bringing before his mind obstacles to his advance in the service of God our Lord, such as labors, shame, fear for his good name in the eyes of the world, etc., the one who is giving the Exercises should not explain to him the rules about different spirits that refer to the Second Week. For while the rules of the First Week will be very helpful to him, those of the Second Week will be harmful, since they deal with matter that is too subtle and advanced for him to understand.

[10] When the one who is giving the Exercises perceives that the exercitant is being assailed and tempted under the appearance of good, then is the proper time to explain to him the rules of the Second Week, which we mentioned above. For commonly the enemy of our human nature tempts more under the appearance of good when one is exercising himself in the illuminative way. This corresponds to the Exercises of the Second Week. He does not tempt him so much under the appearance of good when he is exercising himself in the purgative way, which corresponds to the Exercises of the First Week.

- These three annotations or instructions tell the director when he should be explaining the rules for discernment of spirits, which, as we said, will be tomorrow and the next day, at least for the rules of the First Week. Again, the Exercises are meant to be preached one on one, so the director should pay attention to what the retreatant can handle and when. As Saint Paul wrote to the Corinthians: "I had to feed you with milk, not with solid food, because you weren't ready for anything stronger" (1 Cor 3:2). That's the way it is in the Exercises as well. We can only give what people are ready for.

[14] If the one who is giving the Exercises sees that the exercitant is going on in consolation and in great fervor, he must admonish him not to be inconsiderate or hasty in making any promise or vow. The more unstable in character he knows him to be, the more he should forewarn and admonish him. For though it is right to urge one to enter the religious state in which he knows that vows of obedience, poverty, and chastity are taken, and though a good work done under vow is more meritorious than one done without a vow, nevertheless, it is necessary to consider with great care the condition and endowments of each individual, and the help or hindrance one would experience in carrying out his promises.

- Here, writes Casanovas, we can admire Ignatius's human prudence, something that is indeed exquisite. Again, it relies on knowing the person, and also to measure the natural elements that come into play, and not be fixated on the extremes that sometimes people suggest. The Director should brake the one who is being too hasty, but must also be prudent in not pushing too much.

[15] The director of the Exercises ought not to urge the exercitant more to poverty or any promise than to the contrary, nor to one state of life or way of living more than to another. Outside the Exercises, it is true, we may lawfully and meritoriously urge all who probably have the required fitness to choose continence, virginity, the religious life, and every form of religious perfection. But while one is engaged in the Spiritual Exercises, it is more suitable and much better that the Creator and Lord in person communicate Himself to the devout soul in quest of the divine will, that He inflame it with His love and praise, and dispose it for the way in which it could better serve God in the future. Therefore, the director of the Exercises, as a balance at equilibrium, without leaning to one side or the other, should permit the Creator to deal directly with the creature, and the creature directly with his Creator and Lord.

- Here Ignatius is following Saint Paul when he admits that he is not the spouse of souls, but rather Jesus Christ. To direct a soul isn't to impose our opinion on another's life, or to impose our thoughts on them, or to run after them making sure that in every little detail they are fulfilling God's will. Ignatius says that outside of the Exercises, a director can incline a person to the more perfect life, using the usual rules of discernment. However, in the Exercises, the point is that God should work with the soul directly, so that the person on the Exercises sees what it is that God wants. The director should try to make sure that the communication between God and the soul is not interrupted; even if the director sees things very clearly, he should resist the temptation to say so, and just let God work in the soul.

[18] The Spiritual Exercises must be adapted to the condition of the one who is to engage in them, that is, to his age, education, and talent. Thus exercises that he could not easily bear, or from which he would derive no profit, should not be given to one with little natural ability or of little physical strength.

Similarly, each one should be given those exercises that would be more helpful and profitable according to his willingness to dispose himself for them.

Hence, one who wishes no further help than some instruction and the attainment of a certain degree of peace of soul may be given the Particular Examination of Conscience, # 24–31, and after that the General Examination of

Conscience, # 32–43. Along with this, let him be given for half an hour each morning the method of prayer on the Commandments and on the Capital Sins, etc., # 238–248. Weekly confession should be recommended to him, and if possible, the reception of Holy Communion every two weeks, or even better, every week if he desires it.

This method is more appropriate for those who have little natural ability or are illiterate. Let each of the Commandments be explained to them, and also the Capital Sins, the use of the five senses, the precepts of the Church, and the Works of Mercy.

Similarly, if the one giving the Exercises sees that the exercitant has little aptitude or little physical strength, that he is one from whom little fruit is to be expected, it is more suitable to give him some of the easier exercises as a preparation for confession. Then he should be given some ways of examining his conscience, and directed to confess more frequently than was his custom before, so as to retain what he has gained.

But let him not go on further and take up the matter dealing with the Choice of a Way of Life, nor any other exercises that are outside the First Week. This is especially to be observed when much better results could be obtained with other persons, and when there is not sufficient time to take everything.

- Here Ignatius reminds us that not everyone is the same: some people have different physical dispositions either because of age, physical disabilities or illness, or even a lack of culture, natural talent, or sufficient free time. Likewise, a person might not have the sufficient moral disposition, meaning, simply, the desire to advance in the spiritual life and the generosity to surrender themselves to God their Lord. Something amiss in the physical dispositions means that the Exercises can be adjusted, but often just the right disposition is enough, and God will provide; if something is amiss in the moral disposition, as Ignatius says, if they make the first week but aren't filled with fervor, better just stop preaching and wait a month or two.

[19] One who is educated or talented, but engaged in public affairs or necessary business, should take an hour and a half daily for the Spiritual Exercises.

First, the end for which man is created should be explained to him, then for half an hour the Particular Examination of Conscience may be presented, then the General Examination of Conscience, and the method of confessing and of receiving Holy Communion.

For three days, let him meditate each morning for an hour on the first, second, and third sins, # 45–54. For three more days, at the same time, he should take the meditation on personal sins, # 55–61. Then for three days, at the same hour, he should meditate on the punishment due to sin, # 65–71. Along with all of these meditations, he should be given the ten Additional Directions, # 73–89.

In the mysteries of the life of our Lord, the same order should be observed which is explained later on at great length in the Exercises themselves.

- Some of you might have heard of the 19th annotation in regard to the Spiritual Exercises. Simply put, the 19th annotation—sometimes called an Ignatian Retreat in Daily Life—is a version of the Spiritual Exercises designed for people who cannot be away for 30 days to do the Exercises as they were practiced originally. Most of the time, the "19th" is done by people who work full-time but who want to do the Spiritual Exercises. So the Exercises are extended over several months, and the retreatants do weekly prayer practices, readings, and meditations. I once suggested to a friend that she make the Exercises and she replied, "Oh I have! They are great! I did the 19th annotation not too long ago." The point with these modifications is not to not have them seek perfection, but to adjust the points according to their state and what they can handle. Likewise, in order to be able to do this sort of preaching, the director must really know the Exercises well, and be able to modify and adjust accordingly.

Rules for the Discernment of Spirits – First Week – [313-324]

With commentary adjusted from Fr. Timothy Gallagher, OMV, and Ignacio Casanovas, SJ

Abba Poemen said that Abba Ammonas said, "A person can spend his whole time carrying an axe without succeeding in cutting down the tree; while another, with experience of tree-felling brings the tree down with a few blows. He said that the axe is discernment."
The Sayings of the Desert Fathers

These rules for discernment of spirits are worth their weight in gold. I am personally convinced that, if only for the Exercises and these rules, Ignatius could be named a doctor of the Church. He isn't one, but, no matter: these rules are *extremely valuable*. We should always have them in our toolbox of spiritual instruments so we can know what it is that is affecting our souls or the souls of others, and then apply the proper remedy for their ailments.

Rules for [becoming aware – that's included in some translations] and understanding to some extent the different movements produced in the soul and for recognizing those that are good to admit them, and those that are bad, to reject them. These rules are more suited to the first week.

"Ignatius, then, is assuming that our soul feels any number of different motions (the Spanish word is *mociones*) or movements, for instance, consolation, happiness or sadness, hope or despair, and although this is simply part of life in general, there is special need to pay attention to it during the Exercises, when God *should* be acting in this way (as we mentioned yesterday). These movements are of the spiritual order, and touch on our service of God and the health of our soul. At the same time, these movements can be very different, not only because they are different, one from another, but also because of the impression they produce on us, as well as the effects that follow from them.

The word *movements* seems to refer, at least for the most part, to the emotional and sensitive part of us. This doesn't mean that they are unrelated to our thoughts or imaginations, but, as Ignatius will point out, thoughts 'come from them.'"

** Note the most important part here is the need to *become aware* and then to *understand*. So many people go through life without stopping to consider what it is that's happening in their souls. They just kind of go forward (so they think), going this way and that way, blown about by every little whim, thinking that it's from God if they like it, from the devil if they don't. But things aren't quite that simple . . .

This discernment of spirits stems from Ignatius's own personal experience. While he was recovering in the family castle, the only books available to him were some romance novels, and lives of the saints. He noticed that when he read the romance novels, his imagination would be caught up, and he'd be happy. But, after a few hours, the happiness would go away, and he would be left dry and discontented. However, when he read the lives of the saints, it would make him happy and at peace, and even a while later, he would be at peace. Often, though, other thoughts of worldly things would come to distract him in the course of his thoughts.

Anyways, we can see the three steps Ignatius outlines: **be aware, understand, and then accept or reject.**

The first, and perhaps most important thing we need to determine, is whether a soul is going from bad to worse, or from bad to good or good to better. This sets the stage for everything else that we're going to talk about.

(314) In the case of those who go from one mortal sin to another, the enemy is ordinarily accustomed to propose apparent pleasures. He fills their imagination with sensual delights and gratifications, the more readily to keep them in their vices and increase the number of their sins.

With such persons the good spirit [by this Ignatius means not only God, but also the good angels] uses a method which is the reverse of the above. Making use of the light of reason, he will rouse the sting of conscience and fill them with remorse.

** If a soul is in mortal sin, the devil wants to keep it there. We can think of the example from the *Screwtape Letters* by C. S. Lewis. Screwtape tells his nephew: "I once had a patient, a sound atheist, who used to read in the British Museum. One day, as he sat reading, I saw a train of thought in his mind beginning to go the wrong way. The Enemy, of course, was at his elbow in a moment. Before I knew where I was I saw my twenty years' work beginning to totter. If I had lost my head and begun to attempt a defense by argument I should have been undone. But I was not such a fool. I struck instantly at the part of the man which I had best under my control and suggested that it was just about time he had some lunch. The Enemy presumably made the counter-suggestion (you know how one can never quite overhear What He says to them?) that this was more important than lunch. At least I think that must have been His line for when I said 'Quite. In fact much too important to tackle it the end of a morning', the patient brightened up considerably; and by the time I had added 'Much better come back after lunch and go into it with a fresh mind', he was already half way to the door. Once he was in the street the battle was won. I showed him a newsboy shouting the midday paper, and a No. 73 bus going past, and before he reached the bottom of the steps I had got into him an unalterable conviction that, whatever odd ideas might come into a man's head when he was shut up alone with his books, a healthy dose of 'real life' (by which he meant the bus and the newsboy) was enough to show him that all 'that sort of thing' just couldn't be true. He knew he'd had a narrow escape and in later years was fond of talking about 'that inarticulate sense for actuality which is our ultimate safeguard against the aberrations of mere logic'. He is now safe in Our Father's house."

Now then, we should be aware of this, because, when a person comes from a life of sin, we must convince them that the temptations they face, that call them back to that life, are the devil's way of deceiving them and that, when they feel bad for their sins, that is God calling to them.

It is as Saint Teresa of Jesus remarks in the *Interior Castle*. She mentions that in the second mansion, "are found souls which have begun to practice prayer; they realize the importance of their not remaining in the first mansions, yet often lack determination to quit their present condition by avoiding occasions of sin, which is a very perilous state to be in. However, it is a great grace that they should sometimes make good their escape from the vipers and poisonous creatures around them and should understand the need of avoiding them. In some way these souls suffer a great deal more than those in the first mansions, although not in such danger, as they begin to understand their peril and there are great hopes of their entering farther into the castle. I say that they suffer a great deal more, for those in an earlier stage are like deaf-mutes and are not so distressed at being unable to speak, while the others, who can hear but cannot talk, find it much harder. At the same time, it is better not to be deaf, and a decided advantage to hear what is said to us."

In other words, these souls have started to hear the voice of God, have felt the sting of remorse, but are, perhaps, not quite ready to give up sin and go to God.

[315] In the case of those who go on earnestly striving to cleanse their souls from sin and who seek to rise in the service of God our Lord to greater perfection, the method pursued is the opposite of that mentioned in the first rule.

Then it is characteristic of the evil spirit to harass with anxiety, to afflict with sadness, to raise obstacles backed by fallacious reasonings that disturb the soul. Thus he seeks to prevent the soul from advancing.

"Note how different these two rules are! The souls to whom this rule applies are making an honest, continuous effort to purge their sins. What does the devil do in this case? The opposite of what he does in the first. The evil spirit tries to stir up all sorts of internal tribulations . . . and he isn't content just to attack the imagination and the sensible part of the person; he even wanted, if possible, to disturb the person's mind or reason.

Ignatius' point here is that our life is a warfare, and our soul is a battleground. We should not be surprised at these struggles, because there is a fight going on, and we are in the middle of it."

** There is a lot contained here. Notice what Ignatius says the evil spirit does: "harass with anxiety" [some say 'gnawing anxiety' – the word has this sense of biting], "afflict with sadness," "raise obstacles," and "false reasonings."

In the Bible, Christ never tells us to be anxious or worried; in fact, the word for *anxious* is usually one that literally means *divided*.

In some letters to Teresa Rejadell, a holy woman who really loved God, Ignatius gives some more details about these methods of the devil.

Writing about **anxiety**, he told her:

"The enemy is leading you into error . . . but not in any way to make you fall into a sin that would separate you from God our Lord. He tries rather to *upset* you and to *interfere with* your service of God and *your peace of mind.*"

The devil just wants us to be miserable, to be less effective in God's service. If he can get us to sin, he'll be happy, but if he can't get that, he just wants us to be unhappy, just as he is unhappy.

Regarding **sadness**, Ignatius writes Teresa:

"We find ourselves sad without knowing why. We cannot pray with devotion, nor contemplate, nor even speak or hear of the things of God with any interior taste or relish."

Regarding **obstacles**, Ignatius writes:

"The enemy as a rule follows this course. He places obstacles and impediments in the way of those who love and begin to serve God our Lord, and this is the first weapon he uses in his efforts to wound them. He asks, for instance: 'How can you continue a life of such great penance, deprived of all satisfaction from friends, relative, possession? How can you lead so lonely a life, with no rest, when you can save your soul in other ways and without such dangers?' He tries to bring us to understand that we must lead a life that is longer than it will actually be, by reason of the trials he places before us and which no one ever underwent."

Such as Ignatius' own experience; before his profession of perpetual vows, the devil tempted him with thoughts such as the example he cites: "Will you be able to do this . . . *really* . . . for every day for the rest of your life?" Ignatius was worried, but then replied, "Can you promise me even a day more of life?"

Fr. Lalemont, the spiritual director of a number of the North American martyrs, says, clearly and unequivocally, that any thought or concern regarding the future comes from the devil. It is that simple: concerns about the future come from the evil one.

Finally, for false reasonings, we know that we have our reason, our intellect, as a gift from God. However, sometimes the devil tries to harass with it, sowing the seeds of false reasons. For instance, if we experience peace and calm, he'll try to make us second-guess ourselves and our thoughts.

It is characteristic of the good spirit, however, to give courage and strength, consolations, tears, inspirations, and peace. This He does by making all easy, by removing all obstacles so that the soul goes forward in doing good.
**

Maybe the difficult word there is *consolations*, since it has a very specific meaning. That's why Ignatius, in the next point, goes on to explain what it means.

(316) Spiritual Consolation. I call it consolation when an interior movement is aroused in the soul, by which it is *inflamed with love of its Creator and Lord*, and as a consequence, *can love no creature on the face of the earth for its own sake*, but only in the Creator of them all. It is likewise consolation when one *sheds tears that move to the love of God*, whether it be because of sorrow for sins, or because of the sufferings of Christ our Lord, or for any other reason that is immediately directed to the praise and service of God. Finally, I call consolation every increase of *faith, hope, and love, and all interior joy that invites and attracts to what is heavenly and to the salvation of one's soul by filling it with peace and quiet in its Creator and Lord.*

** Note that Ignatius is talking about spiritual consolation, and not just any consolation whatsoever. If I eat a huge bowl of ice cream, I might feel consoled (or nasty), but I'd be hard pressed to call that a *spiritual* consolation. By spiritual, we mean that it has an impact on my life of faith and my relationship with God. Ditto with spiritual desolation.

Sometimes the natural consolation can lead to a spiritual one. There is a story of St. Therese of Lisieux who, upon looking at a hen protecting its chicks, began to cry. Her sister was there, and said, "You're crying!" and Therese went off to her cell. Later she explained to her sister that, when she began thinking about the hen and her chicks, that that was exactly what God had done for her for so many years: hidden her under the shadow of his wings.

Furthermore, note the supernatural characteristics of this consolation: see the words in italics. This isn't simply a happy feelings; it's something much more profound. Father Casanovas says that "spiritual consolation is *substantially a sensible increase in the theological virtues of faith, hope, and charity*, and particularly of charity, which is the queen of all the virtues and has the greatest consoling force of them all. The other motions that accompany this are merely accidental.

What happens is that the divine love, charity, becomes, as it were, sensible; it burns and extinguishes in us all the other loves for any creature."

(317) Spiritual Desolation. I call desolation what is entirely the opposite of what is described in the third rule, as darkness of soul, turmoil of spirit, inclination to what is low and earthly, restlessness rising from many disturbances and temptations which lead to want of faith, want of hope, want of love. The soul is wholly slothful, tepid, sad, and separated, as it were, from its Creator and Lord. For just as consolation is the opposite of desolation, so the thoughts that spring from consolation are the opposite of those that spring from desolation.

** Again, notice the emphasis on the *spiritual* aspect here. It's not just an emotional sadness or feeling bad. It, just like spiritual consolation, has a direct bearing on our life of faith and our relationship with God.

- *Darkness of soul*: this is confusion characteristic of the evil spirit.
- *Turmoil*: we can think back to the anxiety of the evil spirit.

To give an example of just how bad this can be, we can consider a passage from *Story of a Soul*, by Saint Therese. You know, the Little Flower, Doctor of the Church. We'll see it again at the end, but listen to the description of the way she felt before her first vows: "On the eve of the great day, instead of being filled with the customary sweetness, my vocation suddenly seemed to me as unreal as a dream. The devil—for it was he—made me feel sure that I was wholly unsuited for life in the Carmel, and that I was deceiving my superiors by entering on a way to which I was not called. The darkness was so bewildering that I understood but one thing—I had no religious vocation, and must return to the world."

- *Inclination to what is low*: a lack of delight in doing spiritual things and turning to the things of God.

"The time of desolation is the time that the evil spirit generally picks in order to talk to us, and it is from this reason that Saint John Berchmans took the principle, 'whatever upsets a soul that is given to the spiritual life, has the devil as its author.'"

Note too that desolation is not equivalent to mortal sin. Just because I feel far from God does not mean that I've lost grace in my soul or that I'm a bad person.

[318] In time of desolation we should never make any change, but remain firm and constant in the resolution and decision which guided us the day before the desolation, or in the decision to which we adhered in the preceding consolation. *For just as in consolation the good spirit guides and counsels us, so in desolation the evil spirit guides and counsels. Following his counsels we can never find the way to a right decision.* [This line will be very important when we talk about the discernment of God's will by means of these experiences].

** Now Ignatius has gone from the experience, that is, how I feel, to the thoughts that come from it, the consequences that follow.

Note, too, the categorical nature of the command: we *should never*. No exceptions. Do not pass go, do not collect two hundred dollars.

Being in desolation is, sort of, like being drunk or being sick. You don't see things aright: your vision and perception is all distorted. So, if you don't judge right, you don't want to change things.

There's a funny story about James Cardinal Hickey, the archbishop emeritus of DC who invited us to Washington. He was sick and in a room at Providence Hospital. As he was eating his meal, the Daughter of Charity who ran the hospital stopped in to see, and asked how he was doing, and how he liked the food. The cardinal replied, "Sister, I'm doing fine, and this food is great! It's the best food I've had in a long time!" She just looked at him, and he continued, "Sister, I think you must've flown in a French chief to cook it; it's fantastic!" To which the sister replied, "Your Eminence, now I know that you are very sick."

Let me repeat that: Being in desolation is, sort of, like being drunk or being sick. You don't see things aright: your vision and perception is all distorted. So, if you don't judge right, you don't want to change things.

Casanovas calls desolation "an experiential crisis of love." He adds that, "most of the time, consolation is the voice of God that should be followed, since the Lord never contradicts Himself. The evil spirit is the one who contradicts God and anything that comes from Him. This is why it would be the devil who is inspiring me in the time of desolation against the resolutions and determinations I made in the time of consolation. Ordinarily, then, desolation is the enemy's word, and these are the pieces of advice I should follow in order to get on the right path."

[319] Though in desolation we must never change our former resolutions, it will be very advantageous to intensify our activity against the desolation. We can insist more upon prayer, upon meditation, and on much examination of ourselves. We can make an effort in a suitable way to do some penance.

** While we don't change our decisions in desolation, we can try to change the *situation* or *state* of desolation. Note that Ignatius gives three possible solutions: prayer and meditation, examination of self, and penance.

[320] When one is in desolation, he should be mindful that God has left him to his natural powers to resist the different agitations and temptations of the enemy in order to try him. He can resist with the help of God, which always remains, though he may not clearly perceive it. For though God has taken from him the abundance of fervor and overflowing love and the intensity of His favors, nevertheless, he has sufficient grace for eternal salvation.

** Many, if not all, of the saints recall experiences like this, where they feel that God has abandoned them, and that they have not received any graces from Him, etc. Saint Paul of the Cross, for instance, 45 years of interior desolation, and St. M. Teresa of Calcutta, more than 50 years. Basically the response is to remain firm, and to know that this, too, shall pass.

This is, says Casanovas, the true doctrine regarding desolation. God takes away the sensible overflow of consolation, but man always has enough grace for salvation.

[321] When one is in desolation, he should strive to persevere in patience. This reacts against the vexations that have overtaken him. Let him consider, too, that consolation will soon return, and in the meantime, he must diligently use the means against desolation which have been given in the sixth rule.

[322] The *principal* reasons why we suffer from desolation are three [we will see that what Ignatius proposed as tools against desolation are very suited to these causes]:

The first is because we have been tepid and slothful or negligent in our exercises of piety, and so through our own fault spiritual consolation has been taken away from us.

In this case, then, the best solution is to renew our good resolutions and proposals, to fulfill them, and do what it is we need to do. And how, we might ask, are we to know if desolation is our fault? Because we *examined ourselves and have seen that this is the cause.*

The second reason is because God wishes to try us, to see how much we are worth, and how much we will advance in His service and praise when left without the generous reward of consolations and signal favors.

** God wants to make sure that we don't become attached to the consolations. As Saint Bernard would ask, "What do you seek: the consolations of God, or the God of all consolations?" When we are in consolation, we must "fill up our humps" with the knowledge of God's love for us, like a camel.

So, what do we do in this case? *We should pray and meditate, meaning to think and ponder the truths that we know, the general rules that God is generous and that we need to serve Him and not for a reward. Hence, prayer and meditation would help us.*

The third reason is because God wishes to give us a true knowledge and understanding of ourselves, so that we may have an intimate perception of the fact that it is not within our power to acquire and attain great devotion, intense love, tears, or any other spiritual consolation; but that all this is the gift and grace of God our Lord. God does not wish us to build on the property of another, to rise up in spirit in a certain pride and vainglory and attribute to ourselves the devotion and other effects of spiritual consolation.

** Yes, otherwise, when I have consolations and all sorts of graces, I might start to think, "Wow, I'm the cat's pajamas!" when really you're more like the cat's litterbox. What would keep us humble? *Doing penance, which is last remedy Ignatius proposes, because penance forms us in humility.*

[323] When one enjoys consolation, let him consider how he will conduct himself during the time of ensuing desolation, and store up a supply of strength as defense against that day.

[324] He who enjoys consolation should take care to humble himself and lower himself as much as possible. Let him recall how little he is able to do in time of desolation, when he is left without such grace or consolation.

On the other hand, one who suffers desolation should remember that by making use of the sufficient grace offered him, he can do much to withstand all his enemies. Let him find his strength in his Creator and Lord.

Rules for the Discernment of Spirits —
First Week — [325-327]

With commentary adjusted from Fr. Timothy Gallagher, OMV, and Ignacio Casanovas, SJ

Today we will continue with the rules for the discernment of spirits of the First Week. To finish up the rules, Ignatius gives us three ways that the devil usually acts. He compares the devil to a woman, to a deceitful lover, and to an enemy commander. Each analogy highlights some aspects of how the devil tries to deceive us and lead us astray.

"This part of the rules begins the fourth and final section of the rules of discernment for the first week. The point is to have us see into the depths of our enemy's character and his way of working in souls." Casanovas says that these three rules are the only section that could be called 'literary,' meaning, it's written in a more embellished and flowery way. As we've said, in the rest of the Exercises, Ignatius gets right to the point: he doesn't mince words, and everything he writes is precisely measured. Here, however, we see a richness of expression and picturesque images, with a certain reminisce of Ignatius' days as a knight and his life in the military.

Casanovas goes on to say that the best commentary that could be made on these points, is simply to recommend that they be read over and over, because the more they are read, the more flavor they acquire, and, besides, the teachings contained in them couldn't be more straight forward and clear.

The point is that we see that in the Ignatian method we're not meant to be passive and just sit by. There is a war going on for our souls, and we need to take an active part in defending ourselves and attacking our enemy.

[325] The enemy conducts himself as a woman. He is a weakling before a show of strength, and a tyrant if he has his will. It is characteristic of a woman in a quarrel with a man to lose courage and take to flight if the man shows that he is determined and fearless. However, if the man loses courage and begins to flee, the anger, vindictiveness, and rage of the woman surge up and know no bounds. In the same way, the enemy becomes weak, loses courage, and turns to

flight with his seductions as soon as one leading a spiritual life faces his temptations boldly, and does exactly the opposite of what he suggests. However, if one begins to be afraid and to lose courage in temptations, no wild animal on earth can be more fierce than the enemy of our human nature. He will carry out his perverse intentions with consummate malice.

** When you preach to women, generally speaking, they don't like this comparison. However, if you ask, and if they're honest, usually they'll admit that it's true. The point is that the devil is a weakling, but, if we give him a little room, he takes it and keeps going. Again writing to Teresa, Ignatius says:

"Not only this, but *if he sees that we are weak* and much humbled by these harmful thoughts, he *goes on* to suggest that we are entirely forgotten by God our Lord, and *leads us* to thinking that we are quite separated from him and that all that we have done and all that we desire to do is entirely worthless. He thus *endeavors to bring us* to a state of general discouragement."

What happens often is the *snowball effect*: if we can stop these thoughts at the beginning, nothing happens. But, if we give in to them, we get more and more anxious and nervous. The devil knows this, so he keeps going and going and going . . . and if we don't stop, he won't either.

Don't forget: the devil has no scruples: he will be in hell for all eternity, and if he can get us there with him, he'll be happy. However, if he sees that we aren't going to fall, the next best thing he can do is frighten us into thinking that we've sinned, so that we'll be miserable and not as effective in God's service. There are many cases where people come to confession, all tormented because of temptations that they have had. Sometimes, this is because the temptations are very disturbing, meaning, to do very foul, very base things. However, it's just a temptation. Likewise, sometimes people are frightened thinking they consented to a sin of thought; this borders on the topic of scrupulosity, but, since the devil likes to make us miserable, sometimes this is where he gets involved. In this, we can follow the advice of Fr. Fuentes, who cites Fr. Benedict Groschel.

In *La castidad ¿posible?*, he writes:

In any event, many people are disturbed when faced with this type of imagination, incapable to determine their degree of consent (and feeding, often, unhealthy scruples).

To them Father Groeschel suggests a practical examination of three questions:

a) Have I voluntarily increased my imagination?
b) Have I physically responded to it, either through voluntary sexual stimulation or acts to increase fantasy, for example, by looking at provocative objects?

c) When I realized what I was doing, did I refuse to direct my attention to something else?

If the answer to all these questions (especially the last one) is clearly and unequivocally yes, then I think – says said author [Groschel] – that the person is guilty (...) Without an affirmative answer to these questions, I would presume that nothing morally wrong was done.' You can not commit a mortal sin in a purely accidental way."[1]

"That enemy of our nature is the devil," writes Casanovas, "that lion who prowls around looking for someone to devour. Even more personal, the devil is each one of the temptations that comes to us. If we are filled with the Ignatian spirit, we will easily overcome them, but, if we are frightened or cowardly, they will conquer us."

[326] Our enemy may also be compared in his manner of acting to a false lover. He seeks to remain hidden and does not want to be discovered. If such a lover speaks with evil intention to the daughter of a good father, or to the wife of a good husband, and seeks to seduce them, he wants his words and solicitations kept secret. He is greatly displeased if his evil suggestions and depraved intentions are revealed by the daughter to her father, or by the wife to her husband. Then he readily sees he will not succeed in what he has begun. In the same way, when the enemy of our human nature tempts a just soul with his wiles and seductions, he earnestly desires that they be received secretly and kept secret. But if one manifests them to a confessor, or to some other spiritual person who understands his deceits and malicious designs, the evil one is very much vexed. For he knows that he cannot succeed in his evil undertaking, once his evident deceits have been revealed.

"Our enemy has no sense of nobility, nor how to be upfront and frank. Those who are beginners need to be led by the hand by their superiors and directors, just like little children need help walking and so hold on to their parents' hands. However, we must keep in mind that our parents will never know the temptations that we are suffering if we don't reveal them to them with honesty and trust. Hence it follows that the devil's treachery consists in closing our mouths and convincing us that we're doing just fine by going it alone. These suggestions to keep our mouths shut are born from embarrassment, shrinking, and vain fear, and sometimes from presumption and exaggerated self-confidence. We must open our hearts and present these imaginations, and the devil and the temptation will take flight."

---

1. 73 in the cited text.

** A deceitful lover likes to work in silence. When we reveal these things humbly to our confessor or spiritual director, they often disappear.

Here's a text from Saint Therese of Lisieux, taken from *Story of a Soul*, that describes this perfectly; it's a text that we cited partially earlier, when we were talking about *desolation* and what it does to us:

"Shortly before my profession I received the Holy Father's blessing, through the hands of Brother Simeon; and this precious Blessing undoubtedly helped me through the most terrible storm of my whole life.

On the eve of the great day, instead of being filled with the customary sweetness, my vocation suddenly seemed to me as unreal as a dream. The devil—for it was he—made me feel sure that I was wholly unsuited for life in the Carmel, and that I was deceiving my superiors by entering on a way to which I was not called. The darkness was so bewildering that I understood but one thing—I had no religious vocation, and must return to the world (!!!! This is Saint Therese of Lisieux we're talking about! The saint, doctor of the Church, co-patroness of the missions! She only "understood" one thing, and it was completely and utterly wrong! *That's* how the devil works!). I cannot describe the agony I endured. What was I to do in such a difficulty? I chose the right course, deciding to tell my Novice Mistress of the temptation without delay. I sent for her to come out of choir, and though full of confusion, I confessed the state of my soul. Fortunately she saw more clearly than I did, and reassured me completely by laughing frankly at my story. The devil was put to instant flight by my humble avowal; what he wanted was to keep me from speaking, and thus draw me into his snares. But it was my turn now to ensnare him, for, to make my humiliation more complete, I also told you everything, dear Mother, and your consoling words dispelled my last fears.

[327] The conduct of our enemy may also be compared to the tactics of a leader intent upon seizing and plundering a position he desires. A commander and leader of an army will encamp, explore the fortifications and defenses of the stronghold, and attack at the weakest point. In the same way, the enemy of our human nature investigates from every side all our virtues, theological, cardinal and moral. Where he finds the defenses of eternal salvation weakest and most deficient, there he attacks and tries to take us by storm.

"Our enemy," writes Casanovas, "has the cleverness of a thief, and he knows the best time and place to attack us. He knows perfectly well our weak points of our supernatural life, and he assaults us wherever we are least careful. We must be attentive and cautious. If the head of the household knew when the thief was coming, he would stay awake waiting so that he didn't get into the house to steal. We must also be awake and make a good review of all the possible entrances, all the possible doors in the house of our soul so that the devil cannot enter in and find us unprepared."

This is a two-fold implication for us: First, know yourself! If you tend to pride, know that the devil will use that and play off of it. Have a response prepared.

At the same time, use his attacks to your advantage. If he's tempting you in some way, see why that is. He sees a weakness there that he wants to exploit. Use his attacks to find your weaknesses and strengthen them.

FIRST WEEK

Homilies

Homily for the Start of the Exercises

If we read carefully the history of the Paris Foreign Missions Society, one of the great Catholic missionary organizations of the past three centuries, we find a ritual, a departure ceremony for priests leaving for their assignments in foreign lands, that is at once haunting and strangely beautiful.[1]

On the night before or even the very night when the new missionaries were to depart for their missions, they would all gather in the seminary chapel with their family, friends, and fellow seminarians. It would be their last opportunity to pray night prayer all together. Afterwards, an experienced missionary who had recently returned from the missions would give them a brief exhortation, encouraging them to be faithful to God and to their vocations. When he had finished, the missionaries would climb the steps to the altar and, standing in front of the tabernacle, they would turn and face the congregation. Then, slowly, starting with the other seminarians and then family and friends, one by one, those gathered would climb the steps to the altar and, kneeling down, would kiss the feet of the missionaries. Only God knows how many of these missionaries received that veneration of their feet, something similar to the veneration of hands we have after each ordination; for some, it would be the *proto*-veneration of their relics, the foretaste of the kiss of victory.

The reason for this particular veneration can be found in the anthem that the choir would sing during the ceremony: *Quam speciosi pedes evangelizantium pacem, evangelizantium bona! How beautiful are the feet of them that preach the gospel of peace, of them that bring glad tidings!*

The phrase is adapted from Saint Paul's letter to the Romans (10:13-15), in a passage where he explains the need for missionaries in the first place; he writes: "'Everyone who calls on the name of the Lord will be saved.' But how can they call on Him in whom they have not believed? And how can they believe in Him of whom they have not heard? And how can they hear without

---

1. For details on this ceremony, see Rev. T. J. Mulvey's article "The Departure of Missionaries," in *The Sacred Heart Review*, Volume 21, Number 5, 28 January 1899. Most specifically, we can read about St. Theopane Vénard's experience in Walsh, James. *A Modern Martyr: Theophane Vénard* (Maryknoll, NY: Catholic Foreign Mission Society of America, 1913): 78-79.

someone to preach? And how can people preach unless they are sent? As it is written, 'How beautiful are the feet of those who bring [the] good news!'" God, who calls the missionary in the first place, by that very call sets off a chain reaction: He sends the missionary, who preaches so people can hear and believe and thus call on the Lord's name and be saved. How blessed is the one that God calls to such a task!

As Saint Paul points out, though, that phrase isn't an original idea; he's quoting the prophet Isaiah (52:7). This, then, is an old truth, and one that is worth meditating upon: how beautiful it is to be a missionary! How beautiful is the missionary vocation! As we make our way through this first week of the Exercises, let us seek out all those attachments that keep us from following God fully. These things keep us from fully living out our vocations, and embracing the beauty of the calling that is ours.

Let us ask through the intercession of Mary, whose beauty is so great that, as Saint Bernadette recounts, "to see her again one would be willing to die," for the grace to die to ourselves so as to live fully in Christ and in our vocations.

Homily for the Principal and Foundation

Today, if you go to the town of Loyola, you can still see the castle that belonged to Saint Ignatius's family. Although there is a massive church next door now, the castle itself looks pretty much like it did in the 16th century: walls that are six feet thick, and a beautiful red brickwork on the upper part, where his family would have lived.

Tucked up on the fourth floor is the bedroom where Ignatius recovered from his injury. Where his sickbed used to be, there is now a canopy and a statue of the saint, with a book in one hand, and his eyes turning towards Heaven. On one of the beams overlooking the statue, there is an inscription painted in gold: *Aquí se entregó a Dios Iñigo de Loyola, Here Ignatius of Loyola surrendered himself to God.*[1]

It's sort of an understatement for the conversion of one of the greatest missionary saints the Church has ever seen. For as impressive as the castle is, and as great as everything around it might be, what really matters is what happened in that room. There was no fanfare, no fireworks, no nothing, just Ignatius, God, and a desire for holiness.

As we make our way through the first week of the Exercises, let us go into our inner rooms, pray, and seek God with all our hearts, so that it could be read over the door to our rooms: *Here I surrendered myself to God.* May the Blessed Virgin Mary help us to obtain this grace.

---

1. Cf. James Martin, *The Jesuit Guide to (Almost) Everything: A Spirituality for Real Life,* 13. I only take the description of the room from him!

Homily on the Cost of Sin

What is the most expensive thing in the world? If you ask the mass media, or the Wall Street Journal, you will be given a number of different items that are "the most expensive in the world." The world's most expensive watch, for instance, is valued at 55 million dollars: it is a "platinum quartz watch encrusted in yellow, pink, blue, gray, and orange diamonds in different cuts." The world's most expensive car is the 1963 Ferrari 250 GTO; there are only 39 of them in the world, so each one alone is valued at 70 million dollars. The world's most expensive house is in Mumbai, with 27 floors, a garage for 168 cars, three helipads, and even a temple (to what god, I might add?); the house is worth 2 billion dollars. That's cheap, though, in comparison to the world's most expensive yacht, which boasts a master bedroom with a wall made of meteorites and a statue made from the bones of a T-Rex and is valued at 4.5 billion dollars.

But really, despite what businessmen or Wall Street might say, perhaps the most expensive thing in the world is sin. On one hand, as we've meditated last night and will continue to do so, we can see the terrible, terrible price that the sins of the angels, of Adam and Eve, and a soul condemned paid. A watch does no good in hell, where time is measured by eternity, and a car can't evade the presence of Satan and the damned. The only house really worth having is one in Heaven, and dinosaur bones remind us of the fate of all living beings, but they can't help us to escape it. In any case, the only boat to be taken is the one that floats down the River Styx. They would think little of paying 4.5 billion dollars if they could only have grace and peace restored to them. On the other hand, Someone did pay the price for our sins: Jesus Christ, whose precious blood was shed for us, a blood that, to borrow a phrase from C. S. Lewis, each drop of which was "more precious than the Earth would be if it was a single solid diamond."

As we continue to meditate on the three sins, let us ask, through the intercession of Mary, the Mother of Jesus, for the grace to see how the disordered use of creatures and rejection of the principal and foundation come at a cost that is too high for us to pay. If we can't buy a four billion dollar yacht, even less can we pay the price of sin and disobedience.

Homily on Our Sins and God's Mercy

As we continue to mediate on our own sins, it is worthwhile to consider the relation between God's mercy and our sinfulness.

We'll do this again in one of the meditations, considering just how great God's mercy is, but, for now, we will look only at our own sinfulness. Some people claim, and it's very popular now, that our God is merciful, so merciful in fact that there can't be anything like sin. Well, our God is merciful; this is true.

The problem is that mercy implies or requires something or someone to have mercy on. As Aquinas defines it, mercy means to feel compassion at another's misery and to help alleviate if possible. If we make God so merciful that sin is no more, that there's no right or wrong, then we take away the reason why God is merciful in the first place: by eliminating sin, we eliminate mercy, and God, rather than being a Father, becomes something quite different. C. S. Lewis describes the situation this way:

> "By the goodness of God we mean nowadays almost exclusively His lovingness; and in this way we may be right. And by Love, in this context, most of us mean kindness—the desire to see others than the self happy; not happy in this way or in that, but just happy. What would really satisfy us would be a God who said of anything we happened to like doing, 'What does it matter so long as they are contented?' We want, in fact, not so much a Father in Heaven as a grandfather in Heaven—a senile benevolence, who, as they say, 'liked to see young people enjoying themselves,' and whose plan for the universe was simply that it might be said at the end of each day, 'a good time was had by all. Not many people, I admit, would formulate a theology in precisely those terms: but a conception not very different lurks at the back of many minds. I do not claim to be an exception: I should very much like to live in a universe which as governed on such lines. But since it is abundantly clear that I don't, and since I have reason to believe, nevertheless, that God is Love, I conclude that my conception of love needs correction."

Lewis's point is that if we remove the idea of sin from mercy, God the Father becomes no father at all, and it is only by experiencing God the Father's mercy ourselves that we can hope to share it with others. We can ask ourselves, how do we live our experience of God's mercy? Do we recognize our own sinfulness? Our awareness of our own sinfulness and our personal experience of God's mercy leads us to witness to both the reality of sin and the reality of God's mercy, a mercy that embraces everyone but forces itself on no one.

Let us pray, through the intercession of Mary, Mother of Mercy, for the grace to grow in the awareness of our own sinfulness so as to more fully embrace God's mercy.

SECOND WEEK

Meditations and Contemplations

The Call of Christ the King
In the Book of the Exercises: [91-100]

Usual Preparation Prayer.

First Prelude: The composition of Place: This is a mental representation of the place. Here it will be to see in imagination the synagogues, villages, and towns where Christ our Lord preached.

Second Prelude: The Petition I will ask for the grace I desire. Here, it will be to ask of our Lord the grace not to be deaf to His call, but prompt and diligent to accomplish His most holy will. – "Knowing that His holy will is our sanctification in this life, we look to the example of Jesus Christ, to become prompt and diligent to do God's will, to bring out in reality the work of changing my life and ordering myself in my acts and operations."[1]

"The contemplation on the Kingdom of Christ has been accurately called the heart of Ignatian spirituality," says Servant of God Fr. John Hardon. "It epitomizes two ideals: . . . The first is a willingness to go beyond mediocrity in the service of Christ, the Son of God; the second a projection of personal love into the world outside, so that other souls may also 'yield a higher than ordinary service to Christ their King.'"[2]

Ignatius breaks this contemplation into two parts, the first which is easier to visualize, and then this will help when we compare this with Christ the King. Ignatius himself says that this "will help us to contemplate the life of the eternal king." Remember, to contemplate means to be more involved in the scene, to be a player in it. Before we were meditating with our understanding, our memory, and our will; now, properly speaking, we have a contemplation, meaning, we are involving ourselves in the scene. What are they saying? What are they doing?

1. Calveras, *Practica intensiva*, 187.
2. Fr. John Hardon, SJ.

[092] I can place before my mind a human king or leader chosen by God our Lord Himself, to whom all Christian princes and people pay homage and obedience.

[093] This will be to consider the address this king makes to all His subjects, with the words: "It is my will to conquer all the lands of the infidel. Therefore, whoever wishes to join with me in this enterprise must be content with the same food, drink, clothing, etc. as mine. So, too, he must work with me by day, and watch with me by night, etc., that as he has had a share in the toil with me, afterwards, he may share in the victory with me."

[094] Consider what the answer of good subjects ought to be to a king so generous and noble-minded, and consequently, if anyone would refuse the invitation of such a king, how justly he would deserve to be condemned by the whole world, and looked upon as an ignoble knight.

Notice, the earthly king is undertaking a *personal* campaign against his enemies, and he has called *everyone* to take part, to fight next to him. The response to the call of this king should be that every man, woman, and child offers themselves to fight with him, and not only to *work with their whole being*, fighting against anything that might get in the way, but even *in spite of humiliations, poverty, and suffering.*[3]

For us, in our day and age, it can be difficult to think of Catholic kings who inspire, which is important, because we want to have a clear image in our minds. For this, perhaps the best examples we can think of are Saint Joan of Arc and Saint John Paul the Second.

For Saint Joan of Arc, we have an abundance of testimonies from her contemporaries, who bore witness to her holiness at her retrial. For instance, regarding the privations that Ignatius mentions, Joan was inspiring: although she was young and by all accounts tiny in size, she wore a heavy suit of armor and stayed in the saddle all day, day after day, sometimes even sleeping through the night in her armor. One of her fellow officers noted that through the long weeks of her campaigns she "slept on the straw" as any soldier would without the least complaint. In fact, she never demanded anything special: she was completely simple.

What is perhaps more impressive, though, is the effect she had on her troops. Single-handedly, she raised the morale of the French army and encouraged them to fight as never before. As one of the officer recounted, "I swear

---

3. Calveras, *Practica intensiva*, 188.

that the English, two hundred of whom had previously been sufficient to rout eight hundred or a thousand of the royal army, from that moment became so powerless that four or five hundred soldiers and men at arms could fight against what seemed to be the whole force of England."

Another wrote that King Charles had no money to pay the army; nonetheless, nobles and commoners of all ranks "did not refuse to go with and serve him for that journey in the Maid's company, saying that wherever she went they would go." A young French knight named Guy de Laval wrote a letter home to his mother saying that in the army "never before did men go with a better will to a task than they go to this one." He went on to tell his mother to sell and mortgage his lands if need be to raise troops for the cause.

Even the simplest peasants followed her example. In parts of France occupied by the English, the previously docile peasants rose up in partisan resistance as word of Joan's exploits spread. In those parts of France under the rule of the eventual King, peasants came in droves, of their own volition, to join an army that ostensibly belonged to Charles but that in its soul belonged to Joan. Popular eagerness to fight for France and for Joan became so intense that a force of peasants attempted to storm the walls of Jargeau even before Joan arrived with the army. The peasants were routed, but when Joan came on the scene, so did victory.

Joan was often the first to scale walls, and, if her troops ever began to flee, she would simply turn and charge the enemy to inspire them back to the fight. Once, while attacking, she was hit with an arrow. When she saw how her troops became nervous, she pulled out the arrow and, once the bleeding stopped, continued fighting. No difficulties, no challenges stopped her campaign.

We can also think of Pope Saint John Paul the Great: when he returned to Poland for his first apostolic visit on June 1-10, 1979, fully two-thirds of Poland's population came to see him. Bear in mind that the Poles had suffered greatly during the World Wars, and now under Communism. Yet, on June 2nd, in Victory Square in the Old City in Warsaw, the pope held a mass, and gave what George Weigel called the greatest sermon of his life.

Why, the pope asked, had God lifted a Pole to the papacy? Perhaps it was because of how Poland had suffered for centuries, and through the 20th century had become "the land of a particularly responsible witness" to God. The people of Poland, he suggested, had been chosen for a great role, to understand, humbly but surely, that they were the repository of a special "witness of His cross and His resurrection." He asked if the people of Poland accepted the obligations of such a role in history.

The crowd responded with thunder. "We want God!" they shouted, together. "We want God!" For 11 minutes, the Pope had to stop his homily, because the crowd was cheering so loudly. Mikhail Gorbachev later said that that visit was the beginning of the end of the Soviet Union, and many historians call that visit "nine days that changed the world."

There were tons of sacrifices involved for the Polish people. In his homily the pope alluded to the tomb of the Unknown Solider nearby, and said, "The history of the motherland written through the tomb of an Unknown Soldier! I wish to kneel before this tomb to venerate every seed that falls into the earth and dies and thus bears fruit. It may be the seed of the blood of a soldier shed on the battlefield, or the sacrifice of martyrdom in concentration camps or in prisons. It may be the seed of hard daily toil, with the sweat of one's brow, in the fields, the workshop, the mine, the foundries and the factories. It may be the seed of the love of parents who do not refuse to give life to a new human being and undertake the whole of the task of bringing him up. It may be the seed of creative work in the universities, the higher institutes, the libraries and the places where the national culture is built. It may be the seed of prayer, of service of the sick, the suffering, the abandoned—'all that of which Poland is made.'"

In other words, this is the sacrifice you have to make; if you want God, if you really want Him, you must want and love sacrifice.

These are the sorts of leaders that we're talking about.

We can imagine either case, either listening in the camp to Joan of Arc, or being a part of that crowd with Pope John Paul the Second. With a little modification, we can hear what Saint Ignatius has them say: "See how these leaders speak to their people, saying: "It is my will to conquer all the land of unbelievers. Therefore, whoever would like to come with me is to be content to eat as I, and also to drink and dress, etc., as I; likewise he is to labor like me in the day and watch in the night, etc., that so afterwards he may have part with me in the victory, as he has had it in the labors." Joan wants to reconquer France; the Pope wants his people not to be afraid, to trust in God and bear witness to His power.

Now, try to hear the answer of those who are standing beside this leader. Try to see the two very different reactions:

First of all, the cowardice of some, of those who try to hide themselves from the presence of these holy people. Try to hear the weak arguments that they set. "I am too young or I am too old or too . . . whatever [any adjective will do]." "I don't know if I can endure something so long!" "Many people need me here…" "I never left the country, how I can go to a place that I don't know…"

"We don't know what will happen." "What if I lose everything?" "What if I die?" "What will the future hold for me?"

Try to see their faces, try to see if they are happy or they are sad. Try to hear the commentaries of others about them: "What sort of people are these? Do they not get it? Don't they see what's at stake? Don't they see who's leading them?"

Later, you can see the second group. People with light in their eyes, and with blood in their veins, noble people whose hearts are on fire. And, what is it to be noble?? It is to have heart. They can give themselves because they fully possess themselves. They're the ones who know what things in their lives are worth dying for, worth giving up everything for, worth surrendering their time, talents, and even their very lives for.

These noble princes, hearing the words of the holy leaders, cannot say any other words than these: "Serviam . . . I will serve."

CHRIST THE KING

Ignatius then tells us to apply the example of the earthly king to Christ our Lord.

[095] If such a summons of an earthly king to his subjects deserves our attention, how much more worthy of consideration is Christ our Lord, the Eternal King, before whom is assembled the whole world. To all His summons goes forth, and to each one in particular He addresses the words: "It is my will to conquer the whole world and all my enemies, and thus to enter into the glory of my Father. Therefore, whoever wishes to join me in this enterprise must be willing to labor with me, that by following me in suffering, he may follow me in glory."

[096] Consider that all persons who have judgment and reason will offer themselves entirely for this work.

"The call of the temporal king was fictional; no earthly king has called us to overcome his enemies, we weren't with Joan of Arc or in the crowds with John Paul II. What Christ is asking of us, the call of Christ the King, however, is extremely real and always in effect; His kingdom and His universal reign are also real. His call is universal, to everyone, as if He had them all in front of Him, but also to each and every one of us in particular."[4]

His will is to conquer the whole world, and our lives are part of this world; that's where He wants and needs to start His conquest. And each aspect of

4. Calveras, *Practica intensiva*, 194.

our lives has to be conquered. To follow Him means imitation. It is not an invitation simply to go behind. It is an invitation to imitate Him: to live as He lives. Ignatius tells us "Consider that all persons who have judgment and reason will offer themselves entirely for this work," meaning, if we have really processed the Principle and Foundation, if I have really assimilated the truths contained therein, my judgment and my reason see that it is only logically to decide to follow Christ. It's not rocket science; it's not the fruit of profound years of study. It's simply reasonable.

"Jesus Christ, our redeemer, has done *so much to save us*. He came to earth, suffered, and died to save me from my sins, but He has done even more: He is constantly working for my sanctification. Moreover, He doesn't just work for me; *He Himself is my example*. He shows me how to live, on one hand, because He Himself overcame all manner of difficulties to save me and work my sanctification, suffering from Bethlehem to Calvary, poverty, humiliations, sufferings, but also because He is the most perfect model of all virtues. His actions are a model for me." This is why, for the rest of the Exercises, we follow Christ's life, but it all begins here, with His call to us: *Follow me!*

What does it mean *to follow Christ*? To follow Him means renunciations: the rich young man understood this point perfectly, and "on hearing the invitation of Jesus, he went away sad for he had many possessions" (Mt 19:22; cf. Mk 10:22).

To follow him means sacrifice and sometimes the supreme sacrifice. We have to be aware of this: following Christ will mean sacrifices, privations, difficulties, and challenges, but we can't give up or stop because of them! Christ didn't give up, and He warns us about it. This is why He says to his disciples, "If any man would come after me, let him deny himself and take up his cross and follow me. For whoever would save his life will lose it; and whoever loses his life for my sake will save it . . ." (Mt 16:24-25).

This is what Saint Louis Marie de Montfort points out in his *Letter to the Friends of the Cross*: "You are the members of Christ, a wonderful honor indeed, but one which entails suffering. If the Head is crowned with thorns, can the members expect to be crowned with roses? If the Head is jeered at and covered with dust on the road to Calvary, can the members expect to be sprinkled with perfumes on a throne? If the Head has no pillow on which to rest, can the members expect to recline on feathers and down? That would be unthinkable!

No, no, my dear Companions of the Cross, do not deceive yourselves. Those Christians you see everywhere, fashionably dressed, fastidious in manner, full of importance and dignity, are not real disciples, real members of Christ crucified. To think they are would be an insult to our thorn-crowned

Head and to the truth of the Gospel. How many so-called Christians imagine they are members of our Savior when in reality they are his treacherous persecutors, for while they make the sign of the cross with their hand, in their hearts they are its enemies!

If you are guided by the same spirit, if you live the same life as Jesus, your thorn-crowned Head, you must expect only thorns, lashes and nails; that is, nothing but the cross; for the disciple must be treated like the master and the members like the Head. And if you were to be offered, as was St. Catherine of Siena, a crown of thorns and one of roses, you should, like her, choose the crown of thorns without hesitation and press it upon your head, so as to be like Christ."

What is our response to be? "How should subjects respond to the invitation of a king who is at once so generous to invite others to come, and so human: He doesn't command us, but rather invites, rather pleads with us, begs us, to come join Him." We can't even imagine rejecting that call; it would be illogical and be the greatest mistake of our lives, since our lives are *meant for this*, to follow Christ. To do this, is simply to follow right reason and judgment.

[097] Those who wish to give greater proof of their love, and to distinguish themselves in whatever concerns the service of the eternal King and the Lord of all, will not only offer themselves entirely for the work, but will act against their sensuality and carnal and worldly love, and make offerings of greater value and of more importance in words such as these:

But, Ignatius tells us here, among these who simply follow Christ, there are some who will stand out; they won't simply be a solider on the field, but a leader, a hero, an outstanding warrior. These are the ones who don't simply go to war, which is only logical, but rather give themselves wholeheartedly to the cause.

In a lot of tasks, most tasks, you can decide how you do them. You can do your task, get the job done OK, and that's that. Here, you can go forth in Christ's service, following Him, but not giving yourself entirely. You can let obstacles and impediments get in the way, little attachments here and there.

Sensuality is an inordinate love of this world or the things of this world. It might be a disordered inclination to the satisfactions of the exterior and interior senses, or a sensual love that rejects physical pain and, even worse, interior work, or it could be a carnal love that rejects work and fatigue, the inconveniences of hunger and thirst, the privations of poverty, vain honor, and show. In the very moment of decisions worldly things cry: "You cannot live without us", "You don't know how to live without us.", "You won't be able to."

When the battle begins, or the struggle breaks out, how often our attachments come calling to us!

The main problem is that "this – go forward …" means to die, and you are sure of this. But you came to this battlefield to give up your life, because you love the cause, and you think that is worth dying for. If something is worth living for, it must be worth dying for, and, if it's worth dying for, it's worth dying the daily death, the slow martyrdom, of giving up anything and everything that prevents us from giving ourselves entirely.

Then, only those who have heart will go forward with this prayer in their lips:

[098] Eternal Lord of all things, in the presence of Your infinite goodness, and of Your glorious mother, and of all the saints of Your heavenly court, this is the offering of myself which I make with Your favor and help. I protest that it is my earnest desire and my deliberate choice, provided only it is for Your greater service and praise, to imitate You in bearing all wrongs and all abuse and all poverty, both actual and spiritual, should Your most holy majesty deign to choose and admit me to such a state and way of life.

There is no greater proof. This is the evangelical proof of love, "No man has greater love than this, that a man lay down his life for his friends." (John 15: 13). Looking at the cross of our King and Lord, we are encouraged to renounce ourselves, to take up our cross daily and walk behind him.

How do I respond to Christ's invitation? Am I satisfied with just offering *myself* to the task, or with I *work with my works*, signing up to go in the front lines, next to Christ, in poverty and humiliations? Will I be a hero in this war, or just another one of the soldiers? Christ might have millions of soldiers, but what He needs, and what He is asking for, is heroes. The choice, and the response, is left up to us.

[099]
Note I.

This exercise should be gone through twice during the day, that is, in the morning on rising, and an hour before dinner, or before supper.

[100]
Note II.

During the Second Week and thereafter, it will be very profitable to read some passages from the *Imitation of Christ*, or from the Gospels, and from the *Lives of the Saints*.

The Incarnation [101-109], [262]

[101]: This is a contemplation on the Incarnation. After the preparatory prayer and three preludes, there are three points and a colloquy

Usual Preparation Prayer.

First Prelude. This will consist in calling to mind the history of the subject I have to contemplate. Here it will be how the Three Divine Persons look down upon the whole expanse or circuit of all the earth, filled with human beings. Since They see that all are going down to hell, They decree in Their eternity that the Second Person should become man to save the human race. So when the fullness of time had come, They send the Angel Gabriel to our Lady. Cf. # 262.

Second Prelude. This is a mental representation of the place. It will be here to see the great extent of the surface of the earth, inhabited by so many different peoples, and especially to see the house and room of our Lady in the city of Nazareth in the province of Galilee.

Third Prelude. The Petition: This is to ask for what I desire. Here it will be to ask for an intimate – meaning, profoundly felt and appreciated – knowledge of our Lord – meaning of His person, His divinity and His humanity, His interior and exterior –who has become man for me – meaning, that He went ahead of me, taking on the most difficult tasks, carrying the cross – that I may love Him more and follow Him more closely – by fighting against my carnal, sensual, and worldly loves and perfecting my actions by following His example.

For this contemplation on the Incarnation, Ignatius has us examine a sort of triptych, with the same three scenes three times each: in the first scene, we consider the earth, where the problems are, then the Three Divine Persons, who are "above the world" and who are the ones to come up with a solution because they love us, and then the scene of the Annunciation, back down to the world and wherein the solution is received. We'll see the scenes, then hear the scenes, and then consider the actions of those involved. Obviously, each time, then, we'll be seeing the scene, and adding more elements. It's a sort of increasing intensity as we go back and see the scene again, adding more elements and details.

[106]: First Point: "This will be to see the different persons: First, those on the face of the earth, in such great diversity in dress and in manner of acting. Some are white, some black; some at peace, and some at war; some weeping, some laughing; some well, some sick; some coming into the world, and some dying; etc.

Secondly, I will see and consider the Three Divine Persons seated on the royal dais or throne of the Divine Majesty. They look down upon the whole surface of the earth, and behold all nations in great blindness, going down to death and descending into hell.

Thirdly, I will see our Lady and the angel saluting her.

I will reflect upon this to draw profit from what I *see*."

Let us focus now on what is *seen* in this mediation. Consider the awful state that our world was in after the fall: there are so many people, all over the planet, all engaged in what we could call the "everyday drama of life": some are at peace, some at war, some weeping, laughing, and the like. They are just going about their business, or so they think. They are just going about their business, but really this is the slow, silent path to hell. See how in their blindness they commit any number of sins, how they live in great forgetfulness of God, ignorant of the Trinity's great love for them. They simply walk right into the yawning gates of Hell, which have opened up for them and are happy to receive them. "The safest road to hell," wrote C. S. Lewis, "is the gradual one – the gentle slope, soft underfoot, without sudden turning, without milestones, without signposts." "See their blindness, how they seek happiness only in this world, having forgotten God and surrendered themselves over to their passions; in this way their evil constantly increases, their awful deeds pile up, and then they die and fall into the endless pit of misery."[1]

Notice the Trinity's great mercy: what do They see when They look upon the earth? In Genesis (6:5-6) we read "When the LORD saw how great the wickedness of human beings was on earth, and how every desire that their heart conceived was always nothing but evil, the LORD regretted making human beings on the earth, and his heart was grieved." Or, as Ps 53 reads (3-4): "God looks out from the heavens upon the children of Adam, to see if there is a discerning person who is seeking God. All have gone astray; each one is altogether perverse. There is not one who does what is good, not even one."

1. Cf. Calveras, *Practica intensiva*, 220.

Imagine the pain and sorrow, as we read in the book of Job (15:15-16): "If the heavens are not without blame in his sight, how much less so is the abominable and corrupt: people who drink in iniquity like water!"

However, the Trinity looks down, not to punish, but to do good, to provide a remedy: They "behold all nations in great blindness, going down to death and descending into hell." Rather than leave them to this fate, they send the Second person of the Trinity, the Son, to "save sinners" by going down among them, to live among them in that world of sorrow, to call them back to knowledge and love of God. "The Divine Persons focus their attention, not on the variety of circumstances or the horror of sins, but rather on the only thing that matters: the salvation of men, and to do it, not simply by an act of will, but in the most loving way possible. God would become man, even though it would cost Him dearly. For this, here He takes the first step, becoming like us in all things but sin, and is enclosed in the womb of the Virgin Mary.

See how Gabriel comes to announce the news: see how he comes to a lowly young woman, a poor woman, who, simple and modest, receives Him. See the lowliness of her house, her simple dwelling, her beauty. "The angel is diligent and faithful to his mission; Mary's love is for purity and for prudence; she doesn't ask unnecessary questions, and only later does she ask for the needed clarifications. She is humble, docile to God's will, and she, in her humility, becomes the Mother of God."

[107]: Second Point: "This will be to listen to what the persons on the face of the earth say, that is, how they speak to one another, swear and blaspheme, etc. I will also hear what the Divine Persons say, that is, 'Let us work the redemption of the human race,' etc. Then I will listen to what the angel and our Lady say. Finally, I will reflect upon all I hear to draw profit from their words."

Let us now consider what is *heard* in that scene. Again, notice the contrast: how much hatred fills the world! Anger against each other, anger against the heavens, and anger and hatred against God Himself, who is the most loveable of all! How many lies are told, serious lies that cause scandal, lies that deprive the poor of what is theirs, lies that shatter families, lies that lead to murder! Words of seduction, words of treason, gossip, false rumors meant to inspire fear, betrayals, whispers of temptations, murmurs against the Almighty and His servants . . . and we hear all of these words! Imagine all the sins of the tongue! In the book of Proverbs (18:21) we're told that "Death and life are in the power of the tongue; those who choose one shall eat its fruit." Men had chosen death, and had eaten the fruit of eternal death. What power words have! These men do not realize what they are doing; in their words, they only think of obtaining what they desire for this life, what their passions clamor for: lies, blasphemies, gossip . . . all for pleasure or advantage in this world. That's all.

And yet, God has His words as well. He has "the words of eternal life." Hear the conversation between the Trinity: "Let us work the redemption of the human race." "Let us work the redemption of the human race!" It's as though they don't hear those horrible blasphemies, as though they ignore man's horrible crimes, as though they have covered their ears when faced with those sad diatribes! What mercy! Again, their sole concern is to save man, even in spite of his evil deeds.

Imagine their words: as the prophet Jeremiah recalls (29:11): "For I know well the plans I have in mind for you, plans for your welfare and not for woe, so as to give you a future of hope." Imagine them speaking amongst themselves, all the while concerned for man, although they are perfectly happy in Heaven! What compassion! Consider the words of Isaiah (6:8): "I heard the voice of the Lord saying, "Whom shall I send? Who will go for us?" Then Christ speaks: "Here I am," He said; "send me!", "As is written of me in the scroll, 'Behold, I come to do your will, O God' (Heb 10:9).

In the midst of all the death-dealing words of men, the Word of God comes to earth to save men. As Saint Athanasius writes, Christ is "the word of the good God, who is God in His own right. The Word is different from all created things: He is the unique Word belonging only to the good Father. This is the Word that created this whole world and enlightens it by His loving wisdom."

What power words have! The angel Gabriel comes to Mary, and speaking His words of greeting, asks her to conceive the Word of God, the remedy from Heaven. As Saint Bernard of Clairvaux urges our Lady, "Answer with a word, receive the Word of God. Speak your own word, conceive the divine Word. Breathe a passing word, embrace the eternal Word." Mary, full of charity and freedom, responds, "Fiat. Be it done unto me according to your word."

What power words have! Words can bring condemnation, but now the Word comes to bring life and salvation!

[108]: Third Point: "This will be to consider what the persons on the face of the earth do, for example, wound, kill, and go down to hell. Also, what the Divine Persons do, namely, work the most holy Incarnation, etc. Likewise, what the Angel and our Lady do; how the Angel carries out his office of ambassador; and how our Lady humbles herself, and offers thanks to the Divine Majesty.

Then, I shall reflect upon all to draw some fruit from each of these details." So now we have the vision of the greatest intensity: not only do we see the scene, not only do we hear it, but now we're contemplating the actions of those here.

Let us consider the *actions* of those in this scene. Consider the violence of those on the face of the earth, how, having forgotten God, men and women give into violence. They wound and kill, in so many different ways: they wound and kill the body, of course, but they also wound and kill minds by filling them with lies and hatred, blinding them to truth and goodness. They wound and kill spirits, enslaving them to sin and its seductions. Worst of all, they wound and kill souls, binding them under the burden of mortal sin so they end up in hell. See more clearly now the evils deeds that they do, and how they are dragged down into hell. Again, all these actions for a temporal benefit, but they are ignorant of their last end, what they should really be doing!

What does the Trinity do? Upon seeing the sad state of man, rather than punish, They also begin to act, but to *save* men and women from their fate. See how the Son, although perfectly happy in Heaven and with no need of anything, agrees to become incarnate on the earth, to take a human nature, in order to show men and women the way back to God. Men and women have killed minds with lies and hatred, but Christ will fill them with the light of truth and charity. They have wounded and killed spirits, but Christ will break the bonds of sin and death. They have bound souls under mortal sin, but Christ will free them.

See how Christ comes, not as a king, not born of an earthly queen, but of a lowly maiden! The guilty will not be won back by blows or punishments, but by charity and patience. Christ assumes His human nature, not in a palace, not on a throne, but in poverty and humility.

See how His Mother humbly receives the angelic messenger. In the midst of her daily tasks, her humble work as a lowly maiden, the angel fulfills his task and Mary, full of charity and freedom, responds, "Fiat. Be it done until me according to your word."

Here, we have an excellent transition between the first and second weeks: we see the masses, ignorant of the principal and foundation, ignorant of the real purpose of their lives. Here, Christ becomes man precisely to direct us back to God and to show us the way to the Father, giving us an example to follow.

[109] Colloquy: The exercise should be closed with a colloquy. I will think over what I ought to say to the Three Divine Persons, or to the Eternal Word Incarnate, or to His Mother, our Lady. According to the light that I have received, I will beg for grace to follow and imitate more closely our Lord, who has just become man for me.

Close with an *Our Father*.

The Visitation of Our Lady to Elizabeth
[263] and [162]

Usual Preparatory Prayer.

First Prelude: The composition of Place: Here, we can imagine the scene as we find it in the Gospel (Lk 1:39-45): Mary as she makes her way quickly through the hill country, and arrives at the house of Elizabeth and Zechariah. We can see the simple house, with its most basic furnishing, everything simple, but nonetheless well cared for, and a house that exudes a love for God and for neighbor.

Second Prelude: The petition: This we can borrow from [104], the contemplation of the Incarnation, since the whole week has the same end. The petition "is to ask for what I desire. Here it will be to ask for an intimate knowledge of our Lord, who has become man for me, that I may love Him more and follow Him more closely."

The only thing Ignatius gives us here are three points at [263], based on Lk 1:39–56. They are as follows:

First Point: When our Lady visited Elizabeth, St. John the Baptist in his mother's womb knew the visit of our Lady. "And it came to pass that when Elizabeth heard the salutation of Mary, the babe in her womb leapt and Elizabeth was filled with the Holy Spirit, and she lifted up her voice with a loud cry and said, 'Blessed are you among women and blessed is the fruit of your womb.'"

Second Point: Our Lady chants the *Magnificat*, saying, "My soul magnifies the Lord."

Third Point: "Mary stayed with her about three months, and returned to her own home."

A contemplation on the Visitation of Mary to Elizabeth isn't always considered part of the Exercises. At point 162 he tells us: "Everyone, according to the time he wishes to devote to the contemplations of this Second Week, and according to his progress, may lengthen or shorten this Week. If he wishes to lengthen it, let him take the mysteries of the Visitation of our Lady to Elizabeth, the Shepherds, the Circumcision of the Child Jesus, the Three Kings, and also others.

If he wishes to shorten the Week, he may omit even some of the mysteries that have been assigned. For they serve here to afford an introduction and method for better and more complete meditation later." So, here we will, in fact, consider the Visitation.

In many of her biographies, authors recount that Saint Mother Teresa of Calcutta used to love to ask her fellow Missionaries of Charity: "Who was the first Missionary of Charity?" Oftentimes, the question was met with strange stares and the reply, "Well, you, Mother." To that, Mother Teresa would respond: "No; the Blessed Virgin Mary was the first Missionary of Charity, because she went in haste to serve as a handmaid, and not as the Mother of God."[1] "The moment Jesus came [into Mary's life]," the saint says, "she immediately went in haste to give Him to others."[2] "Mary is the model of all Christian in this scene, not only because she was practicing the most sublime virtue of charity, but also because she was bringing the very presence of Jesus with her, within her, to bring great joy and peace to the one whom she served."[3]

Perhaps the best way to consider this, the best way to orient our thoughts, is to consider what our *Directory of Spirituality* has to say at point 84; here we have more than enough material to contemplate. There we read: "In the womb, Jesus taught us to depend totally and completely on God through Mary. At the same time, Mary taught us the evangelical ministry of visitation. By 'carrying Him Who carried her,' she taught us that all our apostolic enthusiasm is to be founded in Him; she taught us to accomplish the things of God quickly; she taught us to serve our neighbor even in the simplest of tasks; she taught us to praise, thank, sing, and be joyful in the Almighty, Holy, Merciful, Saving and Faithful God, because God 'looked upon' her and did 'great things' – the Incarnation – in her, deploying His power, scattering the proud, casting down the mighty, filling the hungry, lifting up the lowly and protecting His servants forever." That is worth repeating. . . . There is more than enough there to consider for a contemplation.

Pope Saint John Paul II writes that "in the Visitation, St. Luke shows how the grace of the Incarnation, after filling Mary, brings salvation and joy to Elizabeth's house. The Savior of men, carried in his Mother's womb, pours out the Holy Spirit, revealing himself from the very start of his coming into the world."

---

1. Cf. *Come be My Light*, 313.

2. Cf., also citing M. Teresa: Catherine M. Odell, *Praying the Rosary for Intercession*.

3. Cf., alluding to the thoughts of M. Teresa: Susan Conroy, *Mother Teresa's Lessons of Love & Secrets of Sanctity*, 125.

In other words, as soon as Christ comes into the world, He brings joy and salvation to others. Even though He is doing it in a hidden way, since He can't be seen, His mere presence, the fact that He is there, is sufficient reason for joy. No matter in what, no matter where, no matter how awful or nasty the place is, humanly speaking, when Jesus comes, it becomes a place of light and joy.

The pope continues, "In describing Mary's departure for Judea, the Evangelist uses the verb 'anístemi,' which means 'to arise,' 'to start moving.' The same verb is used in the Gospels to indicate Jesus's Resurrection (Mk 8:31; 9:9,31; Lk 24:7, 46) or physical actions that imply a spiritual effort (Lk 5:27-28; 15:18,20), so it's likely that Luke wanted to stress the vigorous zeal which led Mary, under the inspiration of the Holy Spirit, to give the world its Savior.

The Gospel text also reports that Mary made the journey 'with haste' (Lk 1:39). Even the note 'into the hill country' (Lk 1:39), in the Lucan context, appears to be much more than a simple topographical indication, since it calls to mind the messenger of good news described in the Book of Isaiah: 'How beautiful upon the mountains are the feet of him who brings good tidings, who publishes peace, who brings good tidings of good, who publishes salvation, who says to Zion: 'Your God reigns' (Is 52:7)."[4] Thus far the Pope.

Note the enthusiasm, the way she goes about her mission. With Christ's presence within her, she *makes haste*. She isn't slow in her service of Christ. Remember the grace that we asked for in the contemplation on the call of Christ the King: "I will ask for the grace I desire. Here it will be to ask of our Lord the grace not to be deaf to His call, but prompt and diligent to accomplish His most holy will." See how Mary, compelled by Christ, since *the love of Christ compels us* (2 Cor 5:14-15), is prompt and diligent to carry out her mission of service.

The Pope continues: "Like St. Paul, who recognizes the fulfillment of this prophetic text in the preaching of the Gospel (Rom 10:15), St. Luke invites us to see Mary as the first 'evangelist,' who spreads the 'good news,' initiating the missionary journeys of her divine Son." That's a beautiful thought: *Mary initiates the missionary journeys of her Son*, because she takes Him with her in her womb.

Finally, Saint John Paul II concludes: "Lastly, the direction of the Blessed Virgin's journey is particularly significant: it will be from Galilee to Judea, like Jesus' missionary journey (cf. 9:51). Mary's visit to Elizabeth, in fact, is a prelude to Jesus' mission and, in cooperating from the beginning of her motherhood in the Son's redeeming work, she becomes the model for those

---

4. St. John Paul II, Wednesday Audience of October 2nd, 1996.

in the Church who set out to bring Christ's light and joy to the people of every time and place."[5]

In this scene, then, we can see clearly both Mary's humility and her charity. As Saint Francis de Sales comments, "It was these two virtues which motivated her, and made her leave her little Nazareth, for charity is never idle. It burns in the hearts where it dwells and reigns, and the most Blessed Virgin was full of it, because she bore Love Itself in her womb."[6]

John Paul II notes that, "Mary, now bearing the Divine Secret within her, journeyed several days from Nazareth to the city of Hebron, which, according to tradition, rested over the ashes of the founders of the people of God—Abraham, Isaac, and Jacob. Elizabeth, in some mysterious way, knew that Mary was bearing within herself the Messiah. She asked: *Who am I, that the mother of my Lord should visit me?* (Lk 1:43).

In view of Mary's excellence, Elizabeth also understands what an honor her visit is for her. With the expression 'my Lord,' Elizabeth recognizes the royal, indeed messianic, dignity of Mary's Son. In the Old Testament this expression was in fact used to address the king (cf. I Kgs 1:13,20,21 etc.) and to speak of the Messiah King (Ps 10:1). The angel had said of Jesus: 'The Lord God will give to him the throne of his father David' (Lk 1:32). 'Filled with the Holy Spirit,' Elizabeth has the same insight."[7]

Mary's response to this greeting is the *Magnificat*, a song of joy celebrating what God had done for her. She looked back over history, back to Abraham; she saw the activity of God preparing for this moment from generation to generation, she looked also into an indefinite future when all peoples and all generations would call her "Blessed." Israel's Messiah was on His way, and God was about to manifest Himself on earth and in the flesh. She even prophesied the qualities of the Son 'Who was to be born of her as full of justice and mercy. Her poem ends by acclaiming the revolution He will inaugurate with the unseating of the mighty and the exaltation of the humble.

The overwhelming feeling here, as Pope John Paul II points out, is joy: "Joyful in hope: the atmosphere that pervades the evangelical episode of the Visitation is joy: the mystery of the Visitation is a mystery of joy. John the Baptist exults with joy in the womb of St. Elizabeth; the latter, rejoicing in the gift of motherhood, bursts out into blessings of the Lord; Mary pours forth the *Magnificat*, a hymn overflowing with Messianic joy. But what is the mysterious, hidden source of this joy? It is Jesus, whom Mary has already conceived

---

5. Ibid.

6. St. Francis de Sales, *The Sermons of St. Francis de Sales: On Our Lady*.

7. St. John Paul II, Wednesday Audience of October 2nd, 1996.

thanks to the Holy Spirit, and who is already beginning to defeat what is the root of fear, anguish and sadness: sin, the most humiliating slavery for man."[8]

Pope Benedict XVI points out that in the *Magnificat*, Luke uses seven different verbs to describe what as God has done: "He has shown strength with His arm . . . He has scattered the proud . . . He has cast down the mighty from their thrones . . . He has lifted up the lowly . . . He has filled the hungry with good things . . . the rich He has sent empty away . . . He has come to the help of His servant Israel." Although the sense is lost in English, in the Greek the verb forms indicate not simply something that God has done once, but something that He has done again and again throughout history, things that He does constantly. "Evident in these seven divine works," Benedict writes, "is the 'style' in which the Lord of history inspires his conduct: He places himself on the side of the least. Often his plan is hidden under the opaque terrain of human vicissitudes, in which the 'proud,' the 'mighty,' and the 'rich' triumph. However, in the end, his secret strength is destined to manifest who God's real favorites are: [those who are] 'faithful' to his Word, 'the humble,' 'the hungry,' 'his servant Israel,' namely, the community of the People of God that, as Mary, is constituted by those who are 'poor,' pure and simple of heart. It is that 'little flock' which Jesus invites not to be afraid, as the Father has willed to give it his kingdom (cf. Lk 12:32)."

In other words, we see God's *modus operandi*: how He accomplishes His works.

In the *Magnificat* we see a summary and the surpassing of all salvation history: Mary's words are more excellent that those of Judith, more joyful than the song of Miriam, more beautiful that the Song of Songs, and more pure than that of Zechariah.[9]

Judith (ch 16) declares that "the Lord is a God who crushes wars; he sets his encampment among his people; he delivered me from the hands of my pursuers. The Assyrians threatened to burn my territory, put my youths to the sword, Dash my infants to the ground, seize my children as plunder. And carry off my virgins as spoil. But the Lord Almighty thwarted them, by the hand of a woman!" How much can that be said of the Virgin Mary!

Miriam sang (Ex 15) that she would "sing to the LORD, for he is gloriously triumphant; horse and chariot he has cast into the sea. My strength and my refuge is the LORD, and he has become my savior." How much more glorious is the triumph of our God over sin and death, wrought through the Mary!

---

8. Ibid.

9. This general idea, more or less, is from St. Francis de Sales, *The Sermons of St. Francis de Sales: On Our Lady*.

In the Song of Songs (6:3), the bride declares: "I belong to my lover, and my lover belongs to me." Imagine how much more Mary can say this, since she, who was always and ever without sin, completely and entirely belonged to God!

Zechariah's canticle praises God's mercy and love, but how much purer is Mary's song, since she never doubted that mercy and love!

The *Magnificat*, then, must be the greatest hymn of praise that man has ever raised to God. Here we can contemplate the humility and charity of Mary, the mercy of our Lord Jesus Christ, and the joy that follows from the Visitation.

We ask to imitate our Lord Jesus Christ, and we see an excellent imitation, a perfect model, in Mary. Is the joy of Christ the foundation of all my apostolate, or all my actions? Like Mary, are we quick to be about the things of God, in spite of the difficulties? Do I strive to bring Christ's presence wherever I go?

Colloquy: I will think over what I have to say to the three Divine Persons, or to the Eternal Word Incarnate, or to His Mother, Our Lady. According to the light that I have received, I will beg for the grace to follow and imitate more closely our Lord, who has just become man for me. I will close with an Our Father.

The Nativity [110-117], [264], [162]

[110] Usual Preparatory Prayer.

[111] First Prelude: The History: This is the history of the mystery. Here it will be that our Lady, about nine months with child, and, as may be piously believed, seated on an ass, set out from Nazareth. She was accompanied by Joseph and a maid, who was leading an ox. They are going to Bethlehem to pay the tribute that Caesar imposed on those lands. Cf. # 264.

[112] Second Prelude: This is a mental representation of the place. It will consist here in seeing in imagination the way from Nazareth to Bethlehem. Consider its length, its breadth; whether level, or through valleys and over hills. Observe also the place or cave where Christ is born; whether big or little; whether high or low; and how it is arranged.

[113] The petition: This we can borrow from [104], the contemplation of the Incarnation, since the whole week has the same end. The petition "is to ask for what I desire. Here it will be to ask for an intimate knowledge of our Lord, who has become man for me, that I may love Him more and follow Him more closely."

[114] First Point: This will consist in seeing the persons, namely, our Lady, St. Joseph, the maid, and the Child Jesus after His birth. I will make myself a poor little unworthy slave, and as though present, look upon them, contemplate them, and serve them in their needs with all possible homage and reverence.
Then I will reflect on myself that I may reap some fruit.

[115] Second Point: This is to consider, observe, and contemplate what the persons are saying, and then to reflect on myself and draw some fruit from it.

[116] Third Point: This will be to see and consider what they are doing, for example, making the journey and laboring that our Lord might be born in extreme poverty, and that after many labors, after hunger, thirst, heat, and cold, after insults and outrages, He might die on the cross, and all this for me.

- Hunger, thirst, heat, and cold, are all things that carnal love runs away from, worldly love rises up against insults and outrages, and to die on the cross, amid terrible torments, is frightening to sensual love. All of these Christ conquers in the Nativity.

Then I will reflect and draw some spiritual fruit from what I have seen.

If we're looking for a Biblical passage we can consider Lk 2:1-14, and, at [264], Ignatius gives us three different points:

First Point
Our Lady and her spouse Joseph go from Nazareth to Bethlehem. "Joseph also went up from Galilee to Bethlehem to profess his subjection to Caesar with Mary his espoused wife who was with child."

Second Point
"She brought forth her first-born son and she swathed him round and laid him in a manger."

Third Point
"There appeared with the angel a great multitude of the heavenly host praising God and saying, 'Glory to God in the highest.'"

Once again, as we did in the contemplation of the Incarnation, Ignatius tells us to consider the scene three times: once seeing, once hearing, and once seeing what they are doing.

We can consider, first, a little bit of the history of the scene, and then make some general observations regarding this contemplation, so that we can come to know better and imitate more closely Our Lord.

First, so no one freaks out, the maid or midwife that Ignatius mentions isn't found in the Bible, so don't worry. It was a popular belief in the Middle Ages and beyond that Joseph had the maid so she could deliver the baby, and Joseph didn't have to. Likewise, the *Protoevangelium of James*, the same text where we find the Presentation of Mary, mentions Joseph going out to find a midwife, so, no worries.

Second, it is important to note some details about how the journey would have been: "If the journey [of Mary and Joseph] went through Samaria, the journey would have been about 120 kilometers [75 miles]. [Others say the journey would have been even longer: five days and 110 miles].[1] They would have made this journey spending the night just before entering and just after leaving Samaria, so they wouldn't have to spend the night among the Samaritans, the enemies of the Jews, and probably another night in Jerusalem. The day of the journey would have been flat, heading through the Jezreel valley, but the following days through valleys and hills, crossing the mountains of both Samaria and Judea."[2] "For Jews, that journey would have been like a walk through salvation history: they would have passed Shunem, sanctified by Elisha's miracles, Jezreel, stained by Jeezabel's crimes, Mount Gilboa, where Saul and Jonathan were killed, Shechem, with Jacob's well, Shiloh, where the Ark of the Covenant was kept for many years, and where Samuel had his first visions, and Bethel, where Jacob had the dream of Jacob's ladder. . . . It was the rainy season, and although the winter in the Holy Land isn't as bad as it is here, sometimes there is snow and ice, and on occasion even up to a foot and a half of it, with temperatures in the low forties. Of course, being poor, they wouldn't have brought much extra clothing, and so they would have certainly felt the cold intensely."[3] Being poor, too, they wouldn't have brought much food for the journey, or water either.

Thirdly, we might ask ourselves: what am I supposed to take from this particular contemplation? Fr. Calveras tells us that we need to learn virtues from this contemplation: "to accept the contradictions, knowing that God disposes everything, diligence in providing and doing what is fitting, a cordial dealing with our neighbors, but without taking part in their defects, the way to undertake our spiritual journey, but really to consider the fundamental reason for the mystery of the Nativity: that our Lord might come and, being born in poverty, in a cave, in order to die on a cross, and all this for me. What should I do for Him?"[4]

So, bearing in mind what Calveras says, let's consider some aspects of what we see, things that might be useful to our contemplation.

Accepting contradictions: here Joseph heads back to his family's city. These are *his people*. Even if they weren't, the culture demanded hospitality. As one Biblical scholar writes: "Hospitality was one of the most important customs observed throughout Israelite society. Actually, one might look at hospitality as a cornerstone institution of Israelite culture. There is no reason to assume that this was uniquely Israelite, but other cultures did not leave records of

---

1. Cf. Coppens, *Spiritual Exercises*, 71.
2. Calveras, *Ejercicios intensivos*, 221-224.
3. Cf. Oraa, *Ejercicios Espirituales*, 243.
4. Calveras, *Ejercicios intensivos*, 224.

this practice. . . . Hospitality was considered a very old custom," and Biblical stories, like David's desire to kill Nabal for his lack of hospitality, show that the Israelites took it seriously.[5] And yet, here we have Mary and Joseph without any place to rest their heads. Fulton Sheen describes the scene dramatically: "Joseph was full of expectancy as he entered the city of his family, and was quite convinced that he would have no difficulty in finishing lodgings for Mary, particularly on account of her condition. Joseph went from house to house only to find each one crowded. He searched in vain for a place where He, to whom Heaven and earth belonged, might be born. Could it be that the Creator would not find a home in creation? Up a steep hill Joseph climbed to a faint light which swung on a rope across a doorway. This would be the village inn. There, above all other places, he would surely find shelter. There was room in the inn for the soldiers of Rome who had brutally subjugated the Jewish people; there was room for the daughters of the rich merchants of the East; there was room for those clothed in soft garments, who lived in the houses of the king; in fact, there was room for anyone who had a coin to give the innkeeper; but there was no room for Him Who came to be the Inn of every homeless heart in the world. When finally the scrolls of history are completed down to the last words in time, the saddest line of all will be: 'There was no room in the inn.'"[6] As Saint John writes, *He came to what was his own, but his own people did not accept him* (Jn 1:11).

To head to Bethlehem was an annoyance; it wasn't easy, and it certainly wasn't enjoyable. Yet, it was possible, and, in this, one Jesuit commentator tells us that Christ teaches us the value of obedience. The command of the emperor wasn't sinful, and so Joseph and Mary obeyed. In this, we learn, too, to be obedient. Even though our superiors might be filled with human defects and human miseries, we should obey them docilely.[7] We can see how perfectly that "annoying" command fulfilled the promise made centuries before through the prophet Micah (5:1-2): *But you, Bethlehem-Ephrathah, least among the clans of Judah. From you shall come forth for me one who is to be ruler in Israel; Whose origin is from of old from ancient times. Therefore the Lord will give them up, until the time when she who is to give birth has borne, Then the rest of his kindred shall return to the children of Israel.*

In *Everlasting Man*, G. K. Chesterton says that "Bethlehem is emphatically a place where extremes meet." We have the holiest people in the world, Jesus, Mary, and Joseph, whom we talk about bringing into our homes and, indeed,

---

5. Oded Borowski, *Daily Life in Biblical Times*, 22-24.
6. Fulton Sheen, *Life of Christ*, 15-16.
7. Cf. Oraa, *Ejercicios Espirituales*, 243.

the formula for a house blessing asks Jesus to dwell in the house at least three times, and yet, no one was willing to give them any room. We have the Queen of Heaven and Earth give birth to the King of the Universe in a cave, and lay Him in a manger. The key to these extremes lies in Jesus' humility. Fulton Sheen sums it up best in the *Life of Christ*, when he writes: "In the filthiest place in the world, a stable, Purity was born. He, Who was later to be slaughtered by men acting as beasts, was born among beasts. He, Who would call Himself the 'living Bread descended from Heaven,' was laid in a manger, literally, a place to eat.... There was no room in the inn, but there was room in the stable. The inn is the gathering place of public opinion, the focal point of the world's moods, the rendezvous of the world, the rallying place of the popular and the successful. But the stable is a place for the outcasts, the ignored, the forgotten. The world might have expected the Son of God to be born-if He was to be born at all-in an inn. A stable would be the last place in the world where one would have looked for Him. *Divinity is always where one least expects to find it.* No worldly mind would ever have suspected that He Who could make the sun warm the earth would one day have need of an ox and an ass to warm Him with their breath; that He Who, in the language of Scriptures, could stop the turning about of Arcturus would have His birthplace dictated by an imperial census; that He, Who clothed the fields with grass, would Himself be naked; that He, from Whose hands came planets and worlds, would one day have tiny arms that were not long enough to touch the huge heads of cattle; that the feet which trod the everlasting hills would one day be too weak to walk; that the Eternal Word would be dumb; that Omnipotence would be wrapped in swaddling clothes; that Salvation would lie in a manger.... And that is precisely why so many miss Him. *Divinity is always where one least expects to find it.* ... The Son of God made man was invited to enter His own world through a back door. Exiled from the earth, He was born under the earth, in a sense, the first Cave Man in recorded history. There He shook the earth to its very foundations. Because He was born in a cave, all who wish to see Him must stoop. To stoop is the mark of the humility. The proud refuse to stoop and, therefore, they miss Divinity. Those, however, who bend their egos and enter, find that they are not in a cave at all, but in a new universe where sits a Babe on His mother's lap, with the world poised on His fingers."[8]

"Bethlehem is emphatically a place where extremes meet." In particular, as Sheen notes, it is the intersection between the cave and Calvary. Christ laid in a stranger's stable in the beginning of His life, and then in a stranger's tomb at the end. He had swaddling clothes in the beginning, and swaddling clothes in

---

8. Fulton Sheen, *Life of Christ*, 17-18

His tomb. "He was already bearing His Cross," writes Sheen, "the only cross a Babe could bear, a cross of poverty, exile, and limitation."[9]

To end, I would just like to cite two poems by G. K. Chesterton which capture this sense of the Nativity.

The first is called *The Christ Child Lay on Mary's Lap* and it captures the simplicity of the scene, but also the beauty and, in a sense, the contradiction of it:

> The Christ-child lay on Mary's lap,
> His hair was like a light.
> (O weary, weary were the world,
> But here is all aright.)
> The Christ-child lay on Mary's breast,
> His hair was like a star.
> (O stern and cunning are the kings,
> But here the true hearts are.)
> The Christ-child lay on Mary's heart,
> His hair was like a fire.
> (O weary, weary is the world,
> But here the world's desire.)
> The Christ-child stood at Mary's knee,
> His hair was like a crown.
> And all the flowers looked up at Him,
> And all the stars looked down.

The second is called *Christmas Poem*; I won't cite the whole thing, but just a part, where it reminds us that where Christ is, is Heaven, and that is our true home. Where Christ is homeless, come down to earth, is really the place where we need to head, and where we really find the meaning of our lives. It is, at it were, the principle and foundation made concrete:

> *There fared a mother driven forth*
> *Out of an inn to roam;*
> *In the place where she was homeless*
> *All men are at home.*
> *The crazy stable close at hand,*
> *With shaking timber and shifting sand,*
> *Grew a stronger thing to abide and stand*
> *Than the square stones of Rome.*

9. Fulton Sheen, *Life of Christ*, 18.

For men are homesick in their homes,
And strangers under the sun,
And they lay their heads in a foreign land
Whenever the day is done.

. . .

A child in a foul stable,
Where the beasts feed and foam;
Only where He was homeless
Are you and I at home;

. . .

To an open house in the evening
Home shall all men come,
To an older place than Eden
And a taller town than Rome.
To the end of the way of the wandering star,
To the things that cannot be and that are,
To the place where God was homeless
And all men are at home.

[117] Colloquy: Close with a colloquy as in the preceding contemplation, and with the *Our Father.*

I will think over what I have to say to the three Divine Persons, or to the Eternal Word Incarnate, or to His Mother, Our Lady. According to the light that I have received, I will beg for the grace to follow and imitate more closely our Lord, who has just become man for me. I will close with an Our Father.

The Presentation and the Flight into Egypt
[132], [268-269]

[132] On the second day, for the first and second contemplations, the Presentation in the Temple, #268, and the Flight into Exile in Egypt, #269, should be used. Two repetitions will be made of these contemplations, and the Application of the Senses, in the same way as was done on the preceding day. So, we can consider the basic layout for this meditation, based on the previous contemplations.

Usual Preparatory Prayer.

First Prelude: The History: This is the history of the mystery. For the Presentation, it would be good to read Lk 2:22-39; for the flight into Egypt, Mt 2:13-18.

Second Prelude: This is a mental representation of the place. For the Presentation, it will be to see the Temple, the many people coming and going, the smell of the burnt offerings and incense, the noise of the animals, the discourses of the teachers of the Law, and, almost unnoticed, Joseph and Mary with the baby Jesus, and Simeon and Anna, old, out of the way, but watching the couple closely. For the Flight into Egypt, it will be to see Herod's rage and anger, His command to kill the children, Joseph's dream, and their long and hard journey into Egypt, followed by their exile there.

The petition: This we can borrow from [104], the contemplation of the Incarnation, since the whole week has the same end. The petition "is to ask for what I desire. Here it will be to ask for an intimate knowledge of our Lord, who has become man for me, that I may love Him more and follow Him more closely."

First Point: This will consist in seeing the persons, namely, our Lady, St. Joseph, the Child Jesus, as well as Simeon and Anna; or, in the flight, Herod, the Holy Innocents and their agonizing families, and the Holy Family in flight. I will make myself a poor little unworthy slave, and as though present, look upon them, contemplate them, and serve them in their needs with all possible homage and reverence.

Then I will reflect on myself that I may reap some fruit.

[115] Second Point: This is to consider, observe, and contemplate what the persons are saying, and then to reflect on myself and draw some fruit from it.

[116] Third Point: This will be to see and consider what they are doing, for example, presenting the Child in the Temple so that He might have the Law fulfilled with respect to Him, the blessing and praises of Simeon and Anna; or, the hurried flight of the Holy Family, leaving behind so many things and suffering so much, the slaughter of the Holy Innocents, and the sufferings of their families.

Then I will reflect and draw some spiritual fruit from what I have seen.

As for [268], Ignatius presents the following three points:

First Point
They take the Child Jesus to the temple to be offered as the first-born to the Lord, and they offer for him "a pair of turtle doves or two young pigeons."

Second Point
Coming into the temple, Simeon received Him into his arms saying, "Oh Lord, now You let Your servant go in peace."

Third Point
Anna "came upon them and gave thanks to God, and spoke of the Child to all who were awaiting the redemption of Jerusalem."

As for [269], Ignatius presents the following three points:

First Point
Herod wished to kill the Child Jesus and so killed the Innocents, but before their death the angel warned Joseph that he should flee: "Arise, take the child and his mother and flee into Egypt."

Second Point
He withdrew into Egypt: "So he arose . . . by night and withdrew into Egypt."

Third Point

"There he remained till the death of Herod."

Once again, as we did in the contemplation of the Incarnation, the Visitation, and the like, Ignatius tells us to consider the scene three times: once seeing, once hearing, and once seeing what they are doing.

Likewise, as we did previously, we can consider, first, a little bit of the history of the scene, and then make some general observations regarding this contemplation, so that we can come to know better and imitate more closely Our Lord. We will do this for each of the two scenes we are considering:

First, in the Presentation of the Child Jesus, what is also being recalled (and is the reason why the Holy Family is there in the first place) is the *purification of Mary*. It is based on a precept of the law: "When a woman had borne a child, if it was a boy, she was unclean for forty days, if it was a girl, for eighty days. She could go about her household and her daily business but she could not enter the Temple or share in any religious ceremony (Lv 12:1-8). At the end of that time, she had to bring to the Temple a lamb for a burnt offering and a young pigeon for a sin offering. That was a somewhat expensive sacrifice, and so the law laid it down (Lv 12:8) that if she could not afford the lamb she might bring another pigeon. The offering of the two pigeons instead of the lamb and the pigeon was technically called *The Offering of the Poor*. It was the offering of the poor which Mary brought. Again we see that it was into an ordinary home that Jesus was born, a home where there were no luxuries, a home where every penny had to be looked at twice, a home where the members of the family knew all about the difficulties of making a living."[1]

Nonetheless, there is also another, more profoundly theological reason why Mary didn't bring a lamb to sacrifice, and that is, because in bringing her Son, Jesus Christ, she has brought the true and definitive Lamb of God. Likewise, Mary was completely sinless, before and after Jesus' birth; she had no need to be purified, as it were, but, in the *Summa*, Aquinas explains why it was appropriate for her to go, and, indeed, why Christ was circumcised, and fulfilled all the precepts of the law. The Angelic Doctor, asking if it was fitting for Mary to go to the Temple to be purified, writes: "As the fullness of grace flowed from Christ on to His Mother, so it was becoming that the mother should be like her Son in humility: for 'God gives grace to the humble,' as is written in James 4:6. And therefore, just as Christ, though not subject to the Law, wished, nevertheless, to submit to circumcision and the other burdens of the Law, in order to give an example of humility and obedience; and in order to show His approval

---

1. Commentary of William Barclay.

of the Law; and, again, in order to take away from the Jews an excuse for ca-lumniating Him: for the same reasons He wished His Mother also to fulfill the prescriptions of the Law, to which, nevertheless, she was not subject" (*ST*, III, q. 37, a. 4). Again, the same two virtues stand out: humility and obedience, both of Jesus and of Mary, the first and best disciple of Christ.

That should suffice for a little history; we can, for our general observa-tions, consider some remarks given by Pope Benedict XVI on the feast of the Presentation. "It is interesting to take a close look at this entrance of the Child Jesus into the solemnity of the temple, in the great comings and goings of many people, busy with their work: priests and Levites taking turns to be on duty, the numerous devout people and pilgrims anxious to encounter the Holy God of Israel. Yet none of them noticed anything. Jesus was a child like the others, a first-born son of very simple parents.

Even the priests proved incapable of recognizing the signs of the new and special presence of the Messiah and Savior. Alone two elderly people, Simeon and Anna, discover this great newness. Led by the Holy Spirit, in this Child they find the fulfillment of their long waiting and watchfulness. They both contemplate the light of God that comes to illuminate the world and their prophetic gaze is opened to the future in the proclamation of the Messiah: '*Lumen ad revelationem gentium!*' (Lk 2:32). The prophetic attitude of the two elderly people contains the entire Old Covenant which expresses the joy of the encounter with the Redeemer. Upon seeing the Child, Simeon and Anna understood that he was the Awaited One."

Here, we see the need for recollection; Jesus comes into the Temple, and no one notices. All the priests, all the people, are supposedly 'busied with the things of God,' but they miss God Himself. If you've read *Five Loaves and Two Fishes*, by Venerable Francis-Xavier Cardinal Van Thuan, you might recall the scene where he is imprisoned, lamenting the fact that he isn't doing any-thing for God's people. It's at that point that he hears God tell him: "'Why do you torment yourself so? You must distinguish between God and the work of God. You must choose God alone, and not his works." The things, the works Van Thuan had done were good, but it was really God working through him. Now, if God called him to minister to "his cathedral," meaning, the prison boat full of other suffering, dying, and in chains, he would do that, because that's where God was, waiting to be found. In Jn 8:29, we hear that *this is the way Jesus lived:* He tells the crowds "The one who sent me is with me. He has not left me alone, because *I always do what is pleasing to him*." At every moment, I am focused on Him and on His will in the moment. I see Him behind every tree, in every sinner, in every person who comes attacking Me and insulting Me, and I love them nonetheless.

In the Presentation, we see how Christ gives Himself up entirely for us. Benedict continues: "The Presentation of Jesus in the Temple is an eloquent image of the total gift of one's life for all those, men and women, who are called to represent '*the characteristic features of Jesus* — the chaste, poor and obedient one' in the Church and in the world, through the evangelical counsels.

The evangelical image of the Presentation of Jesus in the Temple contains the fundamental symbol of light; the light that comes from Christ and shines on Mary and Joseph, on Simeon and Anna, and through them, on everyone. The Fathers of the Church connected this radiance with the spiritual journey. The consecrated life expresses this journey, in a special way, as '*philokalia,*' love of the divine beauty, a reflection of God's divine goodness. On Christ's Face the light of such beauty shines forth."[2]

There is much there to consider: Fulton Sheen, too, makes mention of this light. "Simeon was like a sentinel whom God had sent to watch for the Light. When the Light finally appeared, he was ready to sing his *Nunc Dimittis*. In a poor child brought by poor people making a poor offering, Simeon discovered the riches of the world."[3] Saint John tells us in his prologue that *What came to be through [the Word] was life, and this life was the light of the human race; the light shines in the darkness, and the darkness has not overcome it* (1:4-5). The Light, Christ Himself, comes into the Temple, into the world, and shines on all men, to show them the way back to the Father. Poverty, chastity, obedience, trust in God, fidelity to His will, a love of the divine beauty, a desire to seek that beauty and service in everything . . . that is what we see here.

We can note, very briefly, two details contained in Simeon's prophecy, as one commentator explains them. In Lk 2:34-35, Simeon tells Mary, "*Behold, this child is destined for the fall and rise of many in Israel, and to be a sign that will be contradicted (and you yourself a sword will pierce) so that the thoughts of many hearts may be revealed.*" There are two things to consider:

"[Christ] will be the cause whereby many will fall. This is a strange and a hard saying but it is true. It is not so much God who judges a man; a man judges himself; and his judgment is his reaction to Jesus Christ. If, when he is confronted with that goodness and that loveliness, his heart runs out in answering love, he is within the Kingdom. If, when so confronted, he remains coldly unmoved or actively hostile, he is condemned. There is a great refusal just as there is a great acceptance.

[Also], Christ will meet with much opposition. Towards Jesus Christ there can be no neutrality. We either surrender to him or are at war with him. And it

2. Homily of Feb. 2, 2011.
3. *Life of Christ,* 34.

is the tragedy of life that our pride often keeps us from making that surrender which leads to victory."[4]

Let us, then, move on to consider the history of the flight into Egypt. We see a contrast here between the loving embrace of Simeon and Anna, and the murderous threats and evil desires of Herod. These are, as it were, the two ways to respond to Christ: love, or hatred. There is no middle ground. Even Herod professed a love of Christ on his lips, *"Go and search diligently for the child. When you have found him, bring me word, that I too may go and do him homage."* We profess a love of Jesus Christ on our lips, but we need to watch over our hearts, and what is really going on in our lives. Do we live in accord with what we preach?

The Gospels reveal to us the massacre of the innocents. It is interesting to note that Herod at times had shown mercy to his people; he had sometimes relived taxes, and even melted his own gold to buy food for the people in a time of famine. Yet, as one author puts it, "Herod had one terrible flaw in his character. He was almost insanely suspicious. He had always been suspicious, and the older he became the more suspicious he grew, until, in his old age, he was, as someone said, 'a murderous old man.' If he suspected anyone as a rival to his power, that person was promptly eliminated. He murdered his wife Mariamne and her mother Alexandra. His eldest son, Antipater, and two other sons, Alexander and Aristobulus, were all assassinated by him. Augustus, the Roman Emperor, had said, bitterly, that it was safer to be Herod's pig than Herod's son. (The saying is even more epigrammatic in Greek, for in Greek *hus* is the word for a pig, and *huios* is the word for a son).

No sooner was Jesus born than we see men grouping themselves into the three groups in which men are always to be found in regard to Jesus Christ. Let us look at the three reactions.

(i) There was the reaction of Herod, the reaction of hatred and hostility. Herod was afraid that this little child was going to interfere with his life, his place, his power, his influence, and therefore his first instinct was to destroy him.

There are still those who would gladly destroy Jesus Christ, because they see in him the one who interferes with their lives. They wish to do what they like, and Christ will not let them do what they like; and so they would kill him. The man whose one desire is to do what he likes has never any use for Jesus Christ. The Christian is the man who has ceased to do what he likes, and has dedicated his life to do as Christ likes.

(ii) There was the reaction of the chief priests and scribes, the reaction of complete indifference. It did not make the slightest difference to them. They

4. William Barclay's commentary.

were so engrossed in their Temple ritual and their legal discussions that they completely disregarded Jesus. He meant nothing to them.

There are still those who are so interested in their own affairs that Jesus Christ means nothing to them. The prophet's poignant question can still be asked: "Is it nothing to you, all you who pass by?" (Lm 1:12).

(iii) There was the reaction of the wise men, the reaction of adoring worship, the desire to lay at the feet of Jesus Christ the noblest gifts which they could bring.

Surely, when any man realizes the love of God in Jesus Christ, he, too, should be lost in wonder, love and praise."[5]

Knowing of the impeding massacre of the Innocents, because he was warned in a dream, Joseph takes the Holy Family to Egypt.

The Gospels do not give many details about the flight into Egypt. The Coptic Orthodox church maintains a number of holy sites, upon and down the Nile, where it claims that Christ and the Holy Family stayed, worked, and lived. If their accounts are to be believed, and we trace out the path, "it is estimated that the whole journey from Bethlehem to the return to Nazareth lasted over three years.

They [would have] covered approximately 1,300 miles. Their means of transport was a weak beast of burden and the occasional sailboat on the Nile. But for much of the way, they must have trudged on foot, enduring the fierce summer heat and the biting winter's cold, suffering the pangs of hunger and the parching affliction of thirst. It was a journey of much deprivation, which the Child Jesus, His Virgin Mother and Saint Joseph endured in view of their divine mission."[6]

Even in the face of the obvious sufferings, this flight into Egypt was used to mock Jesus. "It is an interesting fact that in after days the foes of Christianity and the enemies of Jesus used the stay in Egypt as a peg to attach their slanders to him. Egypt was proverbially the land of sorcery, of witchcraft and of magic. The Talmud says, 'Ten measures of sorcery descended into the world; Egypt received nine, the rest of the world one.' So the enemies of Jesus declared that it was in Egypt that Jesus had learned a magic and a sorcery which made him able to work miracles, and to deceive men.

When the pagan philosopher, Celsus, directed his attack against Christianity in the third century, that attack which Origen met and defeated, he said that Jesus was brought up as an illegitimate child, that he served for hire in Egypt, that he came to the knowledge of certain miraculous powers, and returned

5. Commentary of William Barclay.
6. See https://udayton.edu/imri/mary/f/flight-into-egypt.php

to his own country and used these powers to proclaim himself God (Origen: *Contra Celsum* 1: 38). A certain Rabbi, Eliezer ben Hyrcanus, said that Jesus had the necessary magical formulae tattooed upon his body so that he would not forget them. Such were the slanders that twisted minds connected with the flight to Egypt."[7]

In these contemplations, we are stuck by two very different ways of seeing Christ and His works. Do I look with love upon everything that He has done for me, everything He has suffered, and everything He has endured? Do I let His light, the light of the Divine Beauty, shine upon me? Or do I remain indifferent, which is to say, opposed, to His goodness, His love, and His example?

Colloquy: Close with a colloquy as in the preceding contemplation, and with the *Our Father.*

I will think over what I have to say to the three Divine Persons, or to the Eternal Word Incarnate, or to His Mother, Our Lady. According to the light that I have received, I will beg for the grace to follow and imitate more closely our Lord, who has just become man for me. I will close with an Our Father.

7. Commentary of William Barclay.

The Hidden Life at Nazareth [271]

Usual Preparation Prayer.

First Prelude: The composition of Place: The representation will be to
see in imagination how our Lord went down with his parents and came to
Nazareth; and was subject to them and how He advanced in wisdom, age,
and grace before God and men (Lk 2:51-52). More specifically, it is to see the
house of Nazareth in detail: the place where Jesus and Mary and Joseph dwell;
where they gather together; where they work.

We want to knock reverently at the door of the home of the Word Incarnate, and ask Mary, our Mother, to allow me to step in and spend some time
with Jesus, her Son and our Lord, with her, and with her beloved Spouse St.
Joseph.

Second Prelude: The petition: Here the petition will be is to ask for light
to know intimately my Divine King, Who has become a Man for me, and the
grace to love Him and follow Him in poverty, suffering, and humiliations.

At [271] Ignatius gives three very short points:

First Point
He was obedient to His parents.

Second Point
"Jesus advanced in wisdom and age and grace."

Third Point
He appears to have practiced the trade of a carpenter, as St. Mark seems to
show in chapter six: "Is not this the carpenter?"

As with some of the other contemplations we have considered, Ignatius
doesn't give a very detailed contemplation. He gives only the basic steps and
then reminds us to follow the same model as we did before: to *see* the people,
then to *hear* the people, then to *examine what they are doing*, each time gathering some fruit for my life.

During his visit to Nazareth, Saint Pope Paul VI said that "Nazareth is the school in which we begin to understand the life of Jesus. It is the school of the Gospel. Here we learn to observe, to listen, to meditate, and to penetrate the profound and mysterious meaning of that simple, humble, and lovely manifestation of the Son of God. And perhaps we learn almost imperceptibly to imitate Him. Here we learn the method by which we can come to understand Christ. Here everything speaks to us; everything has meaning." 90% of Christ's life is spent hidden away in Nazareth, and it calls our attention that Ignatius asks us to meditate on this time spent.

We will consider three things: first, the interior life of that home, by which we mean Christ's conformity to the Father's will and the life of prayer, second, the life of love within the Holy Family and in its dealings with its neighbors, and, lastly, thirdly, the life of hardship, with its poverty, its work, and its concealment. So, interior life, life of love, and the life of hardship.

The Interior Life: "This is none other than the house of God, and the door to Heaven" (Gn 28:17). In the sweet and holy house of Nazareth we breathe a divine atmosphere—an atmosphere of joy, of peace, of tranquility and order.

There is nothing in this holy house of Nazareth to strike the eyes accustomed to the marvels of the world—nothing of what the world calls great and heroic. All is interior. And really, true nobility is nobility of the soul. It is only the life of the heart that matters—what we are, not what we do. And we are what we love. The life of the Heart of Jesus, especially in Nazareth, is, then, the infallible criterion of true greatness and nobility—of life, in one word, for it is life and a greater life that He has come to give us: "I have come, that they may have life, and may have it more abundantly" (Jn 10:10).

Paul VI says that here we learn "the lesson of silence: may there return to us an appreciation of this stupendous and indispensable spiritual condition, deafened as we are by so much tumult, so much noise, so many voices of our chaotic and frenzied modern life. O silence of Nazareth, teach us recollection, reflection, and eagerness to heed the good inspirations and words of true teachers; teach us the need and value of preparation, of study, of meditation, of interior life, of secret prayer seen by God alone."

Christ's conformity to His Father's Will: Doing willingly the Will of His Father, in everything and at every moment—this is the life of the Divine Heart. At the first instant of His existence He cried out: "I delight to do your Will, O My God: Your law is within My heart." And now: "I do always the things that please Him." (Jn 8:29).

He lives in a secluded spot, in a lowly village, engaged in humble occupations. Fulton Sheen (*Life of Christ*) notes that "the term 'Nazarene' signified contempt. The little village was off the main roads at the foot of the mountains; nestling in a cup of hills, it was out of reach of the merchants of Greece, the legions of Rome, and the journeys of the sophisticated. It is not mentioned in ancient geographies. It deserved its name, for it was a 'netzer,' a sprout that grows on the stump of a tree." But such is the Will of His Father. Christ loves it and far from desiring that it might be otherwise, He finds it infinitely lovely. And the humble duties of daily life, the humdrum tasks which Mary and Joseph enjoin on Him, the simple furniture His hands turn out, are as beautiful as the stars that came out of the hands of the Word that was in the beginning. They are the colors with which Christ paints things of eternal beauty, the instruments on which He plays a heavenly melody, and the words that form poems of unsurpassed excellence.

In Mary and Joseph He sees the representatives of His Divine Father—their will and their desires are the Will and the Desires of His Father. See how promptly and attentively He listens to their voice. How readily He complies with their commands. How perfectly and how lovingly He conforms His Will to theirs. "And He came to Nazareth, and was subject to them." That is all that the Evangelist, inspired by God, has recorded for us of those long thirty years. Now, as later, Christ can say: "My food is to do the Will of Him that sent Me." (Jn 4:34).

We do well to meditate on this conformity, this obedience: in fact, when we think about it, "the only acts of Christ's childhood which are recorded are acts of obedience – obedience to His Heavenly Father and to His earthly parents."

Christ's perfection and uninterrupted prayer: The life of Jesus in Nazareth is a life of perfect and uninterrupted prayer. To pray is to raise one's mind to God, and to blend our hearts humbly and confidently with the Heart of our Creator and Father. Prayer is natural to Christ—every throb of his Heart is a prayer of the most perfect kind. His prayer is continuous. It is fervent and calm, not something artificial and constrained. It is humble. It is full of gratitude and confidence.

Look at them pouring out their souls to God in the fervent aspirations of the Psalter at dawn, at midday before and after their simple meal, and at evening. See with what devotion they attend Divine Service in the Synagogue, and join in the singing of the Psalms, or listen attentively to the Prophecies which, they know, have begun to be fulfilled. Truly this house is the Temple of God and the Gate of Heaven.

Second – The Life of Love

The Love of the Holy Family: The love of Jesus, Mary and Joseph is kind; it's not fake or pretentious, judgmental or condescending. It is sympathetic. It is helpful. Let us look attentively on them and study with reverence their very feelings. Virtue will even now go out of them to heal our miseries.

Listen to their words—how sweet and kind. Look on their faces—how serene and smiling. Consider their conversation—how joyful and yet how heavenly. See how they help one another in the performance of their daily tasks. There is not the least trace of self-love in this holy house; each one lives and sacrifices himself for the others, and vies with the others in taking upon himself what is most humiliating and hard. "Christ did not please Himself"—His only pleasure is to do His Father's Will and sacrifice Himself in the service of Mary and Joseph: "The Son of Man did not come to be served, but to serve, and to give His life as a ransom for many" (Mt 20:28).

Let us enter into their hearts and see, if we can, how sympathetically they feel for one another, how each one rejoices in the joys of the others and grieves in their sufferings. "Rejoice with them that rejoice; weep with them that weep." (Rom 12:15). How tenderly is this feeling of common suffering conveyed in those words of Mary: "Behold your father and I have sought you sorrowing."

Truly this is "the House of God and the Gate of Heaven," where peace is supreme—the peace of the children of God who repose trustfully in the arms of their heavenly Father, and have but one object in life—to fulfill His Will and to love one another.

The Life of Love with their Neighbors: Happy those who can approach this holy house and experience the kindness, the helpfulness, the sympathy of the love of Jesus, Mary and Joseph!

See the sweet smile with which Mary welcomes the poor women of Nazareth that come to her! How ready she is to please and to help them! What words of comfort and of encouragement come from her lips! How they leave the place happier, stronger, and brought nearer to God! Look on Joseph transacting business with the men of Nazareth. See his constant calm, his straightforwardness, his sense of the presence of God even in the most material actions of life!

But above all keep your eyes constantly on Jesus. How sweet and kind He is to all, even to those who are rude to Him, who refuse to pay what they owe Him. "He shall not content, nor cry out, neither shall any man hear his voice in the streets." (Mt 12:19). He passes along the streets of Nazareth doing good and healing those tormented by the devil, not by means of miracles, but by the sweet odor of His virtues. Already He conquers hearts by the meekness of His own Heart and the charm of His ways.

Third – The Life of Hardship

The Poverty of the Holy Family: "I am poor and in labors from my youth." (Ps 87:16). The life of the Holy Family in Nazareth is a life of hardships, of privations, of toil and of neglect on the part of men. It must be so. To be in want, to work hard, and to live unknown to men, if not actually despised by them, is the lot of most of us. Our Divine Teacher and Savior has, then, to show us how to make these painful circumstances and trials, the means of our salvation and sanctification. He has to gain for us the grace to embrace them lovingly for His love and in union with Him.

First of all, see how poorly the Holy Family lives. The house is that of a poor artisan. The furniture is what is strictly necessary, and even that is of the simplest kind. Their clothes, clean though they be, bear the marks of long years. Their fare is simple and often scanty. Sometimes Jesus goes to His Mother for bread and she has none to give Him.

They experience the bitter effects of poverty—the necessity to work for their daily bread, the knowledge that there is no more food in the cupboard, the need to sell the work of their hands, to deal with hard and cruel men, to beg and be sent away with harsh words, and, what is still worse to tender hearts, the inability to relieve the misery they see around them.

And yet no complaint crosses their lips. They are happy in their poverty, in the feeling that a Father watches over them, and in the knowledge that their trials are golden chains that bind them close to His loving Heart.

Work: "In the sweat of your face will you eat your bread." (Gen 2:19). Labor, manual labor above all, which, since the Fall has been a punishment, is turned by Jesus into a means of expiation. All work hard in the house of Nazareth.

We have contemplated the spiritual activities of the Holy Family—the continued elevation of the Heart of Jesus, of Mary, of Joseph. Let us see now their external activity also. Let us follow our Blessed Mother as she goes about her work from early morning till late at night. She is busy, either in cleaning the house, or in preparing the meals for Jesus and Joseph, or in mending their poor clothes, yet always finding time to help others poorer and needier than herself.

Let us enter the workshop of Joseph. It is early morning and we already hear the sound of the hammer. It is hot midday: big drops of sweat stare on the Saint's forehead, but he continues to work. It is night, but the light within tells us that the Saint is still at work.

Jesus is no less active. Let us see Him, first of all, helping His Mother to go through the humble tasks of a poor housewife. There He is carrying water and firewood, lighting the fire, laying the table, washing the plates. Then, let us look at Him at work with St. Joseph. The hands of Him Who has created the universe handle the hammer, the plane, the saw.

Fr. Walter Ciszek really makes us think of the value of that work. "There is a tremendous truth contained in the realization that when God become a man, he became a workingman. Not a king, not a chieftain, not a warrior or a statesman or a great leader of nations, as some thought the Messiah would be. The Gospels show us Christ the teacher, the healer, the wonder-worker, but these activities of his public life were the work of three short years. For all the rest of the time of his life on earth, God was a village carpenter and the son of a carpenter. He did not fashion benches or tables or beds . . . by means of miracles, but by hammer and saw. . . . He worked long hours to help his father, and then became the support of his widowed mother, by the rough work of a hill country craftsman. Nothing he worked on, as far as we know, ever set any fashions or became a collector's item. He worked in a shop every day, week in and week out, for some twenty years. . . . There was nothing spectacular about it, there was much of the routine about it, perhaps much that was boring. There is little we can say about the jobs we do or have done that could not be said of the work God Himself did when He became a man. Yet, he did not think it demeaning, beneath his dignity, dehumanizing. . . . Once again God worked, and on the seventh day He rested. . . . He worked day in and day out for some twenty years to set us an example, to show us that these routine chores, too, are not beneath man's dignity or even God's dignity, that simple household tasks and the repetitive work of the wage earner are not necessary evils but noble and redemptive works worthy of God Himself. To eat one's bread in the sweat of one's brow is to do nothing more or less than Christ Himself did. And He did it for a reason. He did it for years on end, He did it for more than three-quarters of His life on earth, to convince us that God has not asked of us anything more tedious, more tiring, more routine and humdrum, more unspectacular than God Himself has done. He did it to make it plain that the plainest and dullest of jobs is – or at any rate can be, if viewed properly in respect to God and to eternity – a sharing in the divine work of creation and redemption, a daily opportunity to cooperate with God."

This is really the house of work—of painful and unceasing work. If we want to be in the company of Jesus, Mary and Joseph we must work like them. We must work seriously; we must work constantly; we must declare war on any kind of idleness. How can we possibly remain idle in the presence of these holy Persons who know no rest? The house of Nazareth is not for idle people. But woe to us if we do not seek constantly to live there!

Hiddenness: "Love to be unknown and to be accounted as nothing." This is the last lesson which the Holy Family teaches us, and it is the most difficult of all. We can endure every trial if only it brings our little self into prominence. On the other hand, nothing is harder than self-concealment, and nothing embitters one so much as neglect.

And yet this is the lot of the Holy Family. There is no one on earth, and there never will be anyone that comes near their high dignity. God Almighty looks down on them with infinite complacency. The Angels come down from Heaven to sing the Divine Praises around this blessed abode; and yet their concealment and the neglect which they suffer could not be greater. Their relations are all poor, and so are their acquaintances. Even these seem to make very little account of the Holy Family. Later on they will be offended with Jesus and will say: "Whence has this man this wisdom, and these mighty works? Is not this the carpenter's Son? Is not His mother called Mary?" "Is not this the carpenter, the Son of Mary?" "His very cousins will, for long, refuse to believe in Him." "For neither did His brethren believe in Him." Not only is the splendor and the glory of the world completely absent from this place—even sanctity seems to hide itself. We hear but one voice: "Learn of Me, because I am meek and humble of heart." (Mt 11:29).

"This is my house for ever and ever: here will I dwell, for I have chosen it." (Ps 131:14). Here shall I often come to look upon Jesus and Mary and Joseph, and learn from them the lessons of life.

Colloquy: We can make a colloquy with Jesus, asking Him to constantly live in His Heart and make His conformity with His Father's will, His prayer, and His zeal ours. Ask Him to fill your heart with His love, and to allow you to copy in your life the poverty of the Holy Family. Ask that you might work with Him seriously and constantly—and with Him love to be unknown and accounted as nothing.

Jesus Goes Up to the Temple at the Age of Twelve
(Loss of the Child Jesus)
[272]

For this contemplation, Ignatius gives us very little in terms of structure, so we can sort of fill it out according to the methods and models he has given us elsewhere.

Usual Preparatory Prayer.

First Prelude: The History: This is the history of the mystery. In [272] Ignatius refers to us Lk 2:41-50, wherein we are told that Jesus' parents would go to Jerusalem for the Passover, and, after it was done, they headed back to Nazareth, not knowing that Jesus wasn't with them. When they realized His absence, they returned to Jerusalem to search for Him.

Second Prelude: This is a mental representation of the place. It will consist here in seeing the Temple in Jerusalem, with all the many people there, the sacrifices, the smells, and the tents outside of the city in the caravan of those returning to Nazareth, and yet again Jerusalem, with Christ in the midst of the teachers.

The petition: The petition "is to ask for what I desire. Here it will be to ask for an intimate knowledge of our Lord, who has become man for me, that I may love Him more and follow Him more closely."

First Point: This will consist in seeing the persons, namely, our Lady, St. Joseph, the 12 year old Christ, and the group they are traveling with, and then the teachers and scholars of the law. I will make myself a poor little unworthy slave, and as though present, look upon them, contemplate them, and serve them in their needs with all possible homage and reverence.
Then I will reflect on myself that I may reap some fruit.

Second Point: This is to consider, observe, and contemplate what the persons are saying, and then to reflect on myself and draw some fruit from it.

Third Point: This will be to see and consider what they are doing, for example, visiting the Temple, celebrating the Passover, returning to Nazareth, looking for Jesus, and finding Him in the Temple. Then I will reflect on myself that I may reap some fruit.

[272] First Point
Christ our Lord at the age of twelve years goes up from Nazareth to Jerusalem.

Second Point
Christ our Lord remained in Jerusalem, and His parents did not know it.

Third Point
After three days they found him disputing in the temple, and seated in the midst of the doctors, and when they asked Him where he had been, He answered, "Why were you looking for me? Did you not know that I must be in my Father's house?"

Once again, as we did in the contemplation of the Incarnation, Ignatius tells us to consider the scene three times: once seeing, once hearing, and once seeing what they are doing.

This is an interesting scene, because, after the infancy narratives, it is the only information we have about Jesus before He began His public ministry. It allows us to see the Child Jesus, and how He lives, and thus how to imitate Him. We can consider, first, a little bit of the history of the scene, and then make some general observations regarding this contemplation, so that we can come to know better and imitate more closely Our Lord.

First, let us consider the historical context: "It was laid down by law that every adult male Jew who lived within fifteen miles of Jerusalem [had to] attend the Passover. In point of fact it was the aim of every Jew in all the world at least once in a lifetime to attend that feast.

A Jewish boy became a man when he was twelve years of age. Then he became a son of the law and had to take the obligations of the law upon him. So at twelve Jesus for the first time went to the Passover. We may well imagine how the holy city and the Temple and the sacred ritual fascinated him."[1]

That's probably a huge understatement. It's hard for us to really grasp what this scene is like; the Book of Deuteronomy established that the Passover lamb could only be sacrificed in the Temple in Jerusalem. Hence, the city would

1. Commentary of Barclay on this passage.

have been packed with people. The first-century Jewish historian Josephus helps us to understand the magnitude of what was going on. He writes:

> So these high priests, upon the coming of their feast which is called the Passover, when they slay their sacrifices, from the ninth hour [about 3 pm] to the eleventh [about 5 pm], but so that a company not less than ten belong to every sacrifice (for it is not lawful for them to feast singularly by themselves), and many of us are twenty in a company, found the *number of sacrifices was 256,600;* which, upon the allowance of no more than ten that feast together, amounts to 2,700,200 persons (Josephus, *War* 6:423-37).

It's possible the numbers are somewhat exaggerated, but, still, imagine the number of people packed into the city, or, even fewer, just two million people, crammed into the city; friends and families gathering, the joy of seeing people, celebrating the joy of their redemption. Consider, too, the *river of blood that flowed through the city,* which, we could say, is the source of their joy. At the age of 12, this is the first time that Christ sees this feast, sees the massive gathering of people, sees the river of blood flow through Jerusalem, a blood that brings salvation and forgiveness of sins.

Fulton Sheen says that, since Christ was 12, He would have gone to see the lamb slain. "He must've watched the lamb's blood pour forth from the wound, to be scattered at the foot of the altar in the four directions of the earth. The Cross was once more before His eyes. The Child would also have seen the carcass of the lamb being prepared for supper. This was done, according to the Law, by running two skewers of wood through the body, one through the breast, and the other through the forelegs, so that the lamb had the appearance of being on a cross."[2]

It's worth mentioning, too, that among the Jews there was a tradition that on the Passover, the Messiah would come back again. "For example, in one ancient Jewish commentary on the Book of Exodus, Rabbi Joshua, son of Hananiah . . . says, 'In that night they were redeemed, and in that night they will be redeemed.' In other words, the future redemption will take place on the same night as the original redemption. . . . [The many] rabbinic traditions are apparently based on the face that in the Bible, the night of Passover is called 'a night of watching' (Ex 12:42). The first Passover was a night of watching for the coming of the destroying angel. In later Jewish tradition, the Passover became a night of watching for the coming of the Messiah and the redemption

---

2. Fulton Sheen, *Life of Christ,* 46.

he would bring." Saint Jerome even mentions this in his commentary on Matthew's Gospel: "It is a tradition of the Jews that the Messiah will come at midnight according to the manner of the time in Egypt when the Passover was (first) celebrated" (*Commentary on Matthew 4 on 25:6*).[3]

All of this is going through Jesus' mind during the Passover; everything there in the Temple, in the Passover rite, is, as He and He alone knows, a type of Him. Everything that is being done will find its fulfillment, its completion, its definitive meaning, in Jesus. We can only imagine how seeing the Passover, knowing that it had been celebrated for perhaps a thousand years since the Exodus, that the Jews had kept it alive so that, in the fullness of time, Christ might be revealed as the definite Passover, the real Lamb of God, who delivers His people from slavery to sin, how all of this delighted His mind and made His heart beat with charity and love towards God's chosen people.

"When his parents returned he lingered behind. It was not through carelessness that they did not miss him. Usually the women in a caravan started out much earlier than the men for they travelled more slowly. The men started later and travelled faster and the two sections would not meet until the evening encampment was reached. It was Jesus' first Passover. No doubt Joseph thought he was with Mary, Mary thought that he was with Joseph and not till the evening camp did they miss him.

They returned to Jerusalem to search for him. For the Passover season it was the custom for the Sanhedrin to meet in public in the Temple court to discuss, in the presence of all who would listen, religious and theological questions. It was there they found Jesus."[4]

With these things in mind, let us consider, then, what is it we can contemplate and thus imitate Christ in.

Once again, we see that we have a mystery of obedience: Christ had no need to offer the Passover. In fact, He Himself was to be the Passover, and He could have just proclaimed it at the moment or ignored the requirements of the Law, but He didn't. He submitted Himself to the dictates of the Law, and fulfilled them precisely.

Likewise, we see Christ's obedience also to His Heavenly Father, the first and most important obedience. He goes and is obedient to His parents, but reminds them that His Father is God the Father, and that His first and really only concern is to be about the Father's will. There is something subtle but profound in the way that Mary tells Jesus that "Your father and I have been

3. For this section, see Brant Pitre, *Jesus and the Jewish Roots of the Eucharist: Unlocking the Secrets of the Last Supper.*

4. Barclay's commentary on this passage.

looking for you with great anxiety," and Jesus replies that "Why were you looking for me? Did you not know that I must be in my Father's house?," or, as it could also be translated, "I must be about my Father's work?" Mary uses father to mean Joseph, and Christ turns it back and uses it for His heavenly Father. For Christ, obedience to His heavenly Father takes priority over family ties. This is the single-minded devotion to God that we must have.

We also see, from a young age, how the Cross was what Christ sought and looked for. To know that everything was a reference to Him, that all the sacrifices were to be fulfilled in Him, must have filled Him with a great desire to accomplish His mission. As He tells Mary, "I must be about My Father's business." It is the accomplishment of that business, a work begun before time began, a work that is now coming to fulfillment, that fills Christ with joy and enthusiasm. Symbols, ideas, and temporary designs give way to reality. Christ cuts through misunderstandings, imitations, and false understandings, to get to what God has intended for man's good. To see the Father's business is not to let ourselves be sidetracked or fooled, confused or downcast.

We are also struck by Christ's *humility*: Luke tells us that when Mary and Joseph found Jesus, He was "sitting in the midst of the teachers, listening to them and asking them questions." He was *listening* to them. There was not a single thing that the teachers of the Law could have taught Him that Jesus didn't already know. There were probably things that they said that were wrong, or that missed the point. After all, as God, Jesus is *the Author of the Law*. Yet, He didn't think it beneath His dignity to sit with them, listen to them, and ask them questions. Indeed, He spent a great deal of time with them, and probably a great deal of patience. How do we practice those virtues, especially in our dealings with others? How generous are we in our use of our time? Do we, too, make efforts at study and learning? Are we attached to our opinions, to our ways of seeing things?

Lastly, we would also do well to consider Mary's reaction to this whole affair; although we are trying to imitate Christ's virtues, Mary, as the greatest disciple of Christ, is also an excellent model to follow. We are told that even after Jesus' explanation, the two "did not understand what he said to them." What was Mary's reaction? "His mother kept all these things in her heart." This is the second time that Luke uses that expression. The Servant of God, Fr. John Hardon, has a rather colloquial reflection on this, making the point that we must follow Mary in her abandonment to God's plans. As Fr. Caussade says in *Abandonment to Divine Providence*, "Perfection consists in doing the will of God, not in understanding His designs."

Fr. Hardon explains to us that the hiding in the Temple tells us "that God tries those He loves. Whatever else we should know about God's dealing with souls, we must make sure that we know this. . . . We return to the event of the Finding in the Temple, which we might just as well call the 'Losing in the Temple.' Christ did not have to do what He did. He needn't have stayed on in the Temple in the first place. And, if He had decided to do so, He could have stayed on but simply told Mary and Joseph, 'I have work to do.' But that is exactly the point. God does not generally tell us what He is going to do, He just does it. Then He lets us try to figure it out for ourselves. . . . No matter; this is the way God acts. And the first lesson that the mystery of the 'Finding in the Temple' should teach us is that God's ways are not our ways.

Secondly, God has a purpose in everything He does. We might ask, 'Why did God act in this way? Why exactly did Christ do what He did, as described by the Evangelist, who we are sure was told this by Mary herself?' No one except God knows the full answer. But one thing we do know, the purpose that God has in thus trying His loved ones is not to see them suffer. His purpose is always good, and His designs are always just; even more, they are supremely loving and kind.

[In moments of difficulty] the emphasis should be placed on us: 'I' do not understand. But what is the essence of faith? It is trusting in God that He understands.

In this way God evokes from us the highest reaches of our love. When do we love God the most? Is it not when we love Him for His own sake and not for ours? But these are cheap words. It is bringing these words into action, it is making them live, that matters. This is what trial and testing and temptation are sure to produce in a humble soul bent only on doing the Will of God. Then we tell Him and mean it, 'Lord, the only satisfaction I receive, the only joy in my heart, is the realization that I am doing what you want, because quite frankly, Lord, I don't want it. But I do it.' That is the definition of perfect love of God.

In this way God teaches us that He is master of the universe, that He alone is Lord. How we need this reminder, we who are so prone with our pride to want God to conform to our plans. And people write books on 'proving' that what they want is what God wants, instead of our always adjusting our hearts to the heart of God, our minds to His, our will to His mysterious, but all-wise, holy Will."

As Caussade tells us, when we are thirsty, we quench our thirst by drinking, not by reading about it. In the same way, in the search for holiness, speculation and curiosity are useless: "everything arranged by God as regards actions and sufferings must be accepted with simplicity, for those things that happen at each moment by the divine command or permission are always the most holy, the best and the most divine for us."

Mary simply accepted these things with simplicity, and kept them in her heart, offering her sufferings and sorrows to the God who knew the purpose of them.

Colloquy: Close with a colloquy as in the preceding contemplation, and with the *Our Father.*

I will think over what I have to say to the three Divine Persons, or to the Eternal Word Incarnate, or to His Mother, Our Lady. According to the light that I have received, I will beg for the grace to follow and imitate more closely our Lord, who has just become man for me. I will close with an Our Father.

Introduction to the Consideration of Different States of Life [135] and Two Standards [136-147]

The example which Christ our Lord gave of the first state of life, which is that of observing the Commandments, has already been considered in meditating on His obedience to His parents. The example of the second state, which is that of evangelical perfection, has also been considered, when He remained in the temple and left His foster father and His Mother to devote Himself exclusively to the service of His eternal Father.

While continuing to contemplate His life, let us begin to investigate and ask in what kind of life or in what state His Divine Majesty wishes to make use of us.

Therefore, as some introduction to this, in the next exercise, let us consider the intention of Christ our Lord, and on the other hand, that of the enemy of our human nature. Let us also see how we ought to prepare ourselves to arrive at perfection in whatever state or way of life God our Lord may grant us to choose.

TWO STANDARDS [136-147]

Prayer: the usual preparatory prayer. I will beg God our Lord for grace that all my intentions, actions, and operations may be directed purely to the praise and service of his Divine Majesty.

First prelude: This is the history. Here it will be that Christ calls and wants all beneath His standard, and Lucifer, on the other hand, wants all under his.

Second prelude: This is a mental representation of the place. It will be here to see a great plain, comprising the whole region about Jerusalem, where the sovereign Commander-in-Chief of all the good is Christ our Lord; and another plain about the region of Babylon, where the chief of the enemy is Lucifer.

Prayer of petition: This is to ask for what I desire. Here it will be to ask for a knowledge of the deceits of the rebel chief and help to guard myself against

232 · A Manual of the Spiritual Exercises of Saint Ignatius of Loyola

them; and also to ask for a knowledge of the true life exemplified in the sovereign and true Commander, and the grace to imitate Him.

There are a couple things that we can remark right at the beginning: first, the word that Ignatius uses for *standard* is *bandera*, meaning, *flag.* The standard that Ignatius is referring to is "a military flag carried on a pole or hoisted on a rope." To be under someone's standard, then, meant to follow them in the midst of a battle. This is a great image, because, as Job says, "The life of man upon earth is a warfare." There's a war going on, and we can't be neutral or sit on the sidelines: as Christ Himself says, "Whoever is not with me is against me, and whoever does not gather with me scatters" (Mt 12:30). Christianity is not a spectator sport.

Secondly, this meditation has two parts: first, we examine the battle flag of Satan: what is it that he does, and how does he try to get us to follow him? We need to consider this in order to know how to defend ourselves. Likewise, we need to look at Christ, and His Standard, so we can know how to place ourselves under it, and follow Him all the days of our lives.

Thirdly, this meditation is particularly useful as we consider making an election, or even just how to reform our lives. Here we have Christ presented as the model, and we need to know Him in order to love Him and follow Him more closely.

Calveras tells us that Ignatius wants us to accomplish three things: first, *to learn,* according to Christ's true doctrine, *how we should dispose ourselves* in order to reach perfection in whatever state of life He calls us, namely, through highest spiritual poverty and the desire for insults and humiliations in order to obtain humility, and from there to reach all other virtues; second, *to know Christ's intention,* in the interior inspirations that He gives us, which is to bring us to humility, and to know *Satan's* intentions in his suggestions, which is to give rise to a certain pride in us, and hence to be able to discern, from these effects, how to discern which spirit is acting, and; third, *to correct our natural judgments,* which look upon humiliation and poverty as things opposed to our excellence and happiness, and replace them with the conviction that in Christ's love and desires is where the true life is to be found, and in Him we will find perfection and freedom of spirit.[1]

Let us begin, then, with the consideration of Satan's standard:

---

1. Calveras, *Practica intensiva,* 252.

[140] First Point: "Imagine you see the chief of all the enemy in the vast plain about Babylon, seated on a great throne of fire and smoke, his appearance inspiring horror and terror."

The fire signifies the destruction he has brought upon himself and is trying to impose upon the whole world. True, God allows him to use his power against us in order to try our love. Yet God does not suffer us to be tempted above our strength, but bestows abundant graces and easy victory on them that call upon him with humility and trust.

The smoke signifies the darkness in which Satan covers his evil designs. His victims must be kept in ignorance and perplexity; they must not be clear in their own minds, nor yet go to others for instruction and counsel. Only the children of light are safe against him. Confusion doesn't come from God; it's the devil's way of masking his designs.

[141] Second Point: "Consider how he summons innumerable demons, and scatters them, some to one city and some to another, throughout the whole world, so that no province, no place, no state of life, no individual is overlooked."

What is Satan doing unceasingly at every moment of time? Jealous of us who are called and destined for Heaven, he is determined to drag us into his own misery. Saint John Chrysostom tells us that each one of us has a particular demon who works assiduously for our damnation, and will hang around us right up until the end. Saint Peter says, "Your opponent the devil is prowling like a roaring lion, looking for someone to devour" (1 Pt 5: 8).

[142] Third Point: Consider the address he makes to them, how he goads them on to lay snares for men and bind them with chains. First, they are to tempt them to covet riches (as Satan himself is accustomed to do in most cases) that they may the more easily attain the empty honors of this world, and then come to overweening pride.

The first step, then, will be riches, the second honor, the third pride. From these three steps the evil one leads to all other vices."

Riches represent whatever can be found in the world apart from God. It can be things or peoples, objects that we have as our treasures. It could be comforts or an inordinate attachment to a particular person, place, or work, under the pretext of good, and certainly the attachment to our own ideas or consideration of things. It could even be my talents and skills, my looks, my personality, my feelings . . . anything that's not God.

Then what happens? If I am rich, I have no need of God, as we hear in the Book of Revelation (3:17): "You say, 'I am rich and affluent and have no need

234 · A Manual of the Spiritual Exercises of Saint Ignatius of Loyola

of anything,' and yet do not realize that you are wretched, pitiable, poor, blind, and naked."

Why don't they realize their poverty? Because the world keeps piling up its empty honors. They build themselves up on false riches, things that aren't really worth anything, and then the world gives them praise for it.

This leads to pride, since when a person is proud, they won't submit their minds or wills to others, not even to God. They become a law unto themselves. The good things of others are displeasing to him; meanwhile, whatever he does has his approval. Pride deprives man of supernatural help. Saint Peter says, "God resists the proud" (1 Pt 5: 5).

Let us examine that passage briefly: the Greek word for resists is ἀντιτάσσομαι (antitássomai), and the term is very strong: to means, literally, "squared off," to "reject the entire make-up of something, i.e. its whole arrangement – from its very 'set up' (organization) to the final way it is 'ordered.'" The word itself is a very old military term, "used in antiquity of organized resistance, like an army assuming a specific battle-array position to resist in 'full alignment'; to disagree (oppose) intensely."

"If it is a terrible thing for a man to be forsaken by God, what is it when God begins to resist him? [This divine resistance must fill us with terror]. God is the sole fount of our holiness, because He is the Author of every grace. Now what grace is to be hoped for from God, if God not only does not give Himself to us, but rather resists us, rejects us? What is there then that is so evil, so contrary to God in pride, for God so mightily to thrust it far from Him?"[2]

The opposition or antagonism between God and the proud stems from the very nature of God's holiness. God is the beginning and the end, the First and the Last, the Alpha and the Omega. Everything comes from Him, flows from Him, and is received from Him. He deserves all the glory, and that glory is His alone. Through the prophet Isaiah, God tells us: "I am the LORD; . . . my glory I give to no other."

"Now what is it that the proud man does? He attempts to rob God of this glory which God alone merits and of which He is so jealous, in order to appropriate it to himself. The proud man lifts himself up above others, he makes himself the center; he glories in his own person, in his perfection, his deeds; he sees in himself alone the principle of all that he has and all that he is; he considers that he owes nothing to anyone, not even to God, He would deprive God, of that Divine attribute of being the First Principle and Last End. Doubtless, in theory, he may think that all comes from God, but, in practice, he acts and lives as if all came from himself."

---

2. Adapted from Bl. Columba Marmion's *Christ, the Ideal of the Monk*.

"You see to what a degree pride is opposed to the soul's union with God; there is not, says St. Thomas, any sin, or tendency, that bears more clearly the character of an obstacle to Divine communications. And as God is the principle of all grace, pride is the most terrible of all dangers for the soul; while there is no surer way of attaining holiness and of finding God than humility. It is pride that above all prevents God from giving Himself; if there were no longer any pride in souls, God would give Himself to them fully."

Pride pulls us out of our place, as it were. It makes us the center of attention, and prevents God from working in our souls. Saint Therese of Lisieux said, "The beginning of all holiness is humbly admitting that without God we can do nothing, but that with, in, and through Him, everything is possible!"

The devil's strategy, then, is to get people to become attached to earthly things. He urges them to acquire say material wealth, which is the cheapest kind of riches, or acquire education. How clever the devil is. Or acquire mastery in the use of their emotions, or cultivate gifts in the social order, or, the devil will even tempt people to acquire spiritual riches. But whatever the possession, whether as cheap a thing as money, or special things say as, secular knowledge or even spiritual wisdom, the beginning is to become wealthy and thus to attain to recognition, praise, honor.

Attachment to the things of this world gradually makes a person, not only satisfied with what he or she possesses, but hungry for acceptance, recognition, praise, and honor. And once, as Ignatius says, once a person becomes a victim of empty honors, then pride follows as a matter of course. Because once a person falls into pride, there is no limit to that person's malice. Proud people are the agents of the devil. He uses them to seduce others. In fact, he uses them to work with him.

Second Part: The Standard of Christ

[143] In a similar way, we are to picture to ourselves the sovereign and true Commander, Christ our Lord.

[144] **First Point**: "Consider Christ our Lord, standing in a lowly place in a great plain about the region of Jerusalem, His appearance beautiful and attractive."

Notice how beautiful the scene is, how calm Christ is. He is in a low place, that is, a place of humility, since humility is the first and most important virtue for the followers of Christ.

[145] **Second Point**: "Consider how the Lord of all the world chooses so many persons, apostles, disciples, etc., and sends them throughout the whole

world to spread His sacred doctrine among all men, no matter what their state or condition."

[146] Third Point: "Consider the address which Christ our Lord makes to all His servants and friends whom He sends on this enterprise, recommending to them to seek to help all, first by attracting them to the highest spiritual poverty, and should it please the Divine Majesty, and should He deign to choose them for it, even to actual poverty. Secondly, they should lead them to a desire for insults and contempt, for from these springs humility.

Hence, there will be three steps: the first, poverty as opposed to riches; the second, insults or contempt as opposed to the honor of this world; the third, humility as opposed to pride. From these three steps, let them lead men to all other virtues."

Christ's strategy is the direct opposite of Satan's. It begins by inspiring His followers and future apostles in every age, in every state of life to practice the first beatitude, "blessed are the poor in spirit," detachment of heart from earthly possessions. And even, if it is God's will, attracting them to actual poverty.

In other words, the first requirement is poverty: not just in terms of money, but poverty of spirit: the Greeks had two words for a poor person. The first meant the one who was poor, but had enough money to get by. However, that's not the word that Christ uses here. He uses the word, *ptochos*, meaning the one who is absolutely destitute, who doesn't even have enough to get by. This is our standing with respect to God. We have absolutely nothing that is our own, and hence the first condition is that the person who wants to serve Christ in winning souls for His Divine Majesty is himself, at least internally, detached from everything and I mean everything, and I mean everything, in this world, money is the most obvious but not only. This is so fundamental in the apostolate that in two thousand years there have been no exceptions: the only persons that Jesus Christ uses to spread His gospel are the people detached from the things of this world. As He Himself tells us, "Without me you can do nothing."

You cannot play both sides. You cannot love, as Christ tells us, both God and mammon.

Then Christ inspires His followers to just the opposite of the devil's instigation. Christ inspires His followers to actually desire, under the influence of grace, to be scorned or rejected. You must want "to be scorned, despised, ignored, rejected."

The key to all of this is humility; as Saint Vincent de Paul said, "The most powerful weapon to conquer the devil is humility. For, as he does not know at all how to employ it, neither does he know how to defend himself from it."

It is, in the words of Saint John Vianney, when asked what the three most important virtues are, replied: "The first most important virtue is humility, the second humility, and the third, humility." As Søren Kierkegaard wrote, "God creates everything out of nothing – and everything which God is to use He first reduces to nothing." To be engaged in God's service, we must be humble, completely detached from everything.

[147] Colloquy [actually, three colloquies]: A colloquy should be addressed to our Lady, asking her to obtain for me from her Son and Lord the grace to be received under His standard, first in the highest spiritual poverty, and should the Divine Majesty be pleased thereby, and deign to choose and accept me, even in actual poverty; secondly, in bearing insults and wrongs, thereby to imitate Him better, provided only I can suffer these without sin on the part of another, and without offense of the Divine Majesty. Then I will say the Hail Mary.

Second Colloquy: This will be to ask her Son to obtain the same favors for me from the Father. Then I will say, *Soul of Christ*, that is, the *Anima Christi*.

Third Colloquy: This will be to beg the Father to grant me the same graces. Then I will say the Our Father.

Introduction to the Consideration of Different States of Life [135] and Two Standards [136-147] – Repetition

The example which Christ our Lord gave of the first state of life, which is that of observing the Commandments, has already been considered in meditating on His obedience to His parents. The example of the second state, which is that of evangelical perfection, has also been considered, when He remained in the temple and left His foster father and His Mother to devote Himself exclusively to the service of His eternal Father.

While continuing to contemplate His life, let us begin to investigate and ask in what kind of life or in what state His Divine Majesty wishes to make use of us.

Therefore, as some introduction to this, in the next exercise, let us consider the intention of Christ our Lord, and on the other hand, that of the enemy of our human nature. Let us also see how we ought to prepare ourselves to arrive at perfection in whatever state or way of life God our Lord may grant us to choose.

TWO STANDARDS [136-147]

Prayer: the usual preparatory prayer. I will beg God our Lord for grace that all my intentions, actions, and operations may be directed purely to the praise and service of his Divine Majesty.

First prelude: This is the history. Here it will be that Christ calls and wants all beneath His standard, and Lucifer, on the other hand, wants all under his.

Second prelude: This is a mental representation of the place. It will be here to see a great plain, comprising the whole region about Jerusalem, where the sovereign Commander-in-Chief of all the good is Christ our Lord; and another plain about the region of Babylon, where the chief of the enemy is Lucifer.

– "See," says Calveras, "that this is a general mobilization. Everyone has been rallied." It's like a massive, worldwide draft, of both the good and the bad.

Prayer of petition: This is to ask for what I desire. Here it will be to ask for a knowledge of the deceits of the rebel chief and help to guard myself against them; and also to ask for a knowledge of the true life exemplified in the sovereign and true Commander, and the grace to imitate Him.

"In considering this exercise," writes Calveras, "it is fitting to make a very clear distinction between the real factors, which come every day to souls in real life, and the scene we are considering, with its imagined factors. There are two very real calls to men that are touched upon in this Exercise. The first is a general call made to everyone, no matter their state or condition in life, one from Christ and the other from Lucifer. The result is that in the interior war, men chose one of two options: either submit self-love to perfection and resist its callings, as Christ wants, and this is to be under His standard, or to surrender to its desires and impulses, and this is to pass to be under Satan's standard. Since man must necessarily be one of two things, either a saint or a sinner, enlisting under one standard or the other is inevitable. Christ calls us to resist, very clearly proposing to all a love for poverty and humiliation, against carnal and worldly love, inviting them to fight alongside Him, so that, spurred on by His love and example they might conquer easier and more quickly.

At the same time, Lucifer, with his deceit and under an appearance of good wants to persuade all to follow that self-love that he encourages them to.

However, the other call is that of the emissaries who Christ 'sends them throughout the whole world to spread His sacred doctrine among all men, no matter what their state or condition.' Note that this is *not* a general call for everyone, but rather only those who are chosen. There are certainly many of them, since we are told 'Consider how the Lord of all the world chooses so many persons, apostles, disciples, etc.' This isn't part of the history of the exercise, properly speaking, meaning that the point isn't that we're focusing on the calling of the apostles, but rather to help all to dispose themselves to reach perfection in their state by the only path that leads there, by taking the three steps of poverty as opposed to riches, insults or contempt as opposed to the honor of this world, and humility as opposed to pride."[1]

[140] First Point: "Imagine you see the chief of all the enemy in the vast plain about Babylon, seated on a great throne of fire and smoke, his appearance inspiring horror and terror."

– "Although this is a fictional scene," Calveras reminds us, "Ignatius does it in a way that is perfect for what we are to contemplate. We can see Lucifer's

1. Calveras, *Ejercicios intensivos*, 253-254.

intention to bring us to overwhelming pride (he is seating on a throne), how unsubstantial his offers are (the throne is not of gold or ivory, but rather of fire and smoke, pure appearance, with darkness and discomfort), and the very effective impression as a way to dominate (he is horrible and frightening), because he cannot make use of any of the natural and irresistible attractiveness of true beauty, truth, and good."[2]

Likewise, the scene "is near Babylon, where the tower of Babel once stood, to signify the pride and the confusion which Satan ever labors to stir up in the hearts of men. He is elevated on a throne, to denote the ambition he arouses in all to rise above their fellows. The throne consists of flames, ever restless, and smoke, darkening the mind of his miserable dupes. His monstrous features reflect the ugly vices of his heart."[3]

[141] Second Point: "Consider how he summons innumerable demons, and scatters them, some to one city and some to another, throughout the whole world, so that no province, no place, no state of life [religious, lay, priest, deacon, bishop], no individual is overlooked."

– "This dispersion of demons," Calveras tells us, "without leaving any person without temptation, is a real fact. The call of the numerous demons to his side in order to receive their commission is fictional, in order to make the scene more dramatic. Note that Lucifer doesn't send particular *men* as his emissaries; this is because men usually cooperate in the work of demons wherever they are, be it by praising and criticizing with a worldly spirit, and in this way creating a vast army of slaves. A fear of worldly honor is an open and gross temptation with which the enemy enlists the beginners, and the vain honors of the world is the sneaky resource with which he wants to bring the retreatant of second week to increased pride, whom he knows he should tempt under the appearance of good."[4]

[142] Third Point: Consider the address he makes to them, how he goads them on to lay snares for men and bind them with chains. First they are to tempt them to covet riches (as Satan himself is accustomed to do in most cases) that they may the more easily attain the empty honors of this world, and then come to overweening pride.

The first step, then, will be riches, the second honor, the third pride. From these three steps the evil one leads to all other vices.

2. Ibid., 255-256.
3. Coppens, *Spiritual Exercises of Saint Ignatius*, 92.
4. Calveras, *Ejercicios intensivos*, 256-57.

- Consider what it is that the demons do: "lay snares and bind with chains: beginning with the simple desire or interest for something, in order to later develop in them a particular disordered affection.
- First, they are to tempt them to *greed*: again, if the person making the retreat really has the dispositions of the second week, the devil won't tempt them openly, because those temptations would be rejected. Rather, he will tempt them under the appearance of good, meaning, under a natural sort of fittingness and even under the appearance of serving God, aspiring to have something that is valuable and appreciated by all. Money is just this sort of thing, as are valuables or good family ties, and this is why, in the majority of cases, the first step in temptation is riches. However, the world also values personal riches, like qualities, talents, knowledge, and the like, and so greed in this sense is to cultivate and develop those gifts so that they might be more valuable, can also be the first step for many."[5]
- In all of this, "the demon understands full well that the temptation is to be adapted to each one's character. With many there is from the beginning an inordinate love of honor and distinction; these may at once be assailed on their weak point and more rapidly led into pride. Others are more readily allured by the bait of pleasure; they may first be tempted by innocent amusements, then by more inordinate enjoyment, till they cast off all restraint, loving self to the contempt of the Creator, which is but another form of pride."[6]
- The second step is "the vain honor of the world: the greed of having something that is valuable is in order for a person to be appreciated and praised, in order to be respected and honored vainly by men, meaning, not attributing those good things to God, from whom all good things come, but rather to man, who is their mere repository; here, it is man who is celebrated, or appears to be celebrated.
- Lastly, this leads to overweening pride, that is, a high decree of self-conceit on account of the worldly praises and honors. The one who thinks that they have something valuable, and if others, even just because of that accomplishment, praise them, that person feels superior, fixed on themselves and what they possess, without needing to consult others or seek help, with the right to intervene and impose their thoughts and likes on others, a right to be preferred to others, and dispensed from the

---

5. Ibid., 257-258.
6. Coppens, *Spiritual Exercises of Saint Ignatius*, 93.

obligations and responsibilities that everyone has, refusing submission to all authority, and even reaching the point of despising God Himself."

- "From these three steps they lead to all other vices: pride is the vice that God detests the most, and He promises to punish it, and the punishment is, precisely, to let the person fall into other sins without ceasing, until they fall into the abyss. This happens both on the natural plane, since this pride naturally opens the path for all other sins, but also on the spiritual plane, where it feeds off of peace of conscience and the favors received from God, and thus leads directly to false consolations from the enemy."[7]

Second Part: The Standard of Christ

[143] In a similar way, we are to picture to ourselves the sovereign and true Commander, Christ our Lord.

[144] **First Point**: "Consider Christ our Lord, standing in a lowly place in a great plain about the region of Jerusalem, His appearance beautiful and attractive."

- "This scene," says Calveras, "is taken from reality. After the calling of the Apostles, upon going to preach the Sermon on the Mount and the Beatitudes, of which He is the summary, Christ went to a lowly place and, sitting down and raising His eyes to His disciples, began to teach them (Mt 5:1; Lk 6:17, 20). In this humble place, we can see Christ's intention to lead us to humility, and in the beauty and grace of His person and position, the delight of the true life of the spirit, the fruit of embracing His doctrine regarding love of poverty and humiliation."[8]

[145] **Second Point:** "Consider how the Lord of all the world chooses so many persons, apostles, disciples, etc., and sends them throughout the whole world to spread His sacred doctrine among all men, no matter what their state or condition."

- "Christ makes use of the exterior ministry of men in order to counter Lucifer's emissaries. However, God works directly in souls as well, through grace and the angels."[9]

7. Calveras, *Ejercicios intensivos*, 258-59.
8. Ibid., 260.
9. Ibid., 160.

[146] Third Point: "Consider the address which Christ our Lord makes to all His servants and friends whom He sends on this enterprise, recommending to them to seek to help all, first by attracting them to the highest spiritual poverty, and should it please the Divine Majesty, and should He deign to choose them for it, even to actual poverty. Secondly, they should lead them to a desire for insults and contempt, for from these springs humility.

Hence, there will be three steps: the first, poverty as opposed to riches; the second, insults or contempt as opposed to the honor of this world; the third, humility as opposed to pride. From these three steps, let them lead men to all other virtues."

- "'To seek to help all': all men are called to perfection, and so all should help so that everyone can achieve it, exhorting each other to take the three steps that Christ Our Lord proposes here:
- First, highest spiritual poverty: the first Beatitude that Christ proclaimed was for the poor in spirit (Mt 5:3), those who are in spiritual poverty. In accord with this, Saint Ignatius places the first step in order to reach perfection spiritual poverty, not any sort, though, but highest spiritual poverty, which embraces the complete detachment from any inclination or affection with respect to riches, without placing any trust in them and with the firm resolution not to commit any sin, not even venial, as well as placing all my love and preference in actual poverty, although with the willingness to embrace whatever is more for the divine majesty;
- And, likewise, to seek *actual poverty*: the actual renunciation of goods or their use, and of the free use of money, to live poorly with all the privations and annoyances that follow upon it, if God should call to this state of life.
- A desire for insults and contempt: insults, false witnesses, and affronts are the contempt we seek, to be thought of as crazy and foolish, and think nothing of me. The last of the Beatitudes, that of persecution, is for these who suffer for holiness. This is the second step, which includes detachment from all inclination and desire for honors and to be esteemed by men, with a decided will not to commit any mortal or venial sin, not even to obtain all earthly honors and glory, not to flee from humiliations, and with the sincere preference for contempt, provided, always, that this is for God's greater glory.
- From these two things comes humility: humility of heart, which should be understood as an absolute subjection to God and His representatives, without any sort of internal deliberation about breaking a commandments, divine or law, under penalty of mortal or venial sin, and the complete surrender of one's self to the Divine Will. Such humility

follows from the preceding two steps, that is, highest spiritual poverty and a scorn of riches, and a desire for insults and contempt with an absolute distain for vain worldly honors. In this way, the soul achieves an unbreakable peace and is strengthened to surrender everything is has and is in the fulfillment of the Divine will.

- It is this submission of heart, then, and by means of it and the surrender of the heart to the law and desires of God, that disposes us to keep all of the commandments: poverty removes impediments, and a desire for humiliation keeps our minds and hearts focused on moving heavenward."[10] This is how we become saints and get to Heaven.

[147] Colloquy [actually, three colloquies]: A colloquy should be addressed to our Lady, asking her to obtain for me from her Son and Lord the grace to be received under His standard, first in the highest spiritual poverty, and should the Divine Majesty be pleased thereby, and deign to choose and accept me, even in actual poverty; secondly, in bearing insults and wrongs, thereby to imitate Him better, provided only I can suffer these without sin on the part of another, and without offense of the Divine Majesty. Then I will say the Hail Mary.

Second Colloquy: This will be to ask her Son to obtain the same favors for me from the Father. Then I will say, *Soul of Christ*, that is, the *Anima Christi.*

Third Colloquy: This will be to beg the Father to grant me the same graces. Then I will say the Our Father.

"The point of these colloquies isn't to make a generous offering of ourselves to God, but rather to already see ourselves under His standard, and this takes places in stages. First, we sign up for complete spiritual poverty, to which everyone is called. Actual poverty, which protects our desire for perfection, allows us to give ourselves even more freely to God's service. To actually suffer insults and contempt corrects our self love and sensibility."

"We can ask ourselves: How well do I appreciate the great benefits for the perfection of my soul and its spiritual well-being that come from the *highest spiritual poverty* and the *desire for insults and contempt,* and what understanding do I have of that danger that is to be found in *greed for riches* and the *desire for worldly honors*? Have I been able to correct *my natural judgment* which sees humiliation and poverty as opposed to my excellence and happiness?"[11]

10. Ibid., 261-262.
11. Ibid., 263, 266.

Three Classes of Men [149-157]

This is a meditation for the same fourth day to choose that which is better
(note, this is the subtitle Ignatius himself gives it –
note that the Spanish is *el mejor*, which could also be translated as *best*)

Usual Preparation Prayer.

[150] First Prelude: The history: This is the history of the Three Classes of Men. Each of them has acquired ten thousand ducats [a ducat was a gold or silver coin used for trade back in the day], but not entirely as they should have, for the love of God. They all wish to save their souls and find peace in God our Lord by ridding themselves of the burden arising from the attachment to the sum acquired, which impedes the attainment of this end.

[151] Second Prelude: The composition of place: This is a mental representation of the place. Here it will be to behold myself standing in the presence of God our Lord and of all His saints, that I may know and desire what is more pleasing to His Divine Goodness. – Note that this setting is the one that Ignatius uses for the most important meditations; when there's something really important, really key, he says to place ourselves in the presence of God and all the saints. Calveras notes that this composition of place has nothing really to do with the three classes of men, but rather everything to do with me, and my choices.[1]

[152] Third Prelude: The petition: This is to ask for what I desire. Here it will be to beg for the grace to choose what is more for the glory of His Divine Majesty and the salvation of my soul. – Note the emphasis on the will, "the grace to choose." The point here is on the aspect of *will*, the choice.

Calveras says essentially we are undertaking this meditation to "completely uproot all the particular affections that exist in our hearts: a) so we can be entirely prompt and diligent to fulfill God's will in everything He asks of me, and b) in order to be well-disposed to enter into the elections and to

---

1. Calveras, *Ejercicios Intensivos*, 269.

seek and embrace God's will, for which it is necessary to get rid of all disordered affections."[2]

Many commentators on the Spiritual Exercises call this meditation "a test of sincerity." Ignatius himself gives the meditation to the subtitle "to choose what is best." We could say that the Two Standards gives us an objective standard, the way that things should be. However, this meditation on the three classes of men [or women, if you prefer] is the subjective test, the test of my sincerity, of my willingness to follow through with that standard.

We are to consider three people, each of whom has acquired a sum of money. It's not like they did anything illegal or wrong to get it (since then they'd be obligated to give it back), but nonetheless they didn't do any discernment beforehand; it wasn't acquired only for the love of God. Maybe they inherited it, maybe it was a gift, maybe it was the National Ducat Lottery, whatever. Calveras thinks that maybe it referred to common practice of those who would sail to the colonies and make their living and then return to Spain, using that money to retire on; if they gave it up, it means they'd have to go back to work in their old age, and hence why they find it hard to give up the money. The point is that they have this thing, this object, and they also have an attachment to it, and they know that they need to get rid of the *attachment* they have to said thing. This is important: God might not be calling them to give up the thing itself, but they *need to be detached from it*. They need to get rid of the attachment to it, and, as Ignatius points out, they all *want* to get rid of the attachment and so find peace and save their souls. But, part of wanting, if it's really a desire, is that it becomes action. Let's see what each of the three classes do:

[153] "The First Class: They would like to rid themselves of the attachment they have to the sum acquired in order to find peace in God our Lord and assure their salvation, but the hour of death comes, and they have not made use of any means."

The first Class make procrastination the rule of their conduct. Although they do not positively refuse to employ the means necessary for their reform, they indefinitely put off employing them. They *would like to . . .* as Ignatius says. "It would be nice if I could get rid of this attachment." "I would *like* to be detached, but . . ." This is the class of the dreamers or the procrastinators, who just sit around and think of ways to be detached, but who never put it into action.

This class only wants to be rid of the attachment, and are unwilling to use any means to that effect. They fail in applying the suitable means that must be

2. Ibid., 267

taken to attain a given end. A variety of reasons may account for this: it may be sloth which avoids the effort necessary to remove the obstacles; or avarice which dreads to make a sacrifice of some long-cherished possession; or fear which shrinks from losing an apparently harmless bodily comfort or spiritual consolation; or lack of self-confidence about meeting and overcoming the difficulties; or want of conviction on the importance of becoming internally detached and a certain impracticality on the method to use; or finally a weak faith which distrusts the mercy of God to supply all the graces necessary "to find God our Lord in peace" of mind and heart.

We have a model of this in the rich young man (Mk 10:17-22): he knows exactly what he must do, and yet "his face fell, and he went away sad, for he had many possessions." Attachment, yes; effort to leave it, no. The danger, as Christ Himself tells us, is that "Not everyone who says Lord, Lord, will enter the kingdom of Heaven but he who does the will of my Father" (Mt 7:21).

For those of us who have been in religious life for some time, it's particularly worthwhile to consider what Blessed Joseph Allamano, the founder of the Consolata missionaries, says. In one of his writings to his congregations, he breaks religious down into three groups. We can consider the first here: "The first group is that of those who make for themselves a great idea of perfection, who know the need for it, and have great desire for it, but that's also where they stop, and they do not put into practice the means that lead to holiness. It's one thing to know, however, and another to put into practice; it's one thing to know the need for perfection and another to try to achieve it. One thing is the desire, and the other the fact. It's true that Saint Teresa exhorts us to have great desires, but here she means efficacious desires, those accompanied by works. Hell is full of ephemeral desires and resolutions to convert later. . . . In certain communities, there are always some certain individuals who are always at the same level of virtue or, rather, lack of virtue, from the moment they enter religious life until the end of their lives. They had desires for perfection when they entered, when they entered in the novitiate, when they professed vows . . . and they remain the same as before, with the same defects of pride, laziness, lack of mortification. Certainly, they are not an example to the community, who simply puts up with them, and who doesn't weep when they leave or when they die. They pass their days without taking advantage of the innumerable graces that accompany them, and in the end, they find themselves with empty hands and a terrible rendering of accounts that must be made. They are like the dried fig tree that the Gospel speaks of, or like the land that didn't produce fruits after the dewfall and the rains. Happy the community that knows how to opportunely get rid of such ones! Such ones, who know how to exploit all the protections of religious life, live more time than others in detriment to discipline and religious peace. This is, regrettably, the story of one monastery. . . . May God grant that this never happen in our Institute!"

[154] "The Second Class: They want to rid themselves of the attachment, but they wish to do so in such a way that they retain what they have acquired, so that God is to come to what they desire, and they do not decide to give up the sum of money in order to go to God, though this would be the better way for them."

The second class too desire to get rid of the inordinate affection. They expect, however, that God should suit Himself to their desire to let them keep what they have gained; they are not determined to give it up in order to go to Him, even though this would be the best state for them. We could say that their motto is: "God, ask me to do what *I* want, and I'll do what you ask." "Ask me to do what *I* want, and I'll do what you ask." God is supposed to come to them. This is the class of the compromiser, the pretender, the one who dodges God's will.

The second class will compromise: they want to be rid of the internal impediment but also retain the external possession. They want to shape the course of providence to suit themselves, instead of adapting themselves to the demands of providence. Not all creatures we possess make us inordinately attached to them. The cumulative factors which produce attachment are manifold and frequently beyond our control—assuming that the creature itself is retained. It may well be that a given object, like money, a position or favorite pastime of which I am now enamored, may be kept or continued without sacrificing the object and detachment achieved. But if I am sincere in wanting to be freed of a psychological burden, I must be willing to dispose of the physical entity which causes the unruly interior effect; otherwise when the time comes (if it comes) to sacrifice what I possess, I will not do so even though I know full well there is no other way of deliverance from the attachment.

Imaginary detachment and real attachment, want of straightforwardness and a policy of compromise, are the distinguishing marks of the second Class. Like the first Class they wish to get rid of their inordinate affection for the thing acquired. Unlike the first Class, however, they are sincerely willing to do a deal for this purpose, always provided they are not required to sacrifice what they have gained.

Think of Pilate in the Gospels, a man attached to power, attached to his fears, attached to so many things. He washes his hands, but in vain. He wishes he could save Christ, but, in the end, he does nothing but condemn Him. The danger is that, as we read in the Book of Revelation (3:15), God tells us, "I know that you are neither cold nor hot. I wish you were either cold or hot. So, because you are lukewarm, neither hot nor cold, I will spit you out of my mouth."

Again, returning to Blessed Allamano: "The second group is made up of those who aren't content with mere desires; they do something, and take steps along the path to perfection, but that's it. They try to become perfect, but in their way, trying to strike a deal with the Lord. They are not generous in their response to the divine callings, they won't sacrifice certain inclinations, they are not indifferent to their tasks, they don't strip themselves of the inclination towards their family members; they are bound to small comforts, and lack the courage to test the effects of poverty. Jesus doesn't accept these half-hearted measures; He doesn't want these reservations, and He withdraws from them. Hence, such souls do not enjoy true peace in this life, and they gather a lot of material for purgatory. Unfortunately, in communities there are usually this sort of people."

[155] "**The Third Class:** These want to rid themselves of the attachment, but they wish to do so in such a way that they desire neither to retain nor to relinquish the sum acquired. They seek only to will and not will as God our Lord inspires them, and as seems better for the service and praise of the Divine Majesty. Meanwhile, they will strive to conduct themselves as if every attachment to it had been broken. They will make efforts neither to want that, nor anything else, unless the service of God our Lord alone move them to do so. As a result, the desire to be better able to serve God our Lord will be the cause of their accepting anything or relinquishing it."

Straightforwardness and earnestness are the characteristic traits of the third Class. They really want to get rid of their inordinate affection and to find God in peace, cost what it may. It's possible that God may not demand that they actually sacrifice the ten thousand ducats, but merely to purify their attachment to it.

But how can they be sure that God's love alone moves them to keep the money, and not rather the love of self, under the disguise of God's honor and glory? As far as lies in their power, they first give up in the money, and then, proceed to consider, whether, for the sole reason of serving Him better, it is God's Will that they should take it back. In other words, they live like it's gone, disappeared, vanished.

An example: Fr. Fuentes tells the story of a wealthy man who took the Exercises with Fr. Fuentes preaching. He had a large sum of money that he didn't know whether God wanted him to keep, or to give to charity. So, Fr. Fuentes told him, "Write a letter to the bank, with all the instructions explaining to which charity the money should go, etc., a letter such that, if I mailed it to the bank, the money would be set off to charity." So the man wrote the letter, and Fr. Fuentes said, "Ok, give it to me. If you discern that God wants you to get rid of the money, then I'll mail the letter. If you discern He wants you to keep it, I'll destroy the letter." So, the man did as he was told. During the Exercises, the man discerned that God wanted him to keep the money, so Fr. Fuentes destroyed the letter, but during those days the man lived as if the money were already gone.

That is the third class of man. The third class have the generosity to dispose of the creature (outside themselves) if this is necessary to shake off a dangerous affection (within themselves). They apply without hesitation the basic norms of the Principle and Foundation: the *tantum quantum* rule which measures the use or abstinence from creatures only by their utility to attain the end of man's creation; and the rule of the counsels, which is not satisfied with a minimal service of God, but wants to do whatever is more conducive to salvation and more pleasing to the Divine Majesty.

Such souls are firmly and solidly established in God and His Holy Will, and enjoy complete freedom and peace. They are fit instruments in God's hands. They generously follow Christ wherever He calls them, even in poverty and humiliations, and choose in everything that which is more for the glory of his Divine Majesty and for the salvation of their souls. Far from being sad, their life is one of constant Joy—no matter whether it is the joy of possessing things for God, or the even greater joy of sacrificing them for his love. In giving up all things, they soon realize they have found the All-Good.

Of this group, Allamano writes: "The third group is made up of those who spare no means to become saints; they allow for no delay, and they fight without rest. Of them Saint Ignatius says: 'With great and generous souls in the service of God, they set all their minds and efforts.' They sacrifice everything, especially their good will. This is how they become saints! This isn't so difficult; again, I say, it's enough to take the first step with courage. Referring to these three groups, Saint Robert Bellarmine says that the first are the sick who don't want to take their medicine; the second accept only sweet and flavorful medicines, and the third reject nothing, no matter how bitter it is, provided it cures them. My thoughts are directed to your future, and I ask: will you be part of the third group? Or will some of you come to be part of the second, or the first group? It's a question of having a firm and resolute will."[3]

---

3. Lorenzo Sales, La vida espiritual. *Conversaciones del P. José Allamano con sus misioneros*, Madrid 1977, pp. 149-150. It's clear that the background of this description is taken from the meditation on the "Three Classes of Men" from the Spiritual Exercises of Saint Ignatius of Loyola. Cited in *Duc in Altum!* By Fr. Fuentes.

We can give a couple of rules to see if we're inordinately attached to something. Let us consider:

If the object occupies my mind at times that should be free of such pre-occupation, like prayer or necessary duties like study, caring for my children or spouse; or if the amount of attention I give to the person, place, or thing is out of proportion to its objective value and importance. The standard hierarchy of values: supernatural, spiritual, intellectual and material may be applied here. So that if, for example, I am more concerned with an intellectual project than with my spiritual obligations to the point where it affects my spiritual obligations, there's an attachment that's out of order.

If I find myself habitually taking some happiness in some possession, to the point where I tend to despise or pity others for lacking what I have, this is a sign of inordinate attachment.

If I often lose peace of mind from definable or undefinable causes, on account of what I have or do, I am too attached to the object, person, or practice, since ordinate affection, being orderly, produces tranquility of mind which is the essence of peace. Recall that Saint Augustine said peace is "a tranquility in order"; it's a sort of calm that comes when things are in the right place, when things are made right, and everything is where it should be. A disordered attachment sets things out of place and out of order.

If I am always afraid of losing or being hindered in the use of some gift or possession, or if I feel dissatisfied with what I have, whether its amount, quality or perfection, again, I have a disordered attachment.

If I regularly talk about my achievement along certain lines or advertise what I have for no better reason than the pleasure I get from being recognized, this is a sign of disorder.

If I am inclined to envy others for some kind of talent, production, or property which I feel outshines or obscures my own, disordered attachment.

If I tend to be jealous of what I have, slow to share it with others or fearful that others may acquire the same, I am overly in love with the creature, no matter how lawfully acquired or how holy the thing may be in itself.

[156] Threefold Colloquy: I will make use of the same three colloquies employed in the preceding contemplation on Two Standards.

A colloquy should be addressed to our Lady, asking her to obtain for me from her Son and Lord the grace to be received under His standard, first in the highest spiritual poverty, and should the Divine Majesty be pleased thereby, and deign to choose and accept me, even in actual poverty; secondly, in bearing insults and wrongs, thereby to imitate Him better, provided only I can suffer these without sin on the part of another, and without offense of the Divine Majesty. Then I will say the Hail Mary.

Second Colloquy: This will be to ask her Son to obtain the same favors for me from the Father. Then I will say, Soul of Christ.

Third Colloquy: This will be to beg the Father to grant me the same graces. Then I will say the Our Father.

[157] Note: It should be noted that when we feel an attachment opposed to actual poverty or a repugnance to it, when we are not indifferent to poverty and riches, it will be very helpful in order to overcome the inordinate attachment, even though corrupt nature rebel against it, to beg our Lord in the colloquies to choose us to serve Him in actual poverty. We should insist that we desire it, beg for it, plead for it, provided, of course, that it be for the service and praise of the Divine Goodness.

Three Kinds of Humility [165-168]

Ignatius actually gives an introductory note to this meditation, in 164; it serves as a sort of culmination of the second week of the Exercises.

(164) Before entering upon the Choice of a Way of Life, in order that we may be filled with love of the true doctrine of Christ our Lord, it will be very useful to consider attentively the following Three Kinds of Humility. These should be thought over from time to time during the whole day, and the three colloquies should also be added as will be indicated further on.

Usual Preparation Prayer.
First Prelude: We may see Christ our Lord climbing to Calvary carrying His Cross, followed by Mary and John, the Beloved Disciple.

Second Prelude: We implore our Lord to be pleased to elect us to the third Mode of greater and more perfect humility, the better to imitate and serve Him. We must repeat this petition as often as possible during the day.

Three Kinds of Humility
(165) The First Kind of Humility
This is necessary for salvation. It consists in this, that as far as possible I so subject and humble myself as to obey the law of God our Lord in all things, so that not even were I made lord of all creation, or to save my life here on earth, would I consent to violate a commandment, whether divine or human, that binds me under pain of mortal sin.

(166) The Second Kind of Humility
This is more perfect than the first. I possess it if my attitude of mind is such that I neither desire nor am I inclined to have riches rather than poverty, to seek honor rather than dishonor, to desire a long life rather than a short life, provided only in either alternative I would promote equally the service of God our Lord and the salvation of my soul. Besides this indifference, this second kind of humility supposes that not for all creation, nor to save my life, would I consent to commit a venial sin.

(167) The Third Kind of Humility

This is the most perfect kind of humility. It consists in this. If we suppose the first and second kind attained, then whenever the praise and glory of the Divine Majesty would be equally served, in order to imitate and be in reality more like Christ our Lord, I desire and choose poverty with Christ poor, rather than riches; insults with Christ loaded with them, rather than honors; I desire to be accounted as worthless and a fool for Christ, rather than to be esteemed as wise and prudent in this world. So Christ was treated before me.

(168) Note

If one desires to attain this third kind of humility, it will help very much to use the three colloquies at the close of the meditation on the three Classes of Men mentioned above. He should beg our Lord to deign to choose him for this third kind of humility, which is higher and better, that he may the more imitate and serve Him, provided equal or greater praise and service be given to the Divine Majesty.

Before entering on the work of the Election, or, as is more often the case, on the work of self-reform, St. Ignatius wants us, in order that we may be well affected towards the true doctrine of Christ our Lord, to consider three Modes of Humility, i.e., three attitudes concerning the service of God and the use of created things, one more perfect than the other. It must be remembered that an attitude, such as a Mode of Humility, is not an act but a habitual purpose.

Though the Saint assigns no definite time to the consideration of these three Modes, but simply desires that we keep revolving them in our minds during the day, we may make them the subject of some sort of meditation.

The expression "Degrees of Humility" [this depends on your translation] or "Kinds of Humility" does not occur in either the Spanish autograph or the recognized versions of the original text. The Spanish uses the term *maneras* or types of humility; the various Latin translations use Species or Modes. There is more than subtlety behind these synonyms. By definition, degree implies a quantitative difference (like degrees of temperature, the difference between 0 degrees Celsius and 100 degrees Celsius) whereas mode and species are qualitative. Accordingly, the second mode differs from the first, and the third from the first two, not only in having more humility (in terms of quantity) but in being humility of a *qualitatively* higher kind. In other words, to rise from a lower to a higher type of humility (in the Ignatian sense) means not merely to accumulate more of what we already possess, but to enter into an essentially superior form of moral disposition. Since the term "Degrees of Humility" is commonly acceptable, there is no problem in using it; but there is also some advantage in knowing the proper meaning which the Exercises attach to this name.

The purpose of the meditation on the Three Modes of Humility is still better to prepare the exercitant for a good Election. By contrast with the Three Classes, the Modes represent the last preparatory stage before the actual Election. Whereas the function of the Classes was primarily negative, to remove inordinate affection for the creatures, the Modes are strictly positive, to test and inspire the will for complete dedication to the service of God. In the words of St. Ignatius, "Before any one enters on the Election, that he may be well affected towards the teaching of Christ our Lord, it will be profitable to consider and examine the following modes of humility."

As conceived by the Exercises, humility is the proper disposition that a human will should assume in relation to the divine, and may reach one of three levels of union with the will of God, in ascending order of sublimity.

(165) The First Kind of Humility: This is necessary for salvation. It consists in this, that as far as possible I so subject and humble myself as to obey the law of God our Lord in all things, so that not even were I made lord of all creation, or to save my life here on earth, would I consent to violate a commandment, whether divine or human, that binds me under pain of mortal sin.

Such a determination is absolutely necessary to anyone who wants to be saved. Not to have it, would imply that he is in a state of opposition to God, or at least of apathy towards, and disregard for Him. On the other hand this habitual disposition not to deliberate about offending God grievously is not inconsistent with an actual fall at times. As a matter of fact there are moments and circumstances in life when nothing short of grim courage and true heroism will enable one to remain true to God. Apart from the thousands and thousands of canonized Saints, who endured the loss of goods, imprisonment, and death itself to be faithful to God, there are the uncanonized millions who often undergo a hidden martyrdom to keep themselves chaste, and to be truthful, just, and charitable in their dealings, with others. Fear of God, humble prayer, and control of one's passions will maintain a soul in the disposition of the first Mode of Humility.

The first Mode requires in one the substantial indifference that makes him look upon God as his ultimate and supreme End, and upon all creatures as means to reach Him. The first type of humility, then, means that quality of submission to the Divine Majesty which makes the will ready to sacrifice any created good, even life itself, rather than disobey a commandment of God binding under mortal sin. In terms of indifference, it requires habitual detachment at least from those creatures which may not be enjoyed without loss of sanctifying grace. In other words, if a person has completed the first week of the Exercises, and really obtained their fruit, they must at least have this level of humility.

However, that being presupposed, one who has but the disposition of the first Mode, loves and pursues the good things of the world, and avoids what is hard and humiliating. Such is, after all, the disposition of so many average Christians.

(166) The Second Kind of Humility: This is more perfect than the first. I possess it if my attitude of mind is such that I neither desire nor am I inclined to have riches rather than poverty, to seek honor rather than dishonor, to desire a long life rather than a short life, provided only in either alternative I would promote equally the service of God our Lord and the salvation of my soul. Besides this indifference, this second kind of humility supposes that not for all creation, nor to save my life, would I consent to commit a venial sin.

The second type of humility is essentially higher. It presupposes the first and goes beyond it with a readiness to sacrifice anything rather than offend God by venial sin. Like the first, it also requires detachment from creatures, and not only from those which are sinful but to a certain extent also from such as may legitimately be used without sin. To practice the second mode, I should be no more "inclined to have riches rather than poverty, to seek honor rather than dishonor, to desire a long life rather than a short life, provided in either alternative I would promote equally the service of God and the salvation of my soul."

Such a disposition is far nobler than the previous one. However, we are still within the limits of reasonableness and justice. As a matter of fact, is it not just and reasonable that we avoid everything that offends His Divine Majesty? And is not the smallest venial sin, even in the light of reason, an incomparably greater evil than all the so-called evils of this world, greater than poverty, dishonor, sickness, and death itself?

To act faithfully and constantly according to such a disposition requires greater energy and strength. One must be perfectly indifferent to all created things, i.e., he must have complete control of himself, of his passions, his whims and caprices, not only in serious matters, as in the first Mode, but in light matters as well. In the first Mode, while keeping his eyes and his steps towards God, his final goal, he allows himself many a digression off the straight road: in the second Mode he walks straight on along it.

If the holy fear of God, humble prayer, and self-denial are necessary to anyone who wants to be faithful to the disposition of the first Mode, how much more essential are they to one who desires to maintain himself in the disposition of the second?

(167) The Third Kind of Humility: This is the most perfect kind of humility. It consists in this. If we suppose the first and second kind attained, then whenever the praise and glory of the Divine Majesty would be equally served, in order to imitate and be in reality more like Christ our Lord, I desire and choose poverty with Christ poor, rather than riches; insults with Christ loaded with them, rather than honors; I desire to be accounted as worthless and a fool for Christ, rather than to be esteemed as wise and prudent in this world. So Christ was treated before me.

The disposition required by the first and second Mode of Humility is a positive disposition of the will. It consists, directly, not in avoiding mortal and venial sin, but in submitting one's will more and more perfectly to the Will of God, and in an ever-greater control of self in using the good things of this world and in enduring its hardships and humiliations.

We are created to serve God, i.e., to do His Holy Will, and all other creatures are given us to attain this end.

In the first Mode we obey God's Holy Will commanding under penalty of mortal sin, and make free use of creatures as long as they do not take us entirely away from God. In the second Mode we obey all the commands of God, even those binding under venial sin only. Towards creatures we keep an attitude of perfect indifference so long as God's Will is not known.

Assuming the first and second modes of humility to be already attained, if the will remains not merely indifferent to poverty or riches, honor or dishonor, but positively desires and chooses by preference poverty and dishonor in imitation of Christ, "this is the most perfect kind of humility." As explained by St. Ignatius in a little-known Directory written by himself, the fundamental difference between the second and the third modes lies in the attitude of will towards poverty and humiliations, with all their implications. If the will is ready to accept them, but equally ready to embrace the opposite, we have the second mode; if it is not only willing to accept but actually prefers poverty and humiliations, we have the third. "If it is possible," Ignatius directs, "the exercitant should rise to the third grade of humility, in which, as far as he can, he is more inclined to what is more conformed to the evangelical counsels and the example of Christ our Lord, if the service of God be equal." But if he inclines less to the counsels, as exemplified in the poverty and humiliation of Christ, at least he should be detached from riches and honors according to the second mode.

The author of the Exercises identifies the value of a retreat with a person's willingness to accept the evangelical counsels. He instructs the director professedly to "dispose the retreatant to desire the counsels rather than the precepts, if this be for the greater service of God." Consequently, "whoever has not reached the indifference of the second degree," which implies at least a passive acceptance of certain counsels, "should not be encouraged to make the election and will more profitably be given other exercises until he acquires this indifference."

In the third Mode we submit to God's Holy Will not only when He commands under penalty of sin, mortal or venial, but even when He merely expresses a desire; in other words, we are determined to do everything that pleases Him, to avoid every imperfection, to follow all counsels and obey all inspirations. As regards the use of creatures, knowing well that Christ has chosen what pleases God most, and anxious to be like Him, our Eldest Brother, we choose, as far as lies in us, to be poor with Him poor, to be insulted with Him covered with insults, and to be esteemed as worthless and fools for Him who was first held to be such. The indifference of the second Mode becomes positive acceptance of, and longing for privations, humiliations, and sufferings, i.e., for the higher and harder path, out of pure love for Christ and to be truly like Him in everything.

The three modes can be illustrated by the example of a man who has unjustly suffered a grave injury to his honor:

First Mode: He does not care to retrieve his good name if it cannot be done without serious sin.

Second Mode: He will not try to defend his honor if this would involve committing venial sin; but if it can be done without sin, he wants to restore his reputation.

Third Mode: He considers the loss of reputation as profit in Christ. Instead of defending himself, he will gladly suffer the injury in silence. But on one condition: as long as God's glory is equally served, i.e., when neither a moral obligation nor benefit to others demands that he vindicate his legitimate rights. If such an obligation or benefit exists, then ipso facto there is no longer equal glory to God, and he will defend his reputation without failing in the spirit of the third mode. All the while his internal dispositions are such that if a just defense of his honor were not obligatory in itself or profitable to the neighbor, he will consider it a privilege to suffer in the company of his humiliated Master.

Only such a disposition can make it possible for one to do God's well-pleasing Will in all circumstances. "The third Mode of Humility places a man spiritually in what mechanicians call a position of advantage for doing work, like the position of water on the top of a hill. He will be endowed with that high courage, for lack of which, in the abundance of good men, great Saints are rare." The love of the Cross cuts at the very root of even the slightest opposition to it and prepares one to face great trials bravely.

The third Mode of Humility—perfect obedience to God's Will, with and like Christ poor, humble, and crucified—is the central point of the Exercises. It is the folly of the Cross: "He became obedient unto death, death on a cross."

[168]: Note: If one desires to attain this third kind of humility, it will help very much to use the three colloquies at the close of the meditation on the three Classes of Men mentioned above. He should beg our Lord to deign to choose him for this third kind of humility, which is higher and better, that he may the more imitate and serve Him, provided equal or greater praise and service be given to the Divine Majesty.

[156] Threefold Colloquy: I will make use of the same three colloquies employed in the preceding contemplation on Two Standards.

A colloquy should be addressed to our Lady, asking her to obtain for me from her Son and Lord the grace to be received under His standard, first in the highest spiritual poverty, and should the Divine Majesty be pleased thereby, and deign to choose and accept me, even in actual poverty; secondly, in bearing insults and wrongs, thereby to imitate Him better, provided only I can suffer these without sin on the part of another, and without offense of the Divine Majesty. Then I will say the Hail Mary.

Second Colloquy: This will be to ask her Son to obtain the same favors for me from the Father. Then I will say, Soul of Christ.

Third Colloquy: This will be to beg the Father to grant me the same graces. Then I will say the Our Father.

[157] Note: It should be noted that when we feel an attachment opposed to actual poverty or a repugnance to it, when we are not indifferent to poverty and riches, it will be very helpful in order to overcome the inordinate attachment, even though corrupt nature rebel against it, to beg our Lord in the colloquies to choose us to serve Him in actual poverty. We should insist that we desire it, beg for it, plead for it, provided, of course, that it be for the service and praise of the Divine Goodness.

The Baptism of the Lord [158], [273]

At [158], Ignatius presents us with a contemplation on the Baptism of the Lord. It marks the end of Jesus' hidden life, and, for us, it marks the end of the first half of the second week.

At this point Ignatius says, simply: "The contemplation on the journey of Christ our Lord from Nazareth to the river Jordan and His baptism. Cf. # 273."

However, he also gives three clarifying notes

[159] This matter should be contemplated once at midnight, and again in the morning. There will be two repetitions of it, one about the time of Mass and the other about the time of Vespers. Before supper there will be the Application of the Senses to the same mystery.

In each of these five exercises, there will be at the beginning, the preparatory prayer and the three preludes [history, composition of place, and the petition] as was fully explained in the contemplations on the Incarnation and the Nativity. They will conclude with the three colloquies of the meditation on Three Classes of Men, or according to the note which follows this meditation.

[160] The Particular Examination of Conscience after dinner and after supper will be made upon the faults and negligences with regard to the exercises of the day and on the Additional Directions. The same will be observed on the subsequent days.

Usual Preparation Prayer.

First Prelude: The History: For the history, we can consider the Biblical text that Ignatius points out: Mt 3:13-17. However, to be fair, all the synoptic Gospels mention it, so we could also consider Mk 1:9-11 and Lk 3:21-22. Jesus goes from Galilee to see John the Baptist at the Jordan River, asking to be baptized. John tells Him it should be reversed: John should be baptized, but Jesus replies "Allow it now, for thus it is fitting for us to fulfill all righteousness." As soon as Jesus is baptized, the heavens opened, the Spirit of God descends like a dove, and a voice is heard that says: "This is my beloved Son, with whom I am well pleased."

Second Prelude: The Composition of Place: Here, in our imaginations, we should see the River Jordan, with the many people who are gathered together. We can see John the Baptist, in accord with the description given in the Gospels, as Mark tells us "John was clothed in camel's hair, with a leather belt around his waist. He fed on locusts and wild honey" (Mk 1:6).

Third Prelude: Petition: Here the petition will be is to ask for light to know intimately my Divine King Who has become a Man for me, and grace to love Him and follow Him in poverty, suffering, and humiliations.

At [273] Ignatius gives three very short points:

First Point
After Christ our Lord had bidden farewell to His blessed Mother, He went from Nazareth to the River Jordan where St. John the Baptist was.

Second Point
St. John baptized Christ our Lord. When he wished to excuse himself because he thought himself unworthy to baptize Him, our Lord said to him: "Let it be so at this time; for so it fitting to fulfill all justness."

Third Point
The Holy Spirit descended upon Him, and the voice of the Father from Heaven testified, "This is my beloved Son in whom I am well pleased."

As with some of the other contemplations we have considered, Ignatius doesn't give a very detailed contemplation. He gives only the basic steps and then reminds us to follow the same model as we did before: to *see* the people, then to *hear* the people, then to *examine what they are doing*, each time gathering some fruit for my life.

As we have done for the other meditations, we can consider, first, a little history of the scene and then, second, some elements to help us contemplate and consider Christ so as to imitate Him better. Tonight, we will consider general facts, but will focus on just the third point that Ignatius gives, namely, the miracles that took place. The other two points will be left for the repetition tomorrow.

Biblical archaeologists have considered several places as the site of the baptism of the Lord, but, "since the 4th century, the place indicated often seems to be the right bank of the river, some 4 to 5 miles north from the Dead Sea. John's Gospel gives two different places that John baptized: Bethany, a three day journey from Nazareth (this isn't the village Bethany near Jerusalem, but rather the place called Bethabara in Perea), and Enon, which means springs, and was near Salim, a day's journey from Nazareth, a little further from the mouth of the Dead Sea."[1]

Now, we could ask, why there? Why not somewhere else? In ST III, q. 39, a. 4, Aquinas points out why this was the most fitting place, because it was through the Jordan that the children of Israel were led into the promised land, and, hence, since baptism leads us to Heaven, the Jordan is the best place. He asks why Jesus wasn't baptized in the Red Sea, because that is where the children of Israel crossed out of Egypt, and he replies, yes, but the main point of baptism is to open Heaven to us. The Red Sea represents forgiveness of sins, but it's more important that it opens Heaven to us.

We could also ask about the timing. For thirty years Jesus had waited: on the surface, such a delay seems unreasonable, unfathomable. But, in God's planning, everything is perfect. As the saying goes, "God is never early, and God is never late: He is always exactly on time." In another article, Aquinas says that 30 represents the perfect age: Joseph and David began ruling at 30, and Ezekiel began prophesying at 30, and so we understand that Baptism brings forth perfect men. Everything plays into God's plan, even seeming delays.

We can leave the consideration of the first two points that Ignatius mentions until tomorrow; now, let us just consider three miracles that takes place: when John baptizes Jesus, first, the heavens open, second, the Holy Spirit descends on Him in the form of a dove, and, third, the Father's voice is heard.

"The heavens were opened. The key that opens Heaven to us is humility; God gives His grace to the humble and that grace is the seed of future glory. We must aspire to Heaven!

This opening of the heavens was undoubtedly seen by both Jesus and John, since John testifies that *"Now I have seen and testified that he is the Son of God"* (Jn 1:34). Did everyone there see the heavens open? Most of the Church Fathers and doctors say yes, because that visible sign wasn't necessary for Christ. He didn't need to see the heavens open, but rather we need signs. Hence, it would be fitting that everyone who was there saw this miracle. Even in this first moment, God wanted to reveal His Son to us, and we do well to recall this, thanking God for it and taking advantage of such revelation.

The second miracle is the descent of the Holy Spirit upon Christ in the form of a dove: this is the way God honors those who humble themselves, by sending them His grace and His very spirit.

We shouldn't understand this coming of the Holy Spirit upon Jesus as though with it He received in His soul some increase in grace or that He was anointed by the Holy Spirit in that moment; rather, we should understand this

1. Oraa, *Ejercicios Espirituales*, 342.

scene as a declaration and manifestation of the Spirit's presence in Christ to all those gathered. In other words, it was to reveal the gift of the Holy Spirit, which was with Christ since His conception, by means of a new sensible sign.

It is the same Spirit that is responsible for making us prompt and diligent to follow Christ's call, to heed His voice, and to follow His lead.

The third miracle is the voice that comes from Heaven: *This is My Beloved Son in whom I am well pleased.* Christ humbled Himself to be baptized, and it is precisely for this reason that God exalts Him. It is grace that transforms us and turns us into God's beloved children. Thus grace is more valuable than worldly riches, worldly honor, and all things."[2]

What are we to make of these miracles? Fulton Sheen offers a very profound reflection, one that we can consider, especially in thinking about our own adopted sonship.

Sheen writes: "The sacred humanity of Christ was the connecting link between Heaven and earth. The voice from Heaven which declared Him to be the Beloved Son of the Eternal Father was not announcing a new fact or a new Sonship of Our Blessed Lord. It was merely making a solemn declaration of that Sonship, which had existed from all eternity, but which was now beginning to manifest itself publicly as Mediator between God and man. The Father's good pleasure, in the original Greek, is recorded in the aorist tense, to denote the eternal act of loving contemplation with which the Father regards the Son. The Christ Who came out of the water, as the earth had come out of the water at creation and after the Flood, as Moses and his people had come out of the waters of the Red Sea, was now glorified by the Holy Spirit appearing in the form of a Dove.

The Spirit of God never appears in the figure of a dove anywhere save here. The Book of Leviticus mentions offerings which were made according to the economic and social position of the giver. A man who could afford it would bring a bullock, and a poorer man would offer a lamb; but the poorest of all had the privilege of bringing doves. When the mother of Our Lord brought Him to the temple, her offering was a dove. The dove was the symbol of gentleness and peacefulness, but above all it was the type of sacrifice possible to the lowliest people. Whenever a Hebrew thought of a lamb or a dove, he immediately thought of a sacrifice for sin. Therefore, the Spirit descending upon Our Lord was for them a symbol of submission to sacrifice. Christ had already united Himself symbolically with man in baptism, in anticipation of His submergence into the waters of suffering; but now He was also crowned, dedicated, and consecrated to that sacrifice through the coming of the Spirit.

2. Oraa, *Ejecicios Espirituales*, 346-48.

The waters of the Jordan united Him with men, the Spirit crowned Him and dedicated Him to sacrifice, and the Voice attested that His sacrifice would be pleasing to the Eternal Father

The baptism in the Jordan closed Our Lord's private life and began His public ministry. He had gone down into the water known to most men only as the son of Mary; He came out ready to reveal Himself as what He had been from all eternity, the Son of God. He was the Son of God in the likeness of man in all things, save sin. The Spirit was anointing Him not just for teaching, but for redeeming."[3]

[Colloquy]: Ignatius tells us to end with the colloquy used for the Three Classes of Men, which is the same as the one used for Two Standards.

Threefold Colloquy:

A colloquy should be addressed to our Lady, asking her to obtain for me from her Son and Lord the grace to be received under His standard, first in the highest spiritual poverty, and should the Divine Majesty be pleased thereby, and deign to choose and accept me, even in actual poverty; secondly, in bearing insults and wrongs, thereby to imitate Him better, provided only I can suffer these without sin on the part of another, and without offense of the Divine Majesty. Then I will say the Hail Mary.

Second Colloquy: This will be to ask her Son to obtain the same favors for me from the Father. Then I will say, Soul of Christ.

Third Colloquy: This will be to beg the Father to grant me the same graces. Then I will say the Our Father.

[157] Note: It should be noted that when we feel an attachment opposed to actual poverty or a repugnance to it, when we are not indifferent to poverty and riches, it will be very helpful in order to overcome the inordinate attachment, even though corrupt nature rebel against it, to beg our Lord in the colloquies to choose us to serve Him in actual poverty. We should insist that we desire it, beg for it, plead for it, provided, of course, that it be for the service and praise of the Divine Goodness.

---

3. Fulton Sheen, *Life of Christ.*

The Baptism of the Lord [158], [273] – Repetition

Once again, we come to reflect on the Baptism of Our Lord in the Jordan, the end of His Hidden Life and the beginning of His public ministry.

Usual Preparation Prayer.

First Prelude: The History: For the history, we can consider the Biblical text that Ignatius points out: Mt 3:13-17, Mk 1:9-11, and Lk 3:21-22. Jesus goes from Galilee to see John the Baptist at the Jordan River, asking to be baptized. John tells Him it should be reversed: John should be baptized, but Jesus replies "Allow it now, for thus it is fitting for us to fulfill all righteousness." As soon as Jesus is baptized, the heavens opened, the Spirit of God descends like a dove, and a voice is heard that says: "This is my beloved Son, with whom I am well pleased."

Second Prelude: The Composition of Place: Here, in our imaginations, we should see the River Jordan, with the many people who are gathered together. We can see John the Baptist, in accord with the description given in the Gospels, as Mark tells us "John was clothed in camel's hair, with a leather belt around his waist. He fed on locusts and wild honey" (Mk 1:6).

Third Prelude: Petition: Here the petition will be is to ask for light to know intimately my Divine King Who has become a Man for me, and grace to love Him and follow Him in poverty, suffering, and humiliations.

At [273] Ignatius gives three very short points:

First Point

After Christ our Lord had bidden farewell to His blessed Mother, He went from Nazareth to the River Jordan where St. John the Baptist was.

Second Point

St. John baptized Christ our Lord. When he wished to excuse himself because he thought himself unworthy to baptize Him, our Lord said to him: "Let it be so at this time; for so it fitting to fulfill all justness."

Third Point

The Holy Spirit descended upon Him, and the voice of the Father from Heaven testified, "This is my beloved Son in whom I am well pleased."

In the contemplation, we should recall the structure that Ignatius wants us to follow: to *see* the people, then to *hear* the people, then to *examine what they are doing*, each time gathering some fruit for my life. Last night we considered the miracles related to the baptism itself, which are easier to visualize. For this morning, we can consider the first two points that Ignatius makes: after Christ our Lord had bidden farewell to His blessed Mother, He went from Nazareth to the River Jordan where St. John the Baptist was, and that St. John baptized Christ our Lord.

Regarding the first, it's interesting that Ignatius includes this point. It is an undeniable fact that Jesus had to go from Nazareth to the Jordan, but Ignatius makes us consider this moment; he presents us with Mary, and teaches us the love and reverence that we should have for her.

It must have been a very sad moment for the both of them. We have no record of their many conversations, their prayers, their discussions regarding the coming of the Kingdom, of God's goodness. Mary must have known that at some point Christ would leave, or, as Fr. Oraa says it so nicely, "she knew that Jesus' messianic labors required a bigger field than the little house at Nazareth."[1] At some point, Jesus must have told her, gently, but with sorrow, that He was going to begin His work. It would have been a great sacrifice for both of them, because they loved each other dearly, and they were happy in their home.

Here, we too learn to sacrifice, and that sacrifice is an essential part of the apostolate. Jesus would have been sorrowed at the sight of His mother's suffering, but He nonetheless went about His mission.

This sacrifice teaches us detachment, that even the deepest bonds and most profound loves, should never keep us from doing God's will. This is important, especially as we begin to see, concretely, what it is that God wants us to work on. Any disordered affection, especially for friends or family, will get in the way of our vocation and our service of God.

We also see that the life of an apostle, no matter what vocation that might be, requires all of our strength and time, our body and our soul, our intellect and our will. As we said in our meditation on the Two Standards, the first requirement to follow Christ is spiritual poverty, detachment from everything, friends, house, goods, and parents.

1. Oraa, *Ejercicios Espirituales*, 343. This entire section, though, is adapted from him, 342-346.

In that same phrase, we are told that Christ went to the Jordan; it would have been a long walk, along the dusty road, over rocks, avoiding wild beasts. All this, so Jesus can begin His public ministry with an act of profound humility.

Second, Ignatius tells us that John baptized Jesus. We can imagine the "carpenter of Nazareth," who, at this point, is basically a nobody, appearing on the shores of the Jordan, mixed in with all the penitents who wanted to change their lives and were attracted by John's preaching. John did not personally know his cousin: *I did not know him* (Jn 1:39). But, as Jesus drew near, John would have received the grace to know who He was, and hence Matthew tells us: *John tried to prevent him, saying, "I need to be baptized by you, and yet you are coming to me?" Jesus said to him in reply, "Allow it now, for thus it is fitting for us to fulfill all righteousness." Then he allowed him* (Mt 3:14-15).

Here we can contemplate Jesus' great humility; as we mentioned in the Two Standards, this is what Christ intends for us: to be humble, and so He gives us an example. Having taken the form of a slave, Christ even took, as it were, the form of a penitent.

When John recognizes Jesus, knowing who He is, he is filled with surprise, reverence, and humbles himself. Yet, Jesus tells him to allow this baptism, and, in obedience, he permits it. Here we see, once again, the two virtues on which our lives hinge: humility and obedience. We must subject ourselves, not only to our superiors and our equals, but even, when appropriate, to our subjects.

Here is Jesus, mixed in with the crowds, considered a sinner among sinners! How much more should we always be submissive, always humble, always obedient!

Once again, as we reflect upon how Christ's Baptism is a model for us, we see, as Fulton Sheen says, a parallel with the Finding of Jesus in the Temple. He writes: "Many years before, He had said that He must be about His Father's business; now He was revealing what His Father's business was: the salvation of mankind. He was expressing His relationship to His people, on whose behalf He had been sent. In the temple at the age of twelve, it had been His origin that He emphasized; now in the Jordan, it was the nature of His mission. In the temple He had spoken of His Divine mandate. Under the cleansing hands of John, He made clear His oneness with humanity."

As for our own lives, and how to follow Christ in His Baptism, we are reminded, as Saint Jose Maria Escriva writes, that "all men are children of God. But a child can look upon his father in many ways. We must try to be children who realize that the Lord, by loving us as his children, has taken us into his house, in the middle of the world, to be members of his family, so that what is his is ours, and what is ours is his, and to develop that familiarity and confidence which prompts us to ask him, like children, for the moon!

A child of God treats the Lord as his Father. He is not obsequious and servile, he is not merely formal and well mannered: he is completely sincere and trusting. Men do not scandalize God. He can put up with all our infidelities. Our Father in Heaven pardons any offence when his child returns to him, when he repents and asks for pardon. The Lord is such a good Father that he anticipates our desire to be pardoned and comes forward to us, opening his arms laden with grace. (*Christ is Passing By, 64*)

A Christian knows that he is grafted onto Christ through baptism. He is empowered to fight for Christ through confirmation, called to act in the world sharing the royal, prophetic and priestly role of Christ. He has become one and the same thing with Christ through the Eucharist, the sacrament of unity and love. And so, like Christ, he has to live for other men, loving each and every one around him and indeed all humanity...

You cannot separate the fact that Christ is God from his role as redeemer. The Word became flesh and came into the world "to save all men." With all our personal defects and limitations, we are other Christs, Christ himself, and we too are called to serve all men...

Our Lord has come to bring peace, good news and life to all men. Not only to the rich, nor only to the poor. Not only to the wise nor only to the simple. To everyone, to the brothers, for brothers we are, children of the same Father, God. So there is only one race, the race of the children of God. There is only one color, the color of the children of God. And there is only one language, the language which speaks to the heart and to the mind, without the noise of words, making us know God and love one another" (*Christ is Passing By, 106*).

[Colloquy]: Ignatius tells us to end with the colloquy used for the Three Classes of Men, which is the same as the one used for Two Standards.

Threefold Colloquy:

A colloquy should be addressed to our Lady, asking her to obtain for me from her Son and Lord the grace to be received under His standard, first in the highest spiritual poverty, and should the Divine Majesty be pleased thereby, and deign to choose and accept me, even in actual poverty; secondly, in bearing insults and wrongs, thereby to imitate Him better, provided only I can suffer these without sin on the part of another, and without offense of the Divine Majesty. Then I will say the Hail Mary.

Second Colloquy: This will be to ask her Son to obtain the same favors for me from the Father. Then I will say, Soul of Christ.

Third Colloquy: This will be to beg the Father to grant me the same graces. Then I will say the Our Father.

[157] Note: It should be noted that when we feel an attachment opposed to actual poverty or a repugnance to it, when we are not indifferent to poverty and riches, it will be very helpful in order to overcome the inordinate attachment, even though corrupt nature rebel against it, to beg our Lord in the colloquies to choose us to serve Him in actual poverty. We should insist that we desire it, beg for it, plead for it, provided, of course, that it be for the service and praise of the Divine Goodness.

The Temptations in the Desert [161], [274]

At [161], Ignatius tells us that for the Sixth day, "The contemplation will be on Christ our Lord's departure from the river Jordan for the desert and on the temptations. The same directions that were given for the fifth day will be followed here." The fifth day was the contemplation we just had, namely, on the Lord's baptism. So, all the three steps of the meditation, the preludes, and the three colloquies, all of that, we continue.

Usual Preparation Prayer.

First Prelude: The History: For the history, we can consider the Biblical texts that Ignatius points out: Lk 4:1–13 and Mt 4:1–11

Second Prelude: The Composition of Place: Here, in our imaginations, we should see the desert, with its dry, burning heat in the day, and the cold in the night; the howling winds, the burning sun, the wild beasts.

Third Prelude: Petition: Here the petition will be is to ask for light to know intimately my Divine King Who has become a Man for me, and grace to love Him and follow Him in poverty, suffering, and humiliations.

At [274] Ignatius gives three very short points:

First Point

After He had been baptized, Jesus went to the desert where He fasted for forty days and forty nights.

Second Point

He was tempted by the enemy three times: "The tempter drew near and said to Him, 'If thou art the Son of God command that these stones become loaves.... Cast thyself down.... All these things I will give thee if falling down thou wilt worship me!'"

Third Point

"The angels came and ministered to Him."

As with some of the other contemplations we have considered, Ignatius doesn't give a very detailed contemplation. He gives only the basic steps and then reminds us to follow the same model as we did before: to *see* the people, then to *hear* the people, then to *examine what they are doing*, each time gathering some fruit for my life.

As we have done for the other meditations, we can consider, first, a little history of the scene and then, second, and sort of mixed in with them, some elements to help us contemplate and consider Christ so as to imitate Him better.

We do well to consider, first, the place where Jesus was tempted. One commentator describes the place this way: "The inhabited part of Judaea stood on the central plateau which was the backbone of Southern Palestine. Between it and the Dead Sea stretched a terrible wilderness, thirty-five by fifteen miles. It was called Jeshimmon, which means 'The Devastation.' The hills were like dust heaps; the limestone looked blistered and peeling; the rocks were bare and jagged; the ground sounded hollow to the horses' hooves; it glowed with heat like a vast furnace and ran out to the precipices, 1,200 feet high, which swooped down to the Dead Sea. It was in that awesome devastation that Jesus was tempted."[1]

Just like everything in Jesus' life, the location of the temptations is chosen deliberately, and all the many commentators, saints, authors, see plenty of reasons why this is the place for the temptations. It's for this reason that Luke tells us Christ went into the desert "filled with the Holy Spirit," or, as Matthew says, Christ was "led by the Spirit to be tempted." It is clear that this is the spot; this is where God wants this to take place. Saint John Chrysostom describes this very beautifully in a homily, where he writes: "With a view to our instruction He both did and underwent all things; He endures also to be led up there, and to wrestle against the devil: in order that each of those who are baptized, if after his baptism he have to endure greater temptations may not be troubled as if the result were unexpected, but may continue to endure all nobly, as though it were happening in the natural course of things. [This is why] you took up arms, not to be idle, but to fight. For this cause neither does God hinder the temptations as they come."[2] Or, as another writer puts it, the sons of God are moved by the spirit of God, and they go where they are told. The sons of Adam follow the impulse of the evil spirit.[3]

Aquinas says that there are at least two reasons for the desert location: first, because the devil comes to those who are alone, and, second, quoting Saint

---

1. Barclay's commentary on this passage.
2. Saint John Chrysostom, *Homily 13*, 2.
3. De la Puente, but cited in Oraa, *Ejecicios Espirituales*, 357.

Ambrose, in this Jesus reversed the punishment of Adam, who was driven out into the wilderness from the garden. He also notes that "here we see that the devil envies those who strive to do great things," meaning, the devil causes problems for those who try to follow Christ, and we shouldn't expect to be exempted, even if we do things like fast and pray.

Likewise, the desert is the place of solitude, the place of silence. The Spirit led Jesus, not to Jerusalem, or to speak with people, but into the silence, where God speaks to the heart. The spirit of the world loves noise, and we can ask ourselves how much noise we fill our lives with.

Fr. Oraa notes: "Jesus was there alone, among the wild beasts. What did He do? Maintain absolute silence, speak with God, day and night, in prayer, fast, and do penance. What an odd way to prepare oneself for an apostolic mission! Yet, that is the example for us: we should not dare to undertake any apostolic activity without first giving ourselves to develop the interior life."[4]

It is here, in the midst of nowhere, in the howling desert, that the devil comes to tempt Christ. We live in a world of temptation, and hence Christ, who came to save us, desires to undergo our same hardships, and to leave us an example so that we might overcome the devil as well.

The First Temptation: To change stones into bread:

The first temptation was to turn stones into bread. This wilderness was not a wilderness of sand. It was covered by little bits of limestone exactly like loaves.

Many see in this a temptation for material goods, to be satisfied with the things of this world that are able to be eaten, consumed, and used. Many see in this an image of Adam, stretching out his hand towards a food that was forbidden him. The tempter said to Jesus, "If you want people to follow you, use your wonderful powers to give them material things." He was suggesting that Jesus should bribe people into following him. Back came Jesus' answer in a quotation of Dt 8:3. "A man," he said, "will never find life in material things." However, as Sheen notes, this is to reduce people to the level of animals, to try to find satisfaction in things that ultimately cannot satisfy.

The task of Christianity is not to produce new conditions, although the weight and voice of the church must be behind all efforts to make life better for men. Its real task is to produce new men; and given the new men, the new conditions will follow.[5]

---

4. Cf. Oraa, *Ejercicios*, 358-359. Much of what follows is adjusted from him.
5. Barclay's commentary.

Others, though, see in this a temptation to something else: "The disorder here," says Fr. Prat, "would be to use the divine power without need, moved by a suggestion that arises from curiosity or malice. To perform a miracle just to perform a miracle would be to show off; to perform it simply to satisfy a natural necessity would be a lack of trust in God. In such a situation, one must surrender to providence, who will provide for our needs in unexpected ways. This is the meaning of Christ's reply. In the desert the Hebrews clamored for bread, and God made the manna rain down on them unexpectedly, precisely, as Moses tells them: "He therefore fed you with manna, a food unknown to you and your ancestors, so you might know that it is not by bread alone that people live, but by all that comes forth from the mouth of the LORD."

Our senses, too, clamor to be satisfied. Likewise, our curiosity is often insatiable.

We could also say that the devil tempted Christ to use His powers to benefit Himself. Each one of us has our own talents and gifts: how do we use them to serve others? Here, Christ teaches us, as Saint John Chrysostom writes, that "though we hunger, indeed, whatever we suffer, [we must] never fall away from our Lord." Are we really willing and able to sacrifice anything and everything in order not to fall into sin?[6]

The Second Temptation: To throw Himself off of the Temple (following Matthew's order - Luke has these last two in the reverse order):

In Matthew's Gospel we read: *Then the devil took him to the holy city, and made him stand on the parapet of the temple, and said to him, "If you are the Son of God, throw yourself down."*

Barclays notes that this temptation might have one of two possible locations: first, "the Temple was built on the top of Mount Sion. The top of the mountain was levelled out into a plateau, and on that plateau the whole area of the Temple buildings stood. There was one corner at which Solomon's porch and the Royal porch met, and at that corner there was a sheer drop of four hundred and fifty feet into the valley of the Kedron below. Why should not Jesus stand on that pinnacle, and leap down, and land unharmed in the valley beneath? Men would be startled into following a man who could do a thing like that.

[Or, secondly], on the top of the roof of the Temple itself there was a stance where every morning a priest stood with a trumpet in his hands, waiting for the first flush of the dawn across the hills of Hebron. At the first dawn light he sounded the trumpet to tell men that the hour of morning sacrifice had

6. Saint John Chrysostom, *Homily 13*, 2.

come. Why should not Jesus stand there, and leap down right into the Temple court, and amaze men into following him? Had not Malachi said, 'The Lord whom you seek will suddenly come to his Temple'? (Mal 3:1) Was there not a promise that the angels would bear God's man upon their hands lest any harm should come to him? (Ps 91:11-12)

This was the very method that the false Messiahs who were continually arising promised. Theudas had led the people out, and had promised with a word to split the waters of Jordan in two. The famous Egyptian pretender (Acts 21:38) had promised that with a word he would lay flat the walls of Jerusalem. Simon Magus, so it is said, had promised to fly through the air, and had perished in the attempt. These pretenders had offered sensations which they could not perform. Jesus could perform anything he promised. Why should he not do it?"

It is, we could say, a temptation to vanity, to display, to boasting; but Christ rejects that: the only way He wants to win followers it through the cross. Indeed, Fulton Sheen says this second temptation is "to forget the Cross, and replace it with an effortless display of power that would make it easy for people to believe in Him."

To this temptation, Sheen places the following reply on Christ's lips: "I refuse to perform stunts to win [men], for they would not really be won that way. It is only when I am seen on the Cross that I really draw men to Myself; it is by sacrifice, and not by marvels, that I must make My appeal. I must win followers not with test tubes, but with My blood; not with material power, but with love; not with celestial fireworks, but with the right use of reason and free will. No sign shall be given to this generation but the sign of Jonas, namely, the sign of someone rising up from below, not of someone flinging Himself down from the pinnacles.

I want men who will believe in Me, even when I do not protect them; I will not open the prison doors where My brethren are locked; I will not stay the murderous Red sickle or the imperial lions of Rome, I will not halt the Red hammer that batters down My tabernacle doors; I want My missionaries and martyrs to love Me in prison and death as I loved them in My own suffering. I never worked any miracles to save Myself! I will work few miracles even for My saints."

In a homily, Saint John Chrysostom teaches us that "we must overcome the devil, not by miracles, but by forbearance and long-suffering, and that we should do nothing at all for display and vainglory." This is what Christ teaches us, and we can ask ourselves: am I really patient in the face of temptations, especially the temptation to be impatient? How quickly do I reject those temptations to vanity, vainglory, popularity, and ambition?

The Third Temptation: To worship Satan

If you go to Spain, to the city of Barcelona, you will find a tall mountain with a view that overlooks the entire city. There is a stunning shrine dedicated to the Sacred Heart on the top, a shrine built by Saint John Bosco, and, from the mountain's peak, there is a beautiful view of the other mountains, the city, and everything for miles around. Precisely because of its beauty, the mountain has an odd name: the place is called *Tibidabo, I will give you*, in Latin. The reason for this name is that the Spaniards who live in the area were so proud of its beauty and splendor that they claimed that when the devil tempted Christ, he brought Him to that place, to the mountaintop, and showed Him the splendor and beauty of Barcelona and the area. It was there, they said, that Christ was told *Tibidabo*, I will give you all this. If Christ had been shown just the hills of Galilee, He could have easily said no, but, claim the Spanish, had He been able to say no to the beauty of their mountain and valley, well, then He must truly be the Son of God!

Some find in this temptation the desire to be mediocre, to compromise with evil, to be comfortable and not sacrifice. "It is a constant temptation to seek to win men by compromising with the standards of the world. G. K. Chesterton said that the tendency of the world is to see things in terms of an indeterminate grey; but the duty of the Christian is to see things in terms of black and white."

Likewise, every sin, especially mortal sin, is, in a sense, a worshipping of the devil in place of Christ. Christ will not be shaken from His mission, and He will certainly not, even for all the kingdoms of the world and all creation, consent to worshipping someone or something who is not God the Father.

In short, the *Catechism* gives us a good summary of what we should see in this contemplation: we read that "Jesus is the new Adam who remained faithful just where the first Adam had given in to temptation. Jesus fulfills Israel's vocation perfectly: in contrast to those who had once provoked God during forty years in the desert, Christ reveals himself as God's Servant, totally obedient to the divine will. In this, Jesus is the devil's conqueror: he 'binds the strong man' to take back his plunder. Jesus' victory over the tempter in the desert anticipates victory at the Passion, the supreme act of obedience of his filial love for the Father.

Jesus' temptation reveals the way in which the Son of God is Messiah, contrary to the way Satan proposes to him and the way men wish to attribute to him. This is why Christ vanquished the Tempter *for us*: 'For we have not a high priest who is unable to sympathize with our weaknesses, but one who in every respect has been tested as we are, yet without sinning.'"

Hence, we must not be saddened by temptation, because Christ Himself was tempted. Indeed, Saint John Chrysostom says temptation should encourage us, because, if we are not tempted, it is a sign that we already belong to the devil.

Second, in temptation we should always turn to our Lord, and ask for His help, for He knows what it is like to be tempted.

Third, we should work to prevent temptations and to strengthen ourselves against them through prayer, fasting, and silence.

[**Colloquy**]: Ignatius tells us to end with the colloquy used for the Three Classes of Men, which is the same as the one used for Two Standards.

Threefold Colloquy:

A colloquy should be addressed to our Lady, asking her to obtain for me from her Son and Lord the grace to be received under His standard, first in the highest spiritual poverty, and should the Divine Majesty be pleased thereby, and deign to choose and accept me, even in actual poverty; secondly, in bearing insults and wrongs, thereby to imitate Him better, provided only I can suffer these without sin on the part of another, and without offense of the Divine Majesty. Then I will say the Hail Mary.

Second Colloquy: This will be to ask her Son to obtain the same favors for me from the Father. Then I will say, Soul of Christ.

Third Colloquy: This will be to beg the Father to grant me the same graces. Then I will say the Our Father.

[157] Note: It should be noted that when we feel an attachment opposed to actual poverty or a repugnance to it, when we are not indifferent to poverty and riches, it will be very helpful in order to overcome the inordinate attachment, even though corrupt nature rebel against it, to beg our Lord in the colloquies to choose us to serve Him in actual poverty. We should insist that we desire it, beg for it, plead for it, provided, of course, that it be for the service and praise of the Divine Goodness.

The Vocation of the Apostles
[275]

Usual Preparation Prayer.

First Prelude: The History: For the history, we can consider the Biblical texts that Ignatius points out: there are a number of them, because he wants us to consider a number of different callings: some took place in stages, others right at once, and others we don't know, but we can consider general characteristics of the calls. More on this below.

Second Prelude: The Composition of Place: Here, in our imaginations, we should see the region next to the Jordan, and the shores of the lake of Galilee, where Jesus gathered His Twelve Apostles.

Third Prelude: Petition: Here the petition will be is to ask for light to know intimately my Divine King Who has become a Man for me, and grace to love Him and follow Him in poverty, suffering, and humiliations.

At [275] Ignatius gives three rather lengthy points; note that he doesn't give specifc verses, which I have added for clarification:

First Point

St. Peter and St. Andrew seem to have been called three times. First, to some knowledge of our Lord. This is evident from the first chapter of St. John [Jn 1:35-39]. Secondly, to a following of Christ in some way, but with the intention of returning to the possessions they had left. St. Luke tells us this in the fifth chapter [Lk 5:1-11, which starts with the miraculous catch and end with them coming into shore, leaving everything]. Thirdly, to follow Christ our Lord forever, St. Matthew, chapter four [this would be Mt 4:18-22], and St. Mark, chapter one [Mk 1:16-18, although 18-20 recounts the calling of James and John as well].

Second Point

He called Philip, as we read in the first chapter of St. John [1:43-44, although 1:45-51 tells of Philip calling Nathanael). He called Matthew, as is recorded by St. Matthew himself in the ninth chapter [this would be Mt 9:9-13, if we include the post-calling banquet, but we could also consider it as Lk 5:27-32, if we assume Levi is the same as Matthew; that also includes the banquet Levi throws].

Third Point

He called the other Apostles, of whom no special call is mentioned in the Gospel.

Three other points must also be considered:

I. That the Apostles were uneducated and from a humble condition of life.

II. The dignity to which they were so gently called.

III. The gifts and graces by which they were raised above all the Fathers of the Old and New Testaments.

As with some of the other contemplations we have considered, Ignatius doesn't give a very detailed contemplation. He gives only the basic steps and then reminds us to follow the same model as we did before: to *see* the people, then to *hear* the people, then to *examine what they are doing*, each time gathering some fruit for my life.

As we have done for the other meditations, we can consider, first, a little background to what Ignatius is doing here, and then, second, some elements to help us contemplate and consider Christ so as to imitate Him better.

Fr. Oraa points out that "very gently and with admirable efficacy, Saint Ignatius chooses and proposes for us the steps of Christ's life that help to shed light, direct, and bring about the incredible work of making an election.

In the presentation of the vocations of the Apostles, we can see, in a very practical way, the three times in which we can make an election. In the first example, that of the gradual calling of Peter and Andrew, we see an example of the second time, namely, the discernment of God's will by means of the experience of consolations and desolations. The callings of Matthew and Philip seem to be graces of the first time: God calls, and they go. Lastly, the ones we know little or nothing about, we can assume were of the third time, when they used the reason to figure out God's will for them."[1] This is the general movement of the contemplation, to consider how God calls, and then, especially for the third point, to see *who* He calls and why.

With this in mind, let us consider the different callings that Ignatius presents for us. The first is that of Peter and Andrew and, as Fr. Oraa states, this is a grace of the second time, a discernment made through the different experiences of consolation and desolation, over a period of time.

---

1. Oraa, *Ejercicios Espirituales,* 368 and following.

At first, we are told, in Jn 1:35-39, that John the Baptist points out Christ to two of his disciples, who then head off to follow Christ and see "where He is staying." The two spent the day with Christ, and were overjoyed. We know this because in Jn 1:41, after Andrew has spent the day with Christ, he goes and tells his own brother Simon, "We have found the Messiah," and then brings him to Jesus.

The second encounter between Jesus and Peter and Andrew seems to be recounted in Lk 5:1-11, where Peter and Andrew have the desolating experience of not catching any fish, even after a long night of work. After this miracle, we are told in v. 11 that "when they brought their boats to the shore, they left everything and followed him." However, as Ignatius points out, it seems that they were thinking of returning at some point. There was consolation in the great number of fish caught, and in such a miraculous way, but nonetheless they still needed a confirmation.

As Fr. Oraa puts it, "it could be said that the Lord, through the experience of consolations and desolations, is preparing His chosen ones for the definitive steps. Without Him, they had labored all night and caught nothing: hours of desolation. With Him, at the first cast of the nets, the nets were filled: it was a consolation. Naturally their hearts were disposed to follow Him, and so they did."

Thirdly, as Matthew recounts, they decided to follow Christ forever. The previous experiences prepared their hearts to follow Him without reserve. This is equally true for us; once we have embraced the call to holiness and to perfection, we must strive to continue to live it out. We must continue to listen for the voice of Jesus Christ as He tells us what we should do, and guides us on the way to Heaven.

In the second calling, that of Philip and Matthew, we see that, in both cases, the Apostles were called by a special, extraordinary grace. They both knew they were called to follow Christ, and did so immediately.

Note, too, that both are filled with joy. Upon finding his vocation, Philip promptly goes and tells Nathanael. Nathanael is decidedly less excited, but Philip will not be deterred or saddened. He simply tells Nathanael, "Come and see!" That indicates a great deal of confidence in his experience, something unshakeable.

Likewise, Matthew is so overjoyed at his calling that he promptly throws a banquet for Christ, and it must have been a rather costly affair, since there were a great number of people attending. Yet, for Matthew, the cost would have been nothing in comparison with the joy that he had found; the huge feast was his way of showing his joy.

Our vocations might not have been through a grace of the first time, but, nonetheless, we can ask ourselves about the joy that we experience, since we, too, have been called by Christ to follow Him. Our vocation is like the pearl of great price, and we should rejoice in it constantly.

The third point is the call of the other Apostles, of whom no mention is made in the Scriptures. There is no mention of how they were called, but it seems that Ignatius wants us to consider that they were made aware of their vocation in the third time: after seeing, knowing, listening, and dealing with Christ, they could see that, in accord with the principle and foundation, their happiness and salvation was to be found in following Christ more closely and, indeed, when invited by Christ, they did so.

We know that not everyone who was called this way actually accepted. The rich young man gives an example of just such a person. Christ Himself tells us "Many are called, but few are chosen" (Mt 22:14). What are we to make of that statement? There is a lot that could be said: it seems that many people are called, but do not hear that call, since they are too busy and wrapped up in their own affairs, in their lives, in their works, and they neglect what is really important. Others it seems hear the call, but refuse to pay it any mind. Still others hear it, acknowledge it, but are too weak to give up the impediments that hold them back in Christ's service. They cut corners, make exceptions, try to bend the rules.

A heart divided will always look to be restored: it either goes to God or goes to the world. Of the twelve Apostles chosen by Christ Himself, Judas was a traitor. We can assume that when he was chosen, he wasn't unworthy or a bad guy. He began with good intentions, to follow Christ's teaching, and to spread the Gospel. But at some point, something happened: he no longer continued in his good desires. Fulton Sheen said that it was a crisis of faith in the Eucharist, and then a loss of faith in Jesus Christ. This may very well be so. Others have suggested that it was greed, or pride. In the end, what matters is that Judas, who started off well, joined the Apostolic College, and at some point intended to be a saint, fell short. We must learn from his example, since, as Jesus Himself says, "it would have been better for him not to be born."

Then, we come to the third point, wherein we consider the other apostles. As Ignatius says, we don't know how they were called, but we should bear in mind three truths: first, that the Apostles were uneducated and from a humble condition of life, second, the dignity to which they were so gently called and, third, the gifts and graces by which they were raised above all the Fathers of the Old and New Testaments.

First, Ignatius tells us that the Apostles were uneducated and from a humble condition of life, and that we should consider this. Almost all were poor, although they did well enough to survive on from their work. They were working class men, who put in long days and nights in order to make ends meet.

Some scholars, like Ricciotti, suggest that they were all literate, but probably Matthew the best of the group.

We can also see, from what the Gospels tell us, that some of them were followers of John the Baptist before going to Christ. However, the Gospels also reveal to us that the average level of culture and moral level were fairly low. They were hard workers, men who feared God and were waiting for the Messiah. However, we also see that they are slow to understand, sometimes missing even Christ's clearest explanations.

Likewise, they were weak and cowardly. When Jesus comes walking on the water, they think He is a ghost, and when Jesus wanted to go and cure Lazarus, they were opposed because they feared being stoned to death. The Passion comes, and everyone runs away.

They were also interested in and desirous of earthly goods, wanting positions of power, authority, and to be the greatest among the group.

So, why did Jesus pick such a group? The wisdom of men is shown when they pick the best, most perfect means to an end, but God's wisdom is seen when, united to His omnipotence, it triumphs by showing how to achieve great ends with means that seem to be completely disproportionate, completely unequal to the task. For us, too, we must be docile to God's inspirations and graces, humble to follow Him, because only in this way will we be fit instruments in God's hands.

Second, consider the dignity to which they were so gently called. When Jesus was about to call His apostles, Luke tells us that He spent the night in prayer. In this way, we are to understand the importance of what He was doing. Of course, Jesus was always at prayer, but to make a point of going and spending the whole night in prayer was to show us that what was about to take place was out of the ordinary. He asked for lights and graces for His Apostles.

Some commentators have said that we can see three characteristics of this prayer: first, it was extraordinary (as we have just said). Second, it reminds us that we must always put God first in our works and undertakings. We must consult God about all of our plans, all of our undertakings, and about when to start them. Thirdly, this prayer was full of great love and enthusiasm for the kingdom of God. The only thing Jesus sought in His prayer was that God's glory and the salvation of souls. Hopefully our prayer resembles that.

Consider, too, the great graces that the Apostles were given. Mark tells us that [3:14-15] "He appointed twelve [whom he also named apostles] that they might be with him and he might send them forth to preach and to have authority to drive out demons." They become companions in Jesus' life. They lived with Him, ate their food from the same table, slept under the same roof. They were inseparable. That is why He called them His friends and His brothers: "I have called you friends, because I have told you everything I have heard from my Father," (Jn 15:15), and, after the Resurrection, Matthew recalls, "Go tell my brothers to go to Galilee, and there they will see me" (Mt 28:10).

They were also made participants in Christ's dignity and in His power.

Thirdly, Ignatius tells us to consider the gifts and graces by which they were raised above all the Fathers of the Old and New Testaments. It was a singular grace and gift for them to live in the company of Jesus, to experience His love and patience, to receive His teachings that He imparted so kindly and prudently. Indeed, Matthew summarizes the greatness of these teachings when Christ says, "But blessed are your eyes, because they see, and your ears, because they hear. Amen, I say to you, many prophets and righteous people longed to see what you see but did not see it, and to hear what you hear but did not hear it" (Mt 13:16-17).

Jesus also gave them other amazing gifts: as Matthew recalls (10:8), Christ tells His apostles, right after calling them: "Cure the sick, raise the dead, cleanse lepers, drive out demons. Without cost you have received; without cost you are to give." These gifts, too, on top of sanctifying grace, and then the fullness of the Holy Spirit.

God is wonderful in His saints, and, even though He poured out all these blessings on His apostles, His treasury is not exhausted. Those who faithfully follow their divine vocation will be rewarded with the company of Christ, "grace in place of grace," and more. We only need to be humble, to accept these graces, to work with Christ, asking for perseverance, and giving ourselves entirely to the spreading of God's Kingdom, even to the point of surrendering our lives, if needed. This is what they did.

[Colloquy]: Ignatius tells us to end with the colloquy used for the Three Classes of Men, which is the same as the one used for Two Standards.

Threefold Colloquy:

A colloquy should be addressed to our Lady, asking her to obtain for me from her Son and Lord the grace to be received under His standard, first in the highest spiritual poverty, and should the Divine Majesty be pleased thereby, and deign to choose and accept me, even in actual poverty; secondly, in bearing insults and wrongs, thereby to imitate Him better, provided only I can suffer these without sin on the part of another, and without offense of the Divine Majesty. Then I will say the Hail Mary.

Second Colloquy: This will be to ask her Son to obtain the same favors for me from the Father. Then I will say, Soul of Christ.

Third Colloquy: This will be to beg the Father to grant me the same graces. Then I will say the Our Father.

[157] Note: It should be noted that when we feel an attachment opposed to actual poverty or a repugnance to it, when we are not indifferent to poverty and riches, it will be very helpful in order to overcome the inordinate attachment, even though corrupt nature rebel against it, to beg our Lord in the colloquies to choose us to serve Him in actual poverty. We should insist that we desire it, beg for it, plead for it, provided, of course, that it be for the service and praise of the Divine Goodness.

The First Miracle Performed
at the Marriage Feast of Cana in Galilee
[276]

Usual Preparation Prayer.

First Prelude: The History: For the history, we can consider the Biblical texts that Ignatius points out: Jn 2:1-11. Jesus and the disciples were invited to a wedding feast, and Mary was there too. The hosts ran out of wine, but Mary, aware of what had happened, told Jesus, who then performs His first miracle.

Second Prelude: The Composition of Place: Here, in our imaginations, we should see the wedding feast in Cana.

Third Prelude: Petition: Here the petition will be is to ask for light to know intimately my Divine King Who has become a Man for me, and grace to love Him and follow Him in poverty, suffering, and humiliations.

At [274] Ignatius gives three very short points:

First Point
Christ our Lord and the disciples were invited to the marriage feast.

Second Point
His Mother calls attention to the shortage of wine, saying to Him, "They have no wine." She bids the servants, "Whatsoever He shall say to you do."

Third Point
He changed the water into wine, "And he manifested his glory and his disciples believed in him."

As with some of the other contemplations we have considered, Ignatius doesn't give a very detailed contemplation. He gives only the basic steps and then reminds us to follow the same model as we did before: to *see* the people, then to *hear* the people, then to *examine what they are doing*, each time gathering some fruit for my life.

As we have done for the other meditations, we can consider, first, a little history of the scene and then, second, some elements to help us contemplate and consider Christ so as to imitate Him better.

The location of the miracle is "Cana of Galilee." [The town] is so called to distinguish it from Cana in Coelo-Syria. It was a village quite near to Nazareth. Jerome, who stayed in Palestine, says that he saw it from Nazareth. . . . The scene is a village wedding feast. In Palestine a wedding was a really notable occasion.

The wedding festivities lasted far more than one day. The wedding ceremony itself took place late in the evening, after a feast. After the ceremony the young couple were conducted to their new home. By that time it was dark and they were conducted through the village streets by the light of flaming torches and with a canopy over their heads. They were taken by as long a route as possible so that as many people as possible would have the opportunity to wish them well. But a newly married couple did not go away for their honeymoon; they stayed at home; and for a week they kept open house. They wore crowns and dressed in their bridal robes. They were treated like a king and queen, were actually addressed as king and queen, and their word was law. In a life where there was much poverty and constant hard work, this week of festivity and joy was one of the supreme occasions.

For a Jewish feast wine was essential. 'Without wine," said the Rabbis, "there is no joy." It was not that people were drunken, but in the East wine was an essential. At any time the failure of provisions would have been a problem, for hospitality in the East is a sacred duty; but for the provisions to fail at a wedding would be a terrible humiliation for the bride and the bridegroom."

We should also note that Jesus' words to His mother: "Woman, how does your concern affect me? My hour has not yet come," sounds rather harsh in English.

"The phrase, 'How does your concern affect me?' was a common conversational phrase. When it was uttered angrily and sharply it did indicate complete disagreement and reproach, but when it was spoken gently it indicated not so much reproach but misunderstanding. It means: 'Don't worry; you don't quite understand what is going on; leave things to me, and I will settle them in my own way.' Jesus was simply telling Mary to leave things to him, to trust.

The word woman (*gunai*) is also misleading. It sounds to us very rough and abrupt. But it is the same word as Jesus used on the Cross to address Mary as he left her to the care of John. In Homer it is the title by which Odysseus addresses Penelope, his well-loved wife. It is the title by which Augustus, the Roman Emperor, addressed Cleopatra, the famous Egyptian queen. So far from being a rough and discourteous way of address, it was a title of respect.

We have no way of speaking in English which exactly renders it; but it is better to translate it Lady which gives at least the courtesy in it."

So, with this setting in mind, we can consider what we see of Christ and what we can imitate.

"(i) We note when it happened. It happened at a wedding feast. Jesus was perfectly at home at such an occasion. He was no severe, sour, gloomy man. He loved to share in the happy rejoicing of a wedding feast.

There are certain religious people who shed a gloom wherever they go. They are suspicious of all joy and happiness. As one scholar put it, "An individual who has no happiness about him had better be an undertaker, and bury the dead, for he will never succeed in influencing the living."

We can ask ourselves about how we imitate Christ's joy, especially in those essential moments of recreation and eutrapelia, those moments that are a foretaste of what Heaven will be like.

(ii) We note where it happened. It happened in a humble home in a village in Galilee. This miracle was not wrought against the background of some great occasion and in the presence of vast crowds. It was wrought in a home; this miracle brought God right into the home circle and into the ordinary things of life. Jesus' action at Cana of Galilee shows what he thought of a home. As the Revised Standard Version has it, he 'manifested forth his glory,' and that manifestation took place within a home.

There is a strange paradox in the attitude of many people to the place they call home [or, for us, our communities]. They would admit at once that there is no more precious place in all the world; and yet, at the same time, they would also have to admit that in it they claim the right to be far more discourteous, far more rude, far more selfish, far more impolite than they would dare to be in any society of strangers. Many of us treat the ones we love most in a way that we would never dare to treat a chance acquaintance. So often it is strangers who see us at our best and those who live with us who see us at our worst. We ought ever to remember that it was in a humble home [a lowly community] that Jesus manifested forth his glory. To him home was a place for which nothing but his best was good enough.

It's true: community life is also the maximum penance, but Jesus is to be found there, in the midst of it. Do we really seek to see Him, to live out His example of giving the very best even in the midst of a simple home?

(iii) We note why it happened. We have already seen that in the East hospitality was always a sacred duty. It would have brought embarrassed shame to that home that day if the wine had run done. It was to save a humble Galilaean family from hurt that Jesus put forth his power. It was in sympathy, in kindness, in understanding for simple folk that Jesus acted.

Nearly everyone can do the big thing on the big occasion; but it takes Jesus to do the big thing on a simple, homely occasion like this. There is a kind of natural human maliciousness which rather enjoys the misfortunes of others and which delights to make a good story of them over the teacups. But Jesus, the Lord of all life, and the King of glory, used his power to save a simple Galilaean lad and lass from humiliation. It is just by such deeds of understanding, simple kindliness that we too can show that we are followers of Jesus Christ."

Also, note how abundantly Christ provided: "There were six waterpots; each held between twenty and thirty gallons of water; Jesus turned the water into wine. That would give anything up to one hundred and eighty gallons of wine." Note, too, that the water contained in them was "for ceremonial washings": "Water was required for two purposes. First, it was required for cleansing the feet on entry to the house. The roads were not surfaced. Sandals were merely a sole attached to the foot by straps. On a dry day the feet were covered by dust and on a wet day they were soiled with mud; and the water was used for cleansing them. Second, it was required for the handwashing. Strict Jews washed the hands before a meal and between each course." In other words, it is from this nasty, dirty water that Jesus makes the best wine, and an overflowing, abundant amount. How do we react when faced with situations that seem difficult, that seem like nothing can be done? Do we complain, despair, or throw ourselves into giving our very best, knowing that Jesus will provide and work with us to provide abundant fruit?

We should also note Mary's role. Fulton Sheen points out that "this is the only occasion in the life of Our Lord where Mary is mentioned before her Son. Mary was to be the instrument of His first miracle, or sign, that He was what He claimed to be, the Son of God. She had already been an instrument for the sanctification of John the Baptist in his mother's womb; now, by her intercession, she sounded the trumpet for a long procession of miracles—an intercession so strong that it has inspired souls in all ages to invoke her name for other miracles of nature and grace.

When the wine gave out at Cana, it is interesting to note that Mary was more concerned with the guests than was the wine-steward; for it was she, and not he, who noticed their need of wine. Mary turned to her Divine Son in a perfect spirit of prayer. Completely confident in Him and trusting in His mercy, she said: They have no wine left. It was not a personal request; she was already a mediatrix for all who were seeking the fullness of joy. She has never been just a spectator, but a full participant willingly involving herself in the needs of others. The mother used the special power which she had as a mother over her Son, a power generated by mutual love."

(i) Instinctively Mary turned to Jesus whenever something went wrong. She knew her son. It was not till he was thirty years old that Jesus left home; and all these years Mary lived with him. There is an old legend which tells of the days when Jesus was a little baby in the home in Nazareth. It tells how in those days when people felt tired and worried and hot and bothered and upset, they would say: "Let us go and look at Mary's child," and they would go and look at Jesus, and somehow all their troubles rolled away. It is still true that those who know Jesus intimately instinctively turn to him when things go wrong--and they never find him wanting.

The Jesuit Fr. John Hardon makes the same point, writing that "The marriage feast at Cana tells us everything we need to know about Our Lady as the Mother of Divine Providence. The Church has given her this title because she, better than anyone else, is the perfect teacher of what Providence should mean in our lives. She teaches us to *believe* there is a Providence of God. She teaches us to *trust* in His Providence. And she teaches us to *cooperate* with Divine Providence in our lives.

How does Our Lady teach us to believe that there is a Providence? She does this in showing us by her example to see a Divine purpose in whatever occurs in our lives. When they ran out of wine at the marriage feast in Cana, she might have said to herself, 'Well, what do they expect? The people drank so much there there was no wine left and the marriage feast is still going on.' But instinctively Mary saw in the situation a providential act of God. She recognized what we are so slow to see, God's divinely ordained purpose in every person, every event, every joy, and every pain that we experience.

What this means is that, like Mary, we should understand there is no such thing as chance with God. Nothing just happens. Everything has a divinely intended purpose, and that purpose is to bring us closer to God. Viewed in this way we see that every creature who touches our lives is meant to be a grace from God. Does this include our mistakes and the mistakes of others? Yes, it does. We make mistakes but God never does. He uses even the wrong that we do to mysteriously lead us to Him, at least by giving us the opportunity for a humble repentance if we have done wrong, and patient acceptance when somebody else may wrong us. Moreover, Our Lady is Mother of Divine Providence because she teaches us to trust in God's goodness and wisdom always, no matter how painful or hopeless a situation may seem. Humanly speaking, once the wine ran out at Cana there was nothing else to do except resign oneself to the obvious. But not Our Lady. Knowing her Son to be Who He is, even before asking Him, she told the stewards to fill the jars with water. Talk about trust in God's Providence!

Like her, beyond recognizing the constant and loving activity of God in our favor, we are also to be confident in the future. Mary had no doubt that her Son would work the miracle of changing water into wine. But the pre-condition for the miracle was His mother's confidence in her Son's answering her request.

None of us can see the future, but only God. There are many things He asks us to do here and now and wants us to trust that we shall not be deceived in what we hope for. Does this mean that God will, if need be, work miracles in our favor? Emphatically, yes.

Finally, Our Lady teaches us that beyond believing in Divine Providence and trusting in His loving care, we are to cooperate with the graces that He is frequently putting into our lives. These graces are the persons whose lives touch ours. They are the events that we experience, and too often take for granted all day.

Notice the way Mary acted after she found out that there was no more wine. She realized that something should be done, and she did it."

(ii) Even when Mary did not understand what Jesus was going to do, even when it seemed that he had refused her request, Mary still believed in him so much that she turned to the serving folk and told them to do whatever Jesus told them to do. Mary had the faith which could trust even when it did not understand. She did not know what Jesus was going to do, but she was quite sure that he would do the right thing. In every life come periods of darkness when we do not see the way. In every life come things which are such that we do not see why they came or any meaning in them. Happy is the man who in such a case still trusts even when he cannot understand."

In the third point, Ignatius notes that "Jesus manifested His glory, and His disciples believed in Him." Lest we forget, this opportunity for Him to show His glory and to increase the faith of His disciples was, objectively, a bad thing, an embarrassment, but here, as always and everywhere, Christ gets good out of something bad. Do we believe that, and do we try to imitate it in our attitude towards life and the negative things that happen to us?

[Colloquy]: Ignatius tells us to end with the colloquy used for the Three Classes of Men, which is the same as the one used for Two Standards.

Threefold Colloquy:

A colloquy should be addressed to our Lady, asking her to obtain for me from her Son and Lord the grace to be received under His standard, first in the highest spiritual poverty, and should the Divine Majesty be pleased thereby, and deign to choose and accept me, even in actual poverty; secondly, in bearing insults and wrongs, thereby to imitate Him better, provided only I can suffer these without sin on the part of another, and without offense of the Divine Majesty. Then I will say the Hail Mary.

Second Colloquy: This will be to ask her Son to obtain the same favors for me from the Father. Then I will say, Soul of Christ.

Third Colloquy: This will be to beg the Father to grant me the same graces. Then I will say the Our Father.

[157] Note: It should be noted that when we feel an attachment opposed to actual poverty or a repugnance to it, when we are not indifferent to poverty and riches, it will be very helpful in order to overcome the inordinate attachment, even though corrupt nature rebel against it, to beg our Lord in the colloquies to choose us to serve Him in actual poverty. We should insist that we desire it, beg for it, plead for it, provided, of course, that it be for the service and praise of the Divine Goodness.

Christ Casts the Sellers from the Temple
[277]

Usual Preparation Prayer.

First Prelude: The History: For the history, we can consider the Biblical text that Ignatius points out: Jn 2:13-22. However, similar events are recounted in the three synoptic Gospels as well: Mt 21:12–17, Mk 11:15–19, and Lk 19:45–48 (although these place the event towards the end of Jesus' life, and not towards the beginning, as John does).

Second Prelude: The Composition of Place: Here, in our imaginations, we should see the Temple area, and the money changers, those buying and selling things, and Jesus, who comes in to purify the Temple.

Third Prelude: Petition: Here the petition will be to ask for light to know intimately my Divine King Who has become a Man for me, and grace to love Him and follow Him in poverty, suffering, and humiliations.

At [277] Ignatius gives three short points:

First Point
With a whip made of cords He casts all those who sell out of the Temple.

Second Point
He overturned the tables and scattered the money of the wealthy money-changers who were in the Temple.

Third Point
To the poor venders of doves He said kindly, "Take these away! Make not the house of my Father a house of traffic."

As with some of the other contemplations we have considered, Ignatius doesn't give a very detailed contemplation. He gives only the basic steps and then reminds us to follow the same model as we did before: to *see* the people, then to *hear* the people, then to *examine what they are doing*, each time gathering some fruit for my life.

As we have done for the other contemplations, we can consider, first, a little of the historical background, and then, second, some elements to help us contemplate and consider Christ so as to imitate Him better.

First, in John's Gospel, we are told that "Since the Passover of the Jews was near, Jesus went up to Jerusalem." Earlier, in the contemplation on the Finding of the Child Jesus in the Temple, we mentioned that every adult male Jew (meaning, over the age of 12) who lived within 15 miles of Jerusalem was obligated to go up to the Temple for the Passover. Likewise, the great number of pilgrims who came from all over meant that there might have been as many as two and half million people in Jerusalem for the feast.

We should also bear in mind that the Temple consisted of a series of courts leading into the Temple proper and to the Holy Place. There was first the Court of the Gentiles, then the Court of the Women, then the Court of the Israelites, then the Court of the Priests. When we talk about the cleansing of the Temple, all this buying and selling was going on in the Court of the Gentiles which was the only place into which a Gentile might come. Beyond that point, access to him was barred. So then if there was a Gentile whose heart God had touched, he might come into the Court of the Gentiles to meditate and pray and distantly touch God. The Court of the Gentiles was the only place of prayer he knew.

Likewise, there was also a rather sinister side to the Temple and its worship. Every Jew over the age of 19 needed to pay a Temple tax of one half-shekel to help keep the sacrifices and rituals going. Although it might not seem like much, it was about two days' wages for the day laborer. Likewise, since pilgrims came from all over, they would bring with them coins for Rome, Greece, Egypt, Tyre, Sidon, and Palestine, but the Temple tax could only be paid in Galilean shekels or in shekels of the sanctuary, which were Jewish coins and therefore clean. Hence, the money changers would be in the Temple courts to provide their service, but they would charge almost one day's wages in order to change the currency into money that could be used in the Temple.

In addition to the money changers, there were also the sellers of oxen, sheep, and doves. A visit to the Temple often meant a sacrifice, and so it could have been a nice service to have the animals there for sale. However, this was far from the case. Pilgrims would often bring animals with them, but they were obligated to have them inspected (for a fee, of course), and then, without fail, they would be found flawed, and the pilgrims would need to buy animals from within the Temple, at around twenty times the cost. Hence the poor, who came simply to worship and offer sacrifice, often found themselves much poorer after their visit, if they could offer sacrifice at all.[1]

1. This section cf. Barclay.

All of this is what moved Christ to action, and this is, properly speaking, what we can consider in our contemplation. Again, we can imagine the scene as Fr. Ricciotti describes it as "the usual scene that took place . . . especially during the great feasts. The outer court of the Temple had become a stable fouled and reeking with dung, and it echoed and re-echoed with the bellowing of oxen, the bleating of sheep, the cooing of doves, and above all the noisy cries and shouts of the traders and money changers installed everywhere within its porticoes. In that court it was possible to hear only dimly the feeble echo of the hymns rising within the inner Temple and to glimpse only faintly the pale glow of the distant holy lamps. There were no other visible signs of religion in that vast enclosure, which was more like a cattle market or a convention of swindlers than the antechamber of the house where dwelt the spiritual God of Israel." Then the exegete offers a profound insight: "To be sure, Jesus had certainly witnessed similar scenes on previous pilgrimages to Jerusalem, but then his public life had not yet begun. Now his mission was fully under way."[2]

In other words, since Jesus lived so close, there is no doubt that He would have been to Jerusalem many times during His hidden life. Jesus had seen this before, but before, it wasn't His time to say or do anything. Prudence and patience dictated that He wait. We can think of the words of Saint John Bosco, the exhortation to "pick the best moment. Correct at the proper time, if you wish correction to do any good." How often we simply give vent to our anger, as soon as it comes! We can ask ourselves: how well do we restrain our passions, our emotions? Do we work on developing that virtue of prudence, so that we act and live well?

Another insight can be gathered from what Christ says as He cleanses the Temple: all of the Evangelists recall differently Christ's words, but Mark has an interesting phrase that gives another insight: he tells us that Christ quoted the Prophet Isaiah [56:7]: "My house shall be called a house of prayer for all peoples" (Mk 11:17)." As we mentioned earlier, the court of buying and selling was the only place where Gentiles could come to pray.

"The Temple authorities and the Jewish traders were making the Court of the Gentiles into an uproar and a rabble where no man could pray. The lowing of the oxen, the bleating of the sheep, the cooing of the doves, the shouts of the hucksters, the rattle of the coins, the voices raised in bargaining disputes— all these combined to make the Court of the Gentiles a place where no man could worship. The conduct in the Temple court shut out the seeking Gentile from the presence of God. It may well be that this was most in Jesus' mind; it may well be that Mark alone preserved the little phrase which means so much.

2. Giuseppe Ricciotti, *Life of Christ*, 286.

Jesus was moved to the depths of his heart because seeking men were being shut out from the presence of God."

In our own lives, too, how often is it that the Temple of our hearts is closed to God because of noise, because of distractions. The temples of our hearts ring with so much activity that it becomes a place where no worship of God can take place, where the focus becomes any number of things that aren't God.

In particular, we can think of the danger of superficiality,[3] a lack of interest in entering profoundly into the natures of things, the search for the ultimate causes. We could say that the spirit of superficiality is an inability to have a sense of interiority, and hence the superficial person does that: they remain on the surface of things, without penetrating into the depths. They might appear nice, charming, and pleasant exteriorly, but they are unaware of their real strengths and weaknesses. Indeed, they are prone to follow their whims, to childishness in their humor, to weakly adhere to their resolutions, if they do so at all, to being frivolous in their dealings with others, and often they fall into sensuality and seek out comfort.

This superficiality takes many forms: it could be mere curiosity, a desire to know things that are really not essential or of value, perhaps to seek out the news and know "what's going on in the world." It could also be a lack of *caution*, meaning, *indiscretion*, a lack of prudence that comes from not seeing the consequences of actions, of not taking into account all the factors that are at play.

In the area of the will, the superficial person gives way to *laziness*, because, being superficial, they avoid the effort needed to penetrate into the depths of reality. They reject all real responsibility, and do not really take their commitments, like vows, seriously.

Likewise, in their emotions, they are prone to *flirting*, to trying to be cool, because all of these rely on superficial notions and ideas. Their humor tends to be juvenile and out of place, because these are superficial and are easily given.

Lastly, the superficial person is usually *impatient* and *never at rest*, because their superficiality makes them bounce from topic to topic, from activity to activity, without ever fully penetrating into the depths of one or the other. They don't know the *joy* that comes from real effort, from real work, and from real study, and so they anxiously jump from thing to thing, task to task, in search of immediate joy and instant reward.

What are the causes? Certain temperaments, like the sanguine, are predisposed for this. However, a certain style of life, one that is too sensual, comfortable, and unmortified, also leads to this. It might be an intellectual problem that stems from not valuing properly spiritual realities and goods, or it might

---

3. I take this following the book of Fr. Fuentes, *La Superficialidad*.

be a problem of the will, that it is lazy and lacks generosity and magnanimity, a will that doesn't want to make a serious effort to study or pray. Another cause might be vanity, the desire to look good without needing to really do anything.

What we see in the cleansing of the Temple is that Christ is not a superficial man; indeed, He doesn't tolerate superficiality, since everything He is and does is marked by a deep and profound knowledge and love of God. He is one who profoundly penetrates into the depths of things. Clearly, as God, He is all-knowing, but everything in His actions is perfectly measured and balanced.

We could say that Christ is the antithesis of superficiality: He is prudent, profound, a man of action, but an action that is perfectly balanced.

Christ is a man in control of Himself: He got angry at things that deserved and warranted His anger. Again, we can consider what we mentioned this morning in the homily: the calm man does not get angry without reason; however, when he has a reason, his anger makes him imposing, since the infuriated meek person knows the reason for his anger and that he has no right to calm himself down until justice is restored.

A man who has the time and makes the delay so as to put together a whip of cords and the character of giving a speech explaining his behavior can not be out of his mind with anger. Jesus did both things. The shoves and kicks He needed to scatter the money changers and scare away the cows and pigeons that infected the Father's Temple were all thought, measured and decided.

His mere presence demanded respect; Saint Jerome thinks that the very sight of Jesus made the whip unnecessary: "A certain fiery and starry light shone from his eyes, and the majesty of the Godhead gleamed in his face."

His manliness must have frightened His enemies, first and foremost because it was "manliness" and not mere "bravado." True courage is that anger placed at the service of justice. This is what frightens evil, and such was Jesus' spirit.

Jesus could be energetic and wield His strength, as occurred in the expulsion of the merchants from the Temple (cf. Mt 21:12-13; Mk 11:15-17; Jn 2:14-17). However, the description of that episode made by the evangelists is infinitely removed from the turbulent anger of the bewildered, or the one who channels his nervous energy in a convulsive tantrum. His indignation does not leave its proper margins.

We see that Jesus has no tolerance for things that go against God's will, that take away from the true worship, from really knowing and serving God, things that are unjust.

We can ask ourselves: in our lives, how do we use our emotions? Are we in control of them, or do they control us? Are we superficial people? How well do we try to expel the things that keep us from developing our interior life, of which we could consider laziness, curiosity, superficiality, and the other vices we mentioned earlier? Have we noticed that we are imprudent in speech or word? Do we jump to conclusions or gossip? How well is our life of prayer going; do we really enter into conversation with the living God, or is it just me talking? Do I try to enter profoundly into what it is that I'm doing, or do I just scratch the surface? Do I like to be considered *cool*, or *awesome* in my dealings with others, without really developing what matters?

If we see these vices in ourselves, we need to act like Christ: expel them from our hearts without delay, and restore true worship to God.

[Colloquy]: Ignatius tells us to end with the colloquy used for the Three Classes of Men, which is the same as the one used for Two Standards.

Threefold Colloquy:

A colloquy should be addressed to our Lady, asking her to obtain for me from her Son and Lord the grace to be received under His standard, first in the highest spiritual poverty, and should the Divine Majesty be pleased thereby, and deign to choose and accept me, even in actual poverty; secondly, in bearing insults and wrongs, thereby to imitate Him better, provided only I can suffer these without sin on the part of another, and without offense to the Divine Majesty. Then I will say the Hail Mary.

Second Colloquy: This will be to ask her Son to obtain the same favors for me from the Father. Then I will say, Soul of Christ.

Third Colloquy: This will be to beg the Father to grant me the same graces. Then I will say the Our Father.

[157] Note: It should be noted that when we feel an attachment opposed to actual poverty or a repugnance to it, when we are not indifferent to poverty and riches, it will be very helpful in order to overcome the inordinate attachment, even though corrupt nature rebel against it, to beg our Lord in the colloquies to choose us to serve Him in actual poverty. We should insist that we desire it, beg for it, plead for it, provided, of course, that it be for the service and praise of the Divine Goodness.

The Sermon on the Mount
[278]

Usual Preparation Prayer.

First Prelude: The History: For the history, Matthew tells us that great crowds were following Jesus, from "Galilee, the Decapolis, Jerusalem, and Judea, and from beyond the Jordan ... [and] when he saw the crowds, he went up the mountain, and after he had sat down, his disciples came to him," and He began to teach them. Thus begins the Sermon on the Mount.

Second Prelude: The Composition of Place: Here, in our imaginations, we can consider the mountain, with the crowd that had gathered. Biblical scholars tell us that it was "a hill of Galilee," probably about 500 feet high (more like a hill) on the western shore of Lake Tiberias above Tabgha about 8 miles from Tiberias and 2 from Capharnaum. Jesus probably gave the Sermon, not from the top of the mount, but on a level place on the southwest slope.[1] Likewise, the hill was in a central location, easily accessible by all. The scenery could hardly be better: in front, you have the calm waters of Lake Tiberias, in the back, mountains, on the right, towards the south, a low plane and further away Mt. Thabor, surrounded by shorter mountains. To the left, towards the north, the great Mt. Hermon, covered with snow, and, at the base of the hill of the Beatitudes, flower-covered fields.[2]

Third Prelude: Petition: Here the petition will be to ask for light to know intimately my Divine King Who has become a Man for me, and grace to love Him and follow Him in poverty, suffering, and humiliations; in particular, we can ask for the grace to live our lives in accord with the Sermon on the Mount.

At [278] Ignatius gives three short points:

First Point

He proposes the eight beatitudes to His beloved disciples apart: "Blessed are the poor in spirit ... the meek ... the merciful ... they that mourn ... they that hunger ... the peace-makers ... those that suffer persecution."

---

1. Cf. Ricciota, *Life of Christ*, n. 316.
2. Cf. Oraa, *Ejercicios Espirituales*, 391.

Second Point

He exhorts them to use their talents, "So let your light shine before men in order that they may see your good works and glorify your Father in Heaven."

Third Point

He shows Himself not a transgressor of the Law but a fulfiller. He explains the commandments not to kill, not to commit adultery, not to swear falsely, and commands us to love our enemies: "I say, love your enemies, do good to them that hate you."

As with some of the other contemplations we have considered, Ignatius doesn't give a very detailed contemplation. He gives only the basic steps and then reminds us to follow the same model as we did before: to *see* the people, then to *hear* the people, then to *examine what they are doing*, each time gathering some fruit for my life.

As we have done for the other contemplations, we can consider, first, a little of the historical background and a general introduction, and then, second, some elements to help us contemplate and consider Christ so as to imitate Him better. Tonight we will consider only the prologue, as it were, the Beatitudes, and then, tomorrow, we will consider the remainder of the text. I know we have seen these in our talks on Christian maturity, but we will see this in a different light than we have during the talks.

"Saint Matthew dedicates 107 verses to the Sermon on the Mount. . . . As a sort of introduction, in the Beatitudes, Jesus lays out a rule of ideal perfection that includes the essential conditions under which a person can obtain citizenship in His kingdom, the conditions that should be practiced by all those in the Kingdom. . . . This is a fruitful and easy contemplation," says one commentator, "just lay them out devoutly and simply, and remind yourself of how Jesus Christ Himself lived them out!"[3]

Indeed, the *Catechism* tells us how essential this preaching is. At paragraph 1716 and following we read:

> The Beatitudes are at the heart of Jesus' preaching. They take up the promises made to the chosen people since Abraham. The Beatitudes fulfill the promises by ordering them no longer merely to the possession of a territory, but to the Kingdom of Heaven. . . . The Beatitudes respond to the natural desire for happiness. This desire is of divine origin: God has placed it in the human heart in order to draw man to the One who alone can fulfill it. . . . The Beatitudes reveal the goal of human

3. Oraa, 389-390.

existence, the ultimate end of human acts: God calls us to his own beatitude. This vocation is addressed to each individual personally, but also to the Church as a whole, the new people made up of those who have accepted the promise and live from it in faith.

So, if we are really to follow Christ, if we really want to be under His standard, and to give ourselves entirely in His service, we must live out the Beatitudes. There is no way around it *at all*. Our happiness is to be found there, and no where else.

In 393, Saint Augustine wrote his *Commentary on the Sermon on the Mount*. In this work, he begins with the weighty proclamation that "anyone who piously and earnestly ponders the Sermon on the Mount — as we read in the Gospel according to Matthew — I believe he will find therein… the perfect standard of the Christian Life." Indeed, we can follow his commentary in Sermon 53, and add our own comments occasionally.

Blessed are the poor in spirit, for theirs is the kingdom of Heaven: To be poor in spirit is not to be materially impoverished, but to be humble. St. Augustine explains that "whoever is puffed up is not poor in spirit." The poor in spirit are not weak; they are strong enough to be detached from the material riches of this world. The kingdom of Heaven is on high but as is said in Mathew 23:12, "he that humbles himself shall be exalted." St. Leo the Great further elucidates the maxim: "blessed, therefore, is poverty which is not possessed with a love of temporal things, and does not seek to be increased with the riches of the world, but is eager to amass heavenly possessions." As we mentioned earlier, the Greeks had two words for *poor*; there is the word *penes*. "*Penes* describes a man who has to work for his living; it is defined by the Greeks as describing the man who is *autodiakonos*, that is, the man who serves his own needs with his own hands. It describes the working man, the man who has nothing superfluous, the man who is not rich, but who is not destitute either. But, it is not *penes* that is used in this beatitude, it is *ptochos,* which describes absolute and abject poverty. It is connected with the root *ptossein*, which means to crouch or to cower; and it describes the poverty which is beaten to its knees. As it has been said, *penes* describes the man who has nothing superfluous; *ptochos* describes the man who has nothing at all. So this beatitude becomes even more surprising. Blessed is the man who is abjectly and completely poverty-stricken. Blessed is the man who is absolutely destitute."[4]

4. Cf. Barclay's commentary on this text.

"Blessed are the meek for they shall inherit the earth" The Greek word for meek has a twofold meaning at once as strong as iron, yet as gentle as a feather. "In our modern English idiom the word meek is hardly one of the honorable words of life. Nowadays it carries with it an idea of spinelessness, and subservience, and mean-spiritedness. It paints the picture of a submissive and ineffective creature. But it so happens that the word meek--in Greek *praus*--was one of the great Greek ethical words." It was the balance between being angry all the time, and never getting angry at all. "But, the word *praus* has a second standard Greek usage. It is the regular word for an animal which has been domesticated, which has been trained to obey the word of command, which has learned to answer to the reins. It is the word for an animal which has learned to accept control."[5]

Jesus describes meekness as being "wise as serpents and gentle as doves." St. Francis de Sales further elucidates meekness when he says "there is nothing as strong as true meekness, there is nothing as gentle as true strength." One who is truly meek will possess the earth, "if you are not meek, [the earth] will possess you." St. Augustine notes that the earth refers to the heavenly kingdom and in another sense, self-possession ordered to Christ that unifies and integrates a community of souls.

Blessed are they who mourn for they shall be comforted: "It is first of all to be noted about this beatitude that the Greek word for to mourn, used here, is the strongest word for mourning in the Greek language. It is the word which is used for mourning for the dead, for the passionate lament for one who was loved. In the Septuagint, the Greek version of the Old Testament, it is the word which is used of Jacob's grief when he believed that Joseph, his son, was dead. It is defined as the kind of grief which takes such a hold on a man that it cannot be hid. It is not only the sorrow which brings an ache to the heart; it is the sorrow which brings the unrestrainable tears to the eyes. Here then indeed is an amazing kind of bliss: Blessed is the man who mourns like one mourning for the dead."[6]

St. Augustine cautions us against an improper understanding of mourning. Jesus does not bless every form of sorrow. Despair is sorrow without hope. Self-pity is a most dangerous form of morning. Mourning is the expression of inner discontent, of the gap between desire and satisfaction, in other words for suffering. We are to mourn for our sins and the sins of others. Our "true consolation will be that which gives comfort that will never be lost." "Christianity begins with a sense of sin. Blessed is the man who is intensely sorry for his sin, the

5. Cf. Barclay's commentary.
6. Ibid.

man who is heart-broken for what his sin has done to God and to Jesus Christ, the man who sees the Cross and who is appalled by the havoc wrought by sin.

It is the man who has that experience who will indeed be comforted; for that experience is what we call penitence, and the broken and the contrite heart God will never despise. The way to the joy of forgiveness is through the desperate sorrow of the broken heart."[7]

Blessed are those who thirst and hunger for justice, for they shall be satisfied.

"The fact is that very few of us in modern conditions of life know what it is to be really hungry or really thirsty. In the ancient world it was very different. A working man's wage was the equivalent of three pence a day, and, even making every allowance for the difference in the purchasing power of money, no man ever got fat on that wage. A working man in Palestine ate meat only once a week, and in Palestine the working man and the day laborer were never far from the border-line of real hunger and actual starvation.

It was still more so in the case of thirst. It was not possible for the vast majority of people to turn a tap and find the clear, cold water pouring into their house. A man might be on a journey, and in the midst of it the hot wind which brought the sand-storm might begin to blow. There was nothing for him to do but to wrap his head in his cloak and turn his back to the wind, and wait, while the swirling sand filled his nostrils and his throat until he was likely to suffocate, and until he was parched with an imperious thirst. In the conditions of modern western life there is no parallel at all to that.

So, then, the hunger which this beatitude describes is no genteel hunger which could be satisfied with a mid-morning snack; the thirst of which it speaks is no thirst which could be slaked with a cup of coffee or an iced drink. It is the hunger of the man who is starving for food, and the thirst of the man who will die unless he drinks.

Since that is so this beatitude is in reality a question and a challenge. In effect it demands. 'How much do you want goodness? Do you want it as much as a starving man wants food, and as much as a man dying of thirst wants water?' How intense is our desire for goodness?"[8]

If we hunger for the things of this world we will end in starvation. We ought to hunger for justice, the Bread of Life who is Christ. He tells us in John 6:41, "I am the bread that has come down from Heaven." We ought to thirst for the living water of which our Lord said "whoever drinks of the water that

---

7. Ibid.
8. Ibid.

302 · A Manual of the Spiritual Exercises of Saint Ignatius of Loyola

I shall give him will never thirst." St. Augustine advises us to "pant after the drink of the thirsty as well, for with Thee is the fountain of Life." Christ being the all-encompassing truth and justice is our food and drink, we ought to hunger and thirst for Him.

Blessed are the merciful for they shall obtain mercy. St. Augustine reminds us here of the truth that we are beggars at God's door and someone is begging from us. He entreats us to remember that "as you treat your beggar, so will God treat his." He exhorts: "Out of your own fullness fill an empty man, so that your own emptiness may be filled from the fullness of God." To him that shows mercy, mercy will be shown. The holy appeal to show mercy is well illustrated by the parable of the Good Samaritan.

Remember, too, that this mercy is extended, not only to us, but also to those who hurt us. Fr. Hardon writes: "But, as now almost two thousand years of the Church's commentators have pointed out, the promise, 'they shall obtain mercy,' is not only mercy for ourselves. By our being merciful toward others who can be very offensive to us, that too, but also, we obtain mercy for the very ones who are offensive, who hurt us. . . . In other words, it is not only that mercy is promised to us because we are merciful, but mercy is promised to those toward whom we show mercy. We merit mercy for them and may well be, don't forget this, it may well be, that our merciful forgiveness of those who have maybe cruelly betrayed us, even hated us, may be the condition that Christ attaches to giving these people His grace of merciful repentance. And that, of course, in one sentence is precisely what Jesus Christ did. He did not need to have His own sins forgiven. But, His mercy toward those who were so cruel toward Him, His mercy merited the mercy from His heavenly Father, for the very ones, who except for His mercy toward them, would not have obtained mercy from the heavenly Father to be saved themselves. More than any of us realize we hold the salvation of souls in the palms of our hands. We go on."

Blessed are the pure of heart for they shall see God. St. Augustine explains that "the eyes by which God is seen are within the heart." As if he is speaking to our age he admonishes, "how foolish then are those who try to find God through the use of their bodily eyes!" We must walk by faith not by sight. The purification of our hearts is the true end of our love which will allow us to see God clearly. The brightness of the true light will not be able to be seen by the unclean sight: and that which is joy to minds that are clean, will be a punishment to those that are tarnished. St. Augustine explains, "A simple heart is a heart that is pure; and, just as the light which surrounds us cannot be seen except through eyes that are clear, so neither is God seen unless that through which He can be seen is pure."

Blessed are the peacemakers for they are the children of God. St. Augustine clarifies that "where there is no contention, there is perfect peace. And because nothing can contend against God, the children of God are peace-makers." The Peacemakers of God are the opposite of the peacemakers of the world, for the men of the world cry "peace peace when there is no peace." St. Augustine explains that "man is unable to rule over the lower things unless he in turn submits to the rule of a higher being. And this is the peace promised on earth to men of good will." God's peace is only possible when everything is in its proper order and oriented to Him.

"Second, it must carefully be noted what the beatitude is saying. The blessing is on the peace-makers, not necessarily on the peace-lovers. It very often happens that if a man loves peace in the wrong way, he succeeds in making trouble and not peace. We may, for instance, allow a threatening and dangerous situation to develop, and our defense is that for peace's sake we do not want to take any action. There is many a person who thinks that he is loving peace, when in fact he is piling up trouble for the future, because he refuses to face the situation and to take the action which the situation demands. The peace which the Bible calls blessed does not come from the evasion of issues; it comes from facing them, dealing with them, and conquering them. What this beatitude demands is not the passive acceptance of things because we are afraid of the trouble of doing anything about them, but the active facing of things, and the making of peace, even when the way to peace is through struggle."[9]

In 2000, Pope Saint John Paul the Great celebrated Mass on the Mount of the Beatitudes. He summarizes very well the point of the Beatitudes, and what our response should be:

"Not far from this very place, Jesus called his first disciples, as he calls you now. His call has always demanded a choice between the two voices competing for your hearts even now on this hill, the choice between good and evil, between life and death. Which voice will the young people of the twenty-first century choose to follow? To put your faith in Jesus means choosing to believe what he says, no matter how strange it may seem, and choosing to reject the claims of evil, no matter how sensible or attractive they may seem.

In the end, Jesus does not merely speak the Beatitudes. He lives the Beatitudes. He is the Beatitudes. Looking at him you will see what it means to be poor in spirit, gentle and merciful, to mourn, to care for what is right, to be pure in heart, to make peace, to be persecuted. This is why he has the right to say, 'Come, follow me!' He does not say simply, 'Do what I say". He says, "Come, follow me!'

9. Ibid.

You hear his voice on this hill, and you believe what he says. But like the first disciples at the Sea of Galilee, you must leave your boats and nets behind, and that is never easy—especially when you face an uncertain future. To be good Christians may seem beyond your strength in today's world. But Jesus does not stand by and leave you alone to face the challenge. He is always with you to transform your weakness into strength. Trust him when he says: 'My grace is enough for you, for my power is made perfect in weakness' (2 Cor 12:9)!

Young people: answer the Lord with a heart that is willing and open! Willing and open, like the heart of the greatest daughter of Galilee, Mary, the Mother of Jesus. How did she respond? She said: 'I am the servant of the Lord, let it be done to me according to your word' (Lk 1:38)."

Jesus Christ doesn't simply preach the Beatitudes; He lives them, He is them. We can ask ourselves: how well do we imitate Him in living out the Beatitudes? Do we really embrace poverty of spirit; do we hunger and thirst for righteousness?

[Colloquy]: Ignatius tells us to end with the colloquy used for the Three Classes of Men, which is the same as the one used for Two Standards.

Threefold Colloquy:
A colloquy should be addressed to our Lady, asking her to obtain for me from her Son and Lord the grace to be received under His standard, first in the highest spiritual poverty, and should the Divine Majesty be pleased thereby, and deign to choose and accept me, even in actual poverty; secondly, in bearing insults and wrongs, thereby to imitate Him better, provided only I can suffer these without sin on the part of another, and without offense of the Divine Majesty. Then I will say the Hail Mary.

Second Colloquy: This will be to ask her Son to obtain the same favors for me from the Father. Then I will say, Soul of Christ.

Third Colloquy: This will be to beg the Father to grant me the same graces. Then I will say the Our Father.

[157] Note: It should be noted that when we feel an attachment opposed to actual poverty or a repugnance to it, when we are not indifferent to poverty and riches, it will be very helpful in order to overcome the inordinate attachment, even though corrupt nature rebel against it, to beg our Lord in the colloquies to choose us to serve Him in actual poverty. We should insist that we desire it, beg for it, plead for it, provided, of course, that it be for the service and praise of the Divine Goodness.

The Sermon on the Mount – Repetition
[278]

Usual Preparation Prayer.
First Prelude: The History: For the history, Matthew tells us that great crowds were following Jesus, from "Galilee, the Decapolis, Jerusalem, and Judea, and from beyond the Jordan . . . [and] when he saw the crowds, he went up the mountain, and after he had sat down, his disciples came to him," and He began to teach them. Thus begins the Sermon on the Mount.

Second Prelude: The Composition of Place: Here, in our imaginations, we can consider the mountain, with the crowd that had gathered. Biblical scholars tell us that it was "a hill of Galilee," probably about 500 feet high (more like a hill) on the western shore of Lake Tiberias above Tabgha about 8 miles from Tiberias and 2 from Capharnaum. Jesus probably gave the Sermon, not from the top of the mount, but on a level place on the southwest slope.[1] Likewise, the hill was in a central location, easily accessible by all. The scenery could hardly be better: in front, you have the calm waters of Lake Tiberias, in the back, mountains, on the right, towards the south, a low plane and further away Mt. Thabor, surrounded by shorter mountains. To the left, towards the north, the great Mt. Hermon, covered with snow, and, at the base of the hill of the Beatitudes, flower-covered fields.[2]

Third Prelude: Petition: Here the petition will be is to ask for light to know intimately my Divine King Who has become a Man for me, and grace to love Him and follow Him in poverty, suffering, and humiliations; in particular, we can ask for the grace to live our lives in accord with the Sermon on the Mount.
We recall that at [278] Ignatius gives three short points:

First Point
He proposes the eight beatitudes to His beloved disciples apart: "Blessed are the poor in spirit . . . the meek . . . the merciful . . . they that mourn . . . they that hunger . . . the peace-makers . . . those that suffer persecution."

1. Cf. Ricciota, *Life of Christ*, n. 316.
2. Cf. Oraa, *Ejercicios Espirituales*, 391.

Second Point

He exhorts them to use their talents, "So let your light shine before men in order that they may see your good works and glorify your Father in Heaven."

Third Point

He shows Himself not a transgressor of the Law but a fulfiller. He explains the commandments not to kill, not to commit adultery, not to swear falsely, and commands us to love our enemies: "I say, love your enemies, do good to them that hate you."

As with some of the other contemplations we have considered, Ignatius doesn't give a very detailed contemplation. He gives only the basic steps and then reminds us to follow the same model as we did before: to *see* the people, then to *hear* the people, then to *examine what they are doing*, each time gathering some fruit for my life.

Last night we considered the Beatitudes as the introduction for the Sermon on the Mount, but now we can consider some remaining selections of the text. Ignatius points out two sections in particular: "So let your light shine before men in order that they may see your good works and glorify your Father in Heaven," and that "He shows Himself not a transgressor of the Law but a fulfiller. He explains the commandments not to kill, not to commit adultery, not to swear falsely, and commands us to love our enemies: "I say, love your enemies, do good to them that hate you." Let's consider each of these two points.[3]

The Light Of The World (Mt 5:14-15)

You are the light of the world. A city set on a hill cannot be hid. Nor do men light a lamp and put it under a bushel, but on a stand, and it gives light to all in the house.

It may well be said that this is the greatest compliment that was ever paid to the individual Christian, for in it Jesus commands the Christian to be what he himself claimed to be. Jesus, said, "As long as I am in the world, I am the light of the world" (Jn 9:5) When Jesus commanded his followers to be the lights of the world, he demanded nothing less than that they should be like himself.

When Jesus spoke these words, he was using an expression which was quite familiar to the Jews who heard it for the first time. They themselves spoke of Jerusalem as "a light to the Gentiles," and a famous Rabbi was often called 'a

---

3. The commentary here is taken from Barclay and from Fuentes, *Maturity according to Jesus Christ.*

lamp of Israel." But the way which the Jews used this expression will give us a key to the way in which Jesus also used it.

Of one thing the Jews were very sure--no man kindled his own light. Jerusalem was indeed a light to the Gentiles, but "God lit Israel's lamp." The light with which the nation or the man of God shone was a borrowed light. It must be so with the Christian. It is not the demand of Jesus that we should, as it were, produce our own light. We must shine with the reflection of his light. The radiance which shines from the Christian comes from the presence of Christ within the Christian's heart. We often speak about a radiant bride, but the radiance which shines from her comes from the love which has been born within her heart.

When Jesus said that the Christian must be the light of the world, what did he mean?

(i) A light is first and foremost something which is meant to be seen. The houses in Palestine were very dark with only one little circular window perhaps not more than eighteen inches across. The lamp was like a sauce-boat tiled with oil with the wick floating in it. It was not so easy to rekindle a lamp in the days before matches existed. Normally the lamp stood on the lampstand which would be no more than a roughly shaped branch of wood; but when people went out, for safety's sake, they took the lamp from its stand, and put it under an earthen bushel measure, so that it might burn without risk until they came back. The primary duty of the light of the lamp was to be seen.

So, then, Christianity is something which is meant to be seen. As someone has well said, "There can be no such thing as secret discipleship, for either the secrecy destroys the discipleship, or the discipleship destroys the secrecy." A man's Christianity should be perfectly visible to all men.

Further, this Christianity should not be visible only within the Church, [and, we might add, a religious shouldn't be such only in their community or in church]. A Christianity whose effects stop at the church door is not much use to anyone. It should be even more visible in the ordinary activities of the world. Our Christianity should be visible in the way we treat a shop assistant across the counter, in the way we order a meal in a restaurant, in the way we treat our employees or serve our employer, in the way we play a game or drive or park a motor car, in the daily language we use, in the daily literature we read. A Christian should be just as much a Christian in the factory, the workshop, the shipyard, the mine, the schoolroom, the surgery, the kitchen, the golf course. the playing field as he is in church. Jesus did not say, "You are the light of the Church"; he said, "You are the light of the world," and in a man's life in the world his Christianity should be evident to all.

(ii) A light is a guide. On the estuary of any river we may see the line of lights which marks the channel for the ships to sail in safety. We know how difficult even the city streets were when there were no lights. A light is something to make clear the way.

So then a Christian must make the way clear to others. That is to say, a Christian must of necessity be an example. One of the things which this world needs more than anything else is people who are prepared to be foci of goodness. Suppose there is a group of people, and suppose it is suggested that some questionable thing should be done. Unless someone makes his protest the thing will be done. But if someone rises and says, "I will not be a party to that," another and another and another will rise to say, "Neither will I." But, had they not been given the lead, they would have remained silent.

There are many people in this world who have not the moral strength and courage to take a stand by themselves, but if someone gives them a lead, they will follow; if they have someone strong enough to lean on, they will do the right thing. It is the Christian's duty to take the stand which the weaker brother will support, to give the lead which those with less courage will follow. The world needs its guiding lights; there are people waiting and longing for a lead to take the stand and to do the thing which they do not dare by themselves.

(iii) A light can often be a warning light. A light is often the warning which tells us to halt when there is danger ahead.

It is sometimes the Christian's duty to bring to his fellowmen the necessary warning. That is often difficult, and it is often hard to do it in a way which will not do more harm than good; but one of the most poignant tragedies in life is for someone, especially a young person, to come and say to us, "I would never have been in the situation in which I now find myself, if you had only spoken in time."

If our warnings are, given, not in anger, not in irritation, not in criticism, not in condemnation, not in tile desire to hurt, but in love, they will be effective.

The light which can be seen, the light which warns, the light which guides, these are the lights which the Christian must be.

Shining for God: Mt 5:16

Let your light so shine before men, that they may see your good works and give glory to your Father who is in Heaven.

There are two most important things here.

(i) Men are to see our good deeds. In Greek there are two words for good. There is the word *agathos* which simply defines a thing as good in quality; there is *kalos* which means that a thing is not only good, but that it is also winsome and beautiful and attractive. The word which is used here is *kalos*.

The good deeds of the Christian must be not only good; they must be also attractive. There must be a certain winsomeness in Christian goodness. The tragedy of so much so-called goodness is that in it there is an element of hardness and coldness and austerity. There is a goodness which attracts and a goodness which repels. There is a charm in true Christian goodness which makes it a lovely thing.

We can think of the great saints who attracted people: Saint Philip Neri, Saint John Bosco . . . their loving way of dealing with others attracted people. There was a joy, a love that radiated from their works.

(ii) It is further to be noted that our good deeds ought to draw attention, not to ourselves, but to God. This saying of Jesus is a total prohibition of what someone has called "theatrical goodness," doing good so that others may see us and praise us, delight in us, whatever.

Again, we can think of what was said about Saint Vincent de Paul. Upon seeing him act and work, a man said, "God must be good, if He made Vincent so good!" That is the way that we should be as well.

Secondly, Ignatius tells us that "[Christ] shows Himself not a transgressor of the Law but a fulfiller. He explains the commandments not to kill, not to commit adultery, not to swear falsely, and commands us to love our enemies: 'I say, love your enemies, do good to them that hate you.'"

First and foremost, what stands out in this text is a great truth: Our Lord seeks the *unity of the person*. Indeed, Jesus affirms His relation to the divine law given to the Jews by presenting Himself as the one who *consummates* or *perfects* it. He has not come to "abolish it," but rather to bring it fulfillment. The fulfillment reaches to the point of extending the influence of the law to the source of a person's being and actions: their *interiority*. The Jews who had come before and those contemporary with Christ only paid attention to the law in what was normative for man's external actions: "You have heard that it was said" (bear in mind that this does not always refer to the Old Testament, but rather also to the Rabbinical traditions, as is clear in the last paragraph—"You have heard that it was said, 'You shall love your neighbor and hate your enemy'"—which is not found at all in Scripture but rather in the oral teachings of the Jewish teachers); all of these norms that His listeners "have heard said" are norms that govern man's external actions: do not kill, do not commit adultery, divorce only when the law permits it, to fulfill oaths, to practice strict justice, to love one's neighbor, and hate one's enemy, etc.

Jesus Christ *overcomes* those "limits" demanded by human weakness by bringing order and maturity to the source of human actions: the heart. "You have heard that it was said, *but I say to you.*" This is not an opposition between the Old Law and the New, except in cases where the Old Law was not in reality a divine law, but rather a human one (that is, a Rabbinic interpretation, as we have said). There is no opposition because the Old Law prepared for the coming of Christ, and He is its natural fulfillment; it was a shadow that prefigured the reality. However, the prefiguring is imperfect but not false; it proclaims a truth in a way that is still confusing. Jesus is complete and total clarity. He can also demand more because He is the strength that helps to fulfill that law. For this reason we say that the Old Law was limited in light of the weakness of the human heart; this is precisely what Jesus will say later on regarding one of the points that He overcomes in this section: "Because of the hardness of your hearts [Moses] wrote you this commandment [writing the bill of divorce and dismissing one's wife]" (Mk 10:5), "but from the beginning it was not so" (Mt 19:8).

The demands of Christ, then, reach into man's interior, and for this reason, for Him:

- The good man is not the one who does not kill (or steal or commit any of the acts against one's neighbor that we could connect with this), but rather the one who kicks anger out of his heart, who forgives and asks for forgiveness, and who sets into practice the means in order to be reconciled with his enemy.

- The good man is not the one who does not commit adultery (or who does not fornicate, or touch, or speak impurely, etc., or any of the other acts that we could place under this sort of sin), but rather the one who orders his interior desires, that interior gaze that has a woman (or any neighbor) as its object, as a respectful gaze and desire, full of modesty and reverence.

- The good man is not the one who disavows his wife but rigorously fulfills the requirements indicated by the law, but rather the one who does not reject her in any way at all; the good man is one who is faithful, who forgives her when she sins, asks for forgiveness when he sins, and stays united with her until death separates them.

- The good man is not the one who does not commit perjury or leave his oaths unfulfilled, nor the one who, having made an oath, fulfills it faithfully, but rather the one who has allowed himself to be so filled with the truth that he has no need to swear a oath in order to defend his word; he is naturally faithful to what he says, even if he does not swear an oath. His "yes" is a true and absolute "yes"; his "no" is a categorical "no." He is not a man of ambiguous words.

- The good man is no longer the one who punishes without exceeding the right measure, but rather the one who forgives with magnanimity, the one who overcomes the debts that in justice he could demand with both forgiveness and generous condonation.
- The good man is not the one who loves strictly those who warrant it by reason of blood, friendship, benefit, or race. Rather, the good man embraces everyone in his love, without exception, even those who do not deserve it.
- Earlier, I said that with this Our Lord is directing us towards the *unity of the person*. The old way for living the demands of morality (from without) implies a *break* in the person: the exterior life is something independent of the interior world. In contrast, Jesus Christ points toward an equation where the person could be expressed like this: thought = desire = action. The external action is the expression of the heart's desires, and these are willful expression of reason's judgments.

Even more, the main work will need to take place in the realm of the value judgments in our thoughts, because it is according to these that we must desire, love, and hate, and, consequently, act.

(ii) We could say that the value judgments that Jesus *corrects* or *elevates* in this section of the Sermon on the Mount are six (which serve as a model for all possible judgments):

- Not only is the physical life of one's neighbor valuable (You shall not kill), but rather also his good name, his dignity, and his entire person. Hence, I should not insult him, elicit his anger, or live at odds with him. Do I recognize in him the image of God (cf. Jm 3:9) or not?
- Not only is external purity of the body valuable, a purity that is tainted by inappropriate sexual contact, but also purity of soul, the reputation and the dignity of the whole person. The body is profaned by physical contact; however, honor and dignity are degraded with impure looks and impure desires. Do I recognize my neighbor as a "temple of the Holy Spirit" (1 Cor 6:19), and do I treat him as such?
- Not only is marriage valuable while fidelity, harmony, and love last, but rather always, in spite of infidelity and lack of love. This is because there are no longer two, but one flesh, and no one can divide what is one. Do I understand the depths of marriage as a sacrament (an image) of Christ's indissoluble love for the Church (cf. Eph 5:32)?
- Not only are words supported by an oath valuable, but rather any word whatsoever that comes from our mouths, if the one speaking has really "wedded" the truth. Every man must "belong to the truth" (Jn 18:37: "Everyone who be*longs to the truth li*stens to my voice"). Do we

understand that only the truth will set us free (cf. Jn 8:32)? Do we be-long *to* the truth?

- Not only is strict justice valuable, that justice which does not demand more than what it should, and does not punish more than what is mer-ited, like an exact mathematical formula, but rather, and above all, mag-nanimity and generous forgiveness? Did not God love us when we were yet His enemies (cf. Rm 5:10) and He had not yet pardoned us, then, when we were an object of His wrath (cf. Eph 2:3-5)?
- Lastly, not only is the love born in our hearts for the good and those who are worthy to be loved valuable, but also the love for evil people, for our enemies, and for those who persecute us. Does not God the Father act in this way, making the sun to shine upon both the evil and the good, without taking into account that the first are ungrateful and spoiled?
- (iii) By changing our value judgments regarding these realities, the incli-nations of our hearts also change, since what is loved is what is valued, and what is desired is what is considered as good and fitting.

In this way, then, the rupture of personality is overcome, a rupture with thoughts and desires (interior life) going to one side, and external acts going towards the other. Both the man who acts correctly exteriorly, but not so in his heart, as well as the one who acts well interiorly, but whose interior thoughts are not translated to the exterior, are both fragmented beings, but perhaps for very different motives. The one who thinks, values, judges, and loves poorly, but acts correctly and politely, is a hypocrite, a whitewashed tomb. The one who bows like a knight before a woman, but undresses her with his desires or in his thought, is a profaner, although his hands and mouth might not have ever touched even so much as a hair of his victim. On the other extreme, the one who thinks, values, judges, and loves well, but who acts exteriorly with-out any tact or respect, or simply does not act, and rather freezes up, becomes paralyzed, is timid, pusillanimous, or even someone with a complex who feels unconquerable shame or fear at externally manifesting their good feelings and desires: this could be the manifestation of some inferiority complex. In either case, we have a break between what is exterior and what is within.

(iv) On the other hand, Jesus Christ does not only direct His words to-wards the *unity* of the person, but also to the fullness of their development. The surpassing of the law that Jesus establishes in His "New Law" does not simply go in the direction of the triumph of what is interior, but rather to ob-taining the "greatest" ideal. Indeed, the purely exterior law is a minimalist law: respect for the life of another is the bare minimum we should do for him; not attempting to seduce our neighbor's wife is the least that we should do for her; not dismissing our spouse without serious reasons is the very least we should do for our marriage; to fulfill what we have promised under oath is the bare minimum we should do with our serious commitments; limiting ourselves to only breaking one tooth of the one who only broke one of our teeth is the least we can do to not go against justice; to love those who love us is the least we can do in the practice of love. In none of these cases is there any mention of a *maximum*. Jesus Christ points precisely at a maximum in each of these orders (which are given to us only by way of example, but are not the only aspects of our lives to which they should be applied).

This is the way Jesus Christ lives, and it's the way He wants us to live: the maximum, not the minimum.

[Colloquy]: Ignatius tells us to end with the colloquy used for the Three Classes of Men, which is the same as the one used for Two Standards.

Threefold Colloquy:

A colloquy should be addressed to our Lady, asking her to obtain for me from her Son and Lord the grace to be received under His standard, first in the highest spiritual poverty, and should the Divine Majesty be pleased thereby, and deign to choose and accept me, even in actual poverty; secondly, in bearing insults and wrongs, thereby to imitate Him better, provided only I can suffer these without sin on the part of another, and without offense of the Divine Majesty. Then I will say the Hail Mary.

Second Colloquy: This will be to ask her Son to obtain the same favors for me from the Father. Then I will say, Soul of Christ.

Third Colloquy: This will be to beg the Father to grant me the same graces. Then I will say the Our Father.

[157] Note: It should be noted that when we feel an attachment opposed to actual poverty or a repugnance to it, when we are not indifferent to poverty and riches, it will be very helpful in order to overcome the inordinate attachment, even though corrupt nature rebel against it, to beg our Lord in the colloquies to choose us to serve Him in actual poverty. We should insist that we desire it, beg for it, plead for it, provided, of course, that it be for the service and praise of the Divine Goodness.

Christ Calms the Storm
[279]

Usual Preparation Prayer.

First Prelude: The History: For the history, we can consider the Biblical text that Ignatius points out: Mt 8:23-27. There are also parallel texts in Mk 4:35-41 and Lk 8:22-25. Jesus gets in the boat, and we are told that "His disciples follow Him." Suddenly a storm comes up as Jesus is asleep, and they awaken Him. He calms the storm, and reprimands them for their lack of faith.

Second Prelude: The Composition of Place: Here, in our imaginations, we should see the sea of Galilee. One commentator notes that "the Sea of Galilee is small; it is only thirteen miles from north to south and eight miles from east to west at its widest. The Jordan valley makes a deep cleft in the surface of the earth, and the Sea of Galilee is part of that cleft. It is 680 feet below sea level. That gives it a climate which is warm and gracious, but it also creates dangers. On the west side there are hills with valleys and gullies; and, when a cold wind comes from the west, these valleys and gullies act like gigantic funnels. The wind, as it were, becomes compressed in them, and rushes down upon the lake with savage violence and with startling suddenness, so that the calm of one moment can become the raging storm of the next. The storms on the Sea of Galilee combine suddenness and violence in a unique way."[1]

Third Prelude: Petition: Here the petition will be to ask for light to know intimately my Divine King Who has become Man for me, and grace to love Him and follow Him in poverty, suffering, and humiliations.

At [279] Ignatius gives three brief points for us to consider.

First Point

While Christ our Lord was asleep in the boat on the sea, a great storm arose.

---

1. Barclay's commentary.

Second Point

His terrified disciples awaken Him. He reprehends them for the little faith they have, and says to them, "Why are ye afraid, O ye of little faith?"

Third Point

He commanded the wind and sea to cease, and they obeyed, and the sea became calm. And the men marveled, saying, "What manner of man is this that even the winds and the sea obey him?"

As with some of the other contemplations we have considered, Ignatius doesn't give a very detailed contemplation. He gives only the basic steps and then reminds us to follow the same model as we did before: to *see* the people, then to *hear* the people, then to *examine what they are doing*, each time gathering some fruit for my life.

As we have done for the other meditations, we can consider, first, a little background to what Ignatius is doing here, and then, second, some elements to help us contemplate and consider Christ so as to imitate Him better.

We've already mentioned the physical layout of the sea of Galilee. Commenting on the parallel text in Mark, Fr. Ricciotti notes that "the departure seems to have been sudden and hurried." It's interesting that we are told that "Jesus got in the boat, and His disciples followed Him." Christ, with His divine knowledge, would've known that a storm was coming, and yet He went ahead anyways. In other words, He knew perfectly well what was going to happen, and how He was going to solve the problem. The disciples didn't know that, but they should have known Jesus.

"The crossing is only a matter of a few miles, but it can be dangerous, especially toward nightfall, as in this case, because cold winds come tumbling suddenly down from the snowy heights of Hermon and blow up storms which are extremely violent for that lake and for the frail craft which sail it. This is what happened that evening. Jesus, wearied from the long, laborious day, lay down in the stern of the boat and went to sleep. . . . Suddenly a violent gale strikes the lake and before long Jesus' boat begins to [take on] water and is in danger of sinking. Its crew try to maneuverer it to safety but all in vain."[2]

"In less than half an hour the placid sunshine had become a raging storm. That is what Jesus and his disciples encountered. The words in the Greek are very vivid. The storm is called a *seismos*, which is the word for an earthquake. The waves were so high that the boat was *hidden* (*kaluplesthai*) in the trough as the crest of the waves towered over them. Jesus was asleep. (If we read the

2. *Life of Christ*, 346.

316 · A Manual of the Spiritual Exercises of Saint Ignatius of Loyola

narrative in Mk 4:1 and 35, we see that before they had set out he had been using the boat as a pulpit to address the people and no doubt he was exhausted).

"Jesus lies fast asleep in the little boat on Galilee's sea, seeming entirely oblivious of all that is happening about him; one could, in the darkness, easily mistake him for a coil of rope or a folded sail lying there. The disciples cannot understand how he can sleep through the raging fury of the wind and sea and they hesitate between their desire not to disturb him and their terror of the impeding disaster, between their respect for the Master and their instinctive habit of turning confidently to Him for help. But after a little they are convinced they cannot hesitate any longer. They simply have to waken and warn him so that he may somehow save himself as well." In their moment of terror the disciples awoke him, and the storm became a calm. The parallel texts emphasize the suddenness of the calm; everything settled down right away. If you are familiar with the water and the way that storms arise, you know that, even after the worst of the storm passes, it still takes time for the water to settle down. However, we see Christ's power in that, as soon as He commands, suddenly everything becomes peaceful.

Wherever Jesus is the storms of life become a calm. It means that in the presence of Jesus the most terrible of tempests turns to peace.

When the cold, bleak wind of sorrow blows, there is calm and comfort in the presence of Jesus Christ. When the hot blast of passion blows, there is peace and security in the presence of Jesus Christ. When the storms of doubt seek to uproot the very foundations of the faith, there is a steady safety in the presence of Jesus Christ. In every storm that shakes the human heart there is peace with Jesus Christ.

The lesson of this story is that when the storms of life shake our souls Jesus Christ is there, and in his presence the raging of the storm turns to the peace that no storm can ever take away.

The foundation of this peace, however, is to be confident in Christ. Fr. Jean d'Elbee explains this when he writes, "What does Jesus lament most when He is with His Apostles? Their lack of confidence. 'Men of little faith!' This is the main reproach He makes to them. He does not say to them, 'Men of no character, men without energy, without discipline. No, He says, 'Men of little faith!'

Jesus was crossing the lake of Tiberias in a boat with His disciples. He was asleep in the stern. A great windstorm blew up, and the waves poured into the boat so that it was already filled. Seized with anguish, the disciples awakened Jesus: 'Lord, save us; we are perishing!' And rising up, He reprimands the wind and says to the sea, 'Peace! Be still!' And the wind abated and there was a great calm' Then, turning to His Apostles, He asks, 'Where is your faith?' I can hear Jesus scolding them with gentleness, but with pain, too: 'Why is this?

I was in the boat with you – I slept, but I was there – and you were afraid; you were terrified. You doubted either my omnipotence or my love. Do you not know after all who I am, and do you not know after all with what tenderness my Heart watches over you continually?' It is truly such doubt that pains and offends Him most.

But you see, we have lost so completely the notion of the entire confidence that He expects of us, that we sometimes make a prayer of the words for which He reproached His Apostles: 'Lord, save us; we are perishing!'

This is not how we should pray, but rather, 'With you, Jesus, I cannot perish; You are always in the boat with me; what have I to fear? You may sleep; I shall not awaken you. My poor nature will tremble, oh yes! But with all my will I shall remain in peace in the midst of the storm, confident in You.'

In hours of anguish, think of the Divine Master calming the violent storm with one word. This will be a tremendous source of comfort for you as you wait – peacefully – for Him to waken.

The great tempest is what our sins stir up in our souls. It is there that Jesus must arise in order that 'a great calm may descend.'"3

So, how can we not wake Jesus, and allow ourselves to remain calm in the midst of troubles? The answer lies in *spiritual childhood*, becoming little children before God. "[Spiritual childhood] involves, above all, the recognition of our own nothingness. To remain a child, says St. Therese: 'is to recognize our nothingness, to expect everything from God as a little child expects everything from its father; it is to be disquieted about nothing. . . . To be little is not attributing to oneself the virtues that one practices, believing oneself capable of anything, but to recognize that God places this treasure in the hands of His little child to be used when necessary; but it remains always God's treasure.'

Remaining a child involves maintaining a spirit of poverty; to be poor is the most priceless treasure because one has compassion and mercy on a child because of his lack of strength. And so she frequently repeats [and we have three quotes from her]: 'In the case of children, they will be judged with extreme sweetness'; 'Little children are not damned'; 'Even among the poor, they give the child what is necessary, but as soon as he grows up, his father no longer wants to feed him.'" This, too, is a point that Fr. Kentenich makes: especially in poor families, where it seems that the parents have nothing, somehow, almost miraculously, the parents make food appear. The child probably isn't even aware of this, but, even in the worst circumstances, somehow the parents manage to provide.

---

3. *I believe in Love*, 40–41.

In *Notes about Confidence*, Fr. Fuentes says, "The greatest enemy of this spiritual childhood is to abandon our poverty due to attachment to earthly goods [recall that *earthly goods* doesn't just mean things like money or cars or fancy houses, but anything that isn't God, that could be found apart from Him or separated from Him in some way], that is, due to the loss of what St. Ignatius calls 'indifference.' Spiritual childhood implies a total detachment, even of all that could be called 'extraordinary': [Again, he gives some quotes from the Little Flower]: 'I don't have any desire to see God here on earth. And yet I love Him! I also love the Blessed Virgin very much, and the saints, and I don't desire to see them. [I prefer to live by faith].' "To ecstasy, I prefer the monotony of sacrifice."

It consists in loving and wanting to suffer for God: 'Sanctity does not consist in saying beautiful things, it does not even consist in thinking them, in feeling them! It consists in suffering and suffering everything.'

'It was far from bringing me any consolations since the most absolute aridity and almost total abandonment were my lot. Jesus was sleeping as usual in my little boat; ah! I see very well how rarely souls allow Him to sleep peacefully within them. Jesus is so fatigued with always having to take the initiative and to attend to others that He hastens to take advantage of the repose I offer to Him. He will undoubtedly awaken before my great eternal retreat, but instead of being troubled about it this only gives me extreme pleasure.'

This childlike abandonment to God does not imply passivity but rather completely the opposite, a great strength to practice a stripping of self and to not place obstacles to the action of God. It should not seem strange to us, because of this, that Sr. Genevieve of the Holy Face – her sister Celine – gave evidence in the process of beatification that the characteristic virtue of the saint was *fortitude*. Thus, from the outside, she harnessed the temperament of this great saint not as a 'sweet child' but as a 'strong woman.'"

We can conclude with a poem of Bl. Joseph Kentenich, which reminds us that our attitude must be like that of children who trust without reserve in their father:

Though storms may rage
And winds may howl
And lightning strike again,
I think as does the mariner's child:
My Father is at the helm!

[**Colloquy**]: Ignatius tells us to end with the colloquy used for the Three Classes of Men, which is the same as the one used for Two Standards.

Threefold Colloquy:

A colloquy should be addressed to our Lady, asking her to obtain for me from her Son and Lord the grace to be received under His standard, first in the highest spiritual poverty, and should the Divine Majesty be pleased thereby, and deign to choose and accept me, even in actual poverty; secondly, in bearing insults and wrongs, thereby to imitate Him better, provided only I can suffer these without sin on the part of another, and without offense of the Divine Majesty. Then I will say the Hail Mary.

Second Colloquy: This will be to ask her Son to obtain the same favors for me from the Father. Then I will say, Soul of Christ.

Third Colloquy: This will be to beg the Father to grant me the same graces. Then I will say the Our Father.

[157] Note: It should be noted that when we feel an attachment opposed to actual poverty or a repugnance to it, when we are not indifferent to poverty and riches, it will be very helpful in order to overcome the inordinate attachment, even though corrupt nature rebel against it, to beg our Lord in the colloquies to choose us to serve Him in actual poverty. We should insist that we desire it, beg for it, plead for it, provided, of course, that it be for the service and praise of the Divine Goodness.

The Good Shepherd [Jn 10]
John 10: 1-18

Usual Preparation Prayer.

[150] First Prelude: The history: Jesus gives the discourse regarding the Good Shepherd in John 10. However, it follows immediately after He heals the man born blind on a Sabbath. The Pharisees get angry, question him, and then kick him out of the Synagogue. After this rebuke, we see Jesus meeting with the man again, and the Pharisees ask if they are blind. In response, Jesus replies with the discourse about the Good Shepherd, which is Jn 10:1-18.

[151] Second Prelude: The composition of place: This is a mental representation of the place. We can see Jesus walking and talking with His disciples, and then the angry Pharisees. However, it might be useful to imagine a shepherd leading his flock out to pasture, like in Psalm 23.

[152] Third Prelude: The petition: This is to ask for what I desire. Here it will be to beg for the grace to know the infinite love of our Divine King and grace to put all my trust in Him.

This is an added meditation; Ignatius doesn't include this in the book of the Exercises, but the whole text is worth considering.

As with some of the other contemplations we have considered, Ignatius doesn't give a very detailed contemplation. He gives only the basic steps and then reminds us to follow the same model as we did before: to *see* the people, then to *hear* the people, then to *examine what they are doing*, each time gathering some fruit for my life.

As we have done for the other meditations, we can consider, first, the text itself, and then explain it and apply it to ourselves.

The text itself is brief, but contains many images and ideas. It is worthwhile to consider the text in its entirety.

"Amen, amen, I say to you, whoever does not enter a sheepfold through the gate but climbs over elsewhere is a thief and a robber. But whoever enters through the gate is the shepherd of the sheep. The gatekeeper opens it for him, and the sheep hear his voice, as he calls his own sheep by name and leads them out. When he has

driven out all his own, he walks ahead of them, and the sheep follow him, because they recognize his voice. But they will not follow a stranger; they will run away from him, because they do not recognize the voice of strangers." Although Jesus used this figure of speech, they did not realize what he was trying to tell them.

So Jesus said again, "Amen, amen, I say to you, I am the gate for the sheep. All who came [before me] are thieves and robbers, but the sheep did not listen to them. I am the gate. Whoever enters through me will be saved, and will come in and go out and find pasture. A thief comes only to steal and slaughter and destroy; I came so that they might have life and have it more abundantly. I am the good shepherd. A good shepherd lays down his life for the sheep. A hired man, who is not a shepherd and whose sheep are not his own, sees a wolf coming and leaves the sheep and runs away, and the wolf catches and scatters them. This is because he works for pay and has no concern for the sheep. I am the good shepherd, and I know mine and mine know me, just as the Father knows me and I know the Father; and I will lay down my life for the sheep. I have other sheep that do not belong to this fold. These also I must lead, and they will hear my voice, and there will be one flock, one shepherd. This is why the Father loves me, because I lay down my life in order to take it up again. No one takes it from me, but I lay it down on my own. I have power to lay it down, and power to take it up again. This command I have received from my Father."

Barclay tells us that "There is no better loved picture of Jesus than the Good Shepherd. The picture of the shepherd is woven into the language and imagery of the Bible. It could not be otherwise. The main part of Judaea was a central plateau, stretching from Bethel to Hebron for a distance of about 35 miles and varying from 14 to 17 miles across. The ground, for most part, was rough and stony. Judaea was, much more a pastoral than an agricultural country and was, therefore, inevitable that the most familiar figure of the Judaean uplands was the shepherd.

His life was very hard. No flock ever grazed without a shepherd, and he was never off duty. There being little grass, the sheep were bound to wander, and since there were no protecting walls, the sheep had constantly to be watched. On either side of the narrow plateau the ground dipped sharply down to the craggy deserts and the sheep were always liable to stray away and get lost. The shepherd's task was not only constant but dangerous, for, in addition, he had to guard the flock against wild animals. especially against wolves, and there were always thieves and robbers ready to steal the sheep."[1]

In the Gospel we see two parts: first, Jesus speaks using the figures of the sheepfold, the gate, and the shepherd but, when His hearers don't understand,

---

1. Barclay's commentary on this passage.

Jesus repeats the figures a second time, this time explaining the meaning of His words and, in particular, how they apply to Him.

Regarding the first section, it's interesting that Christ's listeners "did not realize what He was trying to tell them." Presumably they understood the literal meaning of His words, since the Bible contains some 100 references to shepherds and nearly four hundred to flocks, and the entire setting would've been familiar to them.[2] What they failed to see, and what Christ had to explain to them, was how those words applied to our Savior.

Perhaps our difficulty today is the opposite: we know who Christ is, but many of the details of the Good Shepherd are lost on us because we're not familiar with sheep and shepherding. If we look at Christ's words in the context that He spoke them, however, a clearer image of Christ's love and compassion for us begins to emerge. We can look at three points in particular: first, the shepherd's voice and presence, secondly, the care sheep require, and, thirdly, the value of the sheep.

First, Jesus says, "My sheep hear my voice . . . and they follow me." Earlier, Christ tells His listeners that "the sheep follow him, because they recognize his voice."[3] In order to understand this, we need to consider a little bit what life was like in Biblical Palestine; it was common that several flocks would gather at one watering stop or spend the night together in one sheepfold. All the sheep would be mixed together, a confused lot of many different sheep from multiple flocks. In order to separate them, when it was time for a flock to leave, the shepherds would use a peculiar whistle or call. It's nothing intelligible, like a word or phrase, but rather a peculiar sound or cry that would be recognized by the sheep. At that sound, the sheep of that shepherd's flock simply head over to him, and follow the sound of their shepherd wherever he would lead them to. This is interesting, because sheep are notoriously dumb animals, but they can distinguish their shepherd's voice, and so much so that an unfamiliar voice sends the flock running in all directions, but the familiar one brings order and keeps the flock in peace. Moreover, the mere presence of the shepherd is enough to calm the aggressive instincts of the rams, who would otherwise fight and injure each other.[4]

It's interesting too that the shepherd would go first: he would do so in order to make sure the path was safe, and that no harm would come to his animals. Often the animals needed to be encouraged to follow across rough terrain, but if the shepherd guided them, they would come along.

2. *Dictionary of Biblical Imagery*, edited by Leland Ryken, James C. Wilhoit, Tremper Longman III, 782, voce *Sheep, Shepherd*.

3. Cf. *A Guide Through the Old Testament*, Celia Brewer Marshall, Celia B. Sinclair, 121.

4. *A Guide Through the Old Testament*, Celia Brewer Marshall, Celia B. Sinclair, 121.

We can ask ourselves, do we allow ourselves to hear Christ's voice in our daily lives? Do we let ourselves be calmed by His mere presence? Or do we let ourselves be upset by the noise of the world? Do we trust in the path He takes us on?

Second, Christ tells us that He knows His sheep. Again, to understand what Christ is saying, we need to recall that Biblical shepherds knew their sheep personally, or individually, as it were.[5] The shepherds know their sheep more like we would know our pet dog or cat. We know them by name, the way they behave, what things they like or avoid, all their distinctive traits and characteristics. Christ's knowledge of us is like that. We're not loved simply as a group, or in bulk. He knows each one of us intimately, with all our different strengths, weaknesses, fears, and needs. Even the things we don't know about ourselves, He knows, and He wants to use in order to help us get to Heaven. This requires trust on our part: as Psalm 23 tells us: "The LORD is my shepherd. . . . Even though I walk through the valley of the shadow of death, I will fear no evil, for you are with me; your rod and your staff comfort me." We can ask ourselves: do we really trust in God's love for us, in His knowledge of us, and that He wants to help us in all our needs?

We should also recall that sheep are notoriously stupid animals; if left alone, sheep will eat even the roots of the grass, destroying the land, and drink polluted water. A truly good shepherd takes all of this into account, and is constantly on the watch and on the move to ensure the best for his flock. We can ask ourselves, do we allow Christ to move us where He wants us to go? Do we allow Him to direct our lives since He wants the best for us?

Christ also tell us that He is "the good shepherd who lays down his life for the sheep." Sheep were valuable possessions in the Old Testament, and the shepherd would defend them against thieves and wild animals. Even at night, the shepherd was on guard: he would sleep at the gate of the sheepfold, or, if there was no fold, he would spend the night awake.[6] This is because the sheep were valuable for his family and their well-being. Christ, however, sees us, His sheep, as valuable in ourselves. Do we believe that's the care God has for us, that His eyes are ever-watchful over us?

Thirdly, and lastly, Christ says that no one can take His sheep from His hand: "they shall never perish. No one can take them out of my hand." That is a very strong categorical statement: the sheep of Christ's flock belong to Him, and no one can take them: not the devil, not evil people, not terrible suffering, nothing. When we really give ourselves to Christ, when we really

5. Cf. *The Wiersbe Bible Commentary: New Testament*, 255.
6. *A Guide Through the Old Testament*, Celia Brewer Marshall, Celia B. Sinclair, 121.

surrender ourselves to Him and to His gentle paths, He watches over us and protects us. If we are meek and childlike before Him, He can do with us what He wills, and assures us of the final victory, of making it to Heaven forever with Him. Have we really surrendered ourselves that much to Christ, a total surrender, confident, as the Psalm says, that "[Christ] sets a table before me in front of my enemies; Indeed, goodness and mercy will pursue me all the days of my life; I will dwell in the house of the Lord for endless days"? If not, then we must work on surrendering our lives to Christ, the Good Shepherd.

[Colloquy]: Ignatius tells us to end with the colloquy used for the Three Classes of Men, which is the same as the one used for Two Standards.

Threefold Colloquy:

A colloquy should be addressed to our Lady, asking her to obtain for me from her Son and Lord the grace to be received under His standard, first in the highest spiritual poverty, and should the Divine Majesty be pleased thereby, and deign to choose and accept me, even in actual poverty; secondly, in bearing insults and wrongs, thereby to imitate Him better, provided only I can suffer these without sin on the part of another, and without offense of the Divine Majesty. Then I will say the Hail Mary.

Second Colloquy: This will be to ask her Son to obtain the same favors for me from the Father. Then I will say, Soul of Christ.

Third Colloquy: This will be to beg the Father to grant me the same graces. Then I will say the Our Father.

[157] **Note:** It should be noted that when we feel an attachment opposed to actual poverty or a repugnance to it, when we are not indifferent to poverty and riches, it will be very helpful in order to overcome the inordinate attachment, even though corrupt nature rebel against it, to beg our Lord in the colloquies to choose us to serve Him in actual poverty. We should insist that we desire it, beg for it, plead for it, provided, of course, that it be for the service and praise of the Divine Goodness.

Jesus Preaches in the Temple
[288]

Usual Preparation Prayer.

First Prelude: The History: For the history, we can consider the Biblical texts that Ignatius points out, a very brief passage: Lk 19:47-48. After the cleansing of the Temple in Luke's account, we are told that Jesus was preaching every day in the Temple.

Second Prelude: The Composition of Place: Here, in our imaginations, we should see the Temple in Jerusalem, and, as it is near the time of a great feast, the great number of pilgrims, the sacrifices, the noise. We should see Jesus preaching in the midst of all the people, with His disciples, but also those who come to ridicule Him, to challenge Him, and even those who plot His death.

Third Prelude: Petition: Here the petition will be to ask for light to know intimately my Divine King Who has become a Man for me, and grace to love Him and follow Him in poverty, suffering, and humiliations.

At [288] Ignatius gives only gives us two very short points:

First Point
He was teaching daily in the temple.

Second Point
After His teaching, since there was no one in Jerusalem who would receive Him, He returned to Bethania.

As with some of the other contemplations we have considered, Ignatius doesn't give a very detailed contemplation. He gives only the basic steps and then reminds us to follow the same model as we did before: to *see* the people, then to *hear* the people, then to *examine what they are doing*, each time gathering some fruit for my life.

As we have done for the other meditations, we can consider, first, a little history of the scene and then, second, some elements to help us contemplate and consider Christ so as to imitate Him better.

First, we might think that it is a little odd to have this mystery here. After all, chronologically, it is clear in Luke's Gospel that this takes place after Palm Sunday, and that will be the meditation tomorrow night. So, why is it here?

Early Jesuit directories tell us that, beyond a doubt, this is where Ignatius placed it: the tenth day of the second week. Nonetheless, one might ask why. Fr. Oraa comments that a Fr. Codina suggests that it is simply so that the Second Week can close with Palm Sunday, and then enter directly into the Passion Week.

However, Fr. Oraa thinks that the reason is more profound. He writes: "Could it be, perhaps, that, in order to prepare the exercitant for making a good election of a state of life [or reform, we could add], he wants the retreatant to contemplate Jesus in the full exercise of His preaching apostolate, suffering the ingratitude of the people, and that, after a day of tiring work, they don't even offer Him a place to rest, and so He must go to Bethany because they would not receive him in Jerusalem? What is certain is that this change in the order of events isn't because of carelessness or distraction on Ignatius' part, but is rather done deliberately. It seems clear as well that the matter for contemplation of the 11th and 12th days, the Resurrection of Lazarus and the entrance in Jerusalem, do not link up as clearly and directly with the work of the election, with which the exercitant is concerned in these days."[1]

It should be noted as well that, although Ignatius gives only two verses to consider, Christ's preaching in the Temple takes a number of chapters in Luke, from 20:1 through 21:36 (v. 37 and 38 tell us He would have to leave in the night and stay at the Mount of Olives, and that people would come early in the morning to hear Him preach).

With this in mind, that the contemplation should still assist us in our election and reform of life, let us now turn to the contemplation properly speaking.

There are great number of teachings contained in the verses from Luke's Gospel. However, as Fr. Oraa points out, we can concern ourselves perhaps with just the most important, that is, that of the greatest commandment.

"The Sadducees had attempted to surprise Jesus with whimsical questions about the resurrection of the dead, but since the Lord had emerged victorious, they called their allies the Pharisees in order to begin a new attack. For this, they brought over a scribe, who knew much about interpretation of the law, and, drawing near to Jesus, asked Him: "Which is the first of all the

---

1. Oraa, *Ejercicios Espirituales*, 411-412.

commandments?" Jesus replied, "*The first is this: 'Hear, O Israel! The Lord our God is Lord alone! You shall love the Lord your God with all your heart, with all your soul, with all your mind, and with all your strength.' The second is this: 'You shall love your neighbor as yourself.' There is no other commandment greater than these*" (note, this is from Mark's Gospel, 12:29-31).

"Love! This is the word that summarizes all the others, and, when fulfilled, gives the perfect solution to all the other obligations and requirements of the Christian life! Love, and do everything in and for love!

Note, too, the second precept: to love neighbor. We do not love God if we do not love our neighbor. Other men and women are your brothers and sisters; they are God's adopted children. Let us not separate what God has united."

This is something we must keep in mind: everyone is our neighbor, everyone is our brother and sister. One of Saint Teresa of Calcutta's favorite phrases was to say that she and her sisters served Christ in "His most distressing disguise."[2] In her case, it was in the poor, lepers, and the abandoned, people who physically resembled Lazarus. Christ's words remind us that we too must serve Christ in whatever "His most distressing disguise" might be for us.

This might be the person of our superiors, who might be difficult or lack the qualities we think they should have. However, as Saint Ignatius wrote: "The superior is to be obeyed not because he is prudent, or good, or qualified by any other gift of God, but because he holds the place and the authority of God, as Eternal Truth has said: *He who hears you, hears me; and he who rejects you, rejects me* [Luke 10:16]. Nor on the contrary, should he lack prudence, is he to be the less obeyed in that in which he is superior, since he represents Him who is infallible wisdom."[3] Obedience requires that we see Christ in disguise.

This might also mean Christ hidden in our community members. In her autobiography, Saint Thérèse of the Child Jesus candidly recalls how she dealt with such a one in her own convent, writing: "There is in Community a Sister who has the faculty of displeasing me in everything, in her ways, her words, her character, everything seems very disagreeable to me. . . . I told myself that charity must not consist in feelings but in works; then I set myself to doing for this Sister what I would do for the person I loved the most. Each time I met her I prayed to God for her, offering Him all her virtues and merits... I wasn't content simply with praying very much for this Sister who gave me so many struggles, but I took care to render her all the services possible, and

---

2. Mother Teresa, *Where There is Love, There is God* (New York: Doubleday, 2010), 158.

3. *Letter to the Members of the Society of Jesus in Portugal*, or *On Perfect Obedience*. It is "Ignatius' most celebrated and most widely-read letter."

328 · A Manual of the Spiritual Exercises of Saint Ignatius of Loyola

when I was tempted to answer her back in a disagreeable manner, I was content with giving her my most friendly smile. . . . One day at recreation she asked in almost these words: 'Would you tell me, Sister Thérèse of the Child Jesus, what attracts you so much towards me; every time you look at me, I see you smile?' Ah! What attracted me was Jesus hidden in the depths of her soul.'"[4]

The "distressing disguise" might even be a person who could justly be called an "enemy." But, here, too, we must see Christ Himself. The life of Saint Louis Orione offers great examples of this. "When one of his religious abandoned the Congregation, he covered Orione with insults and abuse. Don Orione gave him some money, embraced him with tenderness, kissed him with affection on the forehead, wished him all good things, and told those present to pray for him as for a benefactor." On another occasion, trouble brewed for Orione in the city of Tortona: the bishop was complaining, there was slander, gossip, accusations, hostility, and trials. Yet, in the midst of it all, Orione wrote to a friend saying: "My enemies can even put my eyes out; just let them leave me my heart [with which] to love them." Once, when Orione was betrayed and insulted by one of his religious, a fellow priest told him to respond in kind, and asked what would be done. Don Orione answered: "Nothing. . . . For these people: a) one prays to God; b) one forgives; c) one loves."

Lastly, we should note that "there is something almost incredibly audacious in the action of Jesus in teaching in the Temple courts when there was a price on his head. This was sheer defiance. At the moment the authorities could not arrest him, for the people hung upon his every word. But every time he spoke he took his life in his hands and he knew well that it was only a matter of time until the end should come. The courage of the Christian should match the courage of his Lord. He left us an example that we should never be ashamed to show whose we are and whom we serve."[5]

Ignatius ends the contemplation with the second point, that after teaching, no one would receive Him, so He would have to leave for Bethany. "How ungrateful men are!" says Fr. Oraa. "After a day of preaching which began very early in the morning, since Luke tells us *And all the people would get up early each morning to listen to him in the temple area* (Lk 12:38), in the afternoon He found no one who would invite Him to spend the night in his house, and He would have to go to the Mount of Olives and to Bethany. In this, both the ingratitude and the fear of the Jews had a part.

How often it happens in the apostolic life that an Apostle must reap ingratitude on the part of those he perhaps once called friends, and persecution

---

4. Saint Thérèse of the Child Jesus, *Story of a Soul* (Chapter 10, Clarke 222-223).

5. Baclay's commentary on the passage.

from enemies. From His birth, this was fulfilled in Jesus, *His own received Him not* (Jn 1:11), He came to His home but His own did not want to receive Him. Ingratitude and persecution were His constant companions in His apostolic life, just like the poverty of not having a home, or a bed, or a table. We must learn from this!"

We must seek to be good friends to Christ, to seek Him out, to love Him, and to invite Him to stay with us in our hearts. Likewise, we must also be grateful, giving Him thanks for the many blessings that He has bestowed upon us.

[**Colloquy**]: Ignatius tells us to end with the colloquy used for the Three Classes of Men, which is the same as the one used for Two Standards.

Threefold Colloquy:

A colloquy should be addressed to our Lady, asking her to obtain for me from her Son and Lord the grace to be received under His standard, first in the highest spiritual poverty, and should the Divine Majesty be pleased thereby, and deign to choose and accept me, even in actual poverty; secondly, in bearing insults and wrongs, thereby to imitate Him better, provided only I can suffer these without sin on the part of another, and without offense of the Divine Majesty. Then I will say the Hail Mary.

Second Colloquy: This will be to ask her Son to obtain the same favors for me from the Father. Then I will say, Soul of Christ.

Third Colloquy: This will be to beg the Father to grant me the same graces. Then I will say the Our Father.

[**157**] **Note:** It should be noted that when we feel an attachment opposed to actual poverty or a repugnance to it, when we are not indifferent to poverty and riches, it will be very helpful in order to overcome the inordinate attachment, even though corrupt nature rebel against it, to beg our Lord in the colloquies to choose us to serve Him in actual poverty. We should insist that we desire it, beg for it, plead for it, provided, of course, that it be for the service and praise of the Divine Goodness.

The Raising of Lazarus [285]
John 11:1-45

Usual Preparation Prayer.

[150] First Prelude: The history: Call to mind how our Lord, two days after hearing that His friend, Lazarus, was dangerously ill, went to Bethany and rewarded the faith of Martha and Mary, the dead man's sisters, by raising him to life (Jn 11, 1-45).

[151] Second Prelude: The composition of place: This is a mental representation of the place. Here it will be to see with the eyes of the imagination the road from Peræa to Bethany and Lazarus' tomb—a cavern chiseled out of the rock and sealed with a stone.

[152] Third Prelude: The petition: This is to ask for what I desire. Here it will be to beg for the grace to know the infinite love of our Divine King and grace to put all my trust in Him.

In [285], Ignatius gives us three very simple points to follow:

First Point: Mary and Martha inform Jesus of the sickness of Lazarus. After He was informed of this, He delayed for two days that the miracle might be more evident.

Second Point: Before He raised him, He asked faith of both Mary and Martha, saying, "I am the resurrection and the life. He that believeth in me even though he die shall live."

Third Point: Jesus raises him after He had wept and said a prayer. The way in which He raised him was by a command, "Lazarus, come forth."

As with some of the other contemplations we have considered, Ignatius doesn't give a very detailed contemplation. He gives only the basic steps and then reminds us to follow the same model as we did before: to *see* the people, then to *hear* the people, then to *examine what they are doing*, each time gathering some fruit for my life.

Contemplating the apparition of our Lord to His Disciples on the lake of Gennesaret we have been encouraged to follow the course He has lovingly planned out for us, by the sure knowledge that He constantly watches over us and is ready to come to our help in the darkest moment of despair. Now St. Ignatius wants us to realize that though our work is hard, thankless and apparently fruitless, we are not alone. Jesus is not only the King that watches the progress of the battle and runs to the rescue of His faithful soldiers, but He is our loving Friend also, the tenderest of friends. "I will not now call you servants. ... But I have called you friends." (Jn 15:15) "As the Father has loved Me, I also have loved you. Abide in My love." (Jn 15:9).

The present contemplation is meant to bring out the tender love of our Divine Friend and the infinite power which is His and which He places so to speak at the disposal of those whom He loves.

"Now there was a certain man sick, named Lazarus, of Bethania of the town of Mary and Martha her sister. ... His sisters therefore sent to Him, saying: Lord, behold, he whom You love is sick.

Note that the sisters call Him "Lord," recognizing His deity and authority. . . . The distance separating Our Lord from the house where Lazarus lived was about a day's journey. If, therefore, He remained two days more in Peraea and we add another day for the journey, in all it would have been four days since He received the news. God's delays are mysterious; sorrow is sometimes prolonged for the same reason for which it is sent. God may abstain for the moment from healing, not because Love does not love, but because Love never stops loving, and a greater good is to come from the woe. Heaven's clock is different from ours. Human love, impatient because of delay, would demand speed. The same delay took place when He was on the way to the house of Jairus, whose daughter He restored to life. Here Our Lord, instead of speeding along the way, took His time. The works of evil are sometimes done in a hurry; Our Lord told Judas to go about his dirty work "quickly."

And Jesus hearing it, said to them: This sickness is not to end in death but for the glory of God: that the Son of God may be glorified by it.

"Now Jesus loved Martha, and her sister Mary, and Lazarus. When He had heard therefore that he was sick, He still remained in the same place two days: then after that He said to the disciples: Let us go unto Judea again...

When explaining the situation to His disciples, John notes that "Jesus was talking about his death, while they thought that he meant ordinary sleep. So then Jesus said to them clearly, 'Lazarus has died.'" Our Lord was reluctant to use the word "death," which proved that His whole life was set against it. He used the same word about the daughter of Jairus as He did about Lazarus, namely, they "were asleep." It would be the same word that the followers of Christ would use about Stephen, that he "fell asleep."

"Martha therefore, as soon as she heard that Jesus was come, went to meet Him: but Mary sat at home. Martha therefore said to Jesus: Lord, if You had been here, my brother had not died. But now also I know that whatsoever You will ask of God, God will give it to You." (Jn 11:1-22).

Mary too will tell Him the same: "When Mary came to where Jesus was and saw him, she fell at his feet and said to him, "Lord, if you had been here, my brother would not have died." When Jesus saw her weeping and the Jews who had come with her weeping, he became perturbed and deeply troubled, and said, "Where have you laid him?"

Sometimes Jesus' silences or non-answers tell us a great deal about God's will and love for us. C. S. Lewis, writing about the death of his wife, demanded that God answer his questions about her. "When I lay these questions before God I get no answer. But a rather special sort of 'No answer.' It is not the locked door. It is more like a silent, certainly not uncompassionate, gaze. As though He shook His head not in refusal but waiving the question. Like, 'Peace, child; you don't understand.'"

The whole episode of the raising of Lazarus is brimful of a love as tender and ardent as any that has ever burnt in the heart of man. The message of Mary and Martha is love pleading to Love: "Behold he whom You love is sick." John, the Apostle of love, hastens to remark that "Jesus loved Martha, and her sister Mary, and Lazarus." Christ Himself speaks of Lazarus as a friend: "Lazarus, our friend"; and at the sight of Mary's tearful sorrow He "groaned in spirit and troubled Himself" and wept, so that the Jews could not help saying, "Behold, how He loved him."

The phrase "groaned in spirit" is very strong; literally it means "snorted like a horse interiorly," and usually means anger. In this case, it would be anger at the presence of sin, and of its effect, namely, death.

Active rather than passive, Christ entered into sympathy with death and sorrow, two of the major effects of sin. He hungered because He willed it; He was sorrowful because He willed it; He would die because He willed it. As He was weak in our weakness, poor in our poverty, so He was sorrowful in our sadness. This deliberately willed sharing of the sorrows of those whom He would redeem caused Him to weep. The Greek word that is used implies a calm shedding of tears. Our Lord is described in the Scriptures as weeping three times: once over a nation, when He wept over Jerusalem, once in the Garden of Gethsemane, when He wept over the sins of the world, and in this instance over Lazarus, when He wept for the effect of sin, which is death. None of these tears were for Himself, but for the human nature He assumed.

It is usually imagined that our Lord did not grant the loving request of the two sisters, but stayed in Peræa two days more to give Lazarus, so to speak, time to die, and to Himself, the occasion to work a miracle. One after the other merely says: "Lord, if You had been here, my brother would not have died."

Their faith in Christ's power, however, is still unshaken and their confidence in His loving care, boundless. "But now also I know that whatsoever You shall ask of God, God will give it to You." Martha does not openly ask Christ to raise her brother to life, sure that He sees the wish of her heart and would not fail to grant it.

Loving recourse to our Divine Friend in our needs and boundless confidence in His love and infinite power even when all seems to rise against us, and He Himself, to have forgotten us, must be the breath of our life.

"Who shall separate us from the love of Christ? Shall affliction or anguish or persecution or hunger or nakedness or danger or the sword? …. Yet amidst all this we more than conquer through Him Who has loved us." (Rom 8:35-37).

"Jesus said to her: Your brother shall rise again. Martha said to Him: I know that he shall rise again in the resurrection at the last day. Jesus said to her: I am the Resurrection and the Life: he that believes in Me, although he is dead, shall live: and everyone that lives and believes in Me shall not die forever. Do you believe this?

"She said to Him: Yes, Lord I have believed that You are the Christ the Son of the Living God Who has come into this world." (Jn 11:23-27).

Christ is the Resurrection and the Life. Through Him we rise from the worst of deaths—the death of sin—to live of the very life of God. Through Him we live eternally of His life, and though our body shall have to undergo the penalty of death, it will one day rise by the power of Christ and share in the happiness and glory of the soul. "He that believes in Me has life everlasting." (Jn 6:47); "He that eats My Flesh and drinks My Blood, has everlasting life: and I will raise him up on the last day." (Jn 6:55)

The faith that Jesus requires is not when there is money in the bank, but when there is bankruptcy; not to believe when the sun is shining, but when it is hidden; the seeming heedlessnesss of His Divine power is never loveless or an unwise delay.

To believe that Christ is the principle of resurrection and life is to believe in His Divinity. That is why Martha answers the question of the Savior: "Do you believe this?" with St. Peter's cry, "You are the Christ the Son of the Living God." To reveal Himself to the crowd and to His enemies as the Son of God, our Lord raises Lazarus to life.

"And Jesus lifting up His eyes said: Father, I give You thanks that You have heard Me. And I knew that You hear Me always, but because of the people who stand about have I said it: that they may believe that You have sent Me." (Jn 11:41-42)

Notice that it is only when the stone is rolled away, when those nearby have taken the very first, baby steps of belief, that Christ begins His prayers.

The message of the Church during the last nineteen centuries, the aim of her activities and of her never ending martyrdom is "that you may believe that Jesus is the Christ the Son of God: and that believing you may have life in His name.

The cry of Peter and of Martha must be the constant cry of our souls—the rock on which the edifice of our spiritual life stands unshaken and ever rises towards the throne of God.

[Colloquy]: Ignatius tells us to end with the colloquy used for the Three Classes of Men, which is the same as the one used for Two Standards.

Threefold Colloquy:

A colloquy should be addressed to our Lady, asking her to obtain for me from her Son and Lord the grace to be received under His standard, first in the highest spiritual poverty, and should the Divine Majesty be pleased thereby, and deign to choose and accept me, even in actual poverty; secondly, in bearing insults and wrongs, thereby to imitate Him better, provided only I can suffer these without sin on the part of another, and without offense of the Divine Majesty. Then I will say the Hail Mary.

Second Colloquy: This will be to ask her Son to obtain the same favors for me from the Father. Then I will say, Soul of Christ.

Third Colloquy: This will be to beg the Father to grant me the same graces. Then I will say the Our Father.

[157] Note: It should be noted that when we feel an attachment opposed to actual poverty or a repugnance to it, when we are not indifferent to poverty and riches, it will be very helpful in order to overcome the inordinate attachment, even though corrupt nature rebel against it, to beg our Lord in the colloquies to choose us to serve Him in actual poverty. We should insist that we desire it, beg for it, plead for it, provided, of course, that it be for the service and praise of the Divine Goodness.

Palm Sunday
[287]

Usual Preparation Prayer.

First Prelude: The History: For the history, we can consider the Biblical text that Ignatius points out: Mt 21:1-17. However, the triumphal entry into Jerusalem is recounted in all the Gospels, so we could also consider Mk 11:1-11, Lk 19:28-44 (which includes the Lamentation over Jerusalem), and Jn 12:12-19. We know that Christ was coming from Bethany, where He raised Lazarus from the dead. Then, He told His disciples to prepare for His entry by finding a colt or an ass. As He entered the city, He rode on it, and the people acclaimed Him and laid palm branches in front of Him, while the Pharisees and leaders of the people grew angry.

Second Prelude: The Composition of Place: Here, in our imaginations, we should see the path that leads from Bethany to Jerusalem. "Bethany is a little town about 2 miles from Jerusalem, on the other side of the Mount of Olives."[1] "Jesus chose the shortest and most crowded road – about three thousand yards long – which went from Bethany up the Mount of Olives and then down its western slope, finally entering the city near the northeast corner of the Temple."[2]

Third Prelude: Petition: Here the petition will be is to ask for light to know intimately my Divine King Who has become a Man for me, and grace to love Him and follow Him in poverty, suffering, and humiliations.

At [287] Ignatius gives three short points:

First Point

Our Lord sends for the ass and the foal, saying, "Loose them and bring them to me, and if anyone say ought to you, you shall say, 'The Lord hath need of them,' and straightway he will let them go."

---

1. Oraa, *Ejercicios Espirituales*, 431.
2. Ricciotti, *Life of Christ*, 519.

Second Point

After the ass was covered with the garments of the Apostles, Jesus mounted it.

Third Point

The people came forth to meet Jesus, and spread their garments and the branches of trees in the way, saying, "Hosanna to the Son of David! Blessed is he that cometh in the name of the Lord! Hosanna in the highest!"

As with some of the other contemplations we have considered, Ignatius doesn't give a very detailed contemplation. He gives only the basic steps and then reminds us to follow the same model as we did before: to *see* the people, then to *hear* the people, then to *examine what they are doing*, each time gathering some fruit for my life.

As we have done for the other contemplations, we can consider, first, a little of the historical background, and then, second, some elements to help us contemplate and consider Christ so as to imitate Him better.

It's perhaps hard for us to understand the overwhelming enthusiasm of the crowds when Jesus came entering into Jerusalem, or some of the details, like why the people didn't mind that their donkey was being taken away, or that it hadn't been ridden on before. Fr. Ricciotti explains the scene and the historical importance of these details this way. As the disciples were heading towards Jerusalem (like Ignatius tells us in the first point), "Jesus gave an order which filled them brimful of happiness. Calling two of his disciples to him, he said: 'Go into the village opposite you, and immediately on entering it you will find a colt tied, upon which no man has yet sat; loose it, and bring it. And if anyone say to you: 'What are you doing?' you shall say that the Lord has need of it, and immediately he will sent it here.

In Palestine the donkey had been the mount of important personages since the time of Balaam (Nm 22:21), and in seeking one on this occasion Jesus seemed to be seconding the festive intentions of his company, which was thereupon filled with delight. But Jesus' purpose was far different; Matthew, careful as usual to show how the messianic prophecies come to pass, points out that here was fulfilled the prediction of the ancient prophet Zechariah (9:9) .... The two disciples did exactly as they were bid, and while they were loosing the animal, the owners asked why they were doing it but, hearing it was for Jesus, said no more. Probably they were friends of the family of Lazarus and therefore friendly to Jesus also.... If the colt had never been ridden by anyone before, it was all the more suitable to bear as its first burden the sacred person of Jesus, for the ancients did not consider an animal that had been trained for profane tasks appropriate for religious uses."[3]

With this context in mind, we can consider for our contemplation what is happening. "Here we have Jesus, heading to Jerusalem, as His passion draws near. This last contemplation of the second week marks the end of the apostolic years of Jesus. Now, we turn to His passion, the work of redemption. We are to understand that He is going to suffer for us, but, here, at the beginning of His passion, He is filled with joy just like the crowds, overjoyed to be able to redeem us. Are we prepared to work and to suffer out of love for the one who loves us so much? How many times has the mere foreshadowing, the mere thought of suffering while following Christ embittered our hearts and even made us give up some undertaking or task?

See how even the vast crowds recognize that He is the Messiah, and yet still many others refuse to open their eyes and believe. Likewise, see how His enemies plot to kill Him, but will be unable to do so until He allows them. We do well to remember that for us, too, our enemies are powerless over us; the only control or power over us they have is what Christ permits them to wield.

Christ sends His disciples to bring the colt to Him, and He instructs them to tell the owners, 'The Lord has need of it.' The owners offer no resistance, and, indeed, how can we resist the Lord when He asks something of us? He has given us so much, but how often do we forget what He has done, and, in our ingratitude, abuse the gifts and benefits that He has given us. 'The Lord has need of it': this could be said of all of our gifts and talents, our time, our skills, our minds, and our wills. 'The Lord has need of it': how can we resist that request?"[4]

Again, "everything is fulfilled as Jesus had predicted. The Apostles laid their best cloaks over the animal, and, placing them on the colt's back, Jesus sat on them. They chose the best of their cloaks in order to adorn the Master's procession, happily assisting in the splendor of His triumph. . . . He is a king, and yet He is contented with so little! . . . It is clear His kingdom is not of this earth! If it were, He would undoubtedly have soldiers to accompany and surround Him, and richly dressed courtiers, and magnificent steeds with imposing knights. That is what earthly kings need; since they are men like any other, they need all of that splendor to set themselves apart. But not Christ: King of Kings and Lord of Lords, He needs nothing, since He Himself is the fullness of greatness and splendor!

3. Ricciotti, *Life of Christ*, 519-520.
4. Oraa, *Ejercicios*, 432-433.

338 · A Manual of the Spiritual Exercises of Saint Ignatius of Loyola

Biblical scholars have given us three reasons for this entry into Jerusalem: first, to fulfill the prophecies, second, to leave us an example of humility and meekness, and, third, to clearly affirm His royalty as foreseen by the prophets. This is why He enters on a colt; even though a colt wasn't the choice of animal for a warrior, nonetheless, the prophets foresaw the King entering His city on one. . . . In this, we should see our King full of gentleness and sweetness. He comes preaching peace, as Saint Luke tells us when He entered the city He said: *If this day you only knew what makes for peace—but now it is hidden from your eyes.*

If only we knew what made for peace! Those in Jerusalem did not take advantage of the Lord's offer of peace: may the same not be said of us; may we always seek to find our peace in Jesus Christ.

See and hear the crowds as they come to greet Jesus: see how Jesus enters the city. "The crowd received Jesus like a king. They spread their cloaks in front of him. That is what his friends had done when Jehu was proclaimed king (2 Kgs 9:13). They cut down and waved the palm branches. That is what they did when Simon Maccabaeus entered Jerusalem after one of his most notable victories (1 Mc 13:51).

They greeted him as they would greet a pilgrim, for the greeting: 'Blessed be he who enters in the name of the Lord' (Ps 118:26) was the greeting which was addressed to pilgrims as they came to the Feast.

They shouted 'Hosanna!' We must be careful to see what this word means. Hosanna means *Save now!* and it was the cry for help which a people in distress addressed to their king or their god. It is really a kind of quotation from Ps 118:25: 'Save us, we beseech Thee, O Lord.' The phrase, 'Hosanna in the highest!' must mean, 'Let even the angels in the highest heights of Heaven cry unto God, Save now!'

It may be that the word *hosanna* had lost some of its original meaning; and that it had become to some extent only a cry of welcome and of acclamation, like 'Hail!'; but essentially it is a people's cry for deliverance and for help in the day of their trouble; it is an oppressed people's cry to their savior and their king."[5]

"Let us reflect for a moment in order to get from fruit from the teachings of this wonderful entrance into the city. It is the triumph of our captain, our eternal king, whose life we have been contemplating in order to follow Him into glory. What a difference there is between this glory and the glory of earthly kings! We have seen that the colt would have been a fine animal for those in Palestine, but a Roman, passing by, would have broke out laughing.

5. Barclay's commentary.

Yet, Jesus, the Meek and Humble King, accepts the humble homages, those offerings from the good people who gave Him what they could. His Kingdom doesn't get caught up on the exterior, but rather on souls, in peace, tranquility, in holiness.

The simple people threw their cloaks at Jesus' feet: what will we place there? We should place our love, so that our King might triumphantly march upon it. We have just made our elections or our reform of life; ask Jesus to step triumphantly over the riches that you have surrendered, the ones you want to leave out of love for Him. Ask Him to process upon your will, which you want Him to subject in obedience; upon your sensuality, which you want to dominate in order to remain chaste . . . ask Him to take everything.

Let us imitate the crowds in proclaiming Jesus. However, we must beware: many of those who acclaimed Jesus on Palm Sunday called for His death on Good Friday."[6]

[Colloquy]: Ignatius tells us to end with the colloquy used for the Three Classes of Men, which is the same as the one used for Two Standards.

Threefold Colloquy:

A colloquy should be addressed to our Lady, asking her to obtain for me from her Son and Lord the grace to be received under His standard, first in the highest spiritual poverty, and should the Divine Majesty be pleased thereby, and deign to choose and accept me, even in actual poverty; secondly, in bearing insults and wrongs, thereby to imitate Him better, provided only I can suffer these without sin on the part of another, and without offense of the Divine Majesty. Then I will say the Hail Mary.

Second Colloquy: This will be to ask her Son to obtain the same favors for me from the Father. Then I will say, Soul of Christ.

Third Colloquy: This will be to beg the Father to grant me the same graces. Then I will say the Our Father.

[157] Note: It should be noted that when we feel an attachment opposed to actual poverty or a repugnance to it, when we are not indifferent to poverty and riches, it will be very helpful in order to overcome the inordinate attachment, even though corrupt nature rebel against it, to beg our Lord in

6. Oraa, *Ejercicios*, 429-438. Some sections are very loosely translated, with my own additions and thoughts.

the colloquies to choose us to serve Him in actual poverty. We should insist that we desire it, beg for it, plead for it, provided, of course, that it be for the service and praise of the Divine Goodness.

SECOND WEEK

Conferences

End of the Second Week and Notes
[127-131], [133]
and
Maturity according to Jesus Christ

For today's conference, we will consider, just briefly, some practical changes and modifications that Ignatius makes for us after having passed through the First Week of the Exercises, as we come to the second week (which begins, technically, with the contemplation on the Incarnation). Then, we will move into something that I will continually refer to through this second week, and that is the idea of Christian maturity as proposed by Jesus Christ.

Today, we began with our consideration of the call of Christ the King. As Casanovas explains, this contemplation is sort of like the Principle and Foundation of the First Week; it sort of guides everything we think, do, consider, and the like, because it teaches us "the spirit with which we should contemplate the life of Christ," namely, as an example to imitate. Thus, the Call of Christ the King is like the Principal and Foundation for the remainder of the Exercises. We are debtors to Jesus Christ, as we have seen, and so we must not only repay Him, but also live according to His model of life.[1]

As with the other additional instructions, the ones Ignatius gives now are meant to help us enter more fully into the life of Jesus Christ and obtain the fruits that we want, namely, to *incorporate the life of Jesus Christ into my own life*, that is, to make me into *another Christ*.

This is the motive for the different rules and instructions that Ignatius gives. For instance, last night, we considered [100], wherein Ignatius tells us "During the Second Week and thereafter, it will be very profitable to read some passages from the *Imitation of Christ,* or from the Gospels, and from the lives of the saints," because all of these readings will help us to better assimilate Christ's life into our own, either by seeing and considering it as it is (in the Gospels), by thinking over concrete ways to incorporate it, as we read in the *Imitation of Christ,* or by considering people who really lived out Christ's life in their own in an exemplary way, as we would find in the lives of the saints.

---

1. Cf. Casanovas, *Ejercicos Espirituales,* 236.

Let's, then, consider the directions that Ignatius gives for this week:

[127] Attention must be called to the following point. Throughout this Week and the subsequent Weeks, I ought to read only the mystery that I am immediately to contemplate. Hence, I should not read any mystery that is not to be used on that day or at that hour, lest the consideration of one mystery interfere with the contemplation of the other.

- The point here is that we shouldn't be guided by curiosity, as sometimes happens, or let ourselves be too eager to move on to the next mystery. We should take care, then, when we are reading the Gospels not to skip ahead to the next mystery.

[128] The First Exercise on the Incarnation should take place at midnight, the second at daybreak, the third about the time of Mass, the fourth near the time of Vespers, and the fifth an hour before supper.

The same order should be observed on all the following days.

[129] If the exercitant is old or weak, or even when strong, if he has come from the First Week rather exhausted, it should be noted that in this Second Week it would be better, at least at times, not to rise at midnight. Then one contemplation would be in the morning, another would be at the time of Mass, a third before dinner, with one repetition of them at the time of Vespers, and the Application of the Senses before supper.

- We will see that the second week is divided into two parts: the first, which will consider the mysteries of Christ's life up until His baptism, culminates in the considerations of the three classes of men and the three modes or manners of humility, which are the preparation for making an election. The second half of the second week, which considers Christ's public life up to and including Palm Sunday, is the actual time of elections.
- As we mentioned, this first half considers the life of Christ from the Incarnation to the beginning of His public ministry. The point of Ignatius here is "to give a place for a contemplation that is very intimate, peaceful, and sweet, but also one that is very uplifting." It's also a time, as we read in [129], for a little bit of rest and relief, especially if the first week was very intense.

Now, we can see how Ignatius modifies the additional directives given during the first week.

[130] Of the ten Additional Directions given during the First Week, the following should be changed during the Second Week: the second, the sixth, the seventh, and part of the tenth.

The second will be that as soon as I awake, I should place before my mind the subject of the contemplation with the desire to know better the eternal Word Incarnate in order to serve and follow Him more closely.

- You might recall that the second direction, at [74], tells us: "When I wake up, I will not permit my thoughts to roam at random, but will turn my mind at once to the subject I am about to contemplate in the first exercise at midnight," etc. The point is that no longer are we thinking of ourselves as a knight who is hauled before the king after doing something bad, or a sinner loaded with chains going to meet the judge. That was for the first week. Now, we are going to focus on Christ, so as to know Him better.

The sixth will be to call to mind frequently the mysteries of the life of Christ our Lord from the Incarnation to the place or mystery I am contemplating.

- Again, the sixth direction was found at [78]: "I should not think of things that give pleasure and joy, as the glory of Heaven, the Resurrection, etc., for if I wish to feel pain, sorrow, and tears for my sins, every consideration promoting joy and happiness will impede it. I should rather keep in mind that I want to be sorry and feel pain. Hence it would be better to call to mind death and judgment." The point is that now, we've come out of the first week, so these thoughts aren't as conducive to the end of the second week. Rather, we should be thinking of the mysteries of Christ's life. There isn't a hard and fast rule here, like that of the first week: Ignatius doesn't say don't think on happy things, but nor does he say think of them. We will think of the mysteries of Christ's life, and, based on the subject matter, we will feel happy or sad, depending. This leads us to the next directive:

The seventh will be that the exercitant take care to darken his room, or admit the light; to make use of pleasant or disagreeable weather, in as far as he perceives that it may be of profit, and help to find what he desires.

- [79] gave us the seventh directive: "For the same reason I should deprive myself of all light, closing the shutters and doors when I am in my room, except when I need light to say prayers, to read, or to eat." Here, there is no hard and fast rule; the governing principle should be what we are contemplating, and then what helps me to contemplate it. For instance, the Visitation and the Nativity are happy moments, whereas the Flight into Egypt is not. Based on the subject matter, I can make use of things to help me get into the feel of the contemplation.

In the observance of the tenth Additional Direction, the exercitant must conduct himself as the mysteries he is contemplating demand. Some call for penance; others do not.

Thus all ten Additional Directions are to be observed with great care.

- The rather lengthy tenth directive stretches from [82] to [85], and dealt with penance. Once again, the rule of the thumb is to follow the mysteries we are contemplating. For instance, when we are contemplating the Nativity, it is a time of great joy. Even the very austere Saint Francis of Assisi, when asked by one of his friars what they should do when Christmas fell on a Friday, if they should fast and abstain from meat for Friday or celebrate for Christmas, Francis replied, "I would like that on Christmas even the walls could eat meat." So, based on what we are contemplating, adjust your penances accordingly as it helps you to enter into the contemplation.

[131] In all the exercises, except the one at midnight and the one in the morning, an equivalent of the second Additional Direction should be observed as follows:

As soon as I recall that it is time for the exercise in which I ought to engage, before proceeding to it, I will call to mind, where I am going, before whom I am to appear, and briefly sum up the exercise. Then after observing the third Additional Direction, I shall enter upon the exercise.

- Again, the second directive dealt with what we do as soon as we wake up. Here, Ignatius is telling us to pay attention and consider the mystery we are going to consider as we make our way towards our meditation.

[133] Note

Sometimes it will be profitable, even when the exercitant is strong and well-disposed, to make some changes from the second day to the fourth inclusive in order to attain better what is desired. Thus, the first contemplation would be the one on rising. Then there would be a second about the time of Mass, a repetition about the time of Vespers, and the Application of the Senses before supper.

- Again, here Ignatius' point is that maybe less intense contemplation, taking a set back, might help us to attain more fruit. My recommendation is still that you try to make the midnight contemplation, to have that extra hour of prayer with God.

Now, then, we come to the second half of our conference, a topic that we will be seeing extensively throughout this second week, and this is the topic of Christian maturity: what does it mean to be a mature Christian? In this, we will follow several books by Fr. Fuentes on the topic, but principally *Maturity according to Jesus Christ*, *The Emotional Maturity of Jesus Christ*, and *The Maturation of Personality*.

We can start with the first of those texts, *Maturity according to Jesus Christ*. Essentially what Fr. Fuentes does is take the Sermon on the Mount, and then apply it as a measure of Christian maturity.

"When he saw the crowds, he went up the mountain, and after he had sat down, his disciples came to him. He began to teach them, saying:

Mt 5:1-2

'For were [Christ] to reward us according to our works, we should cease to be. Therefore, having become His disciples, let us learn to live according to the principles of Christianity.'[2] Indeed, if we imitate His way of behaving, not only will we be saved, but we will also achieve the perfection of our human potencies. We learn this 'way of Christ' in the Gospel, and in a particular and singular way in the Sermon on the Mount, where the program of our moral and spiritual configuration with Christ is contained.

The Apostle James says: 'But the one who peers into the perfect law of freedom and perseveres, and is not a hearer who forgets but a doer who acts, such a one shall be blessed in what he does' (Js 1:25). The 'perfect law of freedom' is Christ's law, which is summarized in a special way in this sermon, since the perfect law is the doctrine regarding the Christian life and, as Saint Thomas says, 'this sermon contains the whole process of forming the life of a Christian.'[3] For this reason it is sometimes considered the *Magna carta* of the kingdom founded by Christ.

Certainly this is the most important preaching that has taken place in the history of humanity and, doctrinally, it has divided history into a *before* and an *after*. There are many books that have marked milestones in the history of thought, for better or for worse, but no writing can be compared to the three chapters in which Saint Matthew summarizes the main lines of Jesus of Nazareth's religious thought.

---

2. Saint Ignatius of Antioch, *Epistle to the Magnesians*, 10, 1.

3. "Sermo quem Dominus in monte proposuit, totam informationem christianae vitae continet" (*ST* I-II, q. 108, a. 3).

My goal here is not to offer an exegetical commentary on this Biblical text. On the contrary, my desire is very simple, since I am only attempting to be inspired by the Sermon on the Mount in order to indicate the basic features that define a mature and balanced Christian life according to the thoughts of Our Lord. This is because I start from the position that in this preaching, Jesus has before His eyes a clear and profound idea of what a real man or woman is, one who is mature, balanced, and perfect."

The first real chapter, we could say, is entitled **Eight properties of maturity**, and here Fr. Fuentes cites the Beatitudes; today we will consider just the first three:

> *Blessed are the poor in spirit,*
> *for theirs is the kingdom of Heaven.*
> *Blessed are they who mourn,*
> *for they will be comforted.*
> *Blessed are the meek,*
> *for they will inherit the land.*
>
> Mt 5:3-12

The Beatitudes are the gateway to the Sermon on the Mount, the "aquatint" of Christianity, black on white. Against the background of the Beatitudes, everything stands out sharply.

With reason, then, they have become one of the preferred topics for many exegetes, Biblical commentators, preachers, and theologians. Saint Thomas said that the Beatitudes express the most perfect acts performed by the virtues when they have been perfected by the gifts of the Holy Spirit. In other words, they are the zenith of Christian supernatural actions, or the point of arrival for the whole of the work of Christian maturity.

However, it is also clear that a port is reached only after having navigated the path that leads toward it. The Beatitudes therefore also contain the *direction* in which a person must advance in the itinerary of maturity. Each one of them alludes to an *attitude* that is proper and essential for maturity. Whoever makes an effort to walk by these paths *is on the path to maturity*. From the degree that a person reaches each of these mental and spiritual dispositions, they can also be measured on the scale of human maturity. On the contrary, whoever is missing one of the *attitudes* likewise suffers from immaturity.

Hence, they are not optional, but rather indispensible qualities. They are eight *basic* properties of maturity that describe the relation of the person with the most fundamental fields of life: the material world (i), the emotions (ii), moral failings (iii), holiness (iv), the sufferings of others (v), the emotional and sexual sphere (vi), resentment and division between people (vii), and the mystery of personal suffering (viii).

The phrases that Jesus Christ uses for the Beatitudes help us to probe the thoughts of our hearts and the positions that we have in the face of these pressing realities. Spiritually, they betray our belonging to one of two possible masters: to God, or to the world. Psychically they reveal the maturity or immaturity of our character.

(i) "Blessed are the poor in spirit"; said in other words: "blessed are the detached." This beatitude "probes" the maturity of our relation with created goods, both exterior (material) and interior (psychic and spiritual).

Poverty of spirit implies freedom in the face of earthly goods, of having or not having (that is, what Saint Ignatius labels as "indifference"[4]). It also supposes a certain distrust (and, to a certain point, despair) of the solutions that worldly realities promote, that is, to recognize that these solutions cannot solve our problems completely nor, and indeed even less, can they satisfy our spiritual needs; only God can respond to the needs of our spirit. To live this Beatitude requires, lastly, the spiritual attitude of the *truly poor person*: humility (the "poor" person in the Bible is one who *recognizes* that he is in need and dependent on God, and understands that he receives everything from Him). Its most lucid and important expression is detachment from self, which we can call a "healthy forgetfulness of self" (because there is also a sick forgetfulness[5]).

There follow innumerable goods from this attitude, goods that bring our character to a true blossoming; among them we can point out serenity in the face of material difficulties, peace of soul in moments of want, and trust placed exclusively in God. In turn, humility, which we have pointed out as the condition for being truly poor, flowers in realism, in forgetfulness of self, and gives a great power before God ("God hears the prayer of the humble," cf. Ps 10:17).

In contrast, the lack of this attitude translates into an anxious mood or earthly greed. In the material order, it shows itself in the vices of greed and stinginess. It gives rise to a lack of peace, anguish, lack of trust, and worry. In the spiritual order, we find ourselves with egoism and live completely

---

4. For Saint Ignatius of Loyola, indifference is an interior attitude of detachment and availability in God's hands with respect to all things: to not be more inclined to one thing than to another as long as the Divine will remains unclear.

5. The one who does not "forget themselves" in a healthy way by going outside of themselves in order to seek out an ideal or the good of their neighbor, runs the risk of ending up in a bad form of "forgetfulness of self," which is that in which a person "avoids" themselves, as through alcoholism, drug addiction, and other forms of addiction.

self-absorbed. This is why a lack of a healthy "forgetfulness of self" is at the center of all neurotic behaviors. In fact, the group Neurotics Anonymous—based on the methodology of Alcoholics Anonymous—affirms that neurosis is "caused by a person's innate egoism, which impedes them from having the ability to love."

If we want to probe our heart regarding this particular aspect, we should ask ourselves: Am I attached to a particular thing or person? What are my fears (these betray attachments)? What effects have been caused, both in me and well as in others, by my attachment or trust in earthly things? Do I live thinking of myself? Do I make everything revolve around me, around my tastes, around my concerns? Am I the definitive criteria of my judgments?

When some serious lack of independence is detected, a lack of independence with respect to earthly things, it will be necessary to work not only on poverty but also—and above all else—on forgetfulness of one's self, since the fight against the "obsession with one's self" is at the foundation not only of every spiritual journey but also of any psychological treatment that is supposed to produce serious results. It also depends on working to acquire humility and trust in God.

(ii) "Blessed are the meek"; that is, "blessed are those who control their emotions." The one who is meek controls their anger, their rage, their ire. They are able to forgive. This Beatitude implies the subjection of the passion of anger, that is, "to tame" one's heart, just as is done with an impulsive and unpredictable animal. It supposes the virtue of humility (in fact, the Greek word used in this Beatitude, which we translate as *meekness*, also means humility).

From this follow numerous good things: peace of soul, which flows from the quieting of the passions; a great spiritual strength, since the one who dominates their emotions can count for their service on all the energy that their uncontrolled passions would consume; it makes the soul attractive since, as the saying goes, more flies are caught with a drop of honey than with a barrel of vinegar, and thus it is that this Beatitude has characterized so many saints who exercised a great attraction on others, like Saint Francis de Sales, Saint John Bosco, Saint Francis, and more.

On the other hand, the lack of this attitude represents a form of immaturity that embitters the spirit, making it unbearable for others and even for that person themselves; it enslaves our mind to a tiring passion; it isolates the person, making it hard to deal with them, which is why often they end up abandoned, or, at the very least, avoided; it feeds resentment, exaggerates the faults of the others, gives rise to violence, hate, bitterness, revenge, vengeance, division, and more.

Whoever wants to probe the region of their heart that we call the "irascible appetite" should ask themselves: Do I discover any resentments or bitterness in me? Do I mistreat others with my words, gestures, or attitudes? Am I vengeful, sharp, or violent? Do I have untimely reactions that I later repent of? Is it hard for me to forgive? Do I forgive easily and quickly?

Whoever thinks to cultivate this spiritual trait should discipline themselves in self-control and in the control of their emotions (especially those of anger, fear, and sadness), and, moreover, practice the art of learning to forgive and the basic virtue of humility.

(iii) "Blessed are those who mourn"; that is, "blessed are those who repent of their errors and sins and seek to correct themselves, making amends for their bad deeds."

This spiritual aspect involves three essential characteristics of human maturity: first, the ability to recognize one's own mistakes, sins, and errors, measuring the responsibility that we have had in them. Nonetheless, said recognition should be balanced and realistic, because an awareness of sin should not be confused with a certain *pathological sense of sin* in which case a person tends not to feel forgiven in spite of having received forgiveness from God or from their neighbor. Secondly, we have the ability to repent from those acts. Finally, we have the intention to ask for forgiveness and repair the hurts and offenses (in the measure that it is possible).

From these follows notable goods, such as the ability to constantly correct oneself, and to move forward in life in spite of the mistakes committed; promptly reconciling oneself to God and to neighbor; peace of soul (as Jesus implies in the reward that is attributed to this Beatitude: "they will be consoled").

On the contrary, immaturity in this realm results in important difficulties among which we must highlight a terrible negative mark for the soul: the lack of sorrow for sin, which can reach the point of becoming something pathological; indeed, the person who is unflinching in the face of the suffering that he himself causes in others is called a *psychopath*; at the same time, the lack of repentance or of empathy can lead to sadistic attitudes. Moreover, it encloses the soul in itself, and sets it against God; it makes the person imitate the main psychic characteristic of those who are eternally condemned, namely, the lack of repentance for the evils committed. It produces desolation and despair. From the false understanding of suffering there also follow great evils, such as a pathological guilt for one's own sins, the inability to forgive oneself, or the tendency to continue returning incessantly to past sins upon which God has already poured out His mercy.

The "heart test" should pass through questions such as these: What is my emotional attitude with respect to my sins? What sort of responsibility do I have regarding my acts? Do I understand that, in addition to repenting, I should, in the measure that it is possible, make reparation for the errors committed? Do I do this with serenity, or do I have a disproportionate sense of guilt? Am I aware of the pain that I cause others? Do I avoid making my neighbor suffer, or does their suffering leave me indifferent? And more . . .

In case there are some aberrations found in this realm, a person should work on their understanding of sin, on humility of heart, and in forgetfulness of self. If in this case there is some pathological understanding of guilt, the effort must be made to acquire a true understanding of sin and the ability to forgive.

Rules for the Discernment of Spirits – Second Week – [328-332]

With commentary adjusted from Fr. Timothy Gallagher, OMV, and Ignacio Casanovas, SJ

For today's conference, we will start with the first half of the Rules for Discernment of Spirits of the Second week, and then, if there's time, we'll talk about maturity according to Jesus Christ, continuing with our considerations of the Beatitudes.

Earlier we talked about spiritual consolation and desolation, and we talked about the conduct that we need to have during consolation and during desolation. Now Saint Ignatius takes it up a notch, to analyze these different movements in the soul when the soul has advanced along the path to perfection.

Sometimes things can be a little tricky: Saint Ignatius, after returning from Jerusalem to Barcelona, began studying to help prepare for theology and the priesthood. While studying Latin, though, he noticed that something strange happened:

Returning to Barcelona, he began to study with great diligence. But one thing hindered him a great deal, and it was that when he began to learn by heart, as is necessary in the beginnings of grammar, there came to him new understandings of spiritual things and new delights; and this with such strength that he could not learn by heart, nor could he free himself of them no matter how he tried. And so, thinking this over many times, he said to himself: "Not even when I pray and when I am at Mass do such vivid understandings come to me"; and thus, little by little, he came to recognize that this was a temptation.

"Such experiences awaken in Ignatius an awareness of a significant question in the discernment of spirits. *Spiritual desolation* and the thoughts associated with it are of the enemy and to be rejected – this is the subject of his first set of rules for discernment of spirits. Is not *spiritual consolation*, however, the time when the good guides and counsels us? . . . As spiritual growth continues, a time may come when spiritual consolation can no longer be simply accepted as of the good spirit, but must itself be careful discerned. . . . We reach a point when the first set of rules doesn't provide enough clarity. When we start out on our spiritual journey, desolation is the bigger danger. But, for souls that are advancing in holiness, consolation can become a danger instead. What happens is, as Ignatius notes in point 10 "the enemy of human nature commonly tempts more *under the appearance of good.*" To quote a nice analogy that can be taken from *The Soul of the Apostolate*: "A jeweler will prefer the smallest fragment of diamond to several sapphires. . . . Satan does not hesitate to encourage a purely superficial success, if he can by this success prevent the apostle from making progress in the interior life: so clearly does his rage guess what it is Our Lord values most highly. To get rid of a diamond, he is quite willing to allow us a few sapphires."

Notice how Ignatius describes these rules:

[328] The Second Week: Further rules for understanding the different movements produced in the soul. They serve for a more accurate discernment of spirits and are more suitable for the second week.

** These are *further rules*, meaning, for the same effect. But, they allow for more accurate discernment, and are more suited to advanced souls, meaning, if you've made it to the Second Week, Ignatius is assuming that you are no longer a bad soul going to worse. Hopefully you've given up those bad things. You are now a good soul going to better. In other words, the first set of rules still holds true, but the problem is that, as the soul advances in holiness, the devil will try to change his techniques. Note, they are for the same effect, namely: to be aware, to understand, and then take action.

[329] It is characteristic of God and His Angels, when they act upon the soul, to give true happiness and spiritual joy, and to banish all the sadness and disturbances which are caused by the enemy. It is characteristic of the evil one to fight against such happiness and consolation by proposing fallacious reasonings, subtilties, and continual deceptions.

** Again, we see the outline of how the different spirits operate. Notice, too, how Ignatius distinguishes here between God and His angels, whereas in the first rules it was simply "the good spirit." There's an important reason for this, as we shall see.

Notice how he describes the evil one's work: he "fights" against our happiness, and this by using "apparent reasons." The enemy proposes "reasons" for the choice of a good and holy thing that conceal, under an appearance of truth, something erroneous: they are only *apparent* reasons." "These apparent reasons," says Casanovas, "are usually fantasies from the imagination, which have no other foundation than their own vain impressions. The devil is good at this, and goes to great lengths to have us accept and embrace those fantasies." "These suggestions have a complex, elaborate quality: they are *subtleties* in which ardent persons may be caught unaware." They are, says Casanovas, "like very fine threads that come from far away." Casanovas counts scruples among these subtleties, noting that in [349] Ignatius says the point of scruples is that "the evil one seeks to make [the soul] excessively sensitive, in order to disturb and upset it more easily." *Subtleties* of this nature, says the Jesuit, can never be reasons that follow what is right.

Finally, though seemingly true, these thoughts are in fact *fallacies* that, if not discerned, will recur again and again in such persons' consciousness: they are *persistent* fallacies." Casanovas says that these are "reasons wrapped in words that give a double meaning: the devil is the great master of using double meanings; to fight against this, we should seek out clarity and precision in our ideas and simplicity and firmness in our faith." This recurrent nature is something really to pay attention to: we can think of the case of Saint John Vianney, who, on several occasions, tried to walk away from his parish in order to become a Carthusian or a Trappist, in order to give himself in prayer and penance.

This is the classic case: prayer and penance are good things, *but*, they weren't what God was asking from St. John Vianney. *This* is why we need to discern. See, too, how the devil knew exactly how to tempt him: you don't send a prostitute, since he'll convert her. You don't try to send him a bunch of alcohol, because he won't touch it. So, you appeal, instead, to his desire for solitude and prayer. The devil gave him a half-truth: you need to do prayer and penance. Yes! You need to do it in the monastery . . . no!

[330] God alone can give consolation to the soul without any previous cause. It belongs solely to the Creator to come into a soul, to leave it, to act upon it, to draw it wholly to the love of His Divine Majesty. I said without previous cause, that is, without any preceding perception or knowledge of any subject by which a soul might be led to such a consolation through its own acts of intellect and will. *I said without previous cause, that is, without any preceding perception or knowledge of any subject by which a soul might be led to such a consolation through its own acts of intellect and will.*

** There is a lot here: perhaps an example will help. Saint Francis of Assisi was once walking down the street with his friends. "But little by little he withdrew himself from them, for he was already deaf to all these things and was singing in his heart to the Lord. Suddenly, the Lord touched his heart filling it with such surpassing sweetness that he could neither speak nor move." It was at this point he decided to marry Poverty.

Casanovas explains this ruling by saying, "only God, by Himself, without any intervention whatsoever of creatures, without the feeling or knowledge of some object that influences it in the least, and entirely without any act of our understanding and will, can enter and leave the soul and produce in it the purely holy motions against which our enemy can do nothing."

Again, the key here of this rule is *without previous cause*, which Ignatius promptly proceeds to explain. There is a cause, as Fr. Timothy Gallagher explains, when a person can recognize all three elements that he lists: first, that in the time *immediately preceding* the spiritual consolation there was within them a *"sentiment or knowledge of some [spiritual] object,"* meaning, that they felt or understood something regarding a spiritual "object," like a verse of Scripture, a truth of faith, an aspect of creation, a memory of God's past workings, etc. Second, the consolation they then experience *arose from* this sentiment or knowledge, that is, the consolation is in *some recognizable way derived from what they felt or understood about that object.* Third, that the link between said sentiment or knowledge of the object and the spiritual consolation that followed from it occurred through these persons' *own reflective and affective acts* – meaning, their thoughts, reasonings, desires, stirrings of the heart as a consequence of them focusing their minds and hearts on it.

So, we have some object, something that I saw or thought or whatever, then I thought about it, reflected on it, whatever, and then the consolation. If I have object, then my act, then a consolation that *clearly comes* from that (you can tell because it's proportionate to my act), all three elements, all three things, then we have consolation *with* cause. If something is missing. If any one of the three elements is missing, however, be it the object, be it my own action, be it a proportionality between the object and our reflection, we have consolation without a preceding cause.

Here, I have a wonderful Clipart diagram with how this works (I am a Clipart *master*):

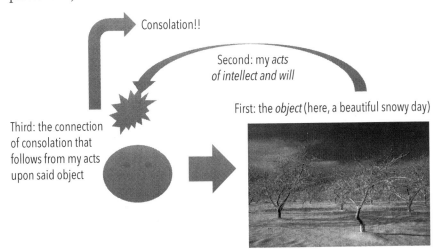

Consolation!!

Second: my *acts of intellect and will*

First: the *object* (here, a beautiful snowy day)

Third: the connection of consolation that follows from my acts upon said object

So, we have the three elements:

- the *object I perceive*
- my *own acts* of will and intellect
- the *connection* (proportion) between my acts and the consolation, meaning, the consolation came from me
- Why does all this matter? A consolation without preceding cause can only come from God, so it should be accepted without hesitation. That's important. I mean, you can and should consult with your spiritual director, but there is no doubt it comes from God, if it *is* this sort of grace (your director might not think that it is this sort of grace, and hence there could be hesitation to accept it, as we will see). Think of the foundational grace of our order. That was a grace of this sort. Anyways, more on this when we talk about the election of state, but if God clearly shows us something this way, there's no need to "wait for it to happen again," because God is *not obligated to do it again.* He knows that we're slow, and He has mercy on us, but it doesn't need to recur. Once is enough.

For instance (and this is a case I have seen): someone is meditating on the Song of Songs, reading the passage about *My lover belongs to me*, and, boom, out of nowhere, the thought occurs to them that they should become a contemplative, and that thought, even though they have never considered it before, fills them with great joy, peace, and love for God. There is an object, the verse of scripture; they were using acts of intellect and will, yes; but there is no proportion between what they were doing and the effects. Consolation without cause.

However, if there is a preceding cause, we need to be careful, as Ignatius points out next.

[331] If a cause precedes, both the good angel and the evil spirit can give consolation to a soul, but for a quite different purpose. The good angel consoles for the progress of the soul, that it may advance and rise to what is more perfect. The evil spirit consoles for purposes that are the contrary, and that afterwards he might draw the soul to his own perverse intentions and wickedness.

** Ignatius had an interesting experience in Manresa. When the time came for him to sleep, his mind would be filled with amazing thoughts about God, so much so that he often wouldn't be able to sleep. Considering this, and that he was giving all day to God, he decided to reject those thoughts and sleep instead.

Each spirit can give consolation, but for their own end. Hence the need to be careful . . . Again, in the rules for the first week, we said that usually the devil produces *desolation,* and that's still the case, but sometimes, if it's more helpful for his evil designs, he can also produce consolation.

[332] It is a mark of the evil spirit to assume the appearance of an angel of light. He begins by suggesting thoughts that are suited to a devout soul, and ends by suggesting his own. For example, he will suggest holy and pious thoughts that are wholly in conformity with the sanctity of the soul. Afterwards, he will endeavor little by little to end by drawing the soul into his hidden snares and evil designs.

** Notice that the devil proposes things that are genuinely good and holy, but eventually tries to pervert them to his own end. An example of this could be when, as a religious, I know that I'm supposed to be in the chapel praying at a certain time, but the thought comes to me to continue spiritual reading. Now, spiritual reading is a good and holy thing, and let's suppose I'm getting a lot of fruit out of it. Great! But . . . the right thing at the wrong time is the wrong thing, and the right thing in the wrong way is the wrong thing: the right thing is only the right thing at the right time and in the right way.

Oftentimes, this is what the devil tries to mess around with: he tries to propose something that looks ok, or even great, but . . . something's just not right. As Ignatius points out, little by little, slowly but surely, the devil tries to lead the soul astray. This means that *time* is something fundamental to the evil spirit's use of good and holy thoughts. As Casanovas points out, the devil is not in a hurry; he has plenty of time, and so he doesn't mind wearing many disguises, hiding himself, waiting. The phrase *angel of light,* is probably taken directly from Saint Paul's second letter to the Corinthians, 11:14, where he writes: "And no wonder, for even Satan masquerades as an angel of light."

We can leave the rules for discernment now, and turn our eyes to the Beatitudes and what they mean in terms of maturity.

(iv) "Blessed are they who hunger and thirst for righteousness"; or, said with other words: "blessed are those who have aspirations to holiness, virtue, and nobility." This Beatitude *probes* our aspirations and, consequently, the maturity that these reveal: are we indifferent, mediocre, or outstanding in our search for holiness?

It implies the desire for holiness (*righteousness* should be understood in this sense); it also implies the existence in our heart of the vital virtue of magnanimity, since it underscores the character of "greatness" and "effort" by speaking of "hunger and thirst," and not just simple "desires" (it is an intense, tenacious, and hard-working desire). It also indicates a *total* desire, since this Beatitude is expressed in the Greek text in the accusative (which

358 · A Manual of the Spiritual Exercises of Saint Ignatius of Loyola

shows that it refers to "the whole of justice," as if it were to say: *those who hunger and thirst for total justice*) and not in the genitive (which would indicate a part of justice).[1] It is not speaking of isolated acts that are just or holy, but rather of holiness in itself; the person who hungers and thirsts for holiness is a person who wants to be a saint, not the one who aspires to perform some good acts once in a while.

This attitude leads *efficaciously* to holiness, because the Kingdom of Heaven is only conquered by those who make the effort (cf. Mt 11:12); consequently, it is a sign of great spiritual maturity. Moreover, this desire manifests a true and effective will, and gives rise to a great spiritual happiness and a true patience in everyday difficulties because whoever aspires to something great considers as little the difficulties that get in the way of that achievement.

On the contrary, the one who lacks this attitude shows various signs of spiritual immaturity. First and foremost, their heart is directed to ideals that are far from those proposed by Jesus Christ. If our most ardent desires (that is, the ones that shake us, make us impatient, seem to put ants in our pants, and do not let us sleep peacefully until we carry them out) *cannot be summarized in "being saints,"* then holiness is something incidental for us. Moreover, perhaps that goal has been cast out from our lives because we considered it as undesirable or impossible. However, to renounce holiness is the first step towards despair. When these desires are lacking, people *immediately*, although at the beginning it might be unconsciously, begin to accommodate themselves to this life, to settle in, to set up shop; in other words, they become worldly. The only thing that can tear us from worldly attachments is an ardent desire for something great, holy, or noble. On the other hand, a lack of ardent desires is a sign of pusillanimity and gives rise to spiritual sloth.

The heart is searched by asking: What are my main desires? What feelings are awakened in me by the thought of holiness: consolation or annoyance; enthusiasm or disinterest; laziness, weariness, boredom or, on the contrary,

---

1. In some languages, in order to express hunger or thirst, something called the "partitive genitive" is used when what is meant to be indicated is that "a part of that" is desired, and the accusative is used when the desire is for the whole. For instance, in Spanish when we say "quiero agua," this rule is implied, and what lies under this simplified expression is the old genitive (which would be expressed by "me da *de* agua," or, "me da *un poco de* agua"); however, we do not say "quiero el agua," because that would give the impression that all of the water is desired. If a thief says "déme *de su* dinero" (genitive), what would be understood is that the thief wants some of the victim's money. However, when the thief says "déme *su* dinero" (accusative), it is clear that he wants all of the money. In Greek, this second nuance, the non-partitive, is expressed in the accusative. This is precisely the case of this Beatitude, expressed in an accusative phrase that does not set limits.

interest and enthusiasm? Do I work seriously to achieve holiness? Do I have noble, great, transcendent, and divine projects? Or do I perhaps live a life that just creeps along, content to fly like a chicken, without interesting aspirations?

When work needs to be done in this area, it will be necessary to meditate on holiness (its nature, necessity, means to obtain it, etc.), to place before our own eyes incarnated examples of holiness that give enthusiasm to our hearts and cultivate—against apathy—real and concrete charity.

(v) "Blessed are the merciful"; or rather: "blessed are those who take pity on the evils that befall others, and seek to provide a remedy for them, those who see their neighbors' needs more than their own."

This Beatitude proposes true mercy, which is not to be confused with *false* tenderness. The Hebrew word used to indicate mercy (*checed*) indicates the ability to place oneself in another's skin in order to see things as they see them, to feel them as they feel them, and to suffer them as they suffer them. Such was Christ's mercy, who suffered understanding what we ourselves suffer, from "within," as the author of the Letter to the Hebrews says (cf. Heb 4:15). It does not refer to a merely sensible attitude, but rather one that is principally spiritual: it is a spiritual pain for a spiritual evil, which is sin or separation from God. For this reason it pushes to action, to remediate the evil in the measure that it is possible.

From this follow innumerable goods. First of all, it is one of the attitudes that makes the soul beautiful: a merciful heart is the one that most closely resembles God, since mercy is the divine attribute that is most perceived by men, given that everything that we know about God, we know because He has *mercifully* inclined Himself to us and opens His heart and His mysteries to us. This quality also protects against one of the most corrupting illnesses of the human soul: *spiritual sclerosis or hardness of heart*, that is, the inability to perceive the sufferings of another. Likewise, it also gives the soul a great spiritual and affective sensitivity in dealing with others: the truly merciful avoid making their neighbor suffer, because their main concern is to alleviate suffering, not to cause it nor to increase it. Likewise, it makes a person loveable and gives them a great ability to form relationships; this is why the merciful person is always sought after and received with veneration, even by those who profess ideas that are completely different (for example, it is notable how religions that differ from Catholicism, like Hinduism or Islam, or even ideologies that persecute it, have sometimes found themselves obligated to respect those who practice mercy, as happened with Saint Mother Teresa of Calcutta in India and China). Lastly, mercy makes a person to be turned towards their neighbor, and not centered on themselves, avoiding a focus only on their own problems; in this sense, it is a safeguard against the different forms of neurosis that flow from egoism.

The lack of this attitude gives rise to the spiritual and psychic illness of "hardness of heart" or "lack of empathy." Likewise, it pushes a person to live centered on their own problems with eyes opened exclusively to their own sufferings; thus, it can give rise to numerous forms of self-pity and neurosis.

In order to probe the heart, we should ask ourselves: Am I indifferent to the sufferings of others? Am I perhaps sensible to the sufferings of others but incapable of helping them effectively? Am I more concerned with my own problems than those of others? Am I capable of carrying the sufferings of others, in spite of the fact that this implies an extra burden for me? Do I think more of myself than others? And the like . . .

If someone notices defects in this area, they will need to work on forgetfulness of self, on the essence of true charity, and on understanding the meaning of suffering.

Rules for the Discernment of Spirits —
Second Week — [333-336]

With commentary adjusted from Fr. Timothy Gallagher, OMV, and Ignacio Casanovas, SJ

For today's conference, we will continue with the second half of the Rules for Discernment of Spirits of the Second week, and then, if there's time, we'll talk about maturity according to Jesus Christ, continuing with our considerations of the Beatitudes.

[333] We must carefully observe the whole course of our thoughts. If the beginning and middle and end of the course of thoughts are wholly good and directed to what is entirely right, it is a sign that they are from the good angel. But the course of thoughts suggested to us may terminate in something evil, or distracting, or less good than the soul had formerly proposed to do. Again, it may end in what weakens the soul, or disquiets it; or by destroying the peace, tranquility, and quiet which it had before, it may cause disturbance to the soul. These things are a clear sign that the thoughts are proceeding from the evil spirit, the enemy of our progress and eternal salvation.

- Again, this is a very dense passage. So, asks Casanovas, how can we know when the bad angel has transformed himself into an angel of light? What indications are there? Well, Ignatius says we must "carefully observe" the entire trajectory, as well as all the motions and movements themselves in our soul. So, everything individually, and as a whole. If, at some individual moment, we notice the signs that Ignatius points out, the devil is there. God and His angels are entirely good, and whatever they propose is entirely good; Ignatius is very wise to note that the devil not only proposes bad things, things that are bad in all levels, but also things that are simply less good than we had proposed. Since God wants our perfection, it doesn't make any sense that He inspire us to do things that are less good than what He originally proposed to our souls.
- ** Practically speaking, there are three moments here: the *beginning*, when the bad spirit first *enters* with such thoughts. Then, there's an *end*

when the bad spirit leaves, having accomplished his mission. But there's also a middle, when the good and holy thoughts unfold *little by little,* which gradually causes a spiritual diminishment.

Sometimes, we undertake a good activity, something that God wants, and then the devil messes around with it and tries to change it. However, if we are careful and pay attention, we will see that point when the devil enters in.

We have to be attentive to our thoughts, not as isolated thoughts, but rather as a chain, or progression. If the three points are all good, then the chain is from the good spirit. If some point is bad, the whole thing is bad.

Of this second set, Ignatius gives two lists: one is objective criteria, the other, subjective. "But the course of thoughts suggested to us may terminate in something evil, or distracting, or less good than the soul had formerly proposed to do. Again, it may end in what weakens the soul, or disquiets it; or by destroying the peace, tranquility, and quiet which it had before, it may cause disturbance to the soul."

What do I mean by objective? In *objective terms,* things are less good, meaning, something evil (a sin), or distracting (objectively something taking us away from what we were doing), or less good (also objective: this thing was X good, this new thing is lower, Y good). *Subjective* means something for the subject to experience and feels. *Weakening of soul,* or *disquieting of the soul* or *a lack of peace* . . . there's not an objective measure to that; they are subjective states or experiences, but the soul who has them will know and recognize them (if they pay attention, of course).

[334] When the enemy of our human nature has been detected and recognized by the trail of evil marking his course and by the wicked end to which he leads us, it will be profitable for one who has been tempted to review immediately the whole course of the temptation. Let him consider the series of good thoughts, how they arose, how the evil one gradually attempted to make him step down from the state of spiritual delight and joy in which he was, till finally he drew him to his wicked designs. The purpose of this review is that once such an experience has been understood and carefully observed, we may guard ourselves for the future against the customary deceits of the enemy.

** Once the devil has been detected, we need to learn from the experience. In other words, when I noticed that my thoughts had ended up in something evil, or distracting, or less good than I had formerly proposed to do, or in something that weakens the soul, or disquiets it, or destroyed the peace, tranquility, and quiet it had, I need find where it is that the devil got involved. Where did he enter in? Ignatius uses a rather poetical way to describe it: he says the devil is known by his *cola serpentina,* literally his snake's tail, we need to follow that tail back to the head . . . where does the devil begin his conversation? This is really important because we can see how the devil tempts us *specifically*, how he tries to lead us astray. What is it that the devil wants to use to get us off-track?

[335] In souls that are progressing to greater perfection, the action of the good angel is delicate, gentle, delightful. It may be compared to a drop of water penetrating a sponge. The action of the evil spirit upon such souls is violent, noisy, and disturbing. It may be compared to a drop of water falling upon a stone.

In souls that are going from bad to worse, the action of the spirits mentioned above is just the reverse. The reason for this is to be sought in the opposition or similarity of these souls to the different kinds of spirits. When the disposition is contrary to that of the spirits, they enter with noise and commotion that are easily perceived. When the disposition is similar to that of the spirits, they enter silently, as one coming into his own house when the doors are open.

** Again, here we're talking about the rules of the second week, for souls that are more advanced and, more importantly, a soul that is going from good to better (since, otherwise, you've failed the first week, and these rules aren't for you). What we see here is the need for reflection. When I'm doing God's work, and the devil tries to get involved, he comes in loudly, with noise. When I'm doing the devil's work that the evil one has proposed for me, it's the good angel that tries to wake me and straighten me out noisily.

This going from "good to better" would be the example of someone doing God's will, growing in their spiritual life and doing what God wants of them. The example of someone going from "bad to worse," would be someone who discerned a particular course of action poorly, and then continues down it. Or, it could be someone who started doing a good, Godly thing, only to let it be corrupted by the evil one.

We could call the effect, then "spiritual consonance" and "spiritual dissonance." If the good spirit is moving me along the good path, he does so silently. If the evil spirit tries to get involved, he must be noisy.

It's worth noting that here, Puhl's translation fails miserably, at least from the Spanish. Ignatius says *el buen angel toca a la tal anima dulce, leve, y suavemente*; literally, he says the good angel *touches* the soul. God speaks to the soul by means of consolation, but here the word *touch* is meant to be more profound, more mystical, notes Casanovas. I would say, too, it implies better the subtlety of what the good angel does. The idea of entering a house, says the Jesuit, also reminds us that God comes to dwell with us, and that

364 · A Manual of the Spiritual Exercises of Saint Ignatius of Loyola

there is nothing sweeter or more consoling than the Presence of the Trinity in our souls.

[336] When consolation is without previous cause, as was said, there can be no deception in it, since it can proceed from God our Lord only. But a spiritual person who has received such a consolation must consider it very attentively, and must cautiously distinguish the actual time of the consolation from the period which follows it. At such a time the soul is still fervent and favored with the grace and aftereffects of the consolation which has passed. In this second period the soul frequently forms various resolutions and plans which are not granted directly by God our Lord. They may come from our own reasoning on the relations of our concepts and on the consequences of our judgments, or they may come from the good or evil spirit. Hence, they must be carefully examined before they are given full approval and put into execution.

** Here, at last, we find the course of action that we must take. A consolation without cause must be from God, but we have to be careful not to attribute to it something that's an aftereffect, and not from the time of the actual consolation.

This can happen when the effects of the consolation remain with us for a while after the actual consolation. We begin to attribute things to it that weren't actually part of the consolation.

In general, then, as Casanovas points out, these rules tell us to *pay close attention and discern attentively*, so that we don't miss any appearance of Satan's *serpentine tail*. God uses the language of consolation to draw us to Himself, but the devil can even take advantage of consolation to draw us astray. That's why we should subject everything to discern, to make sure we are never fooled.

Now, we can continue our considerations of the Beatitudes as the measure of Christian maturity:

(vi) "Blessed are the pure of heart." Even if commentators on the Beatitudes have interpreted this expression differently, I will here consider only one of its meanings, namely, in reference to purity and chastity. In this sense, it is the same as saying: "blessed are those who love and practice the virtue of purity." Purity or chastity is one of the essential elements of human maturity. Lust and lability in the sexual realm is an unmistakable sign of immaturity since it is a fixation upon adolescent or pre-adolescent behaviors.

This attitude implies chastity not only in exterior acts, but also in interior ones, thoughts, and desires; that is, it is a positive decision to be pure, avoiding playing with fire in all fields and degrees; it also supposes the cultivation of modesty and mortification, both exterior and interior. However, it has nothing to do with the neurotic attitude towards sexuality, which sees sin where there is none, or that is disturbed by indeliberate and involuntary movements of our nature.

It would be too much to list all the good that follow from this disposition: the deep practice of chastity (which encompasses the whole of our affectivity) is the cause of a great balance of soul, gives serenity to the heart, a connaturality with respect to spiritual realities, guarantees a homogeneous sexual maturation and, eventually, a full and harmonious living out of sexuality in the vocation of marriage.

On the contrary, the lack of this condition—which presents itself in the vice of impurity in any of its species, including impurity in intentions, desires, thoughts, in flirting with occasions of sins, in curiosity with what entails a danger of sensuality and lust, etc.—is one of the most destructive and degrading disorders of the human person, because it easily leads to disordered conduct, is transformed into a vice, and can become an addiction (in other words, it becomes progressively more serious). For that very reason, it produces callousness in the face of sin: what at the beginning was seen as bad, easily becomes tolerated, and then to being seen as "normal," "inevitable," "necessary," and the like. Nor is it strange that it would push a person to anti-natural behaviors.

If we want to attempt to probe the heart in this field, in addition to considering how we personally judge disorders against chastity (because many have erroneous judgments in this material), we must also examine our dispositions to live out this virtue serenely: Am I modest? What is my attitude when faced with occasions of sin? [For instance, consider the seminarians who you know, during things like Third Order meetings, that, when you need to find them, you know they'll be with the girls. Always. It's not that girls are bad, but it's a dangerous situation.] Do I unnecessarily expose myself to them? Am I curious with respect to questions about sex? Am I lax in my passions, my lack of mortification? Do I grant myself license that prepares my heart to slide into sin? Am I worldly in my thoughts, gestures, and looks? Do I watch television unnecessarily, or alone? Do I use television, the Internet, movies, etc., as an escape from boredom or loneliness? Do I watch my looks at the newspaper, magazines, etc.? Do I engage in worldly and dangerous readings that incite my imagination? And the like . . .

In case it is necessary to educate purity of heart, the work must be done in various areas: to form an understanding of sin, to learn to control the imagination and the emotions [especially the emotions! A priest who was travelling with Saint Mother Teresa said that, once, as they were walking along, M. Teresa very thoughtfully said, "If we look carefully, we will see that all temptations against the vow of chastity, against purity, come when we are sad, because when you are sad, you will look around everywhere to see where you can satisfy your longing for love. *The moody sister is a plaything in the hands of the devil; he can do whatever he wants with her.*" That applies to seminarians and priests as well; the moody seminarian or priest is a play-thing in the hands of the devil), to purify the memory and imagination by means of meditation, serious study, etc., as well as by healthy and balanced physical work: cleaning, sports, etc. Above all, on the positive side, a person must have a noble ideal, to live the life of grace, to practice charity and to lay down their lives for others.

(vii) "Blessed are the peacemakers"; that is: "blessed are those who are ca-pable of reconciliation and of sowing peace in divided hearts." This Beatitude is not so much directed to those who "love peace" as to those who "make" peace. It is one of the most standout qualities of a mature heart.

This ability presupposes the previous pacification of one's own heart. That is where it must start: only when a person has peace in their own heart are they able to sow peace in the hearts of others. The peace that we are speaking of here is that of the soul with God, and also with itself. It is an effect of grace; it is born *in a particular way* by doing God's will at each moment. To avoid doing God's will with respect to us *always produces disturbances, a lack of peace, and an interior struggle.* Moreover, it also demands that we learn to shut our mouths when we would like to say something, and to say something when we would like to keep our mouths shut. It also presupposes the art of correcting well and at the proper time (because to reproach at the wrong time sows rebellion and discord), to be prompt to ask forgiveness from those we offend, to always forgive those who offend us, to never speak evil of a person in front of oth-ers, and to always have good spirit (that is, happiness, comfort, and serenity).

From this attitude there arise great advantages: it makes us "children of God," as the reward attributed to this Beatitude says, because it makes us re-produce one of God's main works, namely, to make peace. It also makes us to resemble Christ, who came to bring peace among men: God did us the good to "through him reconcile all things for [God], making peace by the blood of his cross, whether those on earth or those in Heaven" (Col 1:20). The Messiah is called the "prince of peace" (Is 9:5).

On the contrary, those who are deprived of this attribute are usually those who sow discord, murmur, gossip, attack their neighbors, pour out tensions in communities or groups, and more.

The heart is probed by asking: When I see people who are distant or an-gry with one another, do I, in a certain sense, take delight? Do I seek to make peace between them? Do I deepen the wounds, "adding more fuel to the fire"? Am I one who murmurs or gossips? Am I quick to ask forgiveness, and quick to give it when someone asks me for it?

A person works on this by acquiring charity (it is very fruitful to read, meditate, and to guide oneself as a plan of action by the Hymn of Charity in 1 Cor 13), watching over our words and the spirit that animates us; meditating on forgiveness, and learning to forgive quickly.

(viii) "Blessed are those who are persecuted for the sake of Jesus Christ"; that is: "blessed are we if we are rejected because we resemble Jesus Christ."

This last attitude summarizes all of the other ones: it implies the acceptance of and love for the Cross without any sort of floundering; in other words, it means to love the Cross and *to choose it*. It unites us to Jesus, who became a "Victim" for our sake; indeed, this Beatitude is only correctly understood when a similitude to Christ is being sought.

However, this Beatitude should not be confused with the persecution or punishments that are suffered because of doing bad things, or the rejection of our neighbor caused by our defects or our bad spirit. There are many people who are persecuted to whom this Beatitude doesn't apply. In fact, Christ is not referring to people who "feel that they are being persecuted," because the one "feels" persecuted is, normally, really not in that situation. The saints who were truly persecuted did not exaggerate their condition as such. On the contrary, such a situation demands great happiness: "Rejoice and be glad," says Jesus. If there is no happiness, that is, peace, conformity with the divine will, then this Beatitude is not being lived out, even if the persecution is real and unjust.

From here follow some goods proper to it: a true similitude with Christ crucified and spiritual fruitfulness, since all apostolic fruitfulness derives from the Cross: "When I am lifted up, I will draw all people to myself," says Jesus.

Thus it is clear that a lack of this attitude is the same as living the cross with bitterness and disturbance; it means not to understand Christianity. Speaking of persecutions, Saint Paul tells the Thessalonians: "You yourselves know that we are destined for this" (1 Thess 3:3). Another version translates it: "this is what we are for." If a Christian does not assume this attitude, they will become embittered, because the cross is *inevitable*, and to be in disagreement with what is inevitable is to live a life of opposition. From here it follows that misunderstanding this truth leads to fleeing from all that crucifies us. Others react with dejection, anger, resentment, or even with violence in the face of persecution or calumny. When persecution broke out, the martyrs gave thanks to God. When the immature person hears others speak ill of him, he gets angry and infuriated. The lack of this attitude makes us like the "bad thief" who was crucified with Christ: his way of carrying the cross as a "curse" is the way that it is carried by those who reject it. A lack of understanding of this Beatitude also usually pushes a person to live life with bitterness, to separate themselves from God's plans, to lose perseverance in their vocations or even in the faith itself. In some cases, it can even produce psychic disturbances on account of living for a prolonged period in a state of interior rebellion. It can even spark latent illnesses that might be physical (insomnia, hypertension, gastrisis, ulcers) as well as psychic.

In order to probe the heart, we should ask ourselves: How do I consider the cross? In the face of unjust sufferings (persecution, calumny, unjust criticisms, disproportionate punishments, etc.) what is my reaction? Is it happiness, conformity with God, and forgiveness for those who cause this pain? Or, on the contrary, do I kick and scream and give in to resentment? Do I feel misunderstood and disgusted, unjustly displaced? Do I complain and murmur against my persecutors (even when they are my legitimate superiors, my parents, or my spouse), etc.?

If there is a need to cultivate this attitude, we must work on developing the understanding of suffering (reading of and meditation upon Blessed Carlo Gnocchi's work, *The Pedagogy of Innocent Suffering*, can be very useful[1]); we should contemplate and meditate upon Christ crucified and the attitude of each one of the thieves, seeing with which one of the three is my vision of suffering is identified; finally, one should ask, often, for conformity with the divine will.

* * *

Here, then, we have the outline, in terms of general and basic lines, of a mature personality.

---

1. The book is available in English through IVEPress.

Rules for the Discernment of Spirits – Second Week

With commentary adjusted from Fr. Timothy Gallagher, OMV

Earlier we talked about spiritual consolation and desolation, and we talked about the conduct that we need to have during consolation and during desolation. Now Saint Ignatius takes it up a notch, to analyze these different movements in the soul when the soul has advanced along the path to perfection.

Sometimes things can be a little tricky: Saint Ignatius, after returning from Jerusalem to Barcelona, began studying to help prepare for theology and the priesthood. While studying Latin, though, he noticed that something strange happened:

Returning to Barcelona, he began to study with great diligence. But one thing hindered him a great deal, and it was that when he began to learn by heart, as is necessary in the beginnings of grammar, there came to him new understandings of spiritual things and new delights; and this with such strength that he could not learn by heart, nor could he free himself of them no matter how he tried. And so, thinking this over many times, he said to himself: "Not even when I pray and when I am at Mass do such vivid understandings come to me"; and thus, little by little, he came to recognize that this was a temptation.

"Such experiences awaken in Ignatius an awareness of a significant question in the discernment of spirits. *Spiritual desolation* and the thoughts associated with it are of the enemy and to be rejected – this is the subject of his first set of rules for discernment of spirits. Is not *spiritual consolation*, however, the time when the good guides and counsels us? . . . As spiritual growth continues, a time may come when spiritual consolation can no longer be simply accepted as of the good spirit, but must itself be carefully discerned. . . . We reach a point when the first set of rules doesn't provide enough clarity. When we start out on our spiritual journey, desolation is the bigger danger. But, for souls that are advancing in holiness, consolation can become a danger instead. What happens is, as Ignatius notes in point 10 "the enemy of human nature commonly tempts more *under the appearance of good.*" To quote a nice analogy that can be taken from *The Soul of the Apostolate*: "A jeweler will prefer the smallest fragment of diamond to several sapphires. . . . Satan does not hesitate to encourage a purely superficial success, if he can by this success prevent the apostle from making progress in the interior life: so clearly does his rage guess what it is Our Lord values most highly. To get rid of a diamond, he is quite willing to allow us a few sapphires."

Notice how Ignatius describes these rules:

(328) The Second Week: Further rules for understanding the different movements produced in the soul. They serve for a more accurate discernment of spirits and are more suitable for the second week.

** These are *further rules*, meaning, for the same effect. But, they allow for more accurate discernment, and are more suited to advanced souls, meaning, if you've made it to the Second Week, Ignatius is assuming that you are no longer a bad soul going to worse. Hopefully you've given up those sinful ways. You are now a good soul going to better. In other words, the first set of rules still holds true, but the problem is that, as the soul advances in holiness, the devil will try to change his techniques. Note, they are for the same effect, namely: to be aware, to understand, and then take action.

(329) It is characteristic of God and His Angels, when they act upon the soul, to give true happiness and spiritual joy, and to banish all the sadness and disturbances which are caused by the enemy. It is characteristic of the evil one to fight against such happiness and consolation by proposing fallacious reasonings, subtilties, and continual deceptions.

** Again, we see the outline of how the different spirits operate. Notice, too, how Ignatius distinguishes here between God and His angels, whereas in the first rules it was simply "the good spirit." There's an important reason for this, as we shall see.

Notice how he describes the evil one's work: he "fights" against our happiness, and this by using "apparent reasons." The enemy proposes "reasons" for the choice of a good and holy thing that conceal, under an appearance of truth, something erroneous: they are only *apparent* reasons. These suggestions have a complex, elaborate quality: they are *subtleties* in which ardent persons may be caught unaware. Finally, though seemingly true, these thoughts are in fact *fallacies* that, if not discerned, will recur again and again in such persons' consciousness: they are *persistent* fallacies." This recurrent nature is something really to pay attention to: we can think of the case of Saint John Vianney, who, on several occasions, tried to walk away from his parish in order to become a Carthusian or a Trappist, in order to give himself in prayer and penance.

This is the classic case: prayer and penance are good things, *but*, they weren't what God was asking from St. John Vianney. *This* is why we need to discern. See, too, how the devil knew exactly how to tempt him: you don't

send a prostitute, since he'll convert her. You don't try to send him a bunch
of alcohol, because he won't touch it. So, you appeal, instead, to his desire for
solitude and prayer.

(330) God alone can give consolation to the soul without any previous
cause. It belongs solely to the Creator to come into a soul, to leave it, to act
upon it, to draw it wholly to the love of His Divine Majesty. I said without
previous cause, that is, without any preceding perception or knowledge of any
subject by which a soul might be led to such a consolation through its own
acts of intellect and will. *I said without previous cause, that is, without any preceding perception or knowledge of any subject by which a soul might be led to such
a consolation through its own acts of intellect and will.*

** There is a lot here: perhaps an example will help. Saint Francis of Assisi
was once walking down the street with his friends. "But little by little he withdrew himself from them, for he was already deaf to all these things and was
singing in his heart to the Lord. Suddenly, the Lord touched his heart filling
it with such surpassing sweetness that he could neither speak nor move." It
was at this point he decided to marry Poverty.

Again, the key here of this rule is *without previous cause*, which Ignatius
promptly proceeds to explain. There is a cause when a person can recognize
all three elements that he lists: first, that in the time *immediately preceding* the
spiritual consolation there was within them a *"sentiment or knowledge of some
[spiritual] object,"* meaning, that they felt or understood something regarding
a spiritual "object," like a verse of Scripture, a truth of faith, an aspect of creation, a memory of God's past workings, etc. Second, the consolation they
then experience *arose from* this sentiment or knowledge, that is, the consolation is in *some recognizable way derived from what they felt or understood about
that object.* Third, that the link between said sentiment or knowledge of the
object and the spiritual consolation that followed from it occurred through
these persons' *own reflective and affective acts* – meaning, their thoughts, reasonings, desires, stirrings of the heart as a consequence of them focusing their
minds and hearts on it.

So, we have some object, something that I saw or thought or whatever,
then I thought about it, reflected on it, whatever, and then the consolation. If
I have an object, then my act, then a consolation that *clearly comes* from that
(you can tell because it's proportionate to my act), all three elements, all three
things, then we have consolation *with* cause. If something is missing. If any
one of the three elements is missing, however, be it the object, be it my own
action, be it a proportionality between the object and our reflection, we have
consolation without a preceding cause.

Why does all this matter? A consolation without preceding cause can only come from God, so it should be accepted without hesitation. That's important. I mean, you can and should consult with your spiritual director, but there is no doubt it comes from God. Think of the foundational grace of our order. That was a grace of this sort. Anyways, more on this when we talk about the election of state, but if God clearly shows us something this way, there's no need to "wait for it to happen again," because God is *not obligated to do it again*. He knows that we're slow, and He has mercy on us, but it doesn't need to recur. Once is enough.

However, if these is a preceding cause, we need to be careful, as Ignatius points out next.

(331) If a cause precedes, both the good angel and the evil spirit can give consolation to a soul, but for a quite different purpose. The good angel consoles for the progress of the soul, that it may advance and rise to what is more perfect. The evil spirit consoles for purposes that are the contrary, and that afterwards he might draw the soul to his own perverse intentions and wickedness.

** Ignatius had an interesting experience in Manresa. When the time came for him to sleep, his mind would be filled with amazing thoughts about God, so much so that he often wouldn't be able to sleep. Considering this, and that he was giving all day to God, he decided to reject those thoughts and sleep instead.

Each spirit can give consolation, but for their own end. Hence the need to be careful . . .

(332) It is a mark of the evil spirit to assume the appearance of an angel of light. He begins by suggesting thoughts that are suited to a devout soul, and ends by suggesting his own. For example, he will suggest holy and pious thoughts that are wholly in conformity with the sanctity of the soul. Afterwards, he will endeavor little by little to end by drawing the soul into his hidden snares and evil designs.

** Notice that the devil proposes things that are genuinely good and holy, but eventually tries to pervert them to his own end. An example of this could be when, as a religious, I know that I'm supposed to be in the chapel praying at a certain time, but the thought comes to me to continue spiritual reading. Now, spiritual reading is a good and holy thing, and let's suppose I'm getting a lot of fruit out of it. Great! But . . . the right thing at the wrong time is the wrong thing, and the right thing in the wrong way is the wrong thing: the right thing is only the right thing at the right time and in the right way.

Oftentimes, this is what the devil tries to mess around with: he tries to propose something that looks ok, or even great, but . . . something's just not right. As Ignatius points out, little by little, slowly but surely, the devil tries to lead the soul astray. This means that *time* is something fundamental to the evil spirit's use of good and holy thoughts.

(333) We must carefully observe the whole course of our thoughts. If the beginning and middle and end of the course of thoughts are wholly good and directed to what is entirely right, it is a sign that they are from the good angel. But the course of thoughts suggested to us may terminate in something evil, or distracting, or less good than the soul had formerly proposed to do. Again, it may end in what weakens the soul, or disquiets it; or by destroying the peace, tranquility, and quiet which it had before, it may cause disturbance to the soul. These things are a clear sign that the thoughts are proceeding from the evil spirit, the enemy of our progress and eternal salvation.

** So, there are three moments here: the *beginning,* when the bad spirit first *enters* with such thoughts. Then, there's an *end* when the bad spirit leaves, having accomplished his mission. But there's also a middle, when the good and holy thoughts unfold *little by little,* which gradual causes a spiritual diminishment.

Sometimes, we undertake a good activity, something that God wants, and then the devil messes around with it and tries to change it. However, if we are careful and pay attention, we will see that point when the devil enters in.

We have to be attentive to our thoughts, not as isolated thoughts, but rather as a chain, or progression. If the three points are all good, then the chain is from the good spirit. If some point is bad, the whole thing is bad.

Of this section set, Ignatius gives two lists: one is objective criteria, the other, subjective. "But the course of thoughts suggested to us may terminate in something evil, or distracting, or less good than the soul had formerly proposed to do. Again, it may end in what weakens the soul, or disquiets it; or by destroying the peace, tranquility, and quiet which it had before, it may cause disturbance to the soul."

(334) When the enemy of our human nature has been detected and recognized by the trail of evil marking his course and by the wicked end to which he leads us, it will be profitable for one who has been tempted to review immediately the whole course of the temptation. Let him consider the series of good thoughts, how they arose, how the evil one gradually attempted to make him step down from the state of spiritual delight and joy in which he was, till finally he drew him to his wicked designs. The purpose of this review is that once such an experience has been understood and carefully observed, we may guard ourselves for the future against the customary deceits of the enemy.

** Once the devil has been detected, we need to learn from the experience. This is really important because we can see how the devil tempts us *specifically*, how he tries to lead us astray. What is it that the devil wants to use to get us off-track?

(335) In souls that are progressing to greater perfection, the action of the good angel is delicate, gentle, delightful. It may be compared to a drop of water penetrating a sponge. The action of the evil spirit upon such souls is violent, noisy, and disturbing. It may be compared to a drop of water falling upon a stone.

In souls that are going from bad to worse, the action of the spirits mentioned above is just the reverse. The reason for this is to be sought in the opposition or similarity of these souls to the different kinds of spirits. When the disposition is contrary to that of the spirits, they enter with noise and commotion that are easily perceived. When the disposition is similar to that of the spirits, they enter silently, as one coming into his own house when the doors are open.

** Again, here we're talking about the rules of the second week, for souls that are more advanced. What we see here is the need for reflection. When I'm doing God's work, and the devil tries to get involved, he comes in loudly, with noise. When I'm doing the devil's work that the evil one has proposed for me, it's the good angel that tries to wake me and straighten me out noisily.

This going from "good to better" would be the example of someone doing God's will, growing in their spiritual life and doing what God wants of them. The example of someone going from "bad to worse," would be someone who discerned a particular course of action poorly, and then continues down it. Or, it could be someone who started doing a good, Godly thing, only to let it be corrupted by the evil one.

We could call the effect, then "spiritual consonance" and "spiritual dissonance." If the good spirit is moving me along the good path, he does so silently. If the evil spirit tries to get involved, he must be noisy.

(336) When consolation is without previous cause, as was said, there can be no deception in it, since it can proceed from God our Lord only. But a spiritual person who has received such a consolation must consider it very attentively, and must cautiously distinguish the actual time of the consolation from the period which follows it. At such a time the soul is still fervent and favored with the grace and aftereffects of the consolation which has passed.

In this second period the soul frequently forms various resolutions and plans which are not granted directly by God our Lord. They may come from our own reasoning on the relations of our concepts and on the consequences of our judgments, or they may come from the good or evil spirit. Hence, they must be carefully examined before they are given full approval and put into execution.

** Here, at last, we find the course of action that we must take. A consolation without cause must be from God, but we have to be careful not to attribute to it something that's an aftereffect, and not from the time of the actual consolation.

This can happen when the effects of the consolation remain with us for a while after the actual consolation. We begin to attribute things to it that weren't actually part of the consolation.

Notes on Scruples
[345-351]
Commentary adjusted from Casanovas and Royo-Marin[1]

[345] The following notes will aid us to understand scruples and the temptations of our enemy.

- Well, it doesn't seem like there would be much to say about this, but actually Casanovas has a *lot* to say.
- First, the word Ignatius uses for *temptations* is *suasiones*; in English we have the (very formal) word *suasion*, which means persuasion as opposed to force or compulsion, and, in this, it seems to refer to something more related to thought than to the emotions. Also, these are *notes*, meaning, general indications, and not specific rules.

Note as well the words: in Puhl's version, it says *to understand*; the Spanish that Casanovas is using says *para sentir y entender*, which sort of echoes the rules for discernment of spirit. We see the need to be aware, and then understand what it going on; part of this, too, is to understand the nature and spiritual value of our interior acts. The understanding, Ignatius seems to say, won't be 100% complete (which is why these are notes and not rules), but they will at least open the door to further lights and insights.

[346] It is common for people to speak of something as a scruple though it has proceeded from their own judgment and free will, for example, when I freely decide that something is a sin which is not a sin. Thus it may happen that after one has chanced to step upon a cross formed by straws, he decides according to his own way of thinking that he has sinned. In reality, this is an erroneous judgment and not a real scruple.

- Here, as Casanovas explains, we have the *vulgar*, or common, understanding of scruples. However, this is not, exactly, what a scruple is. Sometimes people have this sort of way of thinking, and Casanovas says it could be on account of temperament, disease, mental handicap, and

---

1. From Casanovas, *Ejercicios Espirituales*, 574-589, and Antonio Royo-Marin, *Nada te turbe, nada te espante* (Madrid: Ediciones Palabra, S.A., 2003), 79-88.

more. However, he also says, rather bluntly, that such people "aren't suitable to make the Exercises, and should go to a doctor before they go to a spiritual director."

- Fr. Royo-Marin, in the book *Nada te turbe, nada te espante,* notes the following: "The scrupulous conscience is distinguished from the *delicate conscience* in that the delicate conscience pays attention to the smallest details, but with serenity and truth, and from the *erroneous conscience,* which issues false, but firm, judgments, whereas the scrupulous conscience continually fluctuates without reaching a stable judgment." So, again: a delicate conscience, which is what we want, judges paying attention to details, but without freaking out, and does so accurately. An *erroneous conscience,* which is what Ignatius says people usually call scrupulosity, means that the conscience gives firm judgments (there's no doubt, at least in their mind), but that are just wrong. An erroneous conscience is a problem, too, and, if it's combined with spiritual pride, forget it, because it won't be corrected. Corrections from superiors, or, in the most serious of cases, formal corrections, help point out the errors, but, if the person won't accept or can't see what they've done . . . forget it. Part of the reason for their error could also be an insistence on their own norms, which, like the Jewish dietary laws, give a certain sense of comfort that they are ok if their erroneous laws are fulfilled.

[347] After I have stepped upon such a cross, or after anything else I may have thought, said, or done, the suggestion may come to me from without that I have sinned, and on the other hand, it may seem to me that I have not sinned. Then if I continue to be anxious about the matter, doubting and not doubting that I sinned, there is a real scruple properly so called and a temptation from our enemy.

- Here, then, Ignatius gives us the definitive definition of scruple, or, as Casanovas calls it, the *ascetical scruple,* in which the person acts and does everything normally, but then is assailed by the devil with a thought from outside that disturbs and makes him think the opposite of what he had thought before. Thus there is an internal debate between two thoughts: the one from the rational, clear-thinking man, and the one from the devil, which Ignatius describes as part of the tricks, false reasoning, and subtleties of the devil.
- If we are well-formed and solid in our thoughts, and a firm and serene temperament, and if we recognize what is going on, scruples won't cause too much of a problem; it'll be a little annoyance, but nothing more. But,

if we aren't well-formed, or our temperament is easily shaken, or we don't know what's going on . . . we are in for a rough journey.

- What characterizes a scruple is this doubt, this uncertainty: the victim says he hasn't sinned, the devil says he has, and everything falls apart, especially when the devil begins to upset the realm of emotions with all the baggage that comes with desolation.

- Fr. Royo-Marin adds some additional clarification. He writes: "The word *scruples* comes from the Latin *scrupulus,* which means a *tiny stone.* What is meant by this expression is a very small weight that only makes the most sensitive and delicate balances move, like the sort of balances used in a pharmacy. This term has been applied to the realm of morality in order to designate a type of conscience that allows itself to be overcome by futile reasons without any sort of consistency or substance. In this sense, the scrupulous conscience can be defined by saying that it is that *conscience which for insufficient and futile motives believes that there is sin where there is not, or believes to be serious or mortal what is only slight.*

- **Signs:** The scrupulous conscience is manifested by a great number of signs. The main ones are the following:
  - Constant and unsettling fear of committing a real sin if certain things or actions are permitted, actions that other prudent and morally upright persons are seen to perform with complete tranquility of spirit.
  - A painstaking anxiety regarding the validity or sufficiency of a good action, mostly regarding past confessions or internal actions.
  - Lengthy and meticulous accusations of circumstances that have nothing to do with the case, but in which the scrupulous person believes they see indispensable complements to the sin, but not the very essence of the sin.
  - Pertinacity of judgment in not calming down at the confessor's decisions out of fear of not having explained things well, of not having been understood, etc., which obliges the scrupulous person to frequently change confessors and to want to repeat their general confessions or the accusation of sins that have already been submitted to the tribunal of penance many times, etc., etc.

- In short, then, this constant back and forth reasoning, without ever reaching a conclusion or without ever being satisfied, is the hallmark of real scruples.

[348] The kind of scruple mentioned in the first note should be much abhorred, since it is wholly erroneous. But the scruple described in the second note may for a while prove to be of no little advantage for a soul devoting itself

to the spiritual life. It may in fact greatly purify and cleanse such a soul by doing much to free it from even the appearance of sin. St. Gregory has said: "It is characteristic of a devout soul to see a fault where there is none."

- So, we see here the appraisal that Ignatius makes of the two sorts of "scruples," as it were. The first is "to be much abhorred," since it's just wrong. Not good, not keeping us from sinning, just wrong. It's like Chesterton says in *Everlasting Man*: "It is as if one were to write a most detailed analysis of the mistakes and misgovernment of the ministers of George the Third, merely with the small inaccuracy that the whole story was told about George Washington; or as if somebody made a list of the crimes of the Bolshevists with no variation except that they were all attributed to the Czar." Erroneous judgment messes everything up: we have no measure, no accuracy, nothing, and we completely miss the point; this is so much so that Ignatius says that people like this can't even make the Exercises, because how are they going to conform themselves to Christ if they can't see straight?
- But, for the one who has real scruples, there are some benefits: Ignatius sees that this temptation helps purge the soul from the remnants of sin, and, since it is a *sort of desolation*, it keeps us humble and cleans us, because we want to avoid even *the appearance of sin and imperfection.* "Scruples is one of the most terrible desolations," writes Casanovas, "it is a true spiritual martyrdom, and this is why it brings with it a great power to purge from sin and pride." When Ignatius says it "greatly purifies and cleanses," he means it does so with great intensity.
- Ignatius' own experience of scruples in Manresa was so intense that it helped lead to the development of the rules for discernment of spirit. Ignatius overcame his own scruples by consulting with learned and holy men, and submitting himself entirely to their judgments. Likewise, he gave himself intensely in prayer, asking for relief.

[349] The enemy considers carefully whether one has a lax or a delicate conscience. If one has a delicate conscience, the evil one seeks to make it excessively sensitive, in order to disturb and upset it more easily. Thus, if he sees that one will not consent to mortal sin, or venial sin, or even to the appearance of deliberate sin, since he cannot cause him to fall in a matter that appears sinful, he strives to make the soul judge that there is a sin, for example, in a word or passing thought where there is no sin.

If one has a lax conscience, the enemy endeavors to make it more so. Thus, if before a soul did not bother about venial sin, the enemy will contrive that it make light of mortal sin. If before it paid some heed to venial sin, his efforts will be that now it cares much less or not at all.

- So, souls that think little of sin don't usually get hit with scruples, because it seems sort of self-defeating. As Casanovas points out: notice how the devil picks his food. The one who suffers from scruples is material for becoming a saint. Indeed, many, if not all, saints have gone through periods of intense scrupulosity. These poor souls suffer immensely, because they discuss within themselves if they should or shouldn't have done this or that, and this every day, throughout the day, about ev*erything*.

[350] A soul that wishes to make progress in the spiritual life must always act in a manner contrary to that of the enemy. If the enemy seeks to make the conscience lax, one must endeavor to make it more sensitive. If the enemy strives to make the conscience delicate with a view to leading it to excess, the soul must endeavor to establish itself firmly in a moderate course so that in all things it may preserve itself in peace.

- So, here we see a classic Ignatian principle, the age*re contra, t*o act against the devil's inclinations and directions. In the case of a lax soul that the devil wants to have become even more lax, one should strive to avoid all *sin, a*nd even the appearance of deliberate sin. This way, if the soul falls, it probably won't fall into mortal sin.
- For a soul that is delicate, and the devil wants it to be overly sensitive, it should be born in mind that the soul is already delicate, as it were: if it tries to avoid all sin and the appearance of sin, that's enough. The soul should attempt "to establish itself firmly in a moderate course so that in all things it may preserve itself in peace." This establishing means it has a peace and calm that isn't shaken by anything – not to the right or to the left, but just solidly concerned with the moderate course.
- Likewise, Royo-Marin suggests confidence in God, and especially confidence in the opinion and advice of our spiritual directors and confessors. Likewise, we should work on developing our understanding of God as a Father, and trust in His mercy.

[351] If a devout soul wishes to do something that is not contrary to the spirit of the Church or the mind of superiors and that may be for the glory of God our Lord, there may come a thought or temptation from without not to say or do it. Apparent reasons may be adduced for this, such as that it is motivated by vainglory or some other imperfect intention, etc. In such cases one should raise his mind to his Creator and Lord, and if he sees that what he is about to do is in keeping with God's service, or at least not opposed to it, he

should act directly against the temptation. According to St. Bernard, we must answer the tempter, "I did not undertake this because of you, and I am not going to relinquish it because of you."

- Up to this point, Ignatius was talking about scruples and sin; now he shifts gears, and talks about positive, good things. When the devil sees he can't get the soul to freak out about bad things, often he changes to tempt it with the suggestion of false humility.
- So, what does Ignatius propose? "If he sees that what he is about to do is in keeping with God's service, or at least not opposed to it," he should continue. This is why the points that immediately follow, namely, [352-370] concern rules *for thinking with the Church*. It's true that we need to discern, because sometimes, many times, inspirations come to us from God, but there could be other motives. But, if what we want to do is good for the Church, good within the traditions, and for God's glory, we should firmly reject the temptation and the apparent reasons that the devil proposes so that we stop. A firm rejection is often enough to make him back away.

Thus ends our discussion on scruples: we can continue to consider another chapter on maturity according to Jesus Christ, entitled, *Overcoming individualism*:

You are the salt of the earth. But if salt loses its taste, with what can it be seasoned? It is no longer good for anything but to be thrown out and trampled underfoot. You are the light of the world. A city set on a mountain cannot be hidden. Nor do they light a lamp and then put it under a bushel basket; it is set on a lampstand, where it gives light to all in the house. Just so, your light must shine before others, that they may see your good deeds and glorify your heavenly Father.

Mt 5:13-16

According to Jesus Christ, we must be salt and light. We know of some very beautiful commentaries on these two short parables. The application that I want to make here, in conformity with the goal that we have traced out regarding maturity, is very simple: understanding that Jesus teaches—in addition to the many other possible applications that His words admit—that our maturity (and, ultimately, our happiness) is linked to the overcoming the individualism that oppresses man as one of the consequences of original sin.

(i) The human being is a being of a social nature, both in the natural order (meaning, he is inclined to live in society with men) as well as in the supernatural realm (he is inclined towards the Mystical Body of the Church). "To operate as is fitting" for the human being demands self-development so as to help the good of one's neighbor. When something does not function according to its nature, according to its intimate, internal structure, it is useless, it becomes frustrated, and unhappiness comes over it. When man does not balance what he does for himself with his efforts for the good of his neighbor, he ends up failing in one of his essential dimensions. Maturity demands that a person go out of themselves; however, they will not go out of themselves except when they seek something that is not themselves, namely, their neighbor.

(ii) The two metaphors are very adequate, because neither salt nor light serve themselves. Salt does not salt itself, and light does not illuminate itself. One gives flavor and prevents the corruption of foods; the other breaks through the darkness and makes things become luminous so that they might be seen by others.

When they do not fulfill this role of service, they receive another role, a humiliating one, as Christ says of the salt: it is only useful for being thrown out and stepped on by men. Indeed, salt serves so that, thrown on a frozen surface or on the snow, the snow won't freeze, the ice melts, and the passers-by do not slip. I think that the application is obvious: if we are not capable of giving flavor to this insipid world and helping it to avoid corruption, the Lord will find a further task for us, useful for others, but not honorable for us: we will serve as an *anecdote* so that others might not slip as happened to us: "You handed us over . . . to become an object lesson, a byword, and a reproach," says Tobit (3:4). "Careful so that what happened to Johnny or Susie does not happen to you." All of those who are in hell "serve" so that those who are still alive might not also be condemned. That is what Dante used them for, setting them as warning signs. "And you, why were you condemned?" "Out of stupidity, because I did what I should not have done." "And you, why have you been so unhappy? Why did you fail? Why have you ruined your life?" "Perhaps because you needed more opportunities to be a saint, to be happy, to *become yourself*?" "Oh, no! Looking back, I see that I left an opportunity at each corner of my life."

(iii) Once salt has lost its flavor, something terrible happens: "it is already too late." The poet Tennyson places the following words on the lips of one who discovers too late the true price of sin:

> *Late, late so late! and dark the night and chill!*
> *Late, late so late! but we can enter still.*
> *Too late, too late! ye cannot enter now.*

The same could be said of the lamp: it should illuminate those who live in the house. Men are lamps when their actions illumine their neighbors, when they "shine." That is, they illuminate when they make clear that path and glorify God, because the first condition in order to shine is to make it clear that the light that we have is from God. When we do things so that others might think that the shine that adorns us comes from ourselves and our work, we cease to enlighten, and rather darken consciences. Hence, maturity means to recognize what we have is a participation from God. On the other hand, immaturity is to believe that it is ours. Maturity cannot exist without humility.

(iv) With these two parables, Jesus reminds us of the social and communitarian aspect of His "way," that is, the religion that He started. If we want to be balanced Christians, we must think of doing good to others. If we think only of being of use to ourselves and our wants, our family, or our country, *and nothing more*, we do not belong to Christ. Jesus was *catholic*, that is, universal: "I have other sheep that do not belong to this fold"; "Go into the whole world and proclaim the gospel to every creature."

(v) Every limit that we might want to place on our light is a bushel basket that we set over the light. Our bushel basket might be small like our heart, or big like our house (or our family). But it is always a basket. When a flame burns within an enclosed space, little by little it consumes the oxygen, and it ends up using it all, after which it goes out. The size of the basket or the jar under which we set our light will only determine whether it goes out sooner or later: no matter what, it will always end up suffocating itself.

This is the reason why so many Christians feel frustrated and do not know why. They feel suffocated by life, that the spiritual air they are breathing is rarefied, that they are burning less and less, and they do not know why! The reason is none other than what Jesus Christ warned about: they burn only for themselves. Jesus said that they must "give light to all in the house." That house is the whole world.

Said with other words: bearing fruit is proper to the Christian and to every man and woman, whether that fruit is to give flavor or prevent corruption, like salt, or rather to illuminate, like a lamp.

When faith is drowned in individualism, in self-interest (even if that interest were something very important, like one's own salvation), the faith dies. Saint John Paul II said: "Faith is strengthened when it is given to others!" While the statue of Buddha is eternally looking at his belly button, the statue of General San Martín looks out at snow-covered mountains.

Reform of Life for Religious
(adapted from Fr. Fuentes)

As we've been making our way through the meditations and contemplations, we've been receiving different lights, different motions of the different spirits, and various fruits (indeed, as was said at the beginning, each meditation or contemplation should have some concrete fruit I can take away from it, something that I have been given). These are all good things, but we can't leave them just at that: we need to take what we've been given and incorporate it into our daily lives, to really live the Exercises beyond the Exercises. In a sense, after living the 30 day Exercises, we need to make sure we live the 31st day well.

1. What is to be reformed?

Saint Ignatius tells us that the Spiritual Exercises "have as their purpose the conquest of self and the regulation of one's life in such a way that no decision is made under the influence of any inordinate attachment" [21].

At this point in the Exercises, it is to be taken for granted that, throughout the meditations we've done, we've identified four things:

a) First, God's will for us **in the past:** we've seen this through the Holy Spirit's inspirations, His lights, and the circumstances of our lives, and the will of our superiors;

b) Second, what God is **clearly** asking from us **now**;

c) Third, those things in which we don't see clearly what God is asking from us. **And it's regarding these things that we need to apply the Rules of Election that Saint Ignatius gives** in order to see what God's will is.

d) Fourth, the concrete obstacles that impede us from completely and totally following Christ.

It's on the basis of all these things that we should reform our lives.

To reform means "to give form to again," "to form anew." It's like when a potter is making something out of clay, and doesn't like the shape, so they go back and form it anew. How is this done? We must look at and examine the different aspects of our formation, taking note if something is missing in one of them, something that we need to start, remove, reform, modify, or perfect. After having those things in mind, we must make a plan of life that is both realistic and concrete.

2. Revision of one's life

The "revision" of one's life means the examination we need to make of the different dimensions of our life, in order to **discover** the things we need to work on. These things are:

a) **Human formation:** this means our human personality, our balance. Concretely what we need to look at here are:
   - What virtues I need to acquire
   - What defects I need to combat
   - What is my dominant defect?
   - Interior and exterior order in my life
   - My emotions: my capacity for friendship, my attachments

b) **Formation in community life:**
   - Life in community: my participation in the life of the community (eutrapelia), giving of my talents
   - Fraternal charity
   - Obedience
   - Generosity and offering of my self

c) **Intellectual formation**
   - How I take advantage of my studies: Am I content just to get by and do the minimum? Do I even reach the minimum? Do I believe C's get degrees, passes say Masses, fails get veils?
   - Personal participation: Do I take interest in those moments of formation: conviviums, melodiums, monthly presentations . . .
   - Personal study: Am I looking to studying something more? To delve more deeply into a topic?
   - Cultural formation: Can I try to reading something more, something additional? Do I do it? Am I interested in doing it?

d) **Pastoral formation**
   - Prayer and mortification for my apostolate
   - Preparation for my apostolate
   - Development and growth of my apostolate
   - Apostolic zeal

3. The plan for my life (the reform, properly speaking)

Once we see the things that stand out from this examination, we must come up with a realistic plan for reforming my life.

a) **Characteristics**
- The plan should be *adjusted* to our duties of state, to my habitual occupations, the dispositions of my soul, my temperament, and my character, to my strengths, and to my real present state of perfection.
- It should be both *flexible* and *rigid*. It should be flexible enough that I'm not a slave to it, when charity to my neighbor requires it, or some serious and unforeseen circumstance, or obedience to my superiors makes it impossible to carry out what I had planned. However, it should be *rigid* enough so that I don't just change it on a whim.

b) **What it should include**
- **A basic daily schedule:** as religious, we already have a basic schedule for each house. However, we might need to adjust it or come up with one during vacations.
- **The basic projects I wanted to accomplish:** these tasks are all of the things that I've seen that I need to work on: which one is the most urgent? And after I accomplish that, where do I go from there? What follows next?
- **The development or progress of that project:** with what means will I accomplish the task that I'm proposing for myself (for instance, to acquire this or that virtue, to overcome this or that vice, what acts must I perform? How often?) The essential and indispensable mean for this is the daily examination of conscience.

c) **Rendering an account**
- Each month, in the monthly retreat, I should examine what I've done, make decisions, to impose some sort of punishment on myself if I need to, examine what steps should be the next ones, etc.

Regarding the reform of life, then, we can consider two more short chapters from Fr. Fuentes' book on maturity according to Jesus Christ: the first regards *responsibility*, since we need to be responsible in our search for holiness and perfection, and, second, we're reminded that seeking perfection is *the difficult path*. We can't take shortcuts.

Not everyone who says to me, 'Lord, Lord,' will enter the kingdom of Heaven, but only the one who does the will of my Father in Heaven. Many will say to me on that day, 'Lord, Lord, did we not prophesy in your name? Did we not drive out demons in your name? Did we not do mighty deeds in your

*name?' Then I will declare to them solemnly, 'I never knew you. Depart from
me, you evildoers.'*

*Everyone who listens to these words of mine and acts on them will be like
a wise man who built his house on rock. The rain fell, the floods came, and
the winds blew and buffeted the house. But it did not collapse; it had been
set solidly on rock. And everyone who listens to these words of mine but does
not act on them will be like a fool who built his house on sand. The rain fell,
the floods came, and the winds blew and buffeted the house. And it collapsed
and was completely ruined.*

Mt 7:21-27

In this last paragraph from the Sermon on the Mount, Jesus distinguishes
between the true disciple and the false one based on their attitude when confronted with the Word of God. "The Word of God" is the same as saying "the
Divine will," since in His Word God expresses His will.

Here Jesus is speaking of "disciples," that is, of those who "accept" God's
will. Those who reject it are not even to be considered in these verses.

(i) Once again we are confronted with the *mature person* and *the immature*
according to the vision of Our Lord. The touchstone in order to distinguish
one from another is, in the end, *responsibility*, and this is the topic that Jesus is
discussing here. "Responsibility" is etymologically derived from "respondere,"
to respond, or perhaps from "res ponderare," *to weigh the thing*.

The responsibility of each individual is measured by the way of weighing—
that is, valuing—that which with God confronts them, and by their awareness
of their duty to respond before God, society, and themselves.

(ii) The immature person spoken of here does not, properly speaking, reject the divine will *outright*; the one who is opposed to God's will in that way
is the *fool* or the *crazy person* of whom Scripture often speaks. However, without rejecting God's will, the immature do not assume it responsibly; they do
not make it efficacious in their own person. The Lord says they "did not act on
it." Perhaps they did not reach the point of "pondering" it with the right value
and urgency. The immature take things in—including the divine will—with
superficiality; perhaps they do so with enthusiasm, as Our Lord says in the
parable of the sower. However, such ones do not let God's will transform them
interiorly, becoming incarnate, as it were, in their own will. In other words,
the two wills do not unite. For this reason, it should not surprise us that the
things that Jesus places on the lips of these immature persons could be considered as usual "priestly" expressions: we prophesized (we preached), we expelled demons (by blessing, exorcising, forgiving), we did miracles (cancelling
out sins, transubstantiating bread into Christ's body, converting souls), etc.

Among priests, there are many who are irresponsible with respect to God's word. God is deployed by means of them (through their priestly power), but this does not transform them, just as the water that passes through a duct does not change it. They build upon sand.

(iii) In contrast, the mature *build upon rock*, as Jesus says. The firmness of the foundations of the balanced person can be understood in different senses. "The Rock is Christ," Saint Paul says, on account of which the short parable of the house built upon rock has often been understood as built upon Christ. However, it also means every stable foundation, like God's word and the divine will. God's plans are immutable, and those who attempt to separate themselves from them work in vain, because men cannot frustrate those plans; these will infallibly be brought about, even though those who are opposed to them contribute to them in a way that is very different from the way that God offers them if they wanted to work according to His Will. This is because God offers everyone salvation, meaning, to freely incorporate themselves into His plans. The one who rejects that will will see it fulfilled *despite himself.* "God frustrates the plans of the nations":

"The LORD foils the plan of nations,
frustrates the designs of peoples.
But the plan of the LORD stands forever,
the designs of his heart through all generations (Ps 33:10-11).

(iv) It could be objected that if these people say that they have performed miracles and have preached in Christ's name, then they could not have been opposed to His plans. Nonetheless, this is the way that it is. The divine plan is principally directed to the conversion of hearts; preaching, miracles, and signs of power are nothing more than "doorways" for transformation of heart. Of what use are those things if souls are not transformed in Christ? The key to understand this is in the Lord's phrase: "I never knew you." Those men who have expelled demons and who have preached Christ, did not know Christ, nor did Christ know them. This is because the knowledge of which Our Lord speaks is a communion of persons. These men build their lives on an externally correct frame, but their building had no soul. They acted like Christ's disciples, without actually becoming true disciples.

(v) From here arises the tremendous drama of *responsibility.* All that God gave them (*power* over demons, *eloquence* of words, *the charism* of healing, etc.) should have been used responsibly. Responsibility demands that those powers should be used first upon oneself: expelling one's own demons, that is, one's vices, letting oneself be transformed by the Word. In Saint John's Gospel the

Lord says: "Whoever rejects me and does not accept my words has something to judge him: the word that I spoke, it will condemn him on the last day" (Jn 12:48). The one who preaches Christ's word can also reject it: they preach it for others, but block it in their hearts. To preach does not mean to accept. To convert is to accept. To transport water does not mean to drink it; the aqueduct brings life to the fields, but within it, nothing ever comes to life. In its stone womb only moss can grow, and, as the water passes more dizzyingly, not even that. Preachers who let the Word of God pass through their minds and from their mouths like a violent river that falls down bathing others but without wetting them are *irresponsible with their own souls*.

(vi) "Everyone who listens to these words of mine and acts on them will be like a wise man." The mature person is the one who is responsible before God for what they have received through Christ's words—that is, God's will. Our responsibility is that that word be transformed into "practice," into "life." "And everyone who listens to these words of mine but does not act on them will be like a fool," immature, irresponsible.

(vii) —"Lord, I have raised someone from the dead." —"But with your life, what have you done?" "—Lord, I have preached marvelously about you." —"But, what have you done with your heart?" What the Lord awaits from us is that His word—His plans, His idea of us—should become reality. What have you made of yourself? What are your interior fruits? What can you present me of yourself?

(viii) Regarding the immature person, Jesus says: "[he] was completely ruined."

Rules for making an Election [169], [170-174], [175-188]

We call Spiritual Exercises every way of preparing and disposing the soul to rid itself of all inordinate attachments, and, after their removal, <u>of seeking and finding the will of God in the disposition of our life for the salvation of our soul.</u>

With commentary taken and modified from Fr. Timothy Gallagher and Fr. Ignacio Casanovas

[169] - Introduction to Making a Choice of a Way of Life

In every good choice, as far as depends on us, our intention must be simple. I must consider only the end for which I am created, that is, for the praise of God our Lord and for the salvation of my soul. Hence, whatever I choose must help me to this end for which I am created.

I must not subject and fit the end to the means, but the means to the end. Many first choose marriage, which is a means, and secondarily the service of God our Lord in marriage, though the service of God is the end. So also others first choose to have benefices, and afterwards to serve God in them. Such persons do not go directly to God, but want God to conform wholly to their inordinate attachments. Consequently, they make of the end a means, and of the means an end. As a result, what they ought to seek first, they seek last.

Therefore, my first aim should be to seek to serve God, which is the end, and only after that, if it is more profitable, to have a benefice or marry, for these are means to the end. Nothing must move me to use such means, or to deprive myself of them, save only the service and praise of God our Lord, and the salvation of my soul.

** These are what we could call the *dispositions* that we need. Casanovas says that these can be summed up in *simple* and *ordered*. *Simple* means looking at only one end, the end for which I was created, and *ordered*, meaning, it goes in order to where I need to go.

We have to keep in mind the principle and foundation, that God created us to know, reverence, and serve Him, and this because He loves us and wants us to be happy. This is the foundation, we could say, of discernment. On the other hand, we must be *open to His will*. It does us no good to say that we're "discerning" something when really the only thing that we want is for God to do what I want. It's the spiritual equivalent of playing Candyland. We must be *indifferent, free from inordinate affections.* Otherwise, we can't possibly make a choice well; we might as well light novena candles to Our Lady of Perpetual Discernment and not go anywhere.

We also have to put the means into place: one of these is or are the *Spiritual Exercises.* As Ignatius says right in the beginning, the Spiritual Exercises "have as their purpose the conquest of self and the regulation of one's life in such a way that no decision is made under the influence of any inordinate attachment" [21].

Other useful means are prayer, daily Communion, silence, reading the Scriptures, and spiritual direction.

By listening to God and doing His will, we come to resemble what He wants us to be: in the lives of the saints we see that holiness doesn't destroy their personalities; on the contrary, saints are more fully themselves. Sinfulness tends to bulldoze our personalities, and sins tend to make people all the same, leveling out the differences; it reduces men and women to that thing which they desire. We can think of, for example, greedy people we know: aren't they all sort of the same? Is there really that much difference between them? We could say that "sin drains the color out of men and women, and replaces it with the color of sin which is a common property. All sinners look less like themselves and more like one another." Saints, however, "are intensely themselves."[1] God created us all as individuals, and all of us are something special. Since holiness means growing close to God, the holier we are, the closer we are to the God who created us, and the closer we become to that perfect individual that He created us to be.

[170] Matters About Which a Choice Should Be Made
The purpose of this consideration is to afford information on the matters about which a choice should be made. It contains four points and a note

First Point
It is necessary that all matters of which we wish to make a choice *be either indifferent or good in themselves, and such that they are lawful within our Holy Mother, the hierarchical Church, and not bad or opposed to her.*

** Again, there's no debate about whether or not I want to decide to go to Mass on Sunday, or whether or not to murder someone. Those aren't things that are indifferent or good in themselves. However, many things in this life are good: to get married or to enter religious life, or enter the seminary for the diocese or for a religious order, to keep working at my present job, or to

---

1. The intro of Frank Sheed's *Saints are not sad* for this point, 11.

cut back some to take up volunteer work. All are good or at least indifferent in themselves. The question is: what does God want?

[171] Second Point

There are things that fall under an unchangeable choice, such as the priesthood, marriage, etc. There are others with regard to which our choice may be changed, for example, to accept or relinquish a benefice, to receive or renounce temporal goods.

** This distinction is important, because some decisions I can change and re-examine, but others, not so much.

[172] Third Point

With regard to an unchangeable choice, once it has been made, for instance, by marriage or the priesthood, etc., since it cannot be undone, no further choice is possible. Only this is to be noted. If the choice has not been made as it should have been, *and with due order, that is, if it was not made without inordinate attachments*, one should be sorry for this, and take care to live well in the life he has chosen.

Since such a choice was inordinate and awry, it does not seem to be a vocation from God, as many erroneously believe. They make a divine call out of a perverse and wicked choice. For every vocation that comes from God is always pure and undefiled, uninfluenced by the flesh or any inordinate attachment.

** Interesting. I've met a lot of people who lived wild lives, but still felt that God was calling them to be priests. Most of them ignored it, and instead got married and had kids. Not a bad thing, getting married, but the point is what is God's will. Most of these, I might add, have families with a lot of problems.

Remember, again, those dispositions we talked about earlier: this is the key for a good discernment.

[173] Fourth Point

In matters that may be changed, if one has made a choice properly and with due order, without any yielding to the flesh or the world, there seems to be no reason why he should make it over. But let him perfect himself as much as possible in the one he has made.

[174] Note

It is to be observed that if a choice in matters that are subject to change has not been made sincerely and with due order, then, if one desires to bring forth fruit that is worthwhile and most pleasing in the sight of God our Lord, it will be profitable to make a choice in the proper way.

[175] Three Times When a Correct and Good Choice of a Way of Life May Be Made

First Time

When God our Lord so moves and attracts the will that a devout soul without hesitation, or the possibility of hesitation, follows what has been manifested to it. St. Paul and St. Matthew acted thus in following Christ our Lord.

** Casanovas notes that *time* here doesn't mean months, weeks, days, or hours, but rather to the diverse spiritual situations in which man might find himself. All are suitable times for making a choice, but each one has a different situation and hence different rules that apply to it.

The first thing that calls our attention, says the Jesuit, is the mystical or passive environment of this first time of election. It is really an extraordinary grace, one that calls our attention, and often the impression remains for years after the fact, if it ever goes away. It is extraordinary.

God calls, and I answer. There's no way that I can doubt that it's Him who has called me to do something. The key here is that something is shown or revealed to the individual, the will is invariably drawn to it, moved towards it, and there can *be no doubt* that it comes from God.

Again, in this case, there's no need to wait and see if God does it again (He's not obligated to!). That's it: we've seen and that's that.

The response is still free; it's not that God imposes it on us or makes us do it. Yet, what is shown gives such peace, joy, confidence, direction, and a sense of being loved by God that that impression remains for years after the fact.

I don't know if there's anyone who has a running tally of these experiences, but I think we can probably say that this is the most uncommon of the three times. Oftentimes God allows us to struggle so that we can really make the decision ours. (*Example of Sister*).

Just as a sort of conclusion, though, I think the words of Saint John Bosco merit some consideration (they sort of summarize what we've been saying). He writes: "I think it is a grave mistake to say it's hard to know if you have a vocation or not. The Lord put us in such circumstances that we don't have to do anything more than go forward; we only have to respond to Him. A vocation is difficult to know when one does not want to follow it, when those first inspirations are rejected. It is there that the tangle gets confusing. . . . Look, when a person is indecisive about whether or not to become a religious, I tell you openly that that person already heard their calling; they didn't follow it immediately, and now they find themselves confused and indecisive."

(176) Second Time

When much light and understanding are derived through experience of desolations and consolations and discernment of diverse spirits.

** In this second mode of discernment, *discernment of spirits* and *discernment of God's will* coincide: through the discernment of consolations and desolations a person attains "sufficient clarity and understanding" for the discernment of God's will.

In a further document, Ignatius amplifies his description of this second mode:

Among the three modes of making a choice, if God does not move a person in the first mode, one should dwell persistently on the second, that of recognizing his vocation by the experience of consolations and desolations; in such manner that, as he continues with his meditations on Christ our Lord, he observes, when he finds himself in consolation, to which part God moves him [meaning, to which option in the choice], and likewise when he finds himself in desolation. And what consolation is should be well explained: that is, spiritual joy, love, hope in things of above, tears, and every interior movement which leaves the soul consoled in our Lord. The contrary of this is desolation: sadness, lack of confidence, lack of love, dryness, etc.

We need to remember, from the rules of the first week, that "in consolation the good spirit guides and counsels us more, so in desolation the bad spirit" (318), and so now this mode of discernment emerges.

Again, Casanovas mentions that this is supernatural, although it is to be counted among the "ordinary" supernatural graces, the usual way of acting.

In reviewing my personal experiences of consolation and desolation, I should ask myself the following: in times of *spiritual consolation*, to which option do I feel inclined? Has the inclination *recurred*? *Enough* so that I can see a clear pattern of inclination? Enough so that, since in consolation the *good spirit* guides and counsels us more, I may confidently judge, with the help of my spiritual director, that God is calling me to this option? Is this judgment further confirmed by the opposite inclination in time of *spiritual desolation* – the time when the *bad spirit* guides and counsels?

Again, we need to look and see the *pattern* that emerges. For instance, if I notice that whenever I'm in consolation, I feel the desire to become a priest, and that fills me with joy, but, when I'm in desolation, I feel like there's nothing I'd rather do less than become a priest, probably God wants me to be a priest. Of course, this is a gross simplification of a process that takes time and prayer, but this is the gist of it.

Again, too, we really need to pay attention: in the rules for the second week, we spoke about how the devil can actually cause consolation for a bad end.

We need to be attentive, and see the pattern. If there's an *odd man out*, then something is up.

Lastly, remember, again, those dispositions we talked about earlier: this is the key for a good discernment.

[177] Third Time

This is a time of tranquility. One considers first for what purpose man is born, that is, for the praise of God our Lord and for the salvation of his soul. With the desire to attain this before his mind, he chooses as a means to this end a kind of life or state within the bounds of the Church that will be a help in the service of his Lord and for the salvation of his soul.

I said it is a time of tranquility, that is, a time when the soul is not agitated by different spirits, and has free and peaceful use of its natural powers.

** Ok, so, now, when there's no clear sign from God, and no consolation and desolation to work with, we come to reason. Remember that our reason, too, is a gift from God, and we need to use it well. Here we are saying that it is a time that is peaceful; there are no different movements of the soul, but that we rely on our natural powers, as it were.

Of course, it goes without saying that those dispositions we talked about earlier must be in place. Otherwise, we can't discern well.

What do we do? We set before ourselves the Principle and Foundation. That needs to be the guiding principle of our lives. It needs to be a *calm* time: if we're bounding through consolations and desolations, that's not the right time for the third mode of discernment.

(178) If a choice of a way of life has not been made in the first and second time, below are given:
Two Ways of Making a Choice of a Way of Life in the Third Time
First Way of Making a Good and Correct Choice of a Way of Life

This contains six points

First Point

This is to place before my mind the object with regard to which I wish to make a choice, for example, an office, or the reception or rejection of a benefice, or anything else that may be the object of a choice subject to change.

** What is it we're trying to discern between (again, they must both be good or at least indifferent in themselves)?

(179) Second Point

It is necessary to keep as my aim the end for which I am created, that is, the praise of God our Lord and the salvation of my soul. Besides this, I must be indifferent, without any inordinate attachment, so that I am not more inclined or disposed to accept the object in question than to relinquish it, nor to give it up than to accept it. I should be like a balance at equilibrium, without leaning to either side, that I might be ready to follow whatever I perceive is more for the glory and praise of God our Lord and for the salvation of my soul.

** Elsewhere, Ignatius recalls that, when he made decisions this way, he would "first empty himself of any passion or attachment which often confuses and obscures judgment so that it cannot discover as easily the radiance and light of the truth, and he placed himself, *without any fixed inclination or predetermined direction*, like *matter ready to take any shape*, in the hands of God our Lord."

(180) Third Point

I should beg God our Lord to deign to move my will, and to bring to my mind what I ought to do in this matter that would be more for His praise and glory. Then I should use the understanding to weigh the matter with care and fidelity, and make my choice in conformity with what would be more pleasing to His most holy will.

** Again, we need to remember that we ask from God a mind that sees clearly, and a will that will choose faithfully. We need to ask God for this grace.

(181) Fourth Point

This will be to weigh the matter by reckoning the number of advantages and benefits that would accrue to me if I had the proposed office or benefice solely for the praise of God our Lord and the salvation of my soul. On the other hand, I should weigh the disadvantages and dangers there might be in having it. I will do the same with the second alternative, that is, weigh the advantages and benefits as well as the disadvantages and danger of not having it.

** This means to make a chart. Literally. Write it out and see. As Ignatius' biographer put it: "He *considered with great attentiveness* and *weighed the reasons* which presented themselves *for one option and for the other*, and *the strength of each, and he compared them among themselves.*"

Option 1 +	Option 1 -
Option 2 +	Option 2 -

We're talking here about spiritual reasons, **_BUT_** sometimes when we make this list, we see that some reasons we've given aren't actually that good, and that others reflect something about us, that we're attached to this, that, or the other.

(182) Fifth Point

After I have gone over and pondered in this way every aspect of the matter in question, I will consider which alternative appears more reasonable. Then I must come to a decision in the matter under deliberation because of weightier motives presented to my reason, and not because of any sensual inclination.

(183) Sixth Point

After such a choice or decision, the one who has made it must turn with great diligence to prayer in the presence of God our Lord, and offer Him his choice that the Divine Majesty may deign to accept and confirm it if it is for His greater service and praise.

** His biographer described it this way: "Finally, Ignatius turned again to our Lord with what he had thought and what he had found, and recently placed it all before his divine gaze, beseeching him that he would give him light to choose what would be most pleasing to him."

Devotion, great tranquility, the absence of an opposed desire, and the sense of completion in the process could be the first indication of how God wishes to confirm the decision.

(184) Second Way of Making a Correct and Good Choice of a Way of Life

This contains four rules and a note.

First Rule

The love that moves and causes one to choose must descend from above, that is, from the love of God, so that before one chooses he should perceive that the greater or less attachment for the object of his choice is solely because of His Creator and Lord.

** Again, this is the affirmation of the basic rules we talked, the basic setting for discernment.

(185) Second Rule

I should represent to myself a man whom I have never seen or known, and whom I would like to see practice all perfection. Then I should consider what I would tell him to do and choose for the greater glory of God our Lord and the greater perfection of his soul. I will do the same, and keep the rule I propose to others.

** This little exercise does two things: first, it helps us to view the situation more objectively, but Ignatius also knows that it's easier for us to give advice than to take it! Hence, oftentimes looking at things this way really helps us to decide what it is we should do.

(186) Third Rule

This is to consider what procedure and norm of action I would wish to have followed in making the present choice if I were at the moment of death. I will guide myself by this and make my decision entirely in conformity with it.

** Again, these things I've decided between aren't evil and good, but all good or indifferent. Which would be a better decision at my moment of death?

(187) Fourth Rule

Let me picture and consider myself as standing in the presence of my judge on the last day, and reflect what decision in the present matter I would then wish to have made. I will choose now the rule of life that I would then wish to have observed, that on the day of judgment I may be filled with happiness and joy.

** Same comment as above. Which choice shows a deeper, more profound love of the One who first loved me?

(188) Note

Guided by the rules given above for my eternal salvation and peace, I will make my decision, and will offer it to God our Lord as directed in the sixth point of the First Way of Making a Choice of a Way of Life.

** Again, I must always put the final decision before the Lord.

(189) Directions for the Amendment and Reformation of One's Way of Living in His State of Life

It must be borne in mind that some may be established in an ecclesiastical office, or may be married, and hence cannot make a choice of a state of life, or, in matters that may be changed and hence are subject to a choice, they may not be very willing to make one.

It will be very profitable for such persons, whether they possess great wealth or not, in place of a choice, to propose a way for each to reform his manner of living in his state by setting before him the purpose of his creation and of his life and position, namely, the glory and praise of God our Lord and the salvation of his soul.

If he is really to attain this end, during the Exercises and during the consideration of the ways of making a choice as explained above, he will have to examine and weigh in all its details how large a household he should maintain, how he ought to rule and govern it, how he ought to teach its members by word and example. So too he should consider what part of his means should be used for his family and household, how much should be set aside for distribution to the poor and other pious purposes.

Let him desire and seek nothing except the greater praise and glory of God our Lord as the aim of all he does. For every one must keep in mind that in all that concerns the spiritual life his progress will be in proportion to his surrender of self-love and of his own will and interests.

Maturity according to Jesus Christ
and the Emotional Maturity of Jesus Christ

For today's conference, we will consider, following Fr. Fuentes's books, first, maturity and prayer, and Jesus and the oblative love of friendship. So, in other words, how maturity and prayer go hand in hand, and then what friendship is like with Jesus Christ as a model.

Maturity and Prayer

In praying, do not babble like the pagans, who think that they will be heard because of their many words. Do not be like them. Your Father knows what you need before you ask him. This is how you are to pray:

Our Father in Heaven, hallowed be your name, your kingdom come, your will be done, on earth as in Heaven.

Give us today our daily bread; and forgive us our debts, as we forgive our debtors; and do not subject us to the final test, but deliver us from the evil one....

Ask and it will be given to you; seek and you will find; knock and the door will be opened to you. For everyone who asks, receives; and the one who seeks, finds; and to the one who knocks, the door will be opened. Which one of you would hand his son a stone when he asks for a loaf of bread, or a snake when he asks for a fish? If you then, who are wicked, know how to give good gifts to your children, how much more will your heavenly Father give good things to those who ask him.

Mt 6:7-13; 7:7-11

The mature person is a person of prayer: prayer reveals a person's maturity or makes them mature; it should be understood that we are speaking of "serious" prayer.

(i) Our prayer shows the level of maturity of our relationship with God, because our way of praying reveals how we understand who God is, and how our religiousness is. By analyzing our prayer, perhaps we will find out that we are very immature. For example: if exclusively sentimental and exterior prayers predominate in our forms of religiosity; if we reduce prayer to formulas; if our prayer seems rather like a contract *"do ut des"* (I give—my prayer—so that you might give me what I ask); if we seek rather consolations or magical solutions without counting on our own personal efforts; and, above all, if what we say in our prayer is incompatible with the style of our life and of our *commitment* to God.

Our prayer can also reveal a distorted image, or even the absence of God. For instance: if it is difficult for us to speak with God as with a tender and most personal Father (as is revealed in the expression Abba, "Dad" – "Daddy," used by Jesus); if we see Him rather as severe and avenging (as often occurs in scrupulous people), or if it simply is hard for us to understand how He is present in our hearts. For many Christians, including many religious, prayer is something empty, or it is a moment where they reflect (meditate) upon God or upon man, but it is not the act in which God is spoken to and God is listened to.

(ii) From the text of the Our Father and from what Saint Matthew says in the passage from chapter 7, verses 7-11, we can grasp six characteristics that are proper to the prayer of a mature person (clearly, Jesus is describing His own experience of prayer):

(a) It is trusting, that is, sure. The way we prayer reflects our trust. "Ask and it will be given to you; seek and you will find; knock and the door will be opened to you." The Lord assures, promises, and guarantees. Do we trust blindly in the value of our prayer? "If you have faith the size of a mustard seed, you will say to this mountain, 'Move from here to there,' and it will move. Nothing will be impossible for you" (Mt 17:20). Trust is a sign of maturity. Among other things, immaturity is doubtful and distrusting.

(b) It is decided. "Ask, seek, knock." It is an activity that the soul undertakes with decision and firmness. It demands overcoming spiritual laziness, called acedia, which becomes afraid in the face of every spiritual activity that is demanding and laborious. The one who wants to pray but without making an effort does not pray: he naps.

(c) It is constant. The verbs used by Jesus do not know limits. He does not say "once in a while," or "every so often." He speaks of them as if they were incessant activities. Barclay translates this verse in the following way: "Keep on asking, and it will be given you; keep on seeking, and you will find; keep on knocking, and it will be opened to you." He bases this translation on the following, saying: "In Greek there are two kinds of imperative; there is the aorist imperative which issues one definite command. 'Shut the door behind you,' would be an aorist imperative. There is the present imperative which issues a command that a man should always do something or should go on doing something. 'Always shut doors behind you,' would be a present imperative. The imperatives here are present imperatives; therefore Jesus is saying, 'Go on asking; go on seeking; go on knocking.'" The immature person becomes discouraged when they see that their requests do not receive an immediate reply, when they ask but God delays His response. How long did God make Abraham pray in order to receive the son that God Himself had promised? Twenty-five years!

Moreover, God demands that we always pray because in the harmonious development of man's life, the discovery that human life is a permanent dialogue with our Creator and Father plays a fundamental role. Jesus prayed without ceasing. Earlier we had spoken about "living facing God." In reaching maturity, man discovers that he is an interlocutor with God ("partner of the Absolute," said John Paul II), or, rather, God is his only absolute interlocutor. The human heart is always saying things that other men cannot understand or respond to properly; only God can. "My heart is restless," wrote Saint Augustine. It is a restlessness that can find no peace apart from God. A person is immature when they are "mute" in their deepest dimension, that aspect in which they ask themselves about the most fundamental things of their existence, questions to which only God can respond.

(d) However, it is not wordy: "In praying, do not babble like the pagans, who think that they will be heard because of their many words" (6:7). The pagans had the habit of prayer by repetition of certain formulas, to the point of fatigue, which ended up producing a sort of self-hypnosis. In their challenge with Elijah, the prophets of Baal spent half a day jumping and shouting: "Baal, answer us," until falling into a sort of diabolic delirium (cf. 1 Kgs 18:26-29). The same is said of the crowd of Ephesians, who for two hours shouted: "Great is Artemis of the Ephesians!" (Acts 19:34). Something similar takes place in some modern religious sects and in certain liturgical misrepresentations. Likewise, many Jews prayed in this way. Jesus teaches that this is opposite of true prayer. The immature person could be a charlatan, talkative, loquacious, verbose, but empty of inner words, of concepts pregnant with existential meaning and responses, because these can only be found in dialogue with God. To pray, few words, even one, are enough: it is the word of the heart that looks to God in an act of adoration.

(e) It is filial. The foundation of trust is the conviction that one is dealing with our Father. We cannot doubt this precisely because prayer consists in asking for necessary things from our Father. Can God, since He is a Father, do anything but listen to us?

(f) It is ordered, as can be seen in the structure of the Our Father: what is most important is first, then what is second, and the order cannot be changed. This idea is already presented to us in the Our Father.

(iii) Indeed, the Our Father teaches us what should be the mature person's desires and the order of their hopes. There is nothing superfluous in the balanced person. What are his concerns?

(a) First and foremost, God. First the things of God; only afterwards the things of man. The immature person sets his worries and desires before divine things. What is the mature person concerned with? (1) With God's glory; (2) with the primacy of God above all things (His kingdom); (3) with God's will (that is, the divine plan, especially regarding the person themselves). Here we have the first three petitions that Jesus teaches.

(b) Only afterwards does what is necessary for man come, synthesized in one phrase ("daily bread") which summarizes what is necessary for the body and for the soul. The mature person is neither anxious nor mistrustful; this is why there is no specification as to what is necessary each day. The mature person asks for "bread," that is, "what You know that I will need today." "You know." It is an act of trust. Once again, the foundation of that trust is the divine fatherhood. That is why Our Lord says: "Which one of you would hand his son a stone when he asks for a loaf of bread, or a snake when he asks for a fish? If you then, who are wicked, know how to give good gifts to your children, how much more will your heavenly Father give good things to those who ask him."

(c) Then he asks for harmony—reconciliation—with God ("forgive us our trespasses"); and the mature person knows that should be asked for in the same way that they themselves forgive others. Only the immature could hope that God would forgive them at the same time they are cruel or hard with others.

(d) Finally, they ask to be freed from evil, meaning both protection so as not to fall into temptations, as well as not ending up being enslaved to the Devil (the Evil one), as happens with sin. The mature know that temptation is inevitable in this life, that it is a part of their daily struggle; hence they do not ask to be spared from temptation but rather not to fall into them.

(iv) The immature easily betray themselves in the priority they give to their desires or in the things that are "missing" from their petitions. For the immature, the center of their concerns tends to be the "bread," what is needed daily; or, they ask for forgiveness, but without having themselves the disposition to give an example by forgiving others from their heart ("from their heart" means without demanding anything in return, that is, just like how we hope God forgives us); or they want to be freed from temptation, meaning, to be exempted from testing (and not just from falling), showing that they are unaware of the human reality and the divine economy. Above all, immaturity is shown in that, for these people, God does not occupy the center of their thoughts and hearts; for them, God is a name written within a beautiful heart carved onto the tree trunk, but He is not the sap that gives life

Jesus and the oblative love of friendship

The difference between an unripe pear and a ripe one is that the first is indigestible and the second can be eaten. Analogously, the immature person is one who cannot go beyond even the borders that mark his or her ego, meaning, they are not in condition to *give themselves*. In contrast, the mature person can give themselves without reserve, because they really possess themselves. The mature person can die to themselves—and they do so—in order to give themselves to a cause, an ideal, or a person. From here it follows that the culmination of emotional development becomes clear in the capacity for friendship and the oblation of self. The love of friendship is the most complete form of love; it is the love that establishes reciprocal emotional and spiritual bonds, as a sort of "circulation" of love. A friend is capable of giving love and of receiving it and, above all, of loving their friend in themselves and not because of the pleasure or benefits that they can obtain from their company or their presence. However, even among friends there are degrees: the lowest degree is held by those who can only respond with love to the love that they receive. The highest, on the other hand, pertains to those who are able to love without needing to be loved first, or even taking the risk that perhaps they will never be paid back with love for the love that they have given.

Jesus was a great friend, meaning, a person with a great capacity for friendship. However, His friendship was the very highest; He gives it even though He does not receive it.

Friendship also has other nuances. There is a love of friendship that unites equals who are not blood relatives; there is a love of friendship among siblings; there is a love of conjugal friendship (Saint Thomas define marriage as a most special form of friendship[1]); there is also a friendship that is proper between the teacher and the disciple; finally, there is a special love between a father—or a mother—and a child.

The sort of friendship that we observe between Christ and His disciples is similar to this last one. Indeed, Peter, John, and James are friends among themselves and also friends of Jesus. However, these bonds are not equal. The first is a friendship *inter pares*, whereas as the second is of filiation. This is in spite of the fact that Jesus should probably be younger than several of the disciples. There are characteristics of the relation between Jesus and them that support this classification. Jesus treats His disciples, and especially those whom He chose as Apostles, like a father: He educates, instructs, defends, encourages, corrects, challenges, and lifts them up; He leads them to the Heavenly Father;

1. Cf. Saint Thomas, *Summa Contra Gentiles*, III, 123.

He gives them wings so that they can fly by themselves. With them He exercises a most delicate providence. In turn, the disciples give Our Lord admiration, respect, and reverence (Lk 5:8: "When Simon Peter saw this, he fell at the knees of Jesus and said, 'Depart from me, Lord, for I am a sinful man'"), trust, and their needs (Jn 6:68: "Master, to whom shall we go? You have the words of eternal life"). They are friends, but like a father is with his dearly beloved children.

This love of paternal friendship leads, as something of His own, to a *certain solitude* of soul. In reality, every human being has an incommunicable dimension of their soul that only God can penetrate. However, in no one is this seen like it is in a father; this is especially true in moments of suffering in which the father, in order not to grieve his children, does not share with them everything he is suffering. The children want the father to unload his burdens on them, but the father, on account of fatherly love itself, feels himself obligated to spare them from that burden.

In no one is that "solitude of heart" perceived like it is in Jesus, even when He is surrounded by men. Even in the moments of greatest feeling, Jesus in a certain sense continues to be alone with God the Father. This is seen at the Last Supper, when Christ's gestures and words, filled to the brim with emotion, find no adequate echo among those who were His own. Even John, who eats while resting on His chest, remains far removed from the depths in which the Lord lives. The gap becomes even deeper in Gethsemane: "Peter, could you not keep watch with Me for an hour?"

Nonetheless, this does not impede the establishment of an intense bond between these hearts. Jesus was not only fully but also completely human; and that perfection makes His capacity for friendship become overflowing for His friends: He gives them more than they can receive. In contrast, their friendship for Him could never fill His heart. It is a friendship that gives infinitely more than it receives, even though it wants and accepts that unequal circulation.

This shines out in His dealings with the Apostles. In spite of the disproportion between Jesus and His friends, He always lowers Himself to them. He recognizes the qualities and personal merits of each one; for this reason He choose Peter as head of the rest on account of the sincerity and generosity of the love of that hardened fisherman, but He privileges John (*the disciple whom Jesus loved*) with a special intimacy owed, perhaps, to the innocence of his age, and He appoints Judas as administrator of the community money because he was skilled for earthly business. He also knows the state of each heart: "You are clean, but not all" (Jn 13:10). However, He is not unaware of the limits and defects of each one, their weak points, weaknesses, and lacks. "Jesus knew from the beginning the ones who would not believe and the one who would betray him" (Jn 6:64). Sometimes, He even predicts it for them: "This night all of you will have your faith in me shaken" (Mt 26:31). Yet, even then, He does not reject them after they have fallen; rather, He touches their hearts in order to invite them to return, as He does to Peter with a simple yet heartfelt look in Caiaphas's patio: "The Lord turned and looked at Peter; and Peter remembered the word of the Lord, how he had said to him, 'Before the cock crows today, you will deny me three times.' He went out and began to weep bitterly" (Lk 22:61-62). The same reproach, directed at Judas in the Garden of Olives, exudes more sorrow for his straying than for the betrayal of which He was the object: "Jesus said to him, 'Judas, are you betraying the Son of Man with a kiss?'" (Lk 22:48).

Jesus establishes an order in His friendship, because authentic love is also ordered.[2] Although He loves all of His friends, He does not love them all equally. To choose always implies making a hierarchy, and the love of charity is a love of *predilection*. By choosing the Twelve, He shows a preference for them with respect to the other disciples. Even among the Apostles, Peter, James, and John were privileged, as Christ made them witnesses of special spiritual experiences (some miracles, His transfiguration, His agony in Gethsemane). However, His love neither absorbs them nor does it become favoritism; if He allows John to rest on His chest, and answers questions that no one else heard (revealing to him who the traitor is: cf. Jn 13:24), He nonetheless did not leave John as His vicar on earth, but rather Peter, *who had denied Him three times*.

Jesus does not show Himself to be jealous with His disciples; He is not overprotective, meddling, or controlling. In the face of misunderstandings He reacts with hurt but also with magnanimity ("But they understood nothing of this; the word remained hidden from them and they failed to comprehend what he said" Lk 18:34). He is forgiving: He does not become resentful in the face of abandonment and denial, and during the apparitions after the Resurrection, He never alludes to the ingratitude or infidelity shown during the Passion by His weak friends.

Jesus' emotional maturity stands out like an intense star in the night sky in the clearest attitude that an extraordinary mature person can offer: *the ability to love without being loved in return*, and even more, *to love while being hated*. The Old Testament considered the one who loved those who were his own and hated his enemies as someone worthy of praise. Taking revenge on an enemy was not seen as a failing; rather, it seemed "normal," the *norm*: "Eye

---

2. "There must needs be some order in things loved out of charity, which order is in reference to the first principle of that love, which is God" (Saint Thomas, *Summa Theologica*, II-II, q. 26, a. 1).

for an eye, tooth for a tooth" (Ex 21:24). The Book of Leviticus orders: "Take no revenge and cherish no grudge against your own people" (Lv 19:18). This would seem to indicate that it was not necessary to apply the same measure with foreigners, and even less to enemies. Jesus knows this way of thinking, but He deliberately overcomes this limitation of the Law by citing an idea that was commonly accepted among His countrymen: "You have heard that it was said, 'You shall love your neighbor and hate your enemy.' But I say to you, love your enemies, and pray for those who persecute you, that you may be children of your heavenly Father, for he makes his sun rise on the bad and the good, and causes rain to fall on the just and the unjust" (Mt 5:43-45). Indeed, He even goes beyond that: "But to you who hear I say, love your enemies, do good to those who hate you, bless those who curse you, pray for those who mistreat you" (Lk 6:27-28). Love, do good, bless, and pray. He did not simply leave it at words: "When they came to the place called the Skull, they crucified him and the criminals there, one on his right, the other on his left. Then Jesus said, 'Father, forgive them, they know not what they do'" (Lk 23:33-34). Saint Paul expresses this fullness and maturity of Christ's love by reminding us: "But God proves his love for us in that while we were still sinners Christ died for us. . . . While we were enemies, we were reconciled to God through the death of his Son" (Rm 5:8-10).

No one loved as He did.

Maturity according to Jesus Christ
and the Emotional Maturity of Jesus Christ

For today's conference, we will consider, following Fr. Fuentes's books, first, maturity and the difficult path, and the conclusions that we have from both of these books, a sort of summary of everything we have been considering this second week of the Exercises.

Maturity and the Difficult Path

Enter through the narrow gate; for the gate is wide and the road broad that leads to destruction, and those who enter through it are many. How narrow the gate and constricted the road that leads to life. And those who find it are few.

Mt 7:13-14

The teaching of these two verses summarizes one of the most ancient ways of teaching the moral life: the doctrine of the two paths. Thus, for example, Psalm 1 says:

> *Blessed is the man who does not walk*
> *in the counsel of the wicked,*
> *Nor stand in the way of sinners,*
> *nor sit in company with scoffers.*
> *Rather, the law of the LORD is his joy;*
> *and on his law he meditates day and night*
> *But not so are the wicked, not so!*
> *They are like chaff driven by the wind.*

(i) There is a path of the just, and another for the unjust, and life sets us at a crossroads, that is, at an intersection of the paths, or, at the very least, a point where the paths divide. If the paths diverge, then so too do men and women diverge; among them are those who take one path, and those who take the other. Jesus Christ is, thus, a "sign of contradiction," (Lk 2:34), "a stumbling block," "a watershed." Regarding the text of Lk 2:34, Barclay says: "It is not so much God who judges a man; a man judges himself; and his judgment is his reaction to Jesus Christ."

(ii) Here freedom intervenes. Jesus commands: "Enter." God always appeals to the use of our free will. The Book of Deuteronomy says: "See, I have today set before you life and good, death and evil. If you obey the commandments of the LORD, your God, which I am giving you today, loving the LORD, your God, and walking in his ways, and keeping his commandments, statutes and ordinances, you will live and grow numerous, and the LORD, your God, will bless you in the land you are entering to possess. If, however, your heart turns away and you do not obey, but are led astray and bow down to other gods and serve them, I tell you today that you will certainly perish; you will not have a long life on the land which you are crossing the Jordan to enter and possess. I call Heaven and earth today to witness against you: I have set before you life and death, the blessing and the curse. Choose life, then, that you and your descendants may live, by loving the LORD, your God, obeying his voice, and holding fast to him. For that will mean life for you, a long life for you to live on the land which the LORD swore to your ancestors, to Abraham, Isaac, and Jacob, to give to them" (30:15-20).

Joshua said the same thing to the Jews a little before they crossed the Jordan: "If it is displeasing to you to serve the LORD, choose today whom you will serve, the gods your ancestors served beyond the River or the gods of the Amorites in whose country you are dwelling. As for me and my household, we will serve the LORD" (Jos 24:15).

Perhaps the most famous text in this regard is that of Jeremiah: "And to this people you shall say: Thus says the LORD: See, I am giving you a choice between the way to life and the way to death" (Jer 21:8).

(iii) Jesus Christ tells us with complete clarity that the path that leads to life is the way of the cross. The following dialogue is found in the "Tablet," attributed to Cebes, a disciple of Socrates:

—Tell us, then the path that leads to True Knowledge.

—Do you see that high mountain pass, where there is no one, that is almost like a desert?

—I see it.

—Do you see a small entrance, facing a seldom-walked path, by which few pass, as with every rugged and steep path, which seems to be quite dangerous?

—Yes, yes.

—Do you not see a mountain, with a lengthy ascent, on either side of which there are deep precipices?

—Yes, I see it.

—That path leads to True Knowledge.

—It truly seems a bitter and difficult path.

Jesus Christ has never tricked us regarding His life program. It is a program of denial, the cross, persecution, and of suffering (which might have the shape of disaster, of death, of illness, of misunderstanding, etc.). Christ never preached ease, but nor did He preach the useless twisting of muddled minds. Hence, this perspective helps us to clarify some important issues.

(iv) First and foremost, contrary to what many think, the mature person is not the who is inclined only to what is difficult and who despises what is easy. This is what the "complicated" person does, because to complicate means precisely that: "to do in a difficult way what could be done easily." When they see the fastest way to do something, the mature person, if they are sure that it is also the right way, does not complicate things. However, the mature person *is* characterized, on the other hand, by "distrusting" what seems easy and attractive because they know that true greatness is the result of effort. For this reason, they know ahead of time that all the advertising that offers "Learn German or Chinese *effortlessly*" or to "speak Russian *in fifteen days*" is phony (in contrast, the immature think that *there should be a way to do important and great things without sacrifice*, and for this reason their library accumulates dozens of these methods, and they seek magical solutions for everything). Virtue, which is the only thing that is really worth the effort, is the fruit of a laborious conquest: there are no happy marriages without great interior struggles to learn how to forgive, to be happy, to tolerate, to be magnanimous. Nor is there perseverance in good without important efforts, just as there do not exist good pianists who have not passed through many tedious hours practicing innumerable exercises and scales.

(v) Nor are the mature the ones who are inclined to take the long route when they can—and it is appropriate—to take the short one; the bad strategist always takes the longer route. Nonetheless, the mature initially *distrust* the shortcut because they know that it is only with great difficulty that something fast and immediate produces a lasting result. In "The Poetic Art," Horace advises Pisos that, when he writes something, to have it in hand nine years before publishing it, so that he can continue perfecting it. Virgil spent the last ten years of his life writing "The Aeneid," and when he was dying, he would have destroyed it if his friends had not prevented him, because it seemed very imperfect to him. Plato's *Republic* begins with a simple phrase: "I went down yesterday to the Piraeus with Glaucon the son of Ariston, that I might offer up my prayers to the goddess." Plato left no less than thirteen different versions of that initial phrase: the great writer corrected it time and again until he achieved the perfect cadence. No one has ever produced a masterpiece by a shortcut. In this world we must constantly confront shortcuts that promise immediate results, and the long journey, the results of which cannot be seen except at a distance. However, the things that last are never done in a hurry; for this reason, *usually*, the best path turns out to be the longer one. The immature do not understand this; as a result, they never reach maturity.

(vi) The mature person does not bind themselves with numerous and unnecessary rules. This is more proper to the perplexed and to the scrupulous. However, the mature know that nothing has even been achieved without discipline, and that all those who do not want to be bound to precise rules, ones that are measured and necessary, that is, those who improvise, those who act following their stomachs, the negligent, never build anything, never finish anything, and never reach any port. A famous example of this is Samuel Coleridge (1772-1834), of whom it was said that "never has so great a mind produced so little." He left Cambridge University to enter the army; he left the army because, in spite of his learning, he did not know how to brush a horse. He returned to Oxford, and then left without any degree. He began to publish a journal entitled "The Watchman," which, after ten issues, collapsed. It was said of him that "he lost himself in visions of work that needed to be done, that were always to be done. Coleridge had all the gifts of poetry except one: that of sustained and concentrated effort." He had all sorts of books in mind, and, as he himself said: "The only thing left is to write them." "I am," he said, "on the verge of sending to the printer two volumes out of eight." However, those books did not exist anywhere except in his head, because he could not submit himself to the discipline of sitting down to write them. His biography seems like so many of ours! No one has ever reached the heights without discipline, and, if they have reached it, they have not remained there.

(vii) However, the real difference between the narrow gate and the narrow path on the one hand, and the wide gate and broad path on the other, will be the end of each. We should not wager all of our discernment of things looking only at the difficulty of their starting point, but rather at their end. We must always look to the end of the path, because what seems easy at first could become quite bitter and hard in the future. Every path might appear very tempting at the beginning, and every difficult path might seem disheartening at first. However, our judgments might change completely if we look to where one and the other path end. If the charming road ends in a ravine and the rough one in a pleasant valley, we will regret very much having taken the easy path and discarded the difficult one. From here arises one last difference in character between the mature person and the immature: the second compares tickets according to the itinerary and the advantages that the travel agency offers, without asking where the trip ends. The first, the mature, on the other hand, choose the company and the itinerary *solely from those that go where they want to go,* and often they find that there is only one risky flight, on an old and uncomfortable glider. However, the mature do not hestitate, because they know where they are going. They see things, not under the light of time, but rather in light of eternity. The immature do not think on eternity, although, sooner or later (and sooner rather than later) they find themselves faced with it, and not in a way that they would have wanted.

(viii) There is one last detail that we find in Saint Luke's version which says: "Strive to enter through the narrow door, for many, I tell you, will attempt to enter but will not be strong enough" (Lk 13:24). It is clear that Saint Luke is looking at things from the point of view of where they arrive. When those who have chosen the wrong path see where they are being lead, if they have the grace to see their final end before they fall into it, they will react like desperate people who want to change their lives in order to enter through the other gate, the uncomfortable one, but they will not be able to go through it since, as it has few suitors, it might happen that it will be closed soon. Here again sounds the echo of those words that we transcribed a few chapters earlier: *Late, late, so late!* The lesson is very clear: do not wait until the last day to change gates.

Conclusions

> *When Jesus finished these words, the crowds were astonished at his teaching, for he taught them as one having authority, and not as their scribes.*
>
> Mt 7:28-29

In the short preceding pages, we have tried to present the Sermon on the Mount from the particular perspective of the "notion" of the mature—that is, perfect—person in Jesus' mind. I think that the connection made, although it is very summarized and general, has brought us to outline the main features of human maturity:

A mature person is one who is . . .
interiorly free in the face of what is earthly and passing;
master of their affections and passions;
able to correct themselves and make reparation for their errors;
a seeker of truth and virtue;
compassionate with the weak;
lord of their heart;
easily forgives injuries;
a friend of sacrifice and of the cross;
not drowned in individualism;
enjoys a great interior unity;

lives facing God and facing eternity;
familiar with God in prayer;
magnanimous and generous;
completely trustful of God;
of a holy sight and without envy;
tough and prudent;
and faithful to their word.

Such a person is the *ideal* that Jesus makes us look at with eyes full of hope and a spirit willing to conquer.

This is what *we must strive to become.*

"The crowds were astonished" at Christ's doctrine. We too are surprised at the excellence and precision of His ideas.

If people were to know and to put into practice the directives of Our Lord, we can be sure that we would not have so many problems of emotional or intellectual immaturity, and that the psychic conflicts that this annoying modern life has accustomed us—and desensitized us—to would be greatly lessened.

Jesus speaks with authority because He has it. That authority—to be understood in the topic that we have studied here—is His because He Himself is the mature Man *par excellence.* The image that He transmits to us is a perfect image of Himself.

Likewise, we can see in the Gospels the "health" of Jesus' affectivity and that, as a consequence, show His emotional, passional, and, if we can be permitted to say so, His sexual balance; in other words, they reveal *His perfect chastity.* Those elements can be broken down into direct and indirect signs of His balance.

Direct signs of His balanced personality are:

- His temperance and mortification: He fasted 40 days and 40 nights in the desert; He spent entire, or, at the very least, large portions of nights in prayer; He had no place to rest His head, He was an extraordinary wayfarer, and put up, without any complain, with thirst, the sun, fatigue, the backtalk of those around Him, etc.
- The organic balance and healthy life which derive from His great physical endurance.
- The incredible prudence, perfect justice, and enormous courage that characterize Him; these virtues suppose an excellent parallel in all the other moral virtues (since they all grow together in perfection), and notably in chastity.

- The great realism with which He judges sin, the weaknesses of others, the situation of men and of the world, the qualities and limits of each person, etc.
- His great understanding of life, and the clear awareness He has with respect to the ultimate end of all things.
- The supernatural criteria by which He is guided (as we can see, summarized, in the Sermon on the Mount).
- The conviction of His personality.
- The ability to capture the beauty of nature, the innocence of children, the honor of marriage, the dignity of women, etc.

Indirect signs of His balance include the absence of the disturbances and vices that usually accompany people with affective and/or sexual disorders. Concretely, in Jesus we see:

- There are no fears that disturb Him. On the contrary, He has an enormous trust (Mt 10:28: "Do not be afraid of those who kill the body but cannot kill the soul"; Mt 17:7: "Do not be afraid.")
- He does not have depressive ideas.
- He does not show any emotional defects and, even less, any lack of fatherly affection or support.
- He shows no misunderstandings regarding evil or sufferings.
- He does not have inferiority complexes.
- He shows no obsessions.
- He does not have a temperamental base that is nervous, tense, anxious, or moody.
- He does not express an understanding of life that is hedonistic, sensual, or materialist.
- He does not encourage weaknesses, comfort, laziness, or sensuality.
- He does not suffer from gluttony or lack of sobriety (vices that often trigger affective and sexual disorders).
- He does not suffer from hatred, resentment, antipathy, harshness, dislikes, anger, etc.
- He does not nourish any pride whatsoever (a vice that usually brings a fall into impurity as a punishment).
- He does not hold erroneous doctrines about sexuality.

In short: in Jesus of Nazareth, such as we discover Him in the Gospels, we see a person with the conditions that make for a perfect psychosexual balance and emotional maturity. So perfect is that balance that He is able to challenge His adversaries who surround Him: "Can any of you charge me with sin?" (Jn

8:46). For this reason, Saint Paul makes Him equivalent to the *state of the perfect man*, with the *maturity of the fullness of Christ* (cf. Eph 4:13).

Only a man like this can be our model and guide us without hesitations through the difficult path of human maturity. This is because in the mystery of Christ His complete perfection and close humanity are joined together. This is why He Himself insists on being followed: "I have given you a model to follow, so that as I have done for you, you should also do" (Jn 13:15). His Apostles have also insisted on this point, as Peter does in proclaiming that Jesus has preceded us so that "[we] should follow in his footsteps" (1 Pt 2:21).

In this sense, we should take as our itinerary those words of the author of the letter to the Hebrews: "keeping our eyes fixed on Jesus . . . consider" Him attentively (Heb 12:2-3).

Poverty

For today's and tomorrow's conferences, we will continue to think about how we can imitate Jesus Christ, and, in particular, through poverty. Following the considerations of Bl. Columba Marmion, we can consider, first, the example Christ sets through poverty, and the virtue that helps us to live it out, and then, second, how we can live it out.

First, let's consider our Lord Jesus Christ as a model of poverty, and, secondly, the virtue that enables us to live according to that example. That virtue is *hope*.

Regarding the first, the good abbot tells us: "Let us contemplate our Lord Who is our Model in all things, Whom we wish to follow for love's sake. What does His life teach us? He, so to speak, espoused Poverty.

He was God . . . Legions of angels are His ministers; with a single word, He drew Heaven and earth out of nothing. He decked them with riches and beauty which are but a pale reflection of His infinite perfections. His power and magnificence are so extensive that, according to the Psalmist's expression, He has but to open His hand to fill 'every living creature with blessing.'

And behold this God, becomes incarnate to bring us to Himself. What way does He choose? That of poverty.

When the Word came into this world, He, the King of Heaven and earth, willed, in His Divine Wisdom, to dispose the details of His birth, life, and death, in such a manner that what most transpired was poverty, contempt for the things of the world. The poorest are born at least under a roof; He first sees the day as He lies upon straw in a manger for 'there was no room' for His Mother in the inn. At Nazareth He leads the obscure life of a poor artisan: *Is this not the carpenter's son?* [At His baptism, He allows the forerunner, John, to pour water over Him, as though He, too, were a sinner among sinners.] Later on, in His public life, He was nowhere to lay His Head although 'the foxes have holes.' At the hour of His death, He is stripped of His garments and fastened naked to the Cross. He leaves His executioners to take possession of that tunic woven by His Mother; His friends have forsaken Him; of His Apostles, He sees only St. John near Him. At least His Mother remains to Him: but no; He gives Her to His disciple: *Behold your mother.* Is not this absolute renunciation? Yet He finds a means of going beyond this extreme degree of destitution. There are still the heavenly joys with which His Father inundates His Humanity. He renounces them, for now His Father abandons Him: *My God, My God, why have You abandoned me?* He remains *alone*, hanging between Heaven and earth.

This is the example that has filled the world with monasteries, and peopled these monasteries with souls in love with poverty. When we contemplate Jesus poor in the manger, poor at Nazareth, poor upon the Cross, holding out His hands to us and saying: 'It is for you,' we understand the follies of the lovers of poverty.

Let us then keep our eyes fixed on this Divine Poor One of Bethlehem, of Nazareth, and of Golgatha. And if we feel some of the effects of poverty, let us accept this generously; do not let us look upon it as a world-wide calamity! And let us not forget that we ought not to be poor merely out of convention, but because we have promised Christ really to leave everything to follow Him. It is at this price that we shall find in Him all our riches; for if He has taken our miseries upon Himself, it is in order to enrich us with His perfection; the poverty of His Humanity services Him as the means of coming near to us and bringing even to our souls the riches of His Divinity."

The practice of poverty must be linked to the practice of the virtue of hope, our second point. The abbot continues: "Now the practice of the virtue of poverty is inseparable from that of hope under a lofty form. What in fact is hope? It is a supernatural habit which inclines the soul to regard God as its one Good, and from Him to hope for all necessary graces whereby to attain the possession of this supreme Good. . . . When in the soul there is living faith, it comprehends that God infinitely surpasses all earthly goods, as St. Gregory says, speaking of St. Benedict, '*all* creatures appear as small' to the soul that contemplates the Creator. Faith shows us in the perfect possession of God that precious pearl of which the Gospel speaks; to gain it, we sell all, we leave all; it is the homage rendered to Divine Goodness and Beauty. Faith blossoms into hope. The soul is so enamored of God that it no longer wishes for any other good, and the privation of any good, except God, does not trouble it. . . . The soul wants God alone.

This is why the soul despoils itself, disengages itself, in order to have more freedom. If, even when God hides Himself, even when He leaves the soul in dryness and desolation, or gives Himself only in the nudity of His Divinity in order to detach it not only from the earth but from itself, if the soul remains faithful to seek God only, to place its beatitude in Him alone, it may be assured of finding at last, never more to lose Him and to enjoy Him in all peace, this God Who surpasses all treasures.

Hope has another aspect: it is that of inclining us to look to God for all that is necessary for our sanctification. Profession, as we have said, is a contract. When, having left all things for Christ Jesus, we remain faithful to our promise, Christ must, if I may thus express myself, bring us to perfection. He has bound Himself to do this. "If you wish to be perfect," He says to us, "Go, sell whatever you have, and come." God is a father, says our Lord Himself; when a child asks his father for bread, will he give him a serpent? And if, adds Jesus, you who are evil, 'know how to give good things to your children, how much more will your Father Who is in Heaven,' give you what is necessary for you.

And how true this is! Saint Paul tells us that the tenderness, as well as the authority, of the fathers of this world has its sources in the Heart of God. And if our Heavenly Father loves us, what will He not give us? While we were enemies He reconciled us to Himself by the death of His Son: He gave Him to us that He might be our salvation and, says St. Paul, 'how much more has He not also given us all things along with Himself.' All that we desire for the perfection and holiness of our souls, we find in Christ Jesus; in Him are all the treasures of the Godhead. The indubitable will of the Enteral Father is that His beloved Son should be *our* redemption, *our* justice, *our* sanctification; that all His merits, all His sanctifications, and their value is infinite, should be ours. You are made so rich in Christ, exclaims St. Paul, 'that nothing is wanting to you in any grace.'

Oh, if we know the gift of God! If we knew the inexhaustible riches we may possess in Christ Jesus, not only should we not go begging happiness from creatures nor seeking it from perishable goods, but we should despoil ourselves of them as much as possible in order to increase our soul's capacity for possessing true treasures. We should be watchful not to attach ourselves to the least thing that could keep us back from God.

It is this that gives assurance to our hope and renders it invincible: when we place our beatitude in God alone; when for love of Him we detach ourselves from every creature, and look but to Him for all necessary graces, then God shows Himself magnificent towards us: He fills us with Himself."

As for our second consideration, how we live out poverty, we'll continue to follow what the Abbot Marmion says. Today, we will see what poverty is, and tomorrow, how to live it out concretely.

So let us begin with the Abbot: "In our seeking after God, we are hindered by the obstacles we find upon our way or within ourselves. To find God perfectly, we must first of all be freed from every creature insofar as it keeps us back on the path of perfection." In the story of the rich young man (Mt 19: 16-22), the man goes away sad because he had many possessions. "Riches held his heart captive, and because of them he could not follow in the footsteps of

Jesus. Our Lord has given us the immense grace of letting us hear His Divine Voice calling us to perfection: *Come after me* (Mk 1:17). By an act of faith in His word and in His divinity, we have come to Him and have said like Saint Peter: "Behold, we have left everything and followed you" (Mt 19:27). We have relinquished material goods, in order that being voluntarily poor, no longer having anything to hold us back, we may fully consecrate ourselves to the pursuit of the one true immutable Good. If we keep ourselves in the fervor with which we totally abandoned all worldly possessions, we shall surely find the Infinite Good even here below."

In Matthew's Gospel (19:27-29), when the rich young man goes away, Peter asks "We have given up everything and followed you. What will there be for us?" Jesus said to them, "Amen, I say to you that you who have followed me ... [that] everyone who has given up houses or brothers or sisters or father or mother or children or lands for the sake of my name will receive a hundred times more, and will inherit eternal life." "God is so magnificent in His dealings with us that in return for the things we leave for Him, He gives Himself to us even now and here with incommensurable generosity. In Mark's Gospel (10:29-30), Jesus doesn't even let Peter finish the question, and simply replies: "Amen, I say to you, there is no one who has given up house or brothers or sisters or mother or father or children or lands for my sake and for the sake of the gospel who will not receive a hundred times more *now in this present age*: houses and brothers and sisters and mothers and children and lands." (That phrase, *now in this present age* is in small caps in the book, which usually indicates that Marmion had it double-underlined in his original writing). I would note, in passing (this Fr. Nate now), that list of goods that Jesus presents: since Peter's question follows right after the rich young man has gone away sad because he had many material possessions, and it's quite probable that Peter has his material goods in mind: his fishing boat, his house, and so on. The word Peter uses just means, "everything" in general. Yet, Jesus replies a specific list of things, the majority of which aren't simply material goods, but, we could say, more spiritual. The list starts with material goods, then more spiritual ones, and ends, oddly, with the Greek ἀγρούς, meaning "fields" or "lands," which would seem to be simply material. Yet, it's important to remember that fields in the Bible aren't simply physical places: they are part of a family's inheritance and future, and fields are not only the place where things are planted and grown, but also where cattle can be raised, battles fought, and the dead buried.[1] In other words, fields are full of potential, full of future possibilities and dreams. In our vocations we surrender all that to Jesus, and it's as though

---

1. Cf. Geoffrey W. Bromiley, *International Standard Bible Encyclopedia*: E-J, 301.

Jesus responds by saying, "I know exactly what you have given up for my sake, even more than you know"; indeed, He's the only one who really knows.

Back to the Abbot: "Only it is important that we always remain in that disposition of faith, hope, and love, whereby we left all to place our [happiness] in God alone; it is important that we should no longer be attached to what we have given us for ever. And this is often very difficult. . . . You see that if voluntary poverty is an indispensable condition for finding God fully, for being perfect disciples of Christ Jesus, it is extremely important in the course of our [religious] life, not to take anything back from what we have once given as regard the renunciation of exterior goods. Let us then see in what this renunciation consists, how far it extends, and with what virtue we ought to link it so as to practice it in its perfection."

Here Columba begins with a reflection on the Rule of Saint Benedict, and how, in general, a monk is to live out poverty. At the moment we profess our vows, "we are bound to seek the perfection of our state. Now the exercise of poverty is necessary for one who wishes to be a perfect disciple of Christ." It's not that possessing things is an evil; when Jesus talks about leaving everything to follow Him, He's speaking of the counsel, and not a precept. Yet, "for us who for love of Christ, and in order to follow Him more freely, have voluntarily renounced this right [to possess things], it would be in some measure a sin to attempt to take it back unduly." The fundamental principle at work here is "that of dependence on authority and detachment of heart. To give or receive anything without the Abbot's [or superior's] consent is an act of independence, and nourishes the spirit of ownership. And nothing is so contrary to the absolute detachment that we have vowed. We must then have nothing of our own. You perhaps say to yourself, 'I am quite at rest on that point.' If it be so, thank God for it, for it is a great grace to be fully detached. However, let us examine things more closely, for there is more than one way of having anything of one's own. It cannot even be a question here of hoarding. At the last Day, we should fear to appear before God if we had possessed the least hoard. But, without going so far as this, there are different fashions of making any object whatsoever 'one's own.' It may happen, for example, that a religious makes himself from the very first so difficult that he surrounds some book or other object with a hedge of thorns, so to speak, and in such a way that no one dare ask him for it. In theory, this object is for the common use; in fact, it has become the property of this religious. Little things in themselves; but the attachment [the original has *detachment* but I think he means attachment] resulting from them can become dangerous for the soul's liberty; the principle of our perfection itself is at stake."

Thus far Blessed Columba. We can already begin to see a couple of themes emerging. First, poverty is something essential for living the religious life. In a sense, we could say that it forms the foundation of the other vows. In a talk to the CFRs, the Franciscans of the Renewal, John Cardinal O'Connor said, "Poverty is the fundamental virtue because all things flow from that: poverty of the will, that we call obedience; poverty of the desires of the body, that we call chastity, and then the obvious poverty, freedom from material possessions. Poverty is the ultimate freedom."[2] In other words, material goods are basically the easiest things to be attached to; if I can't break my attachments to them, I will be in very bad shape regarding obedience and chastity, as well as in the spiritual life in general. This is verified, time and time again, in the Church's tradition. We can think of what Saint Ignatius tells us in the *Spiritual Exercises*, at point 142 (the meditation on the Two Standards): "Consider the address [Satan] makes to [his demons], how he goads them on to lay snares for men and bind them with chains. First they are to tempt them to covet riches (as Satan himself is accustomed to do in most cases) that they may the more easily attain the empty honors of this world, and then come to overweening pride. The first step, then, will be riches, the second honor, the third pride. From these three steps the evil one leads to all other vices." In other words, riches or a lack of poverty, is the starting point to all vices. Again, when Ignatius is talking about "riches," he doesn't mean just cash money. He means anything that is created that can become a source of attachment and preoccupation. More on this in the second talk.

This leads to a second point, namely, we constantly have to be on the lookout for attachments, because they can spring up all over the place. Also, if we leave the attachments for too long, they become harder and harder to uproot. In rather vivid and forceful letter to one of his spiritual daughters, Saint Philip Neri has the following to say regarding attachments: "Now, judge from this whether to get rid of one's self it is enough to do it with a passing thought which flits through our minds once a year, [maybe], or whether we need fire and knife, and to be every moment clipping with shears, and cutting away with a razor that flimsy threads which sprout form our flesh; for if we do not stand heedfully at the mirror of mental prayer, watching them as they spring up, but put up with them and let them along; if without examination of conscience we go heedlessly on, they grow in length and thickness, and become sturdy trees, with roots and fangs so deeply fixed that they can no more be pulled out, but we have to hew them down, and dig all round them, and remove the earth, till we have got to the very bottom, where they have taken fast and complicated hold; whereas, if they had been rooted up when first they appeared,

2. Cited in Timothy Cardinal Dolan, *Priests for the Third Millennium*

you might have plucked them out with two fingers."[3] Not only is the looking for attachments a constant task, it's also an urgent task so they don't take root for very long.

Thirdly, and returning to Marmion's text, we can consider, at least in one respect, the connection between obedience and poverty. It's the superior who is in charge of our community, and who is also responsible for administering the goods of the community.

The blessed abbot makes the following point: "The care of the [community's] goods is . . . confided to the [superior]. It is for him to provide for all the necessities of his monks; he is the shepherd of the flock, the father of the family, and it is from him, says St. Benedict, that the monk must hope for everything. . . . The monk is to look for everything from the Abbot. At our profession, we despoiled ourselves of everything and put ourselves in the hands of [our superior]; it is through him that God will give us what is necessary."

The key word there, as Marmion points out, is *necessary*. What one person needs is not the same as another. Everyone has different needs: "necessities are not mathematically the same; one has need of more, another of less. As the Abbot has not infused knowledge, we ought to tell him our needs with simplicity, and to confide ourselves to him, for he is the father of the monastic family." Likewise, the superior of a convent doesn't have infused knowledge; she needs to be made aware of what people need in order to be able to govern well. She is the mother of the convent family, and if you don't tell her your needs, you don't let her govern well; you impede her in her office and, in a sense, prevent her from acting justly (since justice concerns giving others their due. In some instance, things are distributed with a sort of numerical equality, but sometimes justice requires that things be given proportionally according to need). If this is the case, then do not complain about your superior acting unjustly: the fault lies with you. Marmion continues, "Whatever does not come from the Abbot does not come from God; never let us then try to obtain anything, however small it may be, by roundabout means." Obviously, this means respecting the established order of things, asking permissions and things from the right people, etc.

Although this might seem like a small thing, it's really not, because it touches, not only on poverty, but also on gratitude, humility, and obedience. Marmion explains: "Everything is to be looked for from the father of the monastery [the mother of the convent]. For all that has to do with health, clothing, food, exceptions, and all else, let us with confidence tell our wants to the Abbot or

3. Alfonso Capecelatro, *The Life of Saint Philip Neri Apostle of Rome* (London: Burns and Oates, 1882), 114.

to those whom he has delegated to replace him in this domain." Saint Benedict gives a very supernatural thought on the whole matter when he tells the monks: "Let him who has need of less give thanks to God, and not be grieved thereby; and let him who requires more, be humbled by his infirmity and not be made proud by the mercy shown to him." That's a very profound sentence: if you need less, so, if you see someone else getting special food, or more time to sleep, or a special place to study, don't be upset. Give thanks to God that you don't need that. On the other hand, if you need something extra, ask the superior in humility for what you need. Again, this requires *humility*, because it means accepting our weaknesses and limitations. This shouldn't lead us to pride, though, in thinking that we can somehow get the superior to obey us or condescend to our whims. However, I think that perhaps what Marmion is alluding to is the parable of the unforgiving servant in Matthew 18 (21-35). If your superior gives you an extra permission or something beyond the norm, we can take pride in it, or, which is probably more common, we can still turn around and look down on those others who require special permissions as well. This would be a very clear case of "mercy making someone proud," understood, of course, in the sense that it is really the person shown mercy, and not mercy itself, that makes the person this way.

However, if we follow Marmion's advice, and give thanks for our sufficiency or remain humble in our needs, we will find the path that leads to peace, since, as the Abbot continues, "peace is the fruit of detachment; the soul has no longer any disquietude; it belong altogether to God."

"It certainly requires great faith to conform ourselves perfectly to this program: but we may be persuaded that if we observe all the points of it, God will not fail us in anything, and our soul will taste deep peace because it will look for everything from Him Who is the Beatitude of all the Saints."

At the heart of poverty, is trust in God who never lets Himself be outdone in generosity and who also looks after the concerns of those who love Him. This will be the topic of the homily today, but we can be certain that the more we free ourselves from attachments to creatures, the more we become like the men and women of God that He created us to be. As Saint Augustine said, "You become like what you love. If you love earth, you are earth. If you love Heaven, you are Heaven." If we love material goods, we become like them, namely, fickle, changing, unstable, and temporary. If we free ourselves from attachments to those finite goods, we will find ourselves loving the one true God, who is the source, not only of all happiness and joy, but also all the material things we need. As He says through the prophet: "Mine is the silver, mine is the gold." In the words of Saint Claude de la Colombiere: "I recommend you to begin at once to love poverty. How sweet to be able to say to Jesus Christ:

May Savior, I possess nothing but yourself. . . . Your heavenly Spouse is beautiful above the sons of men, but the beauty is hidden; you will possess Him long before you see Him. He is of high birth but the only dowry He asks you to bring is poverty. From Him you may expect an ardent and faithful love, but He is as jealous as He is tender."[4] We can close with part of a poem by Saint Therese of Lisieux, who wrote it for a novice on her profession day. She writes:
"With heavenly armor am I clad today;
The hand of God has thus invested me.
What now from Him could tear my heart away;
What henceforth come between my God and me?
This armor I shall keep while life shall last;
Thou, Thou, hast given it Me, my King, my Spouse!
My fairest, brightest gems, by naught on earth surpast,
Shall be my sacred vows.
My first dear sacrifice, O Poverty,
Thou shalt go with me till my dying hour.
Detached from all things must the athlete be,
If he the race would run, and prove his power
'Who would My heavenly Kingdom have from Me,
He must use violence,' so Jesus said.
Ah well then! Poverty my mighty lance shall be,
The helmet for my head.

4. Saint Claude de la Colombière, *The Spiritual Direction of Saint Claude de la Colombière* (San Francisco: Ignatius, 1998), 109. The text cited is actually from two separate letters.

Poverty

For today's conference, we will continue to think about how we can imitate Jesus Christ, and, in particular, through poverty. Following the considerations of Blessed Columba Marmion, we can consider how we live it out in our community.

In the following section, the blessed Abbot begins by saying: "Let us return to that individual poverty which the monk ought to embrace so closely and let us try to enter more fully into its spirit. We should understand it wrongly if we limited it to material privation. . . . The man who is perfectly poor will be ready to seek God alone: never let us forget that this is the end that St. Benedict points out to us: to seek God in the sincerity of our heart." "We must remain in that first fervor which made us forsake all things for the love of Christ. Let us then be watchful that the observance of our vow of poverty remains intact. For example, let us often make the inventory of what we have for our use, and if we find that we have a fondness for anything, or that we have such or such an object that has not been given or permitted by the Abbot, let us restore it to common use." Thus far the Abbot.

It's rather interesting, and perhaps sort of ironic, that all religious profess vows of poverty, chastity, and obedience. Although all of these are evangelical counsels, and we all sort of live of chastity and obedience the same way, there's a lot of variation in the way we religious live out poverty. For some communities, an individual might not have anything, but they can have really nice, well-decorated houses. Or, technically an individual has nothing, but the community might have a nice car "for their use" that no one else can use, or they are permitted to have large sums of money for their "personal" use. You also have the opposite end of the spectrum: you have groups that are very poor in the material sense: for instance, you have the Franciscans of the Primitive Observance, an offshoot of the CFRs, who don't touch money. Period.

Our *Constitutions* give us some great indications in points 67 and 68 (in our edition, as least). There, we read: "Religious poverty can be exercised with greater or lesser perfection. There are four main degrees:

1. To abstain from possessing something as one's own or from accomplishing an act of ownership without the Superior's permission. This is the obligatory matter of the vow. Its non-fulfillment, even in small matters, is always a sin that is either grave or venial, depending on the case.

- In legal terms, the owner of an object is "he [or she] who has domin-ion of a thing, real or personal, corporeal or incorporeal, which he has a right to enjoy and do with as he pleases, even to spoil or destroy it."[1] An act of ownership would mean, of course, to buy or sell things without permission, to hold on to money or other items for your own use with-out your superior's permission (and maybe even without your superi-or's knowledge). For those who are interested (and to avoid scruples, because I know someone will recall the time they gave out a handful of prayer cards!), 250 USD (or 200 euros or 313.20 CAD) is considered the line between venial and grave (more or less a day's wages).

- Here, we can also make mention of the goods that belong to the commu-nity. The Roman legal system was the first to introduce the distinction between *res communis*, a community good or a good shared by everyone (like sunshine), and *res nullius*, a good that didn't belong to anyone (like birds in the air and fish in the sea).[2] The point is not to bore you with legal details: I only mention this because sometimes it happens that a *res communis*, common property shared by everyone, becomes a person-al thing, but more often it become a *res nullius*, un-owned, in the sense that it's no one's concern. It can happen that we simply use the goods of the community without caring for them; we might see something that needs to be fixed, or picked up, or cared for, and we just don't do it "be-cause it's not mine." In a sense, though, to permit, allow, or tolerate that some community good be destroyed or damaged *is* to exercise owner-ship over it. That's a privilege that owners have; those who are caring for goods that don't belong to them don't have the luxury of letting them be destroyed or damaged.

2. To deprive oneself of the superfluous (and even of the appearance of riches and luxury), being content with simply what is necessary, and with the heart detached from it. Its non-fulfillment will not break the vow, but rather the virtue of poverty.

- The Constitutions make an interesting distinction that we could over-look. Before, we were talking about the vow of poverty; as the Code of Canon law defines it, is "a vow [is] a deliberate and free promise made to God about a possible and better good" (c. 1191, 1). Here, though, we're talking about the virtue of poverty, meaning, a good habit that makes our

---

1. *Black's Law Dictionary.*

2. You can find this distinction in a number of legal textbooks. This wording of the distinction, and its examples, are adapted from Everett C. Dolman, *Astropolitik: Classical Geopolitics in the Space Age* (Portland: Frank Cass, 2005), 84.

operations good and ourselves good (properly, to practice poverty is to make an act of the virtue of religion; it's not like poverty is some special virtue in that sense). In the *Summa contra gentiles*, Book III, c. 133, Aquinas talks about this "virtue" of poverty, and, to summarize, he says that, strictly speaking, poverty isn't an end to itself; it's a good thing insofar as it frees us from the vices that come from riches and that prevent us from seeking our ultimate end, which is God.[3] When we talk about the virtue of poverty, we mean that good habit or disposition towards material goods that allows us to get to God. In other words, in the second degree of poverty, we might have things that are extra, or that we really don't need. We might have permission to have these things, or the community might have them, so, no sin, but, if they are too nice or beyond what we need, we can allow them to get in the way of our love for God, and hence they go against the virtue of poverty.

- We can also link this in two ways with our apostolate. First, poverty provides an apostolic witness. The early Dominicans, dedicated to the conversion of the Albigensians, were able to bring about the conversion of many of the heretics precisely because they, unlike others who had tried to convert them, lived in accord with the Gospel they preached.
- At the same time, too, as Aquinas says, poverty is a means to an end, namely, it removes impediments for the love of God that arise from material possessions. Another way that I love God and serve Him is through my apostolate. So, if I am in a specialized apostolate that requires, say, a computer, a projector, and other things, to have such a thing with the permission of my superior doesn't break the vow of poverty (since I have permission for it), nor does it break the virtue of poverty, provided that I don't become attached to it, and let it become a hindrance on my way to salvation.
- Lastly, and to repeat, time and again, what poverty is: Aquinas says that it is *a means to an end*; it is not an end to itself. Poverty removes the obstacles for practicing the perfect love of God. I mention this so much because it's the big difference between the way Dominicans (and I would include us as Thomists) and Franciscans view poverty is linked to this. For the

3. In fact, in the aforementioned text, Aquinas is even more blunt: "*Poverty in itself is not good*, but only in so far as it liberates from those things whereby a man is hindered from intending spiritual things. Hence, the measure of its goodness depends on the manner in which man is freed by means of it from the aforementioned obstacles. And this is generally true of all external things: they are good to the extent that they contribute to virtue, but not in themselves."

Franciscans, as one Franciscan author puts it, "poverty was first of all the imitation of Christ.... Thus, for Saint Francis, the significance of poverty is more of a mystical-religious nature rather than ascetical or practical."[4] In other words, Christ was poor and emptied Himself entirely for us, so we should imitate Him and empty ourselves entirely for Him. In this sense, then, the poorer we are, in all senses, but especially in the material sense, the better, because the better we imitate Christ poor; at the risk of oversimplifying, in a sense, poverty becomes an end to itself, because the poorer I am, the more I'm like Christ, period; for Thomas, this isn't necessarily true, because I can be materially poor to a point where my living out of God's will is impeded, and thus poverty ceases to be a good thing and ceases to bring me to perfection; furthermore, I might add, it is difficult to see how lay people and families could imitate Christ in their proper vocations if material poverty is a necessary condition for said imitation. In any event, this whole understanding of poverty occasioned no small number of debates between the Franciscans and Dominicans, but also among the Franciscans themselves (this is part of the reason why you have so many branches of Franciscans: they had debates about poverty, whether the community could own a building, or if someone else had to own it, etc. In fact, one of the earliest debates was whether or not their apostolate should be limited by their poverty, or if apostolate should take precedence over poverty). Obviously the Franciscan family has many branches that have been approved by the Church, and so their path is a valid one for reaching Heaven. The same can be said of the Dominicans and of us (thank God), but just bear in mind that poverty, as we live it, doesn't necessarily mean not having material goods, but rather detaching ourselves for them and using only what we really need, which is also an imitation of Christ in His poverty. Indeed, as we continue to see the perfection of poverty, we'll see that it really can be an imitation of Christ.

Returning to the Constitutions, we read about the third degree of poverty: "3. To prefer for one's own use, and to choose whenever possible, that of least value, that which is least pleasant or least comfortable. In actions, it means to gladly accept, and even to ask for, the lowest offices, the most difficult assignments, anything that makes us most like the poor. The perfection of poverty begins here."

Here begins the perfection of poverty. Poverty isn't simply a negative. As we recall, all of our vows are designed to remove the impediments that prevent

---

4. Jan G. J. van den Eijnden, *Poverty on the Way to God: Thomas Aquinas on Evangelical Poverty* (Leuven; Thomas Instituut Utrecht, 1994), 13.

us from giving ourselves entirely to God. We can be poor in a sort of minimalistic sense, living out the letter of the law, but, here, we really start living out its spirit. Notice, too, that on this point our Constitutions have introduced a shift; now, we're no longer just talking about material goods, but rather spiritual ones too. It's not just things I can touch and hold and hide in my room, "my precious," but rather offices I might have, apostolates I might undertake, spiritual gifts I might have received. In the first talk, I mentioned how Marmion suffered when he entered the monastery. He made an interesting remark later in life, when reflecting on that moment. He wrote: "For over 10 years, I felt a *strong desire* to become a monk; it was my dream, my ideal. As soon as I entered the monastery, all went dark; I felt as thought I were suspended in space, deprived of all that I loved. This it is that gives merit to our cry of 'Lord, we have left all things and followed You.'" Even consolation falls under poverty. So, too, does our own will: Saint Francis used to say that "No one is truly poor until he gives up the purse of his own will." "No one is truly poor until he gives up the purse of his own will." Likewise, returning to Marmion, during those dark days, at one point he threw himself down before the tabernacle and prayed, "And yet, my Jesus, I know that You desire me here. And so I would rather let myself be hacked to pieces than to leave the monastery."[5]

Finally, we come to the fourth degree of poverty, the summit of perfection: "4. To accept with joy, for the love of God, privations of necessary things for the sake of holy poverty. It means to boast as Saint Paul *through hunger and thirst, through frequent fasting, through cold and exposure* (2 Cor 11:27). It was said of Saint Francis of Assisi that "no one was as ambitious for gold as was he zealous for poverty." This degree constitutes the perfection of poverty.

Our Constitutions continue into the next point, saying: "68. We can practice the fourth degree of poverty even more intensely and so gain total detachment not only from material goods (which is the proper object of the virtue of poverty), but also from everything that is not God Himself. This will result in the perfection of charity and a complete, consummated holiness. [Again, notice that poverty and detachment are a means to an end; they lead to, or result in, *the perfection of charity and holiness*]. As Saint John of the Cross expressed, "To love is to labor to divest and deprive oneself for God of all that is not God." The soul will not concern itself with:

- the esteem and good opinion of men,
- health and corporal strength,
- the charges and offices that will be given to or taken from him,
- the events of prosperity or adversity that may happen,
- dying young or old.

5. Both stories are recounted in the aforementioned book by Ann Ball.

"Live as though only God and yourself were in this world, so that your heart is not controlled by anything human." And: "Nothing, nothing until only the skin remains, and the rest for Christ"; "When with self love I did not want it, it was all given to me, not going after it... after I have come to nothing, I have found that I lack nothing." Conclusively, we have to love everything that God wants us to love, without being slaves to our affections for creatures. This means to love without being chained, to possess without remaining imprisoned, to use without selfish pleasure, to keep absolute independence and to look for God's glory in everything and for everything." Thus far our *Constitutions.*

Clearly, we all want to reach perfection: that's why we're here in the first place. The first step, though, is to cultivate that spirit of poverty through detachment. How do we know if our hearts are truly detached from everything? By looking for attachments. How do we know if our hearts are attached to something? We can observe the following things, starting with material goods, but then also moving on to spiritual ones:

"Mental preoccupation, frequent attention, habitual admiration, constant distraction, and being the repeated subject of conversation are all indications that what preoccupies my life and invariably agitates my will is out of order in my life. I am focused inordinately upon myself or some attachment other than God. So, too, whatever regularly arouses envy or jealousy or anger in me is out of control and needs to be regulated if I am to give my heart entirely to God."[6]

Let us consider those again: mental preoccupation . . . frequent attention . . . habitual admiration . . . constant distraction . . . the repeated subject of conversation . . . whatever regularly arouses envy or jealousy or anger in me. These are the signs of something out of order in my soul and in my heart.

We can consider a number of things that we can be attached to (we'll consider them all at some length again):

- Again, we can always start by looking for attachments to material goods. This might be a thing on our desks, places where we like to sit, people we like to hang out with, the foods we particularly enjoy, etc.[7]

6. John A. Hardon, SJ, *Retreat with the Lord* (Ann Arbor, MI: Servant Publications, 1993), 81.

7. Again, I know, we're not machines. The prayer after Communion for the Mass of Saturday of Christmas time reads: "May your people, O Lord . . . experience, both now and in the future, the remedies which you bestow, that, with the needed solace of things that pass away, they may strive with ever deepened trust for things eternal." We need material things, and we can have or use material things without being attached to them. That's the problem: the attachment. This is why Saint Ignatius is so specific in his mediation on the Three Classes of Men. It's the attachment they need to work against, and not necessary rid themselves of the thing.

- We can be attached to our time, either in the sense that we don't want to share it with others, or we want it to be *our* time, so I can do what I want with it when I want to.
- We can be attached to our plans and our future, when, really, all that needs to be placed in God's hands.
- We can be attached to our fears and anxieties, coming up with a million and one situations that have never happened to anyone, and wonder how God will help us. The space in your head also belongs to God, and you can't let something rent space there for free.
- We can be attached to our apostolates, thinking of something as *my* work, or that I'm the only one who can do it. God could have a stone do it for you.
- Lastly, we can be attached to our gifts and talents, or even to our sins and failings.

Let's consider those again. Material attachments: This might be a thing on our desks, places where we like to sit, people we like to hang out with, the foods we particularly enjoy, etc. Again, having things isn't bad, and naturally there's things we like more than others, but all this needs to be *ordered*, and ordered so that it doesn't impede me from loving God. We can ask ourselves: am I worried about certain things that I have, worried about losing them? Am I reluctant to share them for fear that others might lose them? Do I have a "saint's tooth"?[8] If the superior told me that I had to exchange desks with someone else, so their desk and all its junk became mine, and all my junk became theirs, would it bother me? I suppose, too, if I know what cool junk awaits me on the other person's desk, I pay too much attention to what they have! Do I have stockpiles of things that I never use, that are just hanging out there, waiting for the arrival of the Four Horsemen of the Apocalypse, so that I can gift them something? How often do I go through my things, and clean or get rid of what I don't really need? Has anything sat on my desk since the start of the year without me needing it or using it?

8. In a letter to her spiritual director, Saint Gemma Galgani recounts how she attached was to something sort of odd. She writes that she was completely detached from everything, that she had nothing, and yet Jesus found something: "But Jesus – Padre, do you know what He said? – 'That tooth of Ven. Gabriel, tell Me, My daughter, are you not too much attached to that?' (This tooth was a relic of Saint Gabriel Possenti and had been given to her by her director). I was silent for a moment, and then began to complain: 'But Jesus,' I said, almost in tears, 'that's a precious relic!' And Jesus answered rather seriously, 'Daughter, it is your Jesus who tells you so, and that should be sufficient for you.' Alas, it is true Padre. Jesus is right. Sr. Maria asked me for it in order to show it to the nuns, and when I had given it to her I cried because I wanted to have it always near me. But Jesus, Jesus, it is to Him that I must be attached!"

We can also lack poverty in our words: speaking of the life of Saint Joseph Cottolengo, a biographer recounted: "In conversation he was always reserved and delicate, and he exacted a like modesty from others. Even in preaching, his hearers admired his delicacy of language, his modesty of demeanor, and his fervor." Or, speaking of Saint Anthony of Egypt, it was said that "no one had a conversation with him, who didn't leave the better for it." To speak more than necessary, or to talk about useless things, doesn't edify: it's a waste of words. Again, the golden rule: poverty removes material impediments that keep us from God. Sometimes a light-hearted conversation does good to people, and that's fine; however, it's easy to become verbose and waste words. Poverty should exalt the spirit and the person, making others think of God.

Likewise, we can be attached to our time, either in the sense that we don't want to share it with others, or we want it to be *our* time, so I can do what I want with it when I want to. The key to poverty in the use of our time is our community schedule and the expressed commands of our superiors. The ancient Greeks would use two different words for time: *chronos* which is "clock time," chronological time, and *kairos*, which is harder to translate. It means "the suitable time," or "the right moment,"[9] "a qualitative time, time as an opportunity,"[10] in our case, an opportunity to serve God and gain Heaven.

The schedules of our communities, then, are like a bridge or gateway between these two times. We have a clock time, say, 5 am, and the suitable time and way to serve God in it, like, by waking up.

There are two dangers or shortcomings that we can fall into. One is to treat the schedule as a sort of routine in the literal sense of the word. While the word schedule comes from the Greek *skhizein* meaning "to split," routine derives from the French word meaning "the usual course of action," or "a beaten path." The danger of having our schedule become a routine fits both definitions: "a beaten path" is usually the path of least resistance; that's why people use it. We can materially meet the requirements of the schedule, without really taking the opportunity to serve God to the fullest. This is an imperfect practice of poverty in the sense that I keep something for myself. I do what He wants, but not because He wants it, or how He wants it. If we live the schedule as the "usual course of action," the other definition of routine, we don't leave space for God to act. Sometimes charity or our superiors require something beyond what the schedule asks: if I live a routine, I can't move myself into the *kairos* of the moment. I'll be stuck in the *chronos*. However, if we really live the schedule, and this by emptying out we easily make that transition. We're reminded

9. Cf. HELPS Word-studies 2540 for kairos.
10. Strong's Concordance.

that with God, there really isn't anything routine: as C. S. Lewis wrote, "God is the great iconoclast." He destroys the images we make of Him, because He is so much greater.

The second danger that we can fall into is to disobey the schedule or ignore it, and do our own thing. If we do this, then we really separate ourselves from opportunities to serve the God who loves us, who waits for us, as it were, to being the next activity and give us the graces we need.

The story is told that one night at recreation, Aloysius Gonzaga and the other novices were playing games, and the question was asked, "What would you do if you knew Jesus would return in five minutes?" One replied that he would make a general confession, another that he would run to the chapel to spend his last moments in Adoration, but Gonzaga replied, "I would keep playing games." I'm sure they looked at him funny, but he simply said, "That's what the schedule says." Jesus would've known where to find him.

We can be attached to our plans and our future, when, really, all that needs to be placed in God's hands. Poverty means the utter emptying of ourselves, and that includes giving up my own will regarding what my future will be like. Of course, as we said in the first meditation, I need to let my superior (and spiritual director) know if I think that God is calling me to a certain mission or a certain apostolate. To not do so isn't poverty, but rather actively impeding God's will, because I'm not letting the people who need to know know, and thus I don't let them govern well. (Remember that poverty is a means to an end, and not an end unto itself). However, once they know, I just have to give it into God's hands. That doesn't mean I won't feel a longing for it (since presumably God has put it into my heart), or that I won't experience impatience, but my future belongs to God. God never contradicts Himself, and His designs are never frustrated. Everything is unified in a plane that's beyond our understanding.

We can be attached to our fears and anxieties, coming up with a million and one situations that have never happened to anyone, and wonder how God will help us. On one hand, fears take up a lot of our time and energy, both of which belong to God. Our futures, too, belong to God, and we know that He has plans for our welfare, and not for woe. Again, the space in your head also belongs to God, and you can't let something rent space there for free.

We can be attached to our apostolates or our offices, thinking of something as *my* work, or that I'm the only one who can do it. Oftentimes that attitude isn't explicit in us, meaning, it's not like I think myself openly, "This all depends on me." However, I can *think* and *act* like it, implicitly living that belief. If we get overwhelmed, or nervous, or find ourselves distracted or concerned because of them, I don't have those things in the right place. I'm not practicing poverty with respect to them.

I can also be attached to my gifts and talents, thinking that they are all mine. If I notice myself getting angry in class because someone keeps asking questions, or because they don't understand, I need to apply the advice that Marmion gave earlier: "Let him who has need of less give thanks to God, and not be grieved thereby; and let him who requires more, be humbled by his infirmity and not be made proud by the mercy shown to him."

Finally, I can be attached to my sins, failings, and imperfections, thinking that these somehow prevent God from loving me or carrying out His will in me. While it's true that we want to overcome our sins, they can also become an impediment if I don't surrender them to God. The story is told that once Christ appeared to Saint Bernard of Clairvaux and asked him for a gift. The saintly abbot replied, "But, Jesus, I have nothing to give you! I've given you everything." To which Christ replied, "No, you haven't. There's one thing you're holding on to for yourself. Give me your sins and imperfections. Let Me have them." Our loving acceptance of God's mercy is also a surrender of something that we like to hold on to, something that prevents us from being truly poor and from truly loving God.

With all these things in mind, then, we can consider how well we live out poverty: what are we attached to, and how can we break those attachments so as to love God more perfectly in accord with our vocations and our *Constitutions*?

SECOND WEEK

Homilies

Homily for Christ the King

As we continue our contemplation of Christ the King, we can consider the life of a saint who really and truly was a hero in following Christ. That saint is Blessed Miguel Agustin Pro, who died shouting "*Viva Cristo Rey* – Long live Christ the King."

Last night, we mentioned a number of points, but we can consider three in Pro's life: first, the fact that God calls us to join in His service, second, that the best soldiers in Christ's army are the heroes, those who render Him a heroic service by overcoming all difficulties, and, third, to be a hero means sacrifice, and even the ultimate sacrifice of one's life.

First, Pro knew that Christ had called him to serve in His army. Writing to someone who prayed for him, he said, "Does God speak to the soul? . . . Yes, He does indeed speak, and His words are sweet. Yes, He does speak and the soul understands that voice and grasps that language. I know from experience and I can assure you that I didn't have the dispositions that you have to understand that call; rather, on the contrary, I had all the contrary dispositions, all the obstacles in the way, and not from things that didn't depend on me, but rather my actions and way of proceeding were entirely contrary to His call. . . . But, in His infinite mercy God laid His eyes on this dry and sterile trunk of my life, and seeing the statue that He Himself would get out of it with His most holy grace, He gave me my vocation; in spite of my opposition, He took me out of the corrupt world that I was living in, so that the beautiful words of the Psalmist might be fulfilled: *He . . . lifts the poor from the ash heap, seats them with princes, the princes of the people.*" "

Second, to really stand out in Christ's service means to overcome obstacles, to suffer, and to love suffering. Writing to his provincial, Pro speaks of the situation: "The lack of priests is extreme; people die without the sacraments, and those of us who are left aren't enough to meet the need. And those of us who are left? Would that all of them would work just a little, and things wouldn't be so bad; but everyone is the master of their fear." That is, there are priests, but many are too afraid to do anything, to really give themselves to God in service by overcoming difficulties and temptations.

Lastly, to stand out in Christ's service means sacrifice, and sometimes the ultimate sacrifice. Pro knew that the end of his life was to praise, reverence, and serve God, and he saw even his life in that light. In a letter to his provincial he writes: "My life? But what is it? Wouldn't I win it if I gave it for my brothers? Certainly, it doesn't need to be foolishly given, but when are Loyola's sons meant for, if, at the first flash, they come running back? . . . The most they can do to me is to kill me."

As we continue to contemplate the call of Christ the King, may we strive, not only to give ourselves in His service, which is only logical and just, but rather seek to excel in that service, to be a hero in Christ's army. May the Blessed Virgin Mary help us to obtain this grace.

Homily for the Second Week – Beginning of the Second Week

In this second week of the Exercises, as we strive to bring our lives into greater conformity with the life and example of Jesus Christ, to really incarnate Christ's life in our own, I want to take the homilies from Fr. Fuentes' book *The Emotional Maturity of Jesus of Nazareth*. It is a collection of reflections on Jesus Christ, focused on His emotional maturity, and how we can imitate that.

Nowadays, it is common to hear many people be labeled as "emotionally immature," without offering them a clear understanding or an archetype that reflects the aforementioned maturity. This is basically the same as giving these immature persons nothing, because in the education and formation of personality, the path of exemplarity and imitation is essential. Any work to be done in the realms of psychology, emotionality, and morality is, in great part, a process of imitations, like that carried out by children by observing their parents (for better or for worse). Emotional maturity is not achieved if *inspiration* is not received from some attractive, firm, and sure paradigm, in which what the disciple aspires to have materialize in themselves is valued.

These [reflections] are a reply to those who want to find an unmistakable model of emotional and psychological maturity. I consider that Jesus, the Divine teacher, is also an incomparable model in this very delicate realm. In an old and well-known study of characterology, Alejandro Roldán speaks of "Christ's masculine beauty," and of the "masculine and majestic aspect of the Savior . . . a dose of masculinity just right and precisely on point; . . . the perfect man, who possesses in its difficult measure and proportion the precious gift of masculinity." Without a doubt, Christ "fully reveals man to man himself" and reveals the truth about man to him, and thus "anyone who contemplates Christ . . . cannot fail to perceive in him *the truth about man*."

For this task, the Gospels, which are so sparse in their description of Jesus' physical features, nonetheless offer us numerous psychological traces of His rich personality. It is into these writings that we propose to penetrate in order to clarify, at least a little, according to the modest measure of our personal lights, the gigantic mystery of the Teacher's affectivity."

Let us pray, through the intercession of Mary, Mother of God, for the grace to imitate Jesus Christ in this, His emotional maturity.

Homily for the Second Week – The Incarnation

Yesterday, we had the opportunity to contemplate the birth of Jesus Christ. In the Basilica of the Nativity, there is a simple inscription: *Hic De Virgine Maria Jesus Christus Natus – Here Jesus Christ was born of the Virgin Mary.* In the grotto of the Annunciation, we see something similar, *Verbum caro hic factum est – The Word was made flesh here.* They seem like the understandments of the century, or millennia; in few words we see a lot.

This is the way, too, that we see Jesus' emotions in the Gospels. There's not much mentioned, and almost nothing directly. What is missing are conflicts and interior struggles. In order to be emotionally mature, a person must be aware that their masculinity or femininity is a *gift* from God, and that by means of this reality, the will and the mission that the Creator has assigned them in this world is expressed. Effectively, the vocation and mission of every person is tightly bound to their masculinity or femininity, since what must be made concrete in them is either fatherhood in a certain way, or motherhood in a determined mode, be it biological or spiritual, with its consqeuent emotional, psychological, and spiritual imprints, which differ between men and women.

However, maturity in this sense is not limited to awareness of what one has received, but also includes a conformity with the physiological aspect—genitality—that masculinity or femininity expresses; it demands a serene acceptance of one's biological and physical sex, the presence of appropriate intrapsychic experiences, and, finally, attitudes and external gestures that are in agreement with said sex.

The Gospels and apostolic writings of the earliest times say something else about Our Lord. They show Him to us with an emotionality that is normal, pacific, and serene. This is a sufficient indication of His clear emotional and sexual identity. Indeed, men who recognize themselves as men, and women who accept themselves as women, do not make allusions to this topic because they have no need to do so. No one comments that they have only one head, or two lungs, because no one speaks about what is taken as well-known or conventional, or, if you prefer, simply what is normal. On the other hand, those who have doubts about themselves and those who are unhappy with themselves do make such comments. It is when someone is suffering interior conflicts, anxieties, or confusions, that distressing topics are insinuated, be it with indirect questions, complaints, or expectant insinuations.

In contrast, Jesus' gestures and attitudes express a serene and mature experience of His own masculinity. He thinks like a man, acts like a man, has manly gestures, and reveals manly attitudes. Perhaps in many cases the actions shown are not actions exclusive to men, but they are actions that men do with a different tonality than women.

Let us pray, through the intercession of Mary, Mother of God, for the grace to imitate Jesus Christ in this, His emotional maturity.

Homily for the Second Week – The Hidden Life

Yesterday, we had the opportunity to contemplate the mysteries of the Presentation, the Flight into Egypt, and the hidden life of Jesus. In these mysteries, we saw some profound characteristics of Jesus' emotional maturity, first, in His fatherly awareness, we could call it, and, second, in His manly way of living, which will concern our reflections for a few days.

Christ's fully masculine affectivity is expressed in a particular way in His fatherly attitude; this is something we see in the Temple today. On one hand, Jesus is aware of being personally distinct from the Father: "The Father who sent me" (Jn 5:37). Expressions such as "The Father and I," and "Me and My Father" leave no room for doubt regarding this certainty. However, at the same time, He knows Himself to be "one with the Father," by communication in the same divine nature: "The Father and I are one" (Jn 10:30); "I am in My Father" (Jn 14:20).

For this reason, without ceasing to be a person distinct from the Father, Christ is also the Father's face: "Philip . . . Whoever has seen me has seen the Father" (Jn 14:9). Since He is a reflection of the Father, Jesus acts like a father with a paternal attitude and virtues towards men and women: He is provident, a defender, a benefactor, a support, a surety, and a help. It is He who solutions the hunger of His followers (Jn 6), who arranges for His followers to rest (Mk 6:31), and who defends those who are His own even at the cost of His own life: "If you are looking for me, let these men go" (Jn 18:8). In short, His clear understanding of responsibility shines forth: "This was to fulfill what he had said, 'I have not lost any of those you gave me'" (Jn 18:9).

Likewise, in the sufferings He endures, we see that Jesus has a markedly masculine resistence and endurance; we saw some of this in the Flight into Egypt, but it is a recurrent theme, that Christ has a manly way of living. The fatigue that must have been imposed by the tenor of life during His few years of public activity shows forth a magnificent physical complexion. Since ordinarily (although there are exceptions) development in the different spheres of personality is harmonious, we can suppose a correlative development in the other orders. In the expression with which Luke describes the adolescent Jesus, "And Jesus advanced [in] wisdom and age and favor before God and man," (Lk 2:52) Roldán sees a perfect correspondence between His bodily development (age), His psychic development (wisdom), and His spiritual development (grace). He explains, "It is as though [the Gospel] wanted to tell us that the dynamic expansion of the corporeal, immaterial, and spiritual 'components' in Jesus Christ was completely harmonious and balanced, without any deviation or displacement."

Let us pray, through the intercession of Mary, Mother of God, for the grace to imitate Jesus Christ in this, His emotional maturity.

Homily for the Second Week – The Two Standards

In today's Gospel, we hear Jesus tell the scholar of the Law that he must "love his neighbor as himself," and then Christ tells him that that mercy extends even to one's enemies (since the Samaritans were hated by the Jews). Today, as we continue to contemplate the Two Standards and come to make our resolutions, we are reminded that the morality and the doctrine of Jesus Christ isn't a *minimum*; it's a *maximum*, a doctrine and morality of giving the best of one's self, and it precisely in this that Christ's New Law overcomes the Old.

When earlier people and scholars lived by the "Golden Rule," it was usually in a negative form: don't do what you don't like. Don't do to others what you don't want them to do to you. However, this form is not extraordinary; if you don't live by it, you simply can't live in community. Indeed, you could fulfill this negative version by just doing nothing, never doing anything for your neighbors at all.

However, Jesus gives the principle in the positive form: "Do to others whatever you would have them do to you." Laid out this way, the rule is more demanding. Christ's commandment now comes to oblige us to respect others and, what is even more rigorous, *having our very selves as the measure*. It is very easy to know what we want for ourselves, or what we hope for from others: attention, gentleness, help, affection, respect, charity, tolerance, companionship, friendship, loyalty, trust, and many more things. Jesus tells us: do precisely that for others. Here we return to find what we had observed earlier: the doctrine of Jesus Christ is a morality of the *maximum*.

The surpassing of the law that Jesus establishes in His "New Law" does not simply mean the triumph of what is interior, but rather to obtaining the "greatest" ideal. The purely exterior law is a minimalist law: respect for the life of another is the bare minimum we should do for him; not attempting to seduce our neighbor's wife is the least that we should do for her; not dismissing our spouse without serious reasons is the very least we should do for our marriage; to fulfill what we have promised under oath is the bare minimum we should do with our serious commitments. In none of these cases is there any mention of a *maximum*. Jesus Christ points precisely at a maximum in each of these orders.

The minimalism in which many Christians live is a tragedy. It is the experience of living a life of withdrawal, and it is manifested in many attitudes that reveal the desire to live with restrictions: we see this, for instance, in those who ask: "How far can boyfriends and girlfriends go before it is considered a sin?," "What is the minimum dollar amount of alms that we should give?," "Up until what point can someone arrive late in the Mass and still meet the precept?," "Which days are we absolutely required to fast?," "How many times do I need to forgive my brother?," "How much of her body can a woman reveal without committing scandal?," and the like. The people who think like this, think that they have more options for what they can do. However, in reality, acting in this way constricts them, because the action that gives life and fullness is not the sort that is on that side of the fence, but rather on the other. It is not "helping the poor while spending as little as possible" that makes me a better, more decent, freer, more perfect, happier person, but rather "spending on those in need all that we can give without being imprudent." I am not going to be happier by staying 15 minutes more in bed, thinking how I can "make it to Mass" when I arrive halfway through the homily, but rather I will feel joy when I arrive 15 minutes before the Mass starts, so that I can prepare myself in order to live it more fully, etc.

The "men of the minimum" want to breathe deeply in a shirt so small that it suffocates them. They have a very mistaken idea of man, and have learned nothing from God, who always lives to the full: He creates infinite species that we will never be able to know, He has made more stars than man can count, He has made a universe that no telescope can see completely and so great that man has neither the intellect nor imagination to fully measure it, He makes the sun shine on the good and the evil, He gives us an infinite capacity to know, and infinite capacity to love, He has given us His own Son, and this Son shed His blood to the last drop for our salvation.

Minimalism condemns to immaturity, and causes bitterness, because it means to always breathe air rarified with mediocrity; maximalism, the father of maturity, make complete and happy men and women, because it means to conquer the summit in each action, even the most trivial ones.

Today, then, we ask, through the intercession of Mary, Mother of Our Lord, for the grace to place ourselves under Christ's standard, to really embrace the heights of holiness, and resolve to continue to follow Him with all our hearts.

Homily for the Second Week – Jesus as Model #1

In today's Gospel, we hear Jesus lay down the very strict requirements for following Him. Since we know that Jesus is our model, and that He not only tells what to do but actually lives it out Himself. This is tough, but it reminds us, as Fr. Fuentes says and as we will continue to see when we consider Jesus' public ministry, that Jesus Christ *has a manly way of life*.

We see this in what He does: He is able to endure prolonged fasts, like the one that lasted forty days and forty nights that preceded the beginning of His apostolic life (Mt 4). He arises very early in the morning (Lk 6:14); He spends days on His frequent apostolic journeys (Mt 15:21), seemingly with scarce provisions, since that is the way He recommended to His disciples when He sent them out for apostolate (Lk 9:3), and it is witnessed to by the hunger and thirst that would often oppress Him: "Jesus, tired from his journey, sat down there at the well" (Jn 4:6). The evangelists note that sometimes He did not have the time needed in order to eat (Mk 3:20; 6:31). And as a finale, often He would spend entire nights, or a great part of them, in prayer (Lk 6:12), even when the day's work had been exhausting (Mk 6:46).

We can also suppose, and rightfully so, that speaking much would also tire Him greatly, since normally He preached in the open air, to great crowds, under the burning sun of Palestine. It should not surprise us, then, that many could not keep up with His pace, as He seems to warn the scribe who, drawing near to Him, says: "Teacher, I will follow you wherever you go," to which Jesus replied, "Foxes have dens and birds of the sky have nests, but the Son of Man has nowhere to rest his head" (Mt 8:19-20). It seems that this alone was enough to dissuade this superficial admirer, whom we never find again in the Gospel accounts.

It is very likely that during His trips Christ spent the night in uncomfortable and inhospitable public accommodations (*the inns* like those in which His Mother was unable to find a place at the time of His birth) or would even spend nights under the open skies. From here would come that ease with which we see Him fall into a serene and profound sleep, like that of children, able to rest without disturbance in the middle of a storm like that on Lake Gennesaret during which, while the waves threatened to capsize the boat,

"Jesus was in the stern, asleep on a cushion" (Mk 4:38). It seems He greatly enjoyed life outdoors, as is shown by the innumerable allusions to the fields and to agricultural and herding customs that we find in His parables. It was the places of solitude—the desert, the summits of mountains, or the darkness of an olive grove—that He chose to be with His disciples and to which He preferred to withdraw in order to pray.

All of this implies a great tolerance of heat, cold, the wind, the rain, hunger, and fatigue, and we are not talking about a rough man, one raised in the wilderness, or adorned with rough and savage qualities. On the contrary, Jesus never shows Himself unable to deal with people of noble lineage, or uncomfortable in navegating a banquet, as we see in the evangelical texts. Jesus' hosts never reproach him for the awkwardness or ordinariness of His ways, but only for not binding Himself to the customs of the Pharisees, for His excessive condescension with sinners, and for the trust He shows with people leading a bad life.

We do well to bear in mind what Romano Guardini wrote about Christ: "Jesus was emphatically a man. The fact must not be allowed to become obscured either by certain conventional ways of portraying him in art or by the types of piety or devotion which give rise to this portraiture. Jesus is made to appear as a tender, passive, half feminine individual, but this is due to a fatal misinterpretation which empties the notions of Jesus' 'gentleness,' 'humility,' or 'self-sacrifice' of all meaning. It would be equally erroneous, it must be admitted, to conceive of his masculinity exclusively in terms of the man of action, the aggressive type, or the man who is concerned with superficial notions about honor. Jesus' manhood was strong, deep-seated, and inspiring; but, typically, it was not governed by any passion or impulse: it was ruled entirely by the spirit. . . . An unbiased examination of the [*Gospel*] evidence shows clearly that his manhood was without trace of any of the baser passions [*that is, the instinctive attraction towards what is feminine*]. This is not because the evangelists were at pains to cover up such failings; nor is it because he had no feelings at all like other individuals, or because he was an ascetic and overcame them. A primordial warmth and fullness of life pervaded his whole personality. But his masculinity was completely integrated in his whole religious personality, more precisely, in a center which lay deeper and was mightier than the spiritual or religious center to be found in man. His manhood had been taken over by the divine power of love, understood in the purest sense of the word, and permeated by it. The manhood of Jesus was transformed into perfect, selfless, divine love."

Through the intercession of Mary, Mother of Christ, we ask for the grace to imitiate Christ in this, His emotional maturity.

Homily for the Second Week – Jesus as Model #2

Today we have the option to celebrate the memorial of Our Lady of Mount Carmel. It is a fitting moment to consider, then, what Jesus' relation was to women, how He interacted with them, since here we can find a model for ourselves. This consideration will take a few days, and tomorrow we will consider the mystery of the expulsion of the money changers, but this is an important topic, especially for us who are called to be *other Christs*.

It must be recognized that, with respect to women, Jesus was not bound to the customs of His time and place. Among His strictest countrymen, women were discriminated against from birth, which later extended to the nation's political and religious life. "Woe to the one whose descendants are women!" says the Talmud. For some, the birth of a girl caused sadness and annoyance, and, once they grew up, girls would not have access to learning the Law. In the Mishnah it is said, "May the words of the Torah [the Law] be destroyed by fire before they are taught to women. . . . Whosoever teaches the Torah to his daughter is as if he were to teach her [to cause] disasters."

It is certain that expressions like these are sharply contrasted by others, like this one, regarding divorce, which was repeated by the rabbis: "The very altar sheds tears when a man divorces the wife of his youth." However, the great Presbyterian exegete Barclay, speaking precisely of the institution of the Mosaic divorce, points out: "The tragedy was that practice fell so far short of the ideal. One thing spoiled the whole marriage relationship. The woman in the eyes of the law was a thing. She was at the absolute disposal of her father or of her husband. She had virtually no legal rights at all. To all intents and purposes a woman could not divorce her husband for any reason, and a man could divorce his wife for any cause at all. 'A woman,' said the Rabbinic law, 'may be divorced with or without her will; but a man only with his will.' . . . . The process of divorce was extremely simple. The bill of divorcement simply ran: 'Let this be from me thy writ of divorce and letter of dismissal and deed of liberation, that thou mayest marry whatsoever man thou wilt.' All that had to be done was to hand that document to the woman in the presence of two witnesses and she stood divorced."

For this reason, commenting on the apostles' surprise at finding Jesus speaking with the Samaritan woman (cf. Jn 4:27), the same author adds: "There is little wonder that the disciples were in a state of bewildered amazement when they ... found Jesus talking to the Samaritan woman. We have already seen the Jewish idea of women. The Rabbinic precept ran: 'Let no one talk with a woman in the street, no, not with his own wife.' The Rabbis so despised women and so thought them incapable of receiving any real teaching that they said: 'Better that the words of the law should be burned than delivered to women.' They had a saying: 'Each time that a man prolongs converse with a woman he causes evil to himself, and desists from the law, and in the end inherits Gehinnom.' By Rabbinic standards Jesus could hardly have done a more shatteringly unconventional thing than to talk to this woman. Here is Jesus taking the barriers down."

Elsewhere, explaining the Jewish background of the first letter to Timothy, the Scottish scholar adds: "No nation ever gave a bigger place to women in home and in family things than the Jews did; but officially the position of a woman was very low. In Jewish law she was not a person but a thing; she was entirely at the disposal of her father or of her husband. She was forbidden to learn the law; to instruct a woman in the law was to cast pearls before swine. Women had no part in the synagogue service; they were shut apart in a section of the synagogue, or in a gallery, where they could not be seen. A man came to the synagogue to learn; but, at the most, a woman came to hear. In the synagogue the lesson from Scripture was read by members of the congregation; but not by women, for that would have been to lessen 'the honour of the congregation.' It was absolutely forbidden for a woman to teach in a school; she might not even teach the youngest children. A woman was exempt from the stated demands of the Law. It was not obligatory on her to attend the sacred feasts and festivals. Women, slaves and children were classed together. In the Jewish morning prayer a man thanked God that God had not made him 'a Gentile, a slave or a woman.' In the *Sayings of the Fathers* Rabbi Jose ben Johanan is quoted as saying: 'Let thy house be opened wide, and let the poor be thy household, and talk not much with a woman.' .... A strict Rabbi would never greet a woman on the street, not even his own wife or daughter or mother or sister. It was said of woman: 'Her work is to send her children to the synagogue; to attend to domestic concerns; to leave her husband free to study in the schools; to keep house for him until he returns.'"

Undoubtedly not all of the Jews thought this way, as we can see in the gentleness with which some men treated certain women, for instance, Joseph with Mary, Zachariah with Anna, etc. However, it must be agreed that Jewish thought in general at the time of Christ had not advanced very far in the treatment of women. It is for this reason that Jesus' attitude with respect to women strongly contrasts with these expressions.

Through the intercession of Mary, Mother of Christ, we ask for the grace to imitate Christ in this, His emotional maturity.

Homily for the Second Week — Christ Casts the Sellers from the Temple

Today, this morning's contemplation will be on when Christ casts the sellers from the Temple, the cleansing of the Temple. This event is so important that Fr. Fuentes dedicates a great deal of time examining it, so today we will do the same, as a sort of preview of today's contemplation. Jesus bears that unmistakable trait of an authentic man, which is the ability to assert Himself against His enemies when a just cause demands it. For Jesus, the "cause" *par excellence* was His Father's glory. It should not surprise us, then, that we only see Him raise a hand when He sees that fatherly glory trampled. The episode of the expulsion of the merchants from the Temple, who had converted the temple into a market, is recounted by the four evangelists (Jn 2:13-22; Mt 21:12-13; Mk 11:15-19; Lk 19:45-46). The texts allow us to glimpse the stupor and the deranged panic of His adversaries, which is explained, in part, because for the unscrupulous merchant (and these were of that sort), there is nothing more painful than the ruin of their business.

However, and above all else, their fear is because there are few things as fearsome as the *anger of the meek*. The calm man does not get angry without reason; however, when he has a reason, his anger makes him imposing, since the infuriated meek person knows the reason for his anger and that he has no right to calm himself down until justice is restored. The wrathful man can be bribed; however, it is difficult to corrupt a meek person who is angered *with and in accord with reason*. A man who has the time and makes the delay so as to put together a whip of cords and the character of giving a speech explaining his behavior can not be out of his mind with anger. Jesus did both things. The shoves and kicks He needed to scatter the moneychangers and scare away the cows and pigeons that infected the Father's Temple were all thought, measured and decided. Jesus labels the merchants with the less than flattering title of "thieves," and yet, as far as we can see, none of them dared to reply to Him, since, as Mark notes (11:18), "they feared Him." His mere presence demanded respect, and even put a brake on murderous desires, as had happened earlier in Nazareth, when His countrymen wanted to knock Him off, "But he passed through the midst of them and went away" (Lk 4:30). It could not have been easy to get up the courage to place hands on Jesus.

His manliness must have frightened His enemies, first and foremost because it was "manliness" and not mere "bravado." The bully is a braggart and rowdy, and his gestures tend to be the occasion for a brawl because, since his apparent audacity arises from a contrived passion, it gives rise to the passions of others, just as a fire ignites another fire. However, authentic anger, which is imposed by moral superiority and flows from reason and justice, makes those whom it is against languish. True courage is that anger placed at the service of justice. This is what frightens the evil, and such was Jesus' spirit. In order to unleash their fury, His enemies would have to wait until He wished to surrender His life of His own accord (cf. Jn 10:18).

Jesus could be energetic and wield His strength, as occurred in the expulsion of the merchants from the Temple (cf. Mt 21:12-13; Mk 11:15-17; Jn 2:14-17). However, the description of that episode made by the evangelists is infinitely removed from the turbulent anger of the bewildered, or the one who channels his nervous energy in a convulsive tantrum. His indignation does not leave its proper margins. Through the intercession of Mary, Mother of Christ, we ask for the grace to imitiate Christ in this, His emotional maturity.

Homily for the Second Week – Jesus as Model #3

Today, we return to the topic we began to consider on Tuesday, namely, that of Christ' dealings with women. We already saw what the majority of the Jews thoughts about them, but that Christ had a much different view. Now let's consider the changes brought by Christ.

A man's emotional maturity in his dealings with the feminine sex are measured by the ability to form healthy relationships of friendship and respect with women without these entailing disturbances, attachments, dangerous friendships, or a lack of control of his own sensibility.

Our Lord has no qualms about conversing publicly with the Samaritan woman (cf. Jn 4:27), nor does He bear in mind the legal impurity of the woman with the hemorrhage (cf. Mt 9:20-22); He allows a sinful woman to draw near to Him in the house of Simon the Pharisee, and He even lets her touch Him in order to wash His feet and cry over Him (cf. Lk 7:37); He forgives an adulterer, showing that it is unjust to have more severity with the woman's sin than with that of her male accomplice (cf. Jn 8:11). He distances Himself from the Mosaic law into order to affirm the equality of the rights and duties of both man and woman with respect to the marriage bond (cf. Mt 19:3-9; Mk 10:2-11); He was accompanied and maintained in His travelling ministry by several woman (cf. Lk 8:2-3). To women He entrusts the first Pascal message, and even chooses them to announce His resurrection to the rest of the disciples (cf. Mt 28:7-10 and parallels).

Many of the women that Jesus encounters in His journey did not have an exemplar past, and perhaps in some cases they were not even living an exemplar present: the Samaritan woman had already lived with many different men, and Jesus shows that He knows that she is not married to the man with whom she is currently living; the woman who enters into the house of Simon the Pharisee was probably a prostitute, since the host says within himself that she "was a sinner," and he feels a certain repugnance towards her (Lk 7:39); the woman who was caught in adultery, whom Christ's enemies throw at His feet with the hope that He will be caught in a bind because she had been surprised in her crime; our Lord had expelled seven demons from Mary Magdalene (cf. Mk 16:9). Even then, Jesus' enemies, who accuse Him falsely, but fiercely, of being a glutton and a drunk (cf. Lk 7:34), an impostor (Mt 27:63), possessed (cf. Mk 3:22), and a blasphemer (cf. Mt 26:65) ... *never ever* allude even to the most minimal failing against chastity, nor do they even insinuate that Jesus was imprudent in that realm. The very fact that, in order to try the balance between His justice and His mercy, they choose a woman surprised in adultery (cf. Jn 8:1-11), demanding that He apply the Mosaic law to her, in all its harshness, is explained because they were certain that, if Jesus' behavior were in accord with the purity that He preached, He would have to *condemn her*. We know how it ends.

Even John, noting Jesus' special affection towards the three siblings of Bethany, two of whom were women, "Now Jesus *loved* Martha and her sister and Lazarus" (Jn 11:5), never insinuates that that feeling implied some disorder. The words of the same evangelist describing the episode of the Samaritan woman should be understood in the same way: "his disciples ... were amazed that he was talking with a woman" (Jn 4:27); this amazement would not be understandable if Jesus had the custom of speaking to women, or if, as if they say, He were *overfamiliar* with them.

Through the intercession of Mary, Mother of Christ, we ask for the grace to imitate Christ in this, His emotional maturity.

Homily for the Second Week – Jesus as Model #4

Today, we can continue with our meditations regarding Christ and women, especially regarding Christ's emotional balance and His teachings.

Jesus' equilibrium is really extraordinary, since, at the same time it arouses the aforementioned amazement of His apostles, on at least two opportunities He let Himself be touched, kissed, and anointed by some women. The first was in the home of the Pharisee who invited him to dinner: "A Pharisee invited him to dine with him, and he entered the Pharisee's house and reclined at table. Now there was a sinful woman in the city who learned that he was at table in the house of the Pharisee. Bringing an alabaster flask of ointment, she stood behind him at his feet weeping and began to bathe his feet with her tears. Then she wiped them with her hair, kissed them, and anointed them with the ointment" (Lk 7:36-38). The second scene is the one that we alluded to a short while ago, and the protagonist is Lazarus' sister: "Mary took a liter of costly perfumed oil made from genuine aromatic nard and anointed the feet of Jesus and dried them with her hair; the house was filled with the fragrance of the oil" (Jn 12:3). The two episodes are certainly different, and different as well are the motives for the anointings: in one case a poor sinful woman asked for mercy for her sins, while in the second, a young woman shows her gratitude for the one who had just restored her deceased brother to life. In both cases, the women who acted were criticized; one for being bold, for touching the Master although she was a sinner; the other, for being wasteful. However, in both cases Jesus defended them, the one because she had shown great love (cf. Lk 7:47), and the other because she showed mercy to Him by anointing Him in advance of the anointing that would be incomplete at His burial (cf. Mt 26:10-12). However, it is worth mentioning that none of those around Jesus thought ill of Him, which speaks of the high regard they had for His affectivity. Judas himself, who it seems looked at Mary with bitter eyes, did not think ill of her affection, but rather of her extravagance in wasting a jar of purest nard on the Lord's feet (cf. Jn 12:1-7).

In a certain sense, too, we can *deduce Christ's way of life* from His doctrine. What I mean to say is that there should be an extraordinary coherence between Jesus' preaching and His way of life. First and foremost, this is shown in the symmetry between the sermon of the Beatitudes and His death on the Cross, which is the foreseeable outcome of the doctrine contained in His first public preachings. However, we also see this coherence in the fact that, in spite of having so many enemies conspiring in order to be able to accuse Him (Lk 6:7: "The scribes and the Pharisees watched him closely to see if he would cure on the Sabbath so that they might discover a reason to accuse him"), and wanting to set up some false charge that would be believable (Mt 26:59: "The chief priests and the entire Sanhedrin kept trying to obtain false testimony against Jesus in order to put him to death"), He was never accused of not having fulfilled what He Himself preached or demanded from others. If Jesus had been inconsistent, the Sermon on the Mount would be sufficient to have a banquet of reproaches!

From here it follows that it is legitimate to think that Jesus' attitude towards women would have been exactly the attitude He taught. Regarding this point, His doctrine can be summarized in what He proclaimed at the beginning of His public ministry: "Everyone who looks at a woman with lust has already committed adultery with her in his heart" (Mt 5:28). With these words, the Lord overcomes the exteriority of the Jewish teachers—who only pointed out the sin of acts that were external and consummated—condemning in this way the inclination of heart that makes a woman into an object of potential sexual satisfaction, an inclination that is expressed through a look of desire. The interior desire to achieve sensual or sexual satisfaction with a woman who does not belong to him produces a transformation in the man that is so profound, that Jesus expresses it with the strong word of "adultery." This desire, which is translated into a lustful look, reduces a woman to the level of "a thing," and the man who desires her, to the level of a "manipulator." Jesus Christ judges that this attitude is unworthy of a man (which is also true for woman who does the same).

Through the intercession of Mary, Mother of Christ, we ask for the grace to imitiate Christ in this, His emotional maturity.

Homily for the Second Week – Jesus as Model #5

Today, we can continue with our meditations regarding Christ and women, especially regarding Christ's teachings.

Christ's thought is completed with another expression from the same Sermon: "The lamp of the body is the eye. If your eye is sound, your whole body will be filled with light; but if your eye is bad, your whole body will be in darkness" (Mt 6:22-23). "Adultery of soul," the fruit of that sinful look, darkens the heart. The look that is wrongly desirous of a woman who becomes a sexual object, profoundly hurts the will that looks through the eyes. The man's evil eyes spoils the image and the idea that he has of woman, and that vicious and harmful concept enters through the eye's lamp perverting the heart of the lustful man.

It must be highlighted that these expressions of Jesus are part of the *novelty* of His doctrine; they reveal Jesus Christ's heart, and they are, precisely, *new teachings* that Jesus sets against the teaching of the old teachers who did not demand purity of intention but rather only of external acts. "You have heard that it was said, 'You shall not commit adultery.' But I say to you, everyone who looks at a woman with lust has already committed adultery with her in his heart" (Mt 5:27-28). Adultery, like carnal intercourse with someone else's spouse, was condemned in the Old Testament. Our Lord adds (and with that powerful 'But I say to you') that physical contact is not essential to break chastity; the intention is enough. Jesus preaches interior purity because He lives it.

Our look is pure when it is directed to what we judge to be clean and pure; it is reverent in the face of what we consider sacred, and it is caring and understanding with those whom we love tenderly. However, it is greedy of what we value with utilitarian criteria, and voracious of what we calculate sensually. In this sense, it is not the woman's feminine nature that gives rise to lubricious looks, but rather the *meaning* and the *value* that a woman represents for a man. From here it follows that the voluptuous man does not look impurely at his mom, nor his daughter, nor his sister (the pervert is the exception), because they *are appreciated* with holy and spiritual measures. However, in contrast, the lustful man does not do the same with other women. In contrast, the pure man casts a clean eye on his own wife and the women in his life as well as those of others, because he considers them all with the same measure. Thus is Jesus' look: it is pure, because His heart is pure and His intentions are pure. His look is in accord with the *value* that every woman has for Him. In the Samaritan woman, He sees a soul tired and thirsting for transcendental values, and He offers her the pure water that springs up to eternal life; in the woman caught in adultery, He sees fear and shame, and He offers her understanding and forgiveness ("Nor do I condemn you"); in the sinful woman, prostrate at His feet, He sees shame and humiliation, and He praises her love as shown in a repentance capable of wiping away past sins.

Through the intercession of Mary, Mother of Christ, we ask for the grace to imitiate Christ in this, His emotional maturity.

Homily for the Second Week – Jesus as Model #6

Today, we can continue with our meditations regarding Christ and women, especially regarding Christ as a celibate man.

Jesus was celibate. "No woman could say his wife," exclaims Bichlmair. "The mere thought that a woman should share the life of this man is repugnant to our religious sensibility." It's true. More over, not only our religious feeling, but also our theological reasoning is opposed to it, because even though marriage is something sacred, any woman whatsoever would be a limitation to the universal love of the Incarnate God. Even just restricting ourselves to the facts of the Gospels, the idea of a married Jesus is not only repugnant to the health of our imaginations and of our emotions, but even to intellectual honesty and scientific investigation. We cannot invent things in Jesus that the sacred authors do not have, unless we want to confuse exegesis with sensational novels.

Jesus could not belong to any woman; the awareness of His absolute surrender to the mission entrusted to Him by His Father would make it impossible. His vocation is complete and total (cf. Lk. 2:49).

On the other hand, His celibacy is demanded in coherence with the renunciation that He asked from those who wanted to follow Him completely: "Whoever loves father or mother more than me is not worthy of me, and whoever loves son or daughter more than me is not worthy of me" (Mt 10:37). "If any one comes to me without hating his father and mother, wife and children, brothers and sisters, and even his own life, he cannot be my disciple" (Lk 14:26). "Peter began to say to him, 'We have given up everything and followed you.' Jesus said, 'Amen, I say to you, there is no one who has given up house or brothers or sisters or mother or father or children or lands for my sake and for the sake of the gospel who will not receive a hundred times more now in this present age: houses and brothers and sisters and mothers and children and lands, with persecutions, and eternal life in the age to come'" (Mk 10:28-30). Jesus, who considered unworthy of His school anyone who put discipleship on one side of the balance, and any family member or relative on the other, could not, honestly, have been bound to anyone on this earth. Whoever praises those who say that they have given up everything to follow Him, cannot Himself be bound to anything or to anyone.

From this it follows that Jesus' chastity is a necessity that His heart imposes, not as a limitation (because He is unable to love), but rather from *an excess of love* for God and for souls. In His case, it is, truly, a virtuous chastity, because not every chastity is such. As Bruckberger writes, "everything that is materially chaste, is not necessarily virtuous because of it: there is a chastity of stones, and that of dry hearts, that of misers of themselves and that of the impotent, that of blessed cowards who are afraid of hell. All of those sorts of chastity are rotten."

Jesus was celibate on account of a free act of His will. He did not accept chastity, as some think, because *if He had not, He could not have been free to move about.* In other words, they claim it was as a *condition* bound to the sort of life that He had to lead (without a home, without a fixed residence, without money). On the contrary, Jesus chooses it *for itself*, on account of the intrinsic beauty it has as *a way to love God with His whole being, body and soul.* He does it in the same sense that later Saint Paul will call the state of virginity: "eusjémon" (1 Cor 7:35), which means what is noble, decent, decorous, distinguished. The Vulgate translates into Latin as "quod honestum est," that which is worthy (worthy to be loved for itself, regardless of any utility that it might have in addition).

It is true that the New Testament gives Christ the title of "Bridegroom" (John, the forerunner, calls himself "the friend of the bridegroom": Jn 3:29). However, this is always to be understood as the mystical espousal of Christ with the souls of His faithful: "I betrothed you to one husband to present you as a chaste virgin to Christ" (1 Cor 11:2). In other words, He is the spouse of the Church: "Husbands, love your wives, even as Christ loved the Church and handed himself over for her" (Eph 5:25). Christ is spouse in a spiritual sense, as united with the Church through a surrender without reserve. On the other hand, He is not a spouse in the sense of human marriage, between a man and a woman. In this sense, Jesus is both virgin and model of virginity.

It is precisely in Christ that the Apostle seems to be thinking when he praises virginity to the Corinthians: "An unmarried man is anxious about the things of the Lord, how he may please the Lord. But a married man is anxious about the things of the world, how he may please his wife, and *he is divided.* An unmarried woman or a virgin is anxious about the things of the Lord, so that she may be holy in both body and spirit. A married woman, on the other hand, is anxious about the things of the world, how she may please her husband. I am telling you this for your own benefit, not to impose a restraint upon you, but for the sake of propriety and adherence to the Lord *without distraction*" (1 Cor 7:32-35). Even if Saint Paul has a high perception of marriage (1 Cor 7:38: "The one who marries his virgin does well"), he acknowledges, nonetheless, that marital love imposes *a division in the heart of the married person*: between dedication to God and dedication to the spouse. Virgins avoid that division by completely surrendering themselves, without shortcuts, to God. Jesus Christ is not a man of a divided heart, as His life from His infancy bears witness, since at that point He declared Himself totally dedicated to the things of His Father, as we saw earlier, mentioning His being lost and found among the doctors of the law (cf. Lk 2:49); and, as He would repeat on another occasion: "But he said in reply to the one who told him, "Who is my mother? Who are my brothers? . . . Whoever does the will of my heavenly Father is my brother, and sister, and mother" (Mt 12:48, 50).

Jesus was celibate, a virgin, and a virginizer, meaning, He inspires people to virginity.

Through the intercession of Mary, Mother of Christ, we ask for the grace to imitiate Christ in this, His emotional maturity.

Homily for the Second Week — Jesus and the Beatitudes

In 2000, Pope Saint John Paul the Great celebrated Mass on the Mount of the Beatitudes. Speaking to the youth, his homily is very well suited for us as we try to live out the graces of the second week of the Exercises. He said:

Not far from this very place, Jesus called his first disciples, as he calls you now. His call has always demanded a choice between the two voices competing for your hearts even now on this hill, the choice between good and evil, between life and death. Which voice will the young people of the twenty-first century choose to follow? To put your faith in Jesus means choosing to believe what he says, no matter how strange it may seem, and choosing to reject the claims of evil, no matter how sensible or attractive they may seem.

In the end, Jesus does not merely speak the Beatitudes. He lives the Beatitudes. He is the Beatitudes. Looking at him you will see what it means to be poor in spirit, gentle and merciful, to mourn, to care for what is right, to be pure in heart, to make peace, to be persecuted. This is why he has the right to say, "Come, follow me!" He does not say simply, "Do what I say". He says, "Come, follow me!"

You hear his voice on this hill, and you believe what he says. But like the first disciples at the Sea of Galilee, you must leave your boats and nets behind, and that is never easy—especially when you face an uncertain future. To be good Christians may seem beyond your strength in today's world. But Jesus does not stand by and leave you alone to face the challenge. He is always with you to transform your weakness into strength. Trust him when he says: "My grace is enough for you, for my power is made perfect in weakness" (2 Cor 12:9)!

Young people: answer the Lord with a heart that is willing and open! Willing and open, like the heart of the greatest daughter of Galilee, Mary, the Mother of Jesus. How did she respond? She said: "I am the servant of the Lord, let it be done to me according to your word" (Lk 1:38).

We, too, pray, through the intercession of Mary, for the grace to know and live out the Beatitudes in our lives, so that, by knowing Christ, we might love and serve Him all the more.

Made in the USA
Columbia, SC
20 September 2024

42737001R00254